COMPUTER-MEDIATED COMMUNICATION

Pragmatics & Beyond New Series

39

Susan C. Herring (ed.)

Computer-Mediated Communication:
Linguistic, social and cross-cultural perspectives.

√COMPUTER-MEDIATED COMMUNICATION

LINGUISTIC, SOCIAL AND CROSS-CULTURAL PERSPECTIVES

Edited by

SUSAN C. HERRING
University of Texas at Arlington

JOHN BENJAMINS PUBLISHING COMPANY
AMSTERDAM/PHILADELPHIA

The paper used in this publication meets the minimum requirements of American National Standard for Information Sciences — Permanence of Paper for Printed Library Materials, ANSI Z39.48-1984.

Library of Congress Cataloging-in-Publication Data

Computer-mediated communication : linguistic, social, and cross-cultural perspectives / edited by Susan C. Herring.

p. cm. -- (Pragmatics & beyond, ISSN 0922-842X ; new ser. 39)

Includes bibliographical references and index.

Contents: Electronic language : a new variety of English / Milena Collot and Nancy Belmore -- Oral and written linguistic aspects of computer conferencing / Simeon J. Yates -- Linguistic and interactional features of internet relay chat / Christopher C. Werry -- Functional comparisons of face-to-face and computer-mediated decision making interactions / Sherri L. Condon and Claude G. Čech -- Two variants of an electronic message schema / Susan Herring -- Managing the virtual commons : cooperation and conflict in computer communities / Peter Kollock and Marc Smith -- Our passionate response to virtual reality / Nancy R. Deuel -- Cyberfeminism / Kira Hall -- Computer-mediated conversations as a new dimension of inter-cultural communication between East Asian and North American college students / Ringo Ma -- Perceptions of American culture : the impact of an electronically-mediated cultural exchange program on Mexican high school students / Mary Elaine Meagher and Fernando Castaños -- Visible conversation and academic inquiry / Gregory G. Colomb and Joyce A. Simutis -- Group dynamics in an e-mail forum / Joan Korenman and Nancy Wyatt -- Writing to work : how using e-mail can reflect technological and organizational change / Oren Ziv -- The rethorical dynamics of a community protest in cyberspace : what happened with Lotus marketplace / Laura J. Gurak.

1. Communication--Data processing. I. Herring, Susan C. II. Series.

P96.D36C665 1996

302.2'0285--dc20 96-19100

ISBN 90 272 5054 5 (Eur.) / 1-55619-803-5 (US) (Pb; alk. paper) CIP

John Benjamins Publishing Co. • P.O.Box 75577 • 1070 AN Amsterdam • The Netherlands

John Benjamins North America • P.O.Box 27519 • Philadelphia PA 19118-0519 • USA

Contents

Foreword

The present volume traces its genesis to a panel entitled "Cultural and Linguistic Aspects of Computer-Mediated Communication" which I co-organized and chaired at the Fourth International Pragmatics Conference in Kobe, Japan, on July 27, 1993. Four papers were presented in that panel, three of which (Korenman & Wyatt; Meagher & Castaños; Yates) are included in revised form here. My own panel presentation, which was a summary of some previous work, has been replaced in this volume with a chapter reporting previously unpublished research. The remaining 10 chapters were selected for inclusion in response to a call for papers distributed widely on the Internet. At the same time, the theme of the volume was broadened to include social as well as linguistic and cultural issues associated with computer-mediated communication. All 14 chapters present original scholarly research in areas where little or no scholarship has existed in the past.

Jef Verschueren, President of the International Pragmatics Association, deserves much of the credit for the publication of this volume. It was he who first proposed the idea of an edited collection, offering the *Pragmatics and Beyond* series as a publication venue. Recognition is also due to Brenda Danet whose idea it was to organize the Kobe panel, and who did much of the organizational work in the early stages, but who unfortunately was unable to attend the conference.

Many others have contributed to the production of the volume itself. Foremost among these are the contributors, who in addition to writing high-quality professional articles, were prompt and cheerful throughout all stages of the book's production. Thanks are also due to Jacque Lambiase and Robin Lombard for reading and commenting on several of the contributions; to Charles Ess, Laura Gurak, and Nancy Wyatt for useful feedback on the introduction; to Eileen Herring and Holly Herring for proofreading assistance; and to John Paolillo for help in formatting the manuscript as camera-ready copy.

February 1996 Susan C. Herring

Introduction

Susan C. Herring
University of Texas at Arlington

Computer-mediated communication (CMC) is communication that takes place between human beings via the instrumentality of computers. This book focuses on text-based CMC, in which participants interact by means of the written word, e.g., by typing a message on the keyboard of one computer which is read by others on their computer screens, either immediately (synchronous CMC) or at a later point in time (asynchronous CMC).[1] Twenty years ago, this activity was largely unknown outside of a few elite government and academic research institutions in the United States. Today, text-based CMC is engaged in regularly by millions of people around the world, an increasing proportion of whom now gain access to the global network—known as the Internet—through commercial providers rather than through institutional mainframes.[2]

The phenomenal growth of CMC has captured both popular and scholarly imaginations. Cultural theorists and technophiles have been quick to envision sweeping changes in the social order as a result of the democratic and anarchic possibilities inherent in widespread use of a networked medium which allows anyone with access to speak out more or less anonymously, and which is not as yet subject to any centralized authority or control. Utopian visions of class- and gender-free virtual societies have arisen alongside of dystopic visions involving information overload, e-mail addiction, uninhibited aggression, and the eventual breakdown of people's ability to engage one another face-to-face. The popular media contribute to the clamor by focusing on sensational aspects of life in "cyberspace" (as computer networks are collectively and metaphorically known) such as electronic pornography, pirated data, and virtual rape.

While some empirical studies of CMC have been carried out, futuristic speculation and popular stereotyping still far outstrip the availability of factual information. There is thus a pressing need for descriptive and empirical research on computer-mediated interaction, and it is for this reason that the present collection was produced. The 14 papers contained herein are scholarly works which report on empirical observation and analysis of CMC, most in the form of case studies focusing on specific CMC genres. The collection is interdisciplinary in its outlook, with an overall emphasis on language, culture, and social interaction. However, no attempt is made at completeness in any of the areas represented; rather the goal is to bring together a variety of approaches to CMC so that their insights might inform one another and direct future research.

The data examined in this volume represent a broad range of CMC genres—synchronous and asynchronous, local and global, academic and recreational. In other respects the data are more limited: because of ethical issues associated with collecting and analyzing private e-mail correspondence, most of the examples are drawn from public or semi-public group interactions, and with the exception of one chapter which describes interaction on a French-speaking "chat" channel, all of the CMC analyzed here is in English.[3]

A further limitation is the time involved in getting a collection of this sort together and in print. The chapters for this volume were originally written in 1993 and 1994, yet CMC has continued to expand and evolve in the intervening years. For example, the numbers of female users and computer network users of both sexes who access the Internet from their homes have increased dramatically in the past year;[4] these changes in user demographics are not addressed in the volume. Nor does the volume contain many references to the World Wide Web, which first began attracting attention in 1994 and has grown in the intervening two years to rival interactive text-based CMC in popularity.

The passage of time has also worked to our advantage. Because of recent exponential increases in computer network use, many more readers are now familiar with CMC through direct personal experience than would have been the case in 1993. And the significance of CMC itself has been validated through its continued growth: no mere passing trend, CMC has emerged as an important new communication modality that is increasingly permeating everyday life in industrialized societies. Back in 1993, I entertained fears that the subject matter of this volume would appear marginal or arcane to all but a small body of enthusiasts. Such fears have been effectively mooted by recent developments. With a critical mass of readers now Internet literate, the general awareness has caught up with the concerns of this book. Rather than wondering whether CMC scholarship is legimitate, a more appropriate question now is how scholarship can best keep pace with the continued expansion and diversification of CMC.

Historical background on CMC research

When computer networks were first designed in the 1960's, their primary purpose was to facilitate the transfer of information protocols between computers. No one, least of all their inventors, imagined that such networks would come to be used predominantly for human-to-human social interaction (Rheingold 1993b; but cf. Licklider et al. 1968). Some of the earliest researchers to concern themselves with this phenomenon were Starr Roxanne Hiltz and Murray Turoff, sociologists involved in a U.S. government-sponsored project to explore the implications of computer networks for government communications. Hiltz and Turoff's 1978 book, *The Network Nation* (republished in 1993), stands as an early classic in the field of CMC research, although its vision is somewhat idealized. Another major milestone was the publication in the mid-1980's of experimental work by social psychologist Sara Kiesler and her colleagues comparing computer-mediated and face-to-face behavior; Kiesler et al. (1984) is a particularly clear and oft-cited articulation of this early work. Not surprisingly, communications scholars were also among those who took a relatively early interest in CMC (e.g., Cathcart and Gumpert 1983; Chesebro 1985; Rice, ed. 1984), and the mid-to-late 80's also saw a growing practical interest in research on CMC in organizational and business settings (Sproull and Kiesler 1986; Zuboff 1988). Yet another productive branch of CMC scholarship sprouted several years later as composition specialists began to explore the implications of networked classrooms for teaching writing (Batson 1988; Cooper and Selfe 1990; Faigley 1990; Peyton 1989). Surprisingly, although text-based CMC is constructed almost exclusively from linguistic signs, linguists have been slow to consider computer-mediated language a legitimate object of inquiry. Exceptions to this are early articles by Baron (1984) and Murray (1988, 1989), and a special issue of *Written Communication* in 1991 containing a frequently-cited paper by Ferrara, Whittemore, and Brunner characterizing "interactive written discourse" as an emergent discourse genre. Other approaches, such as the analysis of gender and cultural differences in CMC, the dynamics of virtual communities, and psychotherapeutic uses of computer-mediated interaction, have arisen only in the past few years, and numerous potentially fruitful areas of pragmatic and sociolinguistic analysis are currently being identified in ongoing research. As of this writing, scholarly inquiry into CMC is expanding simultaneously in multiple directions, and we can expect new foci of CMC research to continue to emerge in the future.

Key issues in CMC research

What is interesting about CMC? While it is beyond the scope of this introduction to touch even fleetingly on all the issues which have intrigued scholars and provoked heated debates on-line and off, certain properties of CMC draw repeated comment, and are addressed to varying degrees in the papers in this volume. I will mention three of these here.

The first issue concerns the *language* of CMC: it is typed, and hence like writing, but exchanges are often rapid and informal, and hence more like spoken conversation. Moreover, the computer-mediated register has unique features of its own, such as the use of "emoticons" (smiley faces composed of ascii characters) and other graphics, as well as special lexis ("lurking", "flaming", "spamming"[5]) and acronyms (FAQ, IMHO, RTFM[6]). Finally, CMC is not homogeneous, but like any communicative modality, manifests itself in different styles and genres, some determined by the available technologies (e.g., real-time "chat" modes, as opposed to asynchronous e-mail), others by human factors such as communicative purpose and group membership. Separating out the contributions of the medium from those of human users is an important prerequisite to further CMC analysis. It is also important that CMC and its structural variants be accurately described, for what such description stands to contribute to our knowledge of the typological diversity of human communication. A number of the papers in this book (Collot and Belmore; Yates; Werry; Condon and Čech; Herring) are concerned to characterize CMC in linguistic terms.

A second characteristic of the medium that has provoked speculation is the fact that participants interact without the benefit of extra-linguistic cues as to the gender, identity, personality, or mood of their interlocutors (e.g., Hiltz and Turoff 1978/1993). This observation, or some form of it, has led some to hypothesize that text-based CMC is impersonal or distancing, making it useful for the transfer of information but unsuitable for personal relationships. (This hypothesis is belied by most of the papers in this volume, especially the chapter by Deuel on "virtual sex".) The alleged "impersonality" and "anonymity" of the medium have also been claimed to result in decreased inhibition, leading to self-disclosure on the one hand and increased expression of hostility on the other (Kiesler et al. 1984; Kim and Raja 1991). More idealistically, others perceive in the lack of physical cues a potential freedom from limiting gender, class, ethnic, and other status-based prejudices; they claim CMC is inherently democratic—one is judged solely on the merit of what one says, not on who one is. The issue of communication across group and status boundaries is addressed in this volume in the papers by Ma, Meagher and Castaños, and Ziv. However, the democratization view has been substantially undermined by the results of research in at least one area, that of gender. Gender asymmetries have been found to carry over wholesale from face-to-face interaction, and even to be exaggerated in CMC (Herring 1993a inter alia, and this volume; Hall, this volume; cf. Graddol and Swann 1989). These observations give rise to a fundamental question: to what extent does the computer medium alter human interaction, and to what extent do people simply map their existing patterns of behavior onto communication in the new medium?

The last issue of general interest relates to the phenomenon of community formation in cyberspace (Rheingold 1993b). On-line communities take shape, generate norms of interaction (for example, rules of network etiquette, or "netiquette") and conflict resolution procedures, literally before our eyes, in text that can be saved and mined later for insights into the genesis of human social organization. The potential of CMC to bring people together, for better or worse, also has practical consequences both for individuals and the social order. Virtual communities, like communities "in real life", must protect the interests of their members, and ethical dilemmas result when individual and group needs come into conflict, as well as when certain groups dominate in defining the terms of the discourse. The question of "access" in the broader socio-political sense has barely begun to be addressed, yet ultimately it will determine the ends to which the potential of the global network is put. These broader issues are addressed to varying degrees in the papers by Kollock and Smith, Hall, Herring, Korenman and Wyatt, and Gurak in this volume.

CMC as data

At this point, a few words are in order about using CMC as data. Research on computer-mediated communication is still in its infancy, and the authors in this volume have had to devise their own methodologies or adapt methods from other domains to address their research questions about on-line language and social interaction. Some authors have devised sampling techniques for constructing representative corpora, some have made use of questionnaires as data-gathering instruments, some have relied on ethnographic observation of naturally occurring interactions, and some have combined these and other methods. CMC has advantages in respect of each of these methods: large corpora are easily amassed, in that interactions come already entered as text on a computer; surveys can be distributed and returned electronically; and observers can observe without their presence being known, thus avoiding the "Observer's Paradox" that has traditionally plagued research in the social sciences.

In other respects, however, the use of CMC data poses ethical dilemmas. For example, is it ethical to collect data while "lurking" (reading without contributing) on an electronic forum? To the extent that a forum is open to the public, one can argue that this practice is essentially no different from collecting data by eavesdropping on a conversation in a public place such as a restaurant or an airport (Herring, forthcoming). A question still remains, however: how much information about the data sources should be revealed in scholarly publications? Many researchers feel it is best to avoid using participants' real names, especially if the messages are personally revealing or if the analysis is unflattering. King (forthcoming) takes this position to an extreme by advocating that researchers should avoid mention of any specifics concerning the messages or their sources altogether, including the name of the discussion group, so as not to violate the "perceived privacy" of the participants. At the opposite extreme, some consider all CMC to be published written material, and hold that quoting it without crediting the source is in violation of copyright (e.g., Cavazos 1994; Gurak, In press). As this brief discussion illustrates, there are as yet no generally agreed-upon guidelines governing CMC research practices.[7]

The editorial policy followed in citing CMC data in this volume makes a distinction between restricted- and open-access electronic fora, the former of which are considered private, while the latter are public. With data from private or semi-private sources, pseudonyms have been used to refer to participants and groups unless permission to use real names was explicitly granted by the participants involved. Messages posted publicly to Usenet and to open-acess

Listservs are exempt from this requirement, although some authors have elected to mask all participants' identities by the use of pseudonyms regardless, as a matter of courtesy. Finally, if a message is cited to credit (or argue against) its content, rather than as an example of a phenomenon under investigation, its source has been cited as though it were a published reference (e.g., in the chapter by Gurak). In short, an attempt has been made to follow common sense in respecting as much as possible the privacy of those whose messages are cited as examples, while giving credit for ideas where credit is due.

Organization of the volume

This volume is organized into four sections. The first section, *Linguistic Perspectives*, constitutes perhaps the largest collection of linguistic analyses of CMC to appear together in print to date (although I expect and hope that this record, if indeed it is a record, will soon be surpassed). The five papers in this section represent three approaches: corpus linguistics (lexico-grammatical analysis), conversation analysis, and text linguistics; all but one make use of quantitative methods. A common concern expressed in these papers is how CMC compares with other language modalities, especially with spoken and written language.

The second section, *Social and Ethical Perspectives*, contains three papers, each of which is concerned in some way with conflicts of interest between groups, or between individuals and society, in cyberspace. Included in this section are discussions of freedom of speech, including sexually-explicit and hate speech, and the collective interests of a wider community of users. These are the most theoretical papers in the volume, although all maintain a strong descriptive orientation and are based on extended ethnographic observation of computer-mediated communities.

The third section, *Cross-Cultural Perspectives*, is made up of three case studies of computer-mediated interaction between members of different cultures: East Asian and North American college students, Mexican and American high school students, and socially-disadvantaged first-year college students in the United States in interaction with academic institutional culture. A shared concern in these papers is whether CMC in fact facilitates intercultural learning and appreciation, as has been claimed.

The fourth and last section, *CMC and Group Interaction*, applies varied disciplinary approaches to the question of how electronic communication contributes to the construction of group identity by communities of users. The papers in this section address a powerful characteristic of computer networks, which is their ability to bring people together who might not otherwise come together, or who would normally interact in different ways (for example, in more hierarchical or convention-bound roles).

Following the four sections, bibliographic references cited in this introduction and in the individual chapters have been combined into a collective list at the end of the book. This was done so as to eliminate redundant references to commonly-cited works, and to produce a convenient resource for those interested in reading about or researching CMC further. The resulting 29-page list includes approximately 240 references to work on CMC, most of it published since 1992.[8]

Overview of the chapters

The book begins with a chapter by Collot and Belmore on "Electronic Language", in which they analyze lexical and grammatical features of a large corpus of computer-mediated messages sent to an electronic bulletin board system in Canada. Collot and Belmore apply Biber's (1991, 1992) factor analysis to their corpus, comparing the electronic corpus with computerized corpora of spoken and written English. They identify two types of Electronic Language—on-line and off-line—and situate them along six dimensions: informativity, narrativity, explicitness, persuasion, abstraction, and elaboration. The result is a more exact characterization of electronic language than would be possible by simply contrasting it with "spoken" and "written" modalities.

Yates' chapter describes the construction of another large CMC corpus; this one is based on messages exchanged on a computer conferencing system at the Open University in the United Kingdom. Yates compares his corpus with computerized corpora of spoken and written English, following a Hallidayan model that considers textual, interpersonal, and ideational functions of language. His results show that CMC is more like written language with respect to vocabulary use (textual), more like spoken language with respect to the use of personal pronouns (interpersonal), and makes greater use of modal auxiliaries (ideational) than either speech or writing.

Werry takes as his data a synchronous mode of CMC known as Internet Relay Chat (IRC). The chat sessions he analyzes are in English (on an Australian channel) and French. In addition to providing a useful taxonomy of features that characterize this little-studied genre, Werry argues for the essential "orality" of IRC by pointing out ways in which participants attempt to recreate aspects of spoken language through graphic and orthographic means.

The chapter by Condon and Čech directly compares face-to-face and synchronous computer-mediated interaction in an experimental study. Pairs of subjects, some face-to-face and others connected via microcomputers, were asked to complete four decision-making tasks involving planning social events. The authors found that all subjects followed a general decision-making schema, but that subjects under the two experimental conditions differed in their frequency of use of interactional functions such as metalanguage, repetition, and discourse markers. Overall, the CMC interactions were found to be more efficient, while the face-to-face interactions produced more detailed plans.

Herring analyzes the schematic organization of electronic messages posted to two academic mailing lists, one mostly male and the other mostly female, in order to evaluate the popular stereotype that men and women use e-mail for different purposes (information exchange vs. social interaction). The results do not support the stereotype: rather, both genders post electronic messages to exchange views and information in interactive ways. However, women's and men's messages are structured differently, with female users exhibiting alignment, and male users opposition, towards their addressees.

Kollock and Smith take the Usenet and its many newsgroups as the domain in which to situate the problem of "free-riding", or making use of group resources (such as publicly-posted information, free software, and "bandwidth"—the "space" taken up by posting messages) without contributing to their maintenance. They point out that free-riding is rational behavior from the perspective of the individual, but is ultimately detrimental to the common good. By comparing the Usenet with face-to-face communities as described by Ostrom (1990), the authors identify a unique set of issues involved in maintaining the "virtual commons" as a collective resource.

Deuel's chapter is perhaps the first scholarly treatment of the phenomenon of Virtual Sex (VSex) as practiced in recreational MUDs and MOOs (synchronous chat environments in which participants textually construct their identities, physical appearance, and the physical setting). Deuel describes the textual features of VSex interaction, arguing contra Rheingold (1991, 1993a) that VSex is personally beneficial in that it provides valuable opportunities for learning about sex. In concluding, she considers the negative social and political implications of censoring VSex activities.[9]

Hall's chapter identifies and contrasts two varieties of "cyberfeminism": "liberal cyberfeminism", which embraces CMC as a gender-fluid (but sexualized) utopia, and "radical cyberfeminism", in which women-only mailing lists are formed to resist and protect against male-initiated harassment on the Internet. Hall examines the discourse of both movements, the first through the magazine *Future Sex*, cyberpunk literature, and postmodern theory, and the second through the analysis of actual communication on a woman-only mailing list. The analysis of the latter reveals discursive features Hall terms "aggressively collaborative", in opposition to the aggressive "cybermasculinity" exhibited elsewhere on the Internet.

Ma's chapter begins the section on cross-cultural CMC with an investigation of the effects of synchronous relay chat exchanges on cross-cultural communication between East Asian (Chinese, Japanese, and Korean) and North American university students. Ma examines five proposals about cross-cultural CMC, including the hypotheses that both East Asians and North Americans will perceive CMC to be more egalitarian, and will be more direct and self-disclose more in CMC than face to face. Self-reports by students participating in the study largely confirmed the proposals, although U.S students perceived East Asians to be less direct and self-disclosing than East Asians perceived themselves to be.

Meagher and Castaños investigate perceptions of American culture by Mexican high school students before and after participation in a computer-mediated exchange program. Their investigation produced a startling result: perceptions of American culture were *less* rather than more favorable after the exchange. Through triangulation of their results from a variety of diagnostic measures (questionnaires, interviews, analysis of student messages and course work related to the exchange), the authors conclude that the Mexican students have nevertheless undergone significant learning about the target language and culture; their decreased regard for the target culture is attributed to culture shock.

Colomb and Simutis expand the cross-cultural paradigm by examining the effects of interaction in a networked writing class on socially-disadvantaged first-year college students. The students not only belong to diverse cultural groups (African-American, Hispanic, Asian, Anglo-American), but also are encountering an alien academic culture through the discourse they are expected to learn. The authors report on a test case in which CMC was used successfully in conjunction with a special pedagogical design to support novice learning.

The chapter by Korenman and Wyatt begins the last section of the book, which is concerned with group interaction. Their chapter investigates the ways in which interactions by participants on a large women's studies mailing list (one of the two lists analyzed in the chapter by Herring) resemble face-to-face interaction in a small group. The authors analyze questionnaire data and patterns of participation, and propose that feelings of "groupness" can be traced to the exchange of personal messages outside the list, the existence of a core of regular participants who provide continuity, and the establishment of oral discourse practices on the list.

Ziv's chapter examines how the use of e-mail in a workplace setting can reflect organizational change. He reports on a case study involving a technologically less-sophisticated group that has been incorporated under the administrative domain of an academic computing services group. In his study, which focuses on a disagreement over wording for an article in a campus newsletter, Ziv finds that the use of electronic communication by the first group is symbolic of its change in identity. In addition, he finds that CMC does not flatten organizational hierarchies as has been claimed, but rather interacts with existing hierarchies.

Gurak's chapter concludes the volume with a rhetorical analysis of a community protest in cyberspace. She reports on how the electronic medium enabled people who were concerned about privacy violations associated with a commercial product, LotusMarketplace, to come together quickly and in large numbers to force the manufacturer to cancel release of the product. Her examination of the dynamics of the protest reveals limitations of the medium as a "public meeting place", as well as its considerable potential as a forum for community action and political deliberation.

The papers in this volume provide initial answers to intriguing questions, as well as identifying directions for further study. In the meantime, computer-mediated interaction continues to expand and evolve in new directions, and future students of CMC will find no lack of original topics to pursue. My personal vision for the future of this area of scholarship is that it will continue to bring academic disciplines together to learn from one another, at the same time as sub-specializations develop and disciplinary expertise is brought to bear on CMC-related questions. Both breadth and depth are needed if we are to come to understand fully this technologically-based phenomenon with vitally human implications.

NOTES

1. Other forms of CMC not considered in this volume involve graphic, auditory, and/or tactile modalities in addition to or in place of written text.
2. As of December 1995, 46% of the 9.5 million Internet users in the United States accessed the Internet via on-line services, of which America Online is the most popular provider (The American Internet User Survey, 1996).
3. This is in part a reflection of the predominance of English on the Internet (Paolillo 1995). There is a need for published scholarship on computer-mediated interaction in other languages, and on CMC that involves language mixing.
4. The American Internet User Survey (1996).
5. "Flaming", for those readers who may be unfamiliar with the term, refers to the practice of sending hostile or insulting electronic messages, usually in response to a message posted by someone else (Herring 1994, 1996; Kim & Raja 1991; Lea et al. 1992). "Lurking" is observing the interaction on a discussion group without posting messages oneself (Broadhurst 1993). "Spamming" refers to the practice of sending multiple copies of the same message to different electronic destinations; at the present time, this activity is often associated with unsolicited commercial advertising (Elmer-Dewitt 1994).
6. These acronyms stand for "frequently-asked question", "in my humble opinion", and "read the f***ing manual", respectively.
7. For further discussion of the ethics of conducting on-line research, see Thomas (forthcoming).
8. An extensive listing of references to work published up to and including 1992 can be found in the Infolingua bibliography on Computer-Mediated Communication compiled by Sabourin and Lamarche (1994).
9. Since these claims are likely to be controversial, this seems an appropriate point at which to state that the views expressed in the chapters of this volume do not necessarily reflect those of the volume editor, the series editors, or the publishers.

I: Linguistic Perspectives

Electronic Language:
A New Variety of English

Milena Collot
Paris Affiliate, Institute of Advanced Study
University of London

Nancy Belmore
Concordia University, Québec

1. Introduction*

In a prescient article in 1984, Naomi Baron[1] extended the notion of register to computer-based communication and reflected on the possible impact of this new register on traditional spoken and written genres. She suggested that one might wish to find out if there are grammatical differences between computer-mediated communication and other forms of spoken and written language.

This paper describes what is perhaps the most ubiquitous form of computer-mediated communication, the language people use on Bulletin Board Systems (BBSs). We have called this new variety of language Electronic Language.

BBSs have no fixed or identifiable membership. In this respect they differ from electronic discussion forums which serve a particular professional group, some of whose members have actually met and who, even if they have not met, are often familiar with each other's publications. The subject matter of BBSs covers a vast expanse, ranging from discussions of art to political debates and personal advice columns. BBSs are organized into 'conferences', identified by an appropriate title, which gather all the messages with a common theme. For example, in one BBS, all messages concerning advice on personal matters have been grouped under the conference title 'Dear Sue'.

The usual access route to BBSs is a modem. In 1970 there were just 15,000 in operation in the world. By 1987, there were an estimated 10 million (Rosch 1987). By mid-1992, Internet, the largest computer network in the world, linked millions of people through more than 750,000 'host' connections. By the end of 1992, Cukier (1993) reported that the number of computers connected to Internet had increased from 30,000 in 1987 to 1.3 million in 170 countries. As of February 1996, the most frequently-cited estimates of number of Internet users were in the 20-40 million range, according to G. Rowan of the *Globe and Mail* (personal communication), with some estimating as many as 100 million users.

This new form of communication has naturally attracted the interest of scholars around the world. As early as 1986, the *IEEE Transactions on Professional Communication* devoted a special issue to computer conferencing. In the preface to that issue, the editor, Valarie Arms, cited a 1977 article by Turoff and Hiltz which predicted that the new medium would eventually become as widespread and significant as the telephone. Danet (1992) gives an excellent overview of the implications of all forms of computer-mediated communication, not just the subset which we have called Electronic Language.

Electronic Language is characterized by a set of situational constraints which sets it apart from other varieties of English. Messages delivered electronically are neither 'spoken' nor 'written' in the conventional sense of these words. There is an easy interaction of participants and alternation of topics typical of some varieties of spoken English. However, they can not be strictly labelled as spoken messages since the participants neither see nor hear each other. Nor can they be considered strictly written since many of them are composed directly on-line, thereby ruling out the use of planning and editing strategies which are at the disposal of even the most informal writer. Spitzer (1986:19), in the special issue of the IEEE journal cited above, quotes comments from colleagues in which they describe this new variety as "talking in writing", "writing letters which are mailed over the telephone", "a panel discussion in slow motion". He himself observed that participants "...must use language as if they were having conversation, yet their message must be written" (Spitzer 1986:19).

Messages are entered in the BBS chronologically, but participants identify the message to which they are referring. This makes it possible to keep track of the 'thread' of a conference. A participant who wishes to refer to an earlier message uses the same subject header which appeared in that earlier message. To gather together all messages with the same subject header, it is only necessary to type the reference number of one such message. One then gets a copy of all the messages with the same subject header, in sequence and without a miss. Over time, the topics of messages with the same header tend to wander and eventually wane, just as a spoken conversation would. Kenner (1989), in an entertaining account of Electronic Language, describes telecommunications networks as a modern version of the old-fashioned telephone party line. The notable difference is that interlocutors are not only speaking from different places, but at different times.

Although messages can be sent to a specific addressee, everyone on a BBS has access to all messages; none are private. The participants come from widely varying backgrounds, and there are no obvious restrictions of age: anyone old enough to use a computer can have access to the boards. Since the participants do not see or hear each other, it is impossible to guess one's age or infer one's status from physical clues.

Topics vary with each conference and the purposes are as varied as the topics. One detects an overall feeling of enthusiasm for this new form of communication, a sense that it sets the participants apart from other language users. Table 1 describes the components of the speech situation which characterize BBSs.

2. Purpose

Because Electronic Language has unique situational features, it seems reasonable to assume that it embodies a distinctive set of linguistic features as well. If so, what are these features and how does this new variety of English differ from other varieties of English which have already been analyzed?

A pilot study (Collot 1991a) indicated how a description of this new variety might be approached. This study compared the types of comparative adjectives which occurred in a privately collected corpus of Electronic Language with those which Rusiecki (1985) had found in the Survey of English Usage corpus (Quirk 1960). The study revealed clear differences in the relative frequency of occurrence of inflectional ('newer', 'newest') and periphrastic comparison ('more new') in the two corpora. However, because the study focused on a single linguistic feature, it did not of course provide an adequate basis for a characterization of Electronic Language. Moreover, while the observed differences may be a function of the type of language, it is also possible that the differences simply reflect changes in grammatical usage over the past 30 years. There is thus a need for a more extensive study comparing contemporary data.

3. Descriptive framework

3.1. Biber's multidimensional-multi-feature model (MD-MF)

An empirical study of Electronic Language requires a suitable model for the study of situationally-determined language variation, and an adequate corpus. The model chosen was Biber's multidimensional-multi-feature (MD-MF) analysis as described in his *Variation Across Language and Speech* (1988). To our knowledge, our study is one of the first to apply his model to a corpus other than the ones he himself has analyzed (see references in Biber 1991, 1992), and the first to apply it to the study of Electronic Language. Ours is also, so far as we know, the first large-scale, corpus-based study of Electronic Language.

Table 1. Components of the speech situation which characterize Bulletin Board Systems (adapted from Biber 1988)

- Participants
  - Roles
    - Addressor, addressee, audience
  - Personal characteristics
    - Diverse
  - Group characteristics
    - Canadian and American
- Relations among participants
  - Social relations
    - Egalitarian
  - Personal relations
    - Generally friendly
  - Degree of shared interests
    - High
  - Degree of shared knowledge
    - Variable but often high
- Setting
  - Physical context
    - Participant's own desktop
  - Temporal context
    - Any time of day or night
  - Extent to which space and time are shared by participants
    - Zero
- Topic
  - Topics are classified into 'conferences' and vary accordingly
- Purpose
  - To request and give information, to make announcements, to engage in discussion
- Social Evaluation
  - Attitude towards communicative event
    - Acknowledgment of the unique nature of the event
  - Attitude towards content
    - Varies according to topic
- Relations of participants to the text
  - Type 1
    - Planned text, prepared beforehand
  - Type 2
    - Unplanned text, composed on-line
- Channel
  - Keyboarding

In their pioneering work, *Investigating English Style*, Crystal and Davy (1969) foreshadowed Biber's approach. Like Biber, they proposed the classification of texts in terms of what they called 'dimensions of situational constraint' (1969:64), which Biber (1988) calls 'components of the speech situation'. They too hypothesized that differences in situational variables would correlate with both the presence and absence of particular configurations of linguistic features. A similar approach has been used by Kittredge, Lehrberger and others who are interested in the grammatical and lexical features of what they call sub-languages (Kittredge and Lehrberger 1982).

Biber's particular innovation has been the analysis of computer-readable corpora to determine sets of linguistic features whose presence or absence correlates with what he calls 'textual dimensions'. A textual dimension is a functional categorization which cuts across traditional genre classifications. The assumption is that if a particular set of linguistic features consistently co-occurs in a group of texts, that set of features serves a particular communicative function. For example, academic prose, press reportage and official documents, however much they may differ in other respects, all have in common such features as a varied vocabulary and a high frequency of prepositional phrases, but a low frequency of such features as first and second person pronouns and present tense verb forms. Biber's analysis indicates that these features characterize all prose, regardless of genre, that is intended to be highly informational.

The principal technique used in Biber's approach is exploratory factor analysis. The purpose of factor analysis is to reduce a large number of variables, in this case, linguistic features, to a small set of derived variables, or factors. Factor analysis reveals which linguistic features tend to co-occur and which tend to be mutually exclusive. Each such set of features is a factor, and underlying each factor is a textual dimension. By summing the frequencies of each of the linguistic features in a text belonging to a particular genre, a factor score can be computed for that text. Biber selected 67 linguistic features, 59 of which he retained in his actual computation of factor scores. The average factor score for all texts in a genre yields what Biber calls the mean dimension score for the particular genre. Saukonnen (1989, 1993) has adapted Biber's approach to his own study of textual dimensions. However, he has examined a different set of linguistic features, in part, no doubt, because his texts are Finnish, and the dimensions he has identified only partially overlap Biber's.

Biber identified six factors and thus six dimensions. He labels each dimension in terms of what he considers the communicative function of the linguistic features associated with that dimension. One such dimension is 'involved versus informational production'. A text which rates high on the 'involved' end of the scale would contain, among its most prominent features, a relatively large number of private verbs like 'believe', 'feel' and 'know', i.e., verbs which express states or acts which are not observable (Quirk, Greenbaum,

Leech and Svartvik 1985:1181), contractions, first and second person pronouns, hedges like 'sort of' and 'kind of', if-clauses, and emphatics like 'for sure' and 'a lot'. Conversely, a text which rates high on the 'informational' end of the scale would be characterized by many nouns, attributive adjectives, and prepositional phrases, longer words, and many different words. The score of different genres on each dimension allows a comparison of genres both within and across dimensions.

A key feature of Biber's approach is that it does not assume a simple dichotomy between speech and writing. His characterization of texts in terms of the relation between communicative function and linguistic features reveals that there is no absolute distinction between speech and writing. Thus, written genres such as personal letters are more similar to spoken genres such as face-to-face conversation than they are to other written genres, and in each dimension he has found that written and spoken texts overlap.

Biber applied his model to a considerable body of computer-readable English texts, consisting of the one-million word Lancaster-Oslo-Bergen (LOB) corpus of written English (Johansson, Leech and Goodluck, 1978; Johansson, 1986), the 500,000 word London-Lund corpus of spoken English (Svartvik, 1990), and a collection of personal and professional letters. Biber's model makes it possible to rephrase the question initially posed. "What are the linguistic features of Electronic Language and how do they compare with other varieties of English?" can now be understood to mean, "Where does Electronic Language fit on each of the dimensions identified by Biber?"

3.2. The Electronic Language corpus (ELC)

Once a descriptive framework had been selected, the next task was the compilation of an adequate corpus of Electronic Language. The task was one of data selection rather than collection proper. Preliminary texts were downloaded from an international BBS called Input Montreal. Although the BBS is located in Montreal, it is international in the sense that it gathers and posts messages from across Canada and the United States, channeled through the larger networks Fidonet and Metrolink. As a result, Montreal speakers happen not to be represented in this corpus.

From the 86 conferences which appeared on the menu of Input Montreal, conferences were selected which would be as comparable as possible to the LOB and London-Lund corpora in terms of subject matter. For example, the Chit-Chat conference, an agglomeration of four minor conferences, Netchat, Gossip, Late Nite and Students, has unrestricted subject matter and is probably most comparable to the face-to-face or telephone conversations in the London-Lund corpus. Photo and Cooking, in which non-professionals seek information and give instructions, is represented in Biber's corpus by the LOB genre 'skills and hobbies'. Current Events concerns issues in the news, and the aim is primarily suasive. Many of the messages contain well-developed arguments, and as such this conference is comparable to the London-Lund category 'Public Debates'. Science is a general discussion of the physical sciences by science students, professionals and laymen. The topic is academic and the purpose is expository; it is loosely comparable to the academic prose genre of the LOB corpus.

The final corpus came from nine different conferences and contains about 200,000 words. Table 2 identifies each conference by its actual name, and indicates the number of words, messages and authors excerpted from each conference.

The corpus consists of two subsets, 'off-line' (90,075 words) and 'other' (115,618 words). Off-line messages are pre-written and can be positively identified by the presence of a tag, inserted after the last line of a message, which indicates that an electronic mail reader was used. Off-line mail reader programs always add this 'signature' as a form of advertisement, so it would seem reasonable to assume that messages not explicitly identified as off-line are on-line, i.e., like ordinary conversation, they are composed 'on the fly'. However, there is always the possibility that certain messages were pre-written using an ordinary word processor or editor in a multi-tasking environment, in which case a mail-reader tag would not appear. Since this means that the on-line category could not be positively identified, we designated it 'other' rather than on-line.

Table 2. Profile of the Electronic Language corpus

	Off-line				Other	
Messages	Authors	Words	Conference	Messages	Authors	Words
192	21	5115	Chit-Chat	464	55	12594
44	61	2591	Current Events	257	22	9245
135	21	15724	Science	137	56	12587
190	34	10937	Science Fiction	198	48	15535
99	30	10643	Finance	166	45	14460
233	27	10722	Film and Music	220	67	14333
172	28	12254	Photo and Cooking	396	81	12510
63	32	4804	Medical	210	69	5639
116	17	7285	Sports	288	79	18715
1244	216	90075	Totals	2336	522	115618

4. Method

To apply Biber's analysis to the ELC, it was first necessary to tag the corpus, i.e., to assign a part-of-speech label to each word in the corpus. The CLAWS1 tagging programs (Garside 1987), the suite of programs used to tag the LOB corpus, were used.

The untagged ELC was edited so that it would conform to the input requirements of CLAWS1. This included computer programs to handle special features of the ELC, among them many non-standard spellings ('thar', 'yer', 'fer'), invented words ('offensitivity'), and sound symbolic spelling ('I'm not n-n-n-nervous at all'). Some post-editing of the CLAWS1 output was also required. Figure 1 is an extract from the edited corpus. The character '|' has been inserted to indicate the beginning of a paragraph, '^' to indicate the beginning of a sentence.

|^Pal ol boy, as I said to another in a similar predicament to your own, check the batteries in your sarcasm detector. ^If anyone was really upset you'd know it. ^You have the unfortunate condition of being bothered by something relatively trivial, and many folks (myself included) are more than happy to give those with trivial concerns a bit of ribbing.
|^Probably because there is a marked difference between textbook English and colloquial English. ^You have made the mistake of assuming that since these messages are written that they should adhere to proper grammatical form. ^Such might be the case where there was formal debate on a particular topic (science, politics, theology). ^As it is, this conference is a catch-all blow-off zone, where most of the posts are idle chitchat, jokes, and informal discussion. ^Thus, colloquialism reigns.
|^Don't take it so hard, Joelerini.

Figure 1. An extract from the Electronic Language Corpus after it had been edited for input to the LOB Tagging Suite, CLAWS1

The final output yielded four versions of the tagged corpus: a tagged horizontal version, a tagged vertical version, only the tags, and only the words. All four versions were used to extract the specific linguistic features which were required in order to apply Biber's MD-MF model.

Using the tagged ELC as input, a search program called Gopher, and some special programs, the absolute frequencies of Biber's 59 features were determined for the ELC corpus. Then, from a list of normalized frequencies, the following statistics were computed: mean, minimum, maximum, range, and standard deviation and the feature deviation score (FDS). The feature deviation score was calculated on the basis of the figures for mean frequencies and standard deviations in Biber's corpus, as well as the mean frequency per 1000 words in each of the conferences in the ELC. The formula used was FDS = (Frequency - Mean)/Std. Dev. For example, the mean frequency of prepositions in the Off-line Chat conference is 116 per 1000 words. In Biber's corpus, the mean frequency of prepositions is 110.5 per 1000 words, and the standard deviation is 25.4. If we apply the formula above, the FDS will be (116-110.5)/25.4. The FDS is therefore 0.2.

Table 3 displays an extract from the comparative statistics for Biber's corpus and the ELC. Features which are common in Biber's corpus are usually common in the ELC; features which are rare are usually rare in the ELC. However, as would be expected in a subset of English with unique situational constraints, there are some striking differences. FDS is the feature deviation score.

Table 3. An extract from the comparative statistics for Biber's corpus and the ELC

Linguistic feature	Biber Mean	ELC Mean	Biber Std. Dev.	ELC Std. Dev.	FDS
Past tense	40.1	28.0	30.4	11.6	-0.4
Time adverbials	5.2	5.9	3.5	3.1	0.2
First person pronouns	27.2	57.5	26.1	21.2	1.2
Third person pronouns	29.9	25.5	22.5	9.4	-0.2
Agentless passives	9.6	7.0	6.6	5.2	-0.4
THAT verb complements	3.3	7.0	2.9	2.9	1.3
Present participial clauses	1.0	1.2	1.7	1.0	0.1
THAT relative–object position	0.8	1.7	1.1	0.9	0.8
Sentence relative	0.1	1.9	0.4	1.4	4.5
Prepositions	110.5	118.2	25.4	62.3	0.3

Feature deviation scores were computed for the entire corpus of messages, for the 'off-line' subset and the 'other' subset, and for each conference. Factor scores were computed by adding up the FDSs for each of the linguistic features in a factor for each of the conferences in the corpus. The third and final step was the calculation of the mean dimension score for each conference. This was computed by averaging the factor scores for each conference. It was then possible to plot the dimension scores extracted from the ELC onto Biber's graphic representation of these dimensions for his corpus, thereby answering the question: Where does Electronic Language fit on each of Biber's dimensions?

5. Results

Any attempt to interpret the findings of this study on the basis of previous research on speech and writing would have to heed Biber's admonition that there is no absolute difference between speech and writing. Electronic Language displays some of the linguistic features which have been associated with certain forms of written language, and others which are more usually associated with spoken language. The genres which it most closely resembles are public interviews and letters, personal as well as professional.

5.1. Textual dimensions

5.1.1. Dimension 1: Informational vs. involved production

In Biber's factorial structure, nouns, word length, prepositions, high type/token ratios and attributive adjectives were all assigned substantial negative weights. A high frequency of these features would therefore represent a great density of information. In the ELC, the frequencies for these features were largely comparable to Biber's corpus, with the exception of nouns, which were far more frequent in the ELC (225 per 1000 words) than in Biber's corpus (180 per 1000 words). However, if we consider the features in Factor 1 with positive weights, the balance is redressed. The ELC is replete with indicators of involvement such as first and second personal pronouns, contractions, hedges ('sort of', 'kind of') and amplifiers ('utterly', 'very'). Thus, although one of the primary purposes for participating in a BBS is to seek and impart information, the language in which this information is couched is more similar to that of spontaneous genres such as interviews, spontaneous speeches, and personal letters, than it is to that of informative genres such as official documents, academic prose, or press reportage. Figure 2 shows the position of the ELC (underlined) on Biber's continuum for Dimension 1.

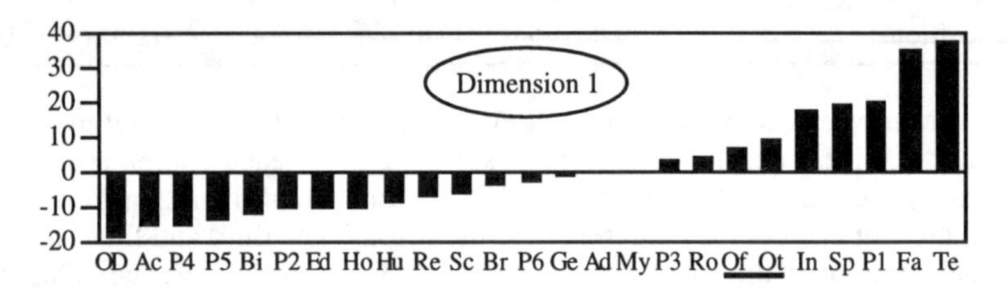

Figure 2. Informational vs. involved production

Abbreviations for Figures 2 through 7:

Ac	Academic prose	P1	Personal letters
Ad	Adventure fiction	P2	Popular lore
Bi	Biographies	P3	Prepared speeches
Br	Broadcasts	P4	Press reportage
Ed	Editorials	P5	Press reviews
Fa	Face-to-face conversations	P6	Professional letters
Ge	General fiction	Re	Religion
Ho	Hobbies	Ro	Romantic fiction
Hu	Humor	Sc	Science fiction
In	Interviews	Sp	Spontaneous speeches
My	Mystery fiction	Te	Telephone conversations
OD	Official Documents		
Of	Off-line ELC ←		
Ot	Other ELC ←		

5.1.2. Dimension 2: Non-narrative vs. narrative

There are a number of features with strong positive weights on this dimension, and none with negative weights. Biber sees all of these features as markers of narrative action. For example, past tense and perfective aspect describe past events, while third person pronouns (other than 'it') refer to animate, typically human referents. Public verbs like 'admit' and 'say' are also important on this dimension, because they function as markers of reported speech, while synthetic negation ('he said nothing' vs. 'he did not say anything') is often seen as the preferred style in literary narrative. In the ELC, all of these features are considerably less frequent than in Biber's corpus. As a result, the ELC has a relatively low score on this dimension. With respect to narrative features, the genres it most resembles are professional letters, telephone conversations, press reviews, and interviews. It is very far indeed from romantic fiction, which has the highest score on this dimension. Figure 3 shows the position of the ELC on Biber's continuum for Dimension 2.

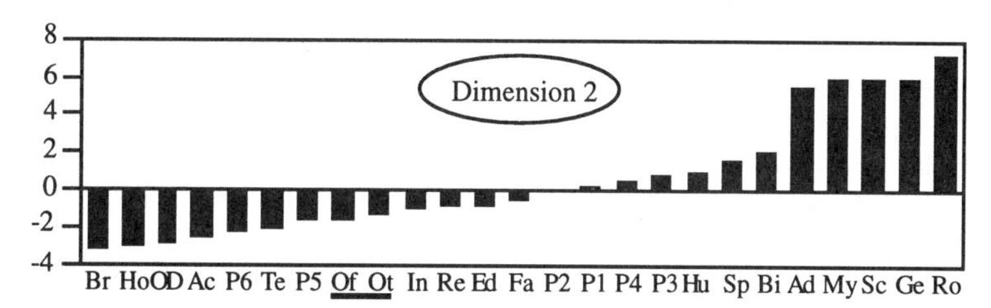

Figure 3. Non-narrative vs. narrative discourse

5.1.3. Dimension 3: Situation-dependent vs. explicit

The features which carry large positive weights on this dimension are relative constructions. WH-relative clauses in object position ('the man whom Sally likes'), pied-piping relative clauses ('the manner in which he was told'), and WH-relative clauses in subject position ('the man who likes popcorn') are all seen as devices for the explicit, elaborated identification of referents in a text. In contrast, the three features with negative weights—time and place adverbials such as 'later', 'yesterday', 'above' and certain other adverbs—are considered markers of reference to times, places and events which can only be correctly interpreted if the addressee has sufficient knowledge of the text (e.g., 'see above') or the external circumstances ('just below us here') to be able to infer, on the basis of context, the intended message. The scores for this dimension reveal that the ELC lies between the two extremes. It has the same or nearly the same score as humor, press reportage and interviews. Humor is, of course, an amorphous category. In the LOB corpus, it includes selections from books and articles which were apparently intended for a highly literate audience, e.g., an article by Doris Lessing which appeared in *The New Statesman*. Figure 4 shows the position of the ELC on Biber's continuum for Dimension 3.

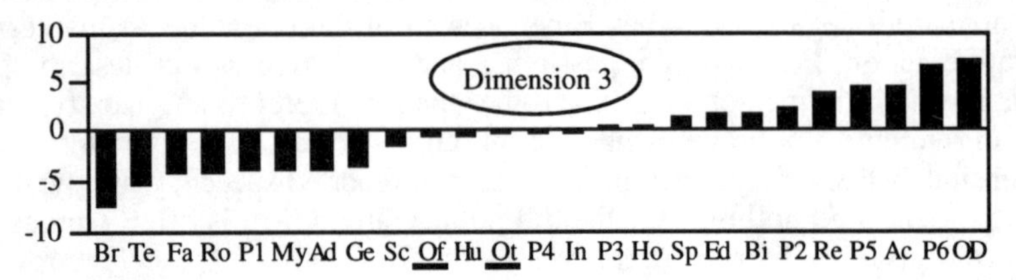

Figure 4. Situation-dependent vs. explicit

5.1.4. Dimension 4: Overt expression of persuasion

This dimension is characterized by prediction and necessity modals, suasive verbs ('command', 'demand'), conditional subordination, and infinitives, most commonly used as adjective and verb complements, which are seen as marking the speaker's attitude towards the proposition encoded in the infinitive clause ('happy to do it', 'hope to see you'). In the ELC, many of these features have a higher frequency than in Biber's corpus. However, three features are less frequent: suasive verbs, necessity modals and split auxiliaries ('they are objectively shown to'). As a consequence of these differences, the ELC is situated between personal letters and editorials, near the high end of the scale. Figure 5 shows the position of the ELC on Biber's continuum for Dimension 4.

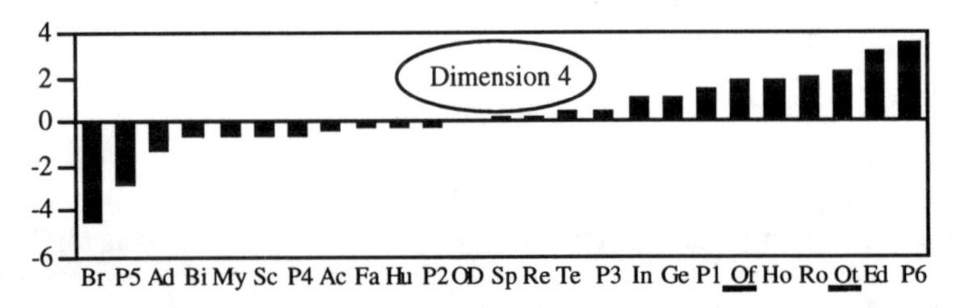

Figure 5. Overt expression of persuasion

5.1.5. Dimension 5: Non-abstract vs. abstract information

Agentless passives, BY-passives, past participial clauses ('built in a single week') and past participial clauses with relative deletion ('the solution produced by this process') are the most important features associated with abstract information. No feature has a large negative weight on this dimension. According to Biber, these forms are frequently used in procedural discourse, where emphasis on the agent is reduced because the same agent is presupposed across several clauses. These features are generally as rare in the ELC corpus as they are in Biber's. However, two features which factor analysis reveals as frequently co-occurring with passive constructions—conjuncts ('however', 'in contrast') and adverbial subordinators ('since', 'while')—do occur considerably more frequently in the ELC than in Biber's corpus, and thus account for the ELC's relatively high score on this dimension. However, neither of these features appears to play a major functional role. Biber included them only because they co-occur with features which do play a major role. It would seem therefore that the ELC score on this dimension would have to be interpreted with caution, since the only features which occur frequently are those which do not play a crucial functional role, and therefore have little interpretive value. Figure 6 shows the position of the ELC on Biber's continuum for Dimension 5.

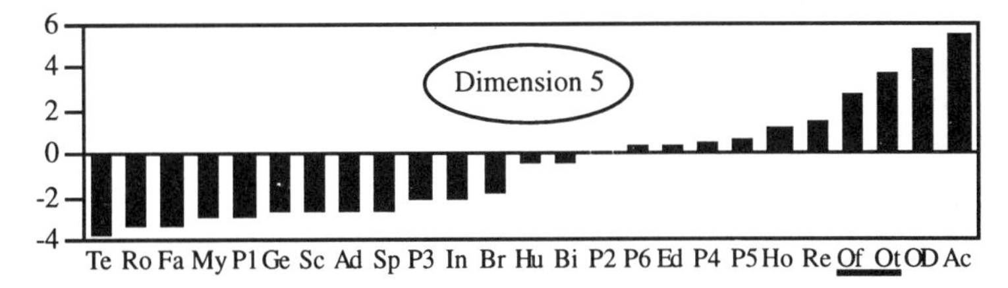

Figure 6. Non-abstract vs. abstract information

5.1.6. Dimension 6: On-line informational elaboration

Four features underlie this dimension: demonstratives, THAT clauses as verb complements, THAT relative clauses in object position, and THAT clauses as adjective complements. Biber sees the co-occurrence of these features as marking informational elaboration in relatively unplanned types of discourse, hence the word 'on-line'. The ELC has a greater number of all four features than Biber's corpus. Accordingly, the ELC scores fairly high on this dimension, between spontaneous speeches and editorials. The off-line subset is at the same level as professional letters. Figure 7 shows the position of the ELC on Biber's continuum for Dimension 6.

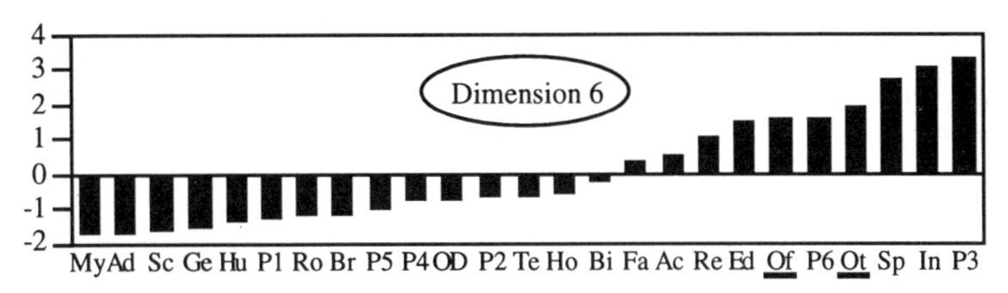

Figure 7. On-line informational elaboration

5.2. Situational features

There seem to be at least four situational features which play an important role in explaining the linguistic manifestations of the ELC. The first is the degree of common interests and shared knowledge among the participants. People who have been using a BBS for a while know each other's nicknames, mannerisms and ideas. They have followed each other's arguments on different subjects and have accumulated a wealth of shared knowledge. Even people who are new to the board know that their audience will be generally sympathetic because they are bound to them by common interests. This may account for the high degree of involvement in the ELC, as well as for its relative situation-dependency, despite the fact that participants are separated by time and space.

The second important feature is the purpose of communication, which is to request and impart information and to discuss specific issues. These purposes seem to play an important role in shaping Electronic Language as a non-narrative and highly persuasive discourse type.

The third important component of the speech situation is the tripartite nature of the roles played by the participants, which include an addressor, an addressee and an audience. This may explain the similarities between the ELC and public interviews, in which the interviewees respond specifically to the interviewer but do so for the benefit of a wider audience. Finally, the fact that time and space are not shared by the participants may explain the resemblance between the ELC on the one hand and personal and professional letters on the other.

One component which was expected to play a large role in the make-up of Electronic Language was the relationship of the speakers to the text. Thus, from the very beginning of the study, as noted in Section 3.2, steps were taken to ensure that messages produced directly on-line be kept separate from those produced beforehand, or off-line. However, while on-line messages (designated 'other') were typically placed along each textual dimension in a position which brought them slightly closer to other spoken genres, the differences between on-line and off-line were very slight.

There are two plausible explanations for this unanticipated result. One is that a significant but unidentifiable group of messages in the category 'other' may not in fact have been composed on-line. The other, and perhaps more likely, explanation for the slight difference between the two categories is that other components of the ELC speech situation, such as the presence of an audience and the disembodiment of messages in space and time, together exercise an influence which outweighs that of time constraints alone.

6. Extending the description

This study has identified the situational features which appear to have a significant impact on the linguistic make-up of Electronic Language. However, what it has not determined is the degree to which each situational feature affects the overall linguistic configuration of Electronic Language. Further studies should examine some of these situational features more closely. A particularly interesting feature, and one which has eluded us here, is the relationship of the participants to the text. As noted above, messages composed off-line could be positively identified, but the inference that messages not so identified were definitely composed extemporaneously could not be made with an adequate degree of certainty.

Another interesting extension of this study would be to examine variation within Electronic Language. This kind of study would produce a description of the internal coherence of the ELC from which it would be possible to infer the importance of particular situational variables such as topic. The sample size of each conference in the ELC is too small to test for differences which might be accounted for in this way, but it is reasonable to assume that such differences may exist. It is also likely that there are differences between Electronic Language as we have defined it and other types of computer-mediated exchanges. The scope of the term Electronic Language should thus be extended to include all such exchanges, since it is by now apparent that, like ordinary spoken and written language, there are different varieties of Electronic Language. While we have investigated one of the most wide-spread varieties, others are equally worthy of investigation.

Since this study was initially completed, Herring (1992, 1993a, 1993c) has established the role of gender in shaping the linguistic and rhetorical features of messages posted on computer-mediated discussion lists with an academic focus. Her studies suggest a new textual dimension, a functional continuum ranging from 'adversarial' to 'attenuated', in which gender and type of discussion play a major role in the distribution of linguistic features. The use of Biber's model to study Electronic Language subsets such as this could reveal other textual dimensions worthy of attention.

As automated linguistic analysis becomes more sophisticated, Biber's model could be extended to include linguistic features of potential significance which it was not feasible for him to include in his original study. For example, a corpus which had been syntactically analyzed, and not just tagged, would permit making a distinction between direct and indirect speech. It would also be of interest to apply other MD-MF systems to the study of Electronic Language. Saukkonen's (1993) dimensions are, as noted, similar to Biber's yet the system as a whole is quite different.

Biber's new measure of 'discourse complexity' (Biber 1992), a five dimensional model, could be interestingly applied to Electronic Language as a whole or to particular sub-sets. As in his earlier studies, none of the dimensions is associated with an absolute difference between speech and writing. However, when taken as a whole "...they identify a fundamental distinction between spoken and written registers: spoken registers are apparently limited in the kinds of complexity they can exploit" (Biber 1992:160). Where would Electronic Language, which seems so clearly a 'hybrid' variety of English, fit on a measure which *does* appear to differentiate between speech and writing consistently?

Regardless of the direction future studies may take, telecommunications are steadily and dramatically gaining in importance the world over. Electronic Language, which gives voice to such communication, is therefore worthy of further exploration.

ACKNOWLEDGMENTS

* This is a revised version of an article which originally appeared in 1993 under the same title in *English Language Corpora: Design and Exploitation.* We would like to express our appreciation to the editors, Jan Aarts, Pieter de Haan and Nelleke Oostdijk, for permission to include the article in this volume. Special thanks are due to G. N. Leech, Professor of English and Director of the Unit for Computer Research on the English Language at the University of Lancaster, for permission to use the CLAWS1 tagging programs. We are also grateful to Adrian Saldanha for his technical expertise, and to Anne G. Barkman of Concordia's Computing Services Department, who modified the CLAWS1 programs so that they would run on Concordia's VAX2 computer. Thanks are also due to Prof. Margery Fee of Queen's University and Prof. John Upshur of Concordia for their helpful comments and suggestions as readers of Collot's master's thesis on Electronic Language.

NOTES

1. We learned about Baron's article and several other early articles on computer-mediated communication in "The language of electronic mail", a paper which Natalie Maynor contributed to the TESL-L electronic discussion forum for Teachers of English as a Second Language in March 1993. In this paper, Maynor comments on some apparent features of what she calls 'e-mail style'. She notes that some of the features "...seem to be attempts to make writing more like speech". Readers who would like a copy can obtain one by joining TESL-L (listserv@cunyvm.bitnet or listserv@cunyvm.cuny.edu).

Oral and Written Linguistic Aspects of Computer Conferencing: A Corpus Based Study

Simeon J. Yates
Open University, UK

1. Introduction

Unlike previous studies of computer-mediated communication (CMC) which have concentrated on either psychological factors, or on the perceived attributes of the medium, and which have often used small and specific data sets, this chapter reports the findings of a large corpus-based comparison between spoken, written and CMC discourse. The various factors across which comparisons are made were drawn from a Hallidayan model of language use and focus upon the textual, interpersonal and ideational (Halliday 1978) aspects of speech, writing and CMC.

The chapter initially describes the construction of a corpus of CMC interactions. The textual aspects of CMC discourse are then considered through such measures as type/token ratios and lexical density. The interpersonal in CMC is explored through the examination of pronoun use. Last, the presentation of the ideational within CMC discourse is considered through an exploration of modal auxiliary use within the CMC corpus. All of these results are comparatively analyzed against similar results from spoken and written corpora.

2. Collecting the data

2.1. Building a corpus of CMC interactions

Over and above the specific needs of this study, there is a more general need to consider the building of a CMC corpus. As Johansson (1991) notes:

> The computer revolution has brought with it new forms of discourse which also deserve systematic study. One of these is electronic mail ... Electronic mail reveals features of both speech and writing. Like other forms of discourse, new as well as old, it deserves the attention of future corpus workers. (307-308)

There are a considerable number of different sources that could be used to build a corpus of CMC interactions and utterances. These possibilities include electronic mail (e.g., Microsoft Mail, VAX Mail, etc.), bulletin boards, computer conferencing (e.g., CoSy, VAX Notes, Confer, etc.), synchronous messaging systems (e.g., VAX Phone, Macintosh Broadcast), and so forth. Though collecting data from such sources has many advantages, especially as the data come already transcribed, there are specific difficulties in relation to each form of communication. The collection of data from direct synchronous forms of communication is for most purposes a difficult task. Such systems tend not to store the messages created and, akin to using the telephone, once they are finished no record remains.

Electronic mail systems do, on the whole, store received messages, allowing the recipient to decide upon which to keep or to delete. However, there is one main problem with using such a source, namely privacy. Most electronic mail is sent directly from individual to individual. To collect such a corpus would require access to others' mail exchanges, or to those messages they wished to release. This would also be the case for synchronous forms of CMC.

Electronic mail in the form of "listserve" interactions and bulletin boards gets around many of these problems as it mostly involves open multi-party communication. There are fewer data collection problems as any one person can be connected to a large number of different discussions. Computer conferencing, like listserve discussions, also tends to consist of open, multi-party discussions. In many respects these two types of CMC are very similar systems of communication, differing mainly in the form of their administration and technical operation. Unlike listserve interactions, computer conferencing messages are stored centrally in a database and accessed by users there. Messages from earlier in the interaction are readily viewable and whole conference discussions can be downloaded at will. This makes computer conferencing a convenient data source for an initial CMC corpus.

There were three main computer conferencing systems available to the research project. These were the CoSy system and the VAX Notes system—both running on the VAX cluster at the Open University in the United Kingdom—and the Confer system used at the University of Michigan in the USA. Very little use is made of the VAX Notes system at the Open University, and no data were therefore collected from that source. A large data set was provided from the Michigan Confer system which is yet to be fully analyzed. The main data source was therefore interactions taking place on the CoSy system at the Open University in the United Kingdom.

Given the above discussion of possible sources, the choice of CoSy might seem a somewhat arbitrary decision. There are, however, important methodological reasons for this choice. First, CoSy has a large user base spread across the whole of the United Kingdom. The system is now used directly for student support on several Open University courses, as well as indirectly by those students with CoSy access on other courses. It also provides a forum for much discussion and communication among both academic and non-academic staff. There were over 2,000 registered users of the CoSy system at the time the research was conducted. A second reason for using CoSy as a data source is the possibility for the collection of background data on users. The main course taught via CMC, through practicals and projects, provides a large database of information on student use and attitudes, containing approximately 900 responses each year. These data have been used to conduct evaluations (see Mason 1989) as well as studies of specific issues (see Yates 1993a).

2.2. Creating the CMC corpus

While one obvious method for the creation of a CMC corpus would be to download all available material, this would produce a data set of excessively large proportions that might prove too unwieldy. It also ignores the fact that the corpus must be to some extent comparable to the written and spoken corpora already in existence. It was decided to use only those conferences which had been designated as "open". Though it was possible for the researcher to have access to "closed" discussions, the use of such data did not seem appropriate for ethical reasons. All open discussions are accessible to all CoSy users.

2.2.1. The 50 message selection

The first task in creating the corpus consisted of collecting a sample from each open conference topic. Given that the size of text samples for the written and spoken corpora was 2,000 and 5,000 words respectively, it was decided that the CoSy samples should be comparable in size. An initial general examination revealed that 50 CoSy messages contained an average of 3,500 words. The sampling technique used was therefore to cut off interactions at 50 messages.

Such an arbitrary cut-off point might seem problematic and does raise some methodological concerns. However, the written corpus to be examined, the Lancaster-Oslo/Bergen (LOB) corpus, arbitrarily cut off text samples at 2,000 words. On the other hand the spoken corpus, the London-Lund corpus, amalgamated spoken interactions of a certain type until they contained some 5000 words. The cutting off of interactions at 50 messages was therefore comparable to the arbitrary sampling techniques used in the other target corpora.

There were 152 conference topics with 50 messages or more. From all of these the first 50 messages were taken. This provided a total of 648,550 words and an average of 4,267 words per sample text, somewhat higher than expected though still within the required range. (A full description of the corpus including individual details for each interaction is given in Yates 1993b.) This corpus will from now on be referred to as the CoSy:50 corpus.

2.2.2. *The full conference selection*

Given that the above selection consisted of only partial discussions, and given some of the possible methodological problems the sampling method might raise, it was decided to create a corpus of full conferencing interactions. Rather than randomly sampling a set of conferences, it seemed more useful to collect data from specific sources. Various considerations bore on this decision. In the first case it seemed best to choose material of which the researcher had a good clear knowledge. It was necessary to choose material of both an academic and non-academic nature. There was also a need to collect data from both novice and expert users, and last, it seemed necessary to collect data from more than one time period.

Two sources were chosen: samples from the discussions taking place on the main course using CMC (DT200: An Introduction to Information Technology: Social and Technological Issues) of 1988, 1990, 1991, and 1992, as well as discussions from a wide-ranging multi-topic conference named Phoenix.[1] In choosing the DT200 data set, a large amount of data produced mainly by novice student users discussing academic and non-academic issues could be analyzed. Each year's data would include a fresh set of discussants. The Phoenix conference contained an open discussion of a variety of subjects from the serious through to the frivolous. The members of this conference consisted in the main of experienced CoSy users who remained present over several years of data. Many, but not all these participants, were employees of the Open University. In total, 66 conference topics were collected totalling some 1,573,499 words for an average of 23,840 words per topic (see Yates 1993c for full details).

2.2.3. *Sample from full conferences*

Last, it was necessary to construct a sub-set of the CoSy:Full corpus. This was necessary as several of the linguistic analyses to be conducted produced results which were sensitive to text length. This made it important that there be a set of CoSy samples equal in average length to the smaller samples of the two other corpora. Given that the LOB corpus averaged 2,000 words, a similar sized corpus was constructed from the CoSy:Full corpus. This contained 61 samples averaging 2,262 words for a total of 137,974 words. The lower number of texts compared to the CoSy:Full was due to the fact that 5 of the CoSy:Full texts did not contain 2,000 words. All of these were DT200 texts. This corpus will from now on be referred to as the CoSy:Sample corpus.

In the end, most analyses used a combination of the CoSy:50 and CoSy:Full corpora. This provided a total of 218 files and 2,222,049 words.

2.2.4. Spoken and written corpora

Two large corpora of spoken and written material were used in the research reported here. These were made available on a CD-ROM provided by the Norwegian Computing Centre for the Humanities. The CD-ROM provided four different corpora, these being the Brown Corpus of written American English, the Lancaster-Oslo/Bergen corpus of written British English, the London-Lund corpus of spoken British English, and the Kolhapur corpus of Indian English. The texts came in various operating system formats and in a number of differently tagged forms. It was decided to use the Lancaster-Oslo/Bergen corpus to represent written texts and the London-Lund corpus to represent spoken texts. These were used because they represented examples of British rather than American or other forms of English. This was an obvious choice given that the CoSy corpus was created by people living within the United Kingdom.

3. The textuality of CMC

3.1. Type/token ratios of vocabulary use

One difference between speech and writing that many researchers have commented upon is that of the differing modes of production and consumption. Speech is produced "on the fly" and is intended to be consumed, heard, in the same rapid and dynamic manner. Writing on the other hand is static; it is produced at the pace set by the writer alone and can be consumed at any speed that the reader chooses. The effects of such differences in production are likely, it is claimed, to generate differences in the language used. One aspect of this concerns vocabulary use. Chafe and Danielewicz (1987) claim that

> [a]s a consequence of these differences, speakers tend to operate with a narrower range of lexical choices than writers. Producing language on the fly, they hardly have time to sift through all of the possible choices they might make, and may typically settle on the first words that occur to them. The result is that the vocabulary of spoken language is more limited in variety. (88)

In order to examine the differing use of vocabulary more empirically, Chafe and Danielewicz make use of the *type/token ratio.* The type/token ratio used by Chafe and Danielewicz is that of the number of different words (*types*) divided by the total number of words (*tokens*). In this calculation, all words of all types were counted (Chafe and Danielewicz 1987:88). The main problem with such an analysis concerns the lack of reference to the structure of most written English. Given that clauses are generated through specific constructions of both grammatical and lexical words, and that these clause constructions may, and do, differ between speech and writing, such a crude measure of the type/token ratio is problematic. A more rigorous measure of vocabulary use would be to calculate the ratio of the number of different lexical items (*lexical types*) to the total number of lexical items (*lexical tokens*).

3.2. Results of a type/token ratio analysis across three media

Using specifically designed software tools, data were collected on the numbers of lexical items in three of the corpora. The three corpora used were the CoSy:Sample, the London-Lund and the LOB corpora. The reason for choosing the CoSy:Sample corpus concerns the effects of length upon type/token ratios. A small text of a few hundred words will not indicate much in terms of vocabulary use in the type of quantitative analysis being conducted here. On the other hand, though there are a greater number of words in total in a longer text, the numbers of *new* words will be less. This makes a type/token measure length sensitive. That is to say that for any set of texts of the same length, one would expect lower type/token ratios for the spoken texts and higher ones for the written texts, but the actual values of the ratios would be proportional to the length of the text. In order to avoid this problem, the sampled set of CoSy conferences was used. The average length of the sampled conferences was 2,262 words, compared to 2,000 for the LOB and 5,000 for the London-Lund corpora. As Zipf (1935) (See below) indicated, this length sensitivity is a function of the natural log of the text length, and therefore the differences in average text length between these three corpora should not affect the result. The general result is presented in Table 1.

Table 1. Mean type/token ratios for three corpora

Corpus:	CoSy:Sample (CMC)	LOB (Writing)	London-Lund (Speech)
Mean Type/Token Ratio:	0.590	0.624	0.395
Standard Deviation:	0.051	0.084	0.051

Conducting a one-way analysis of variance across the data produced a significant result ($F = 367.370$, $df=658$, $p < 0.0001$) indicating a clear statistical difference between the three groups. Further comparisons using t-tests between the three media also produced statistically significant results. Finally a Tukey-Honestly-Significant-Difference test was conducted to check these results. This test also found that all three groups were significantly different at the 0.05 level.

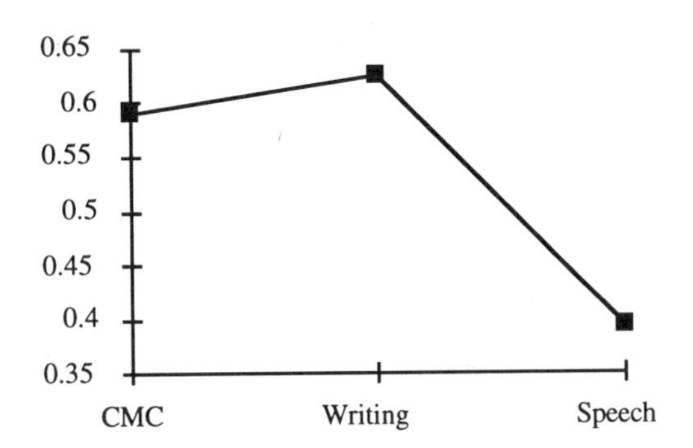

Figure 1. Interaction plot of type/token ratios for three corpora

This result would seem to indicate that CMC is more akin to writing than speech in terms of range of vocabulary used. The most obvious conclusion is to follow Chafe and Danielewicz and see this as a product of the medium itself, and the opportunity it brings for longer gestation over the content of utterances. Careful thought about this point however raises a complication. The texts contained within the LOB corpus were mostly produced prior to the advent of the word processor or the electronic text. The CMC corpus contains only word-processed electronic texts. Electronic text brings an even greater set of opportunities to correct, change, restructure and review utterances. Following the reasoning of Chafe and Danielewicz, one would expect to see an even greater variety of vocabulary used in CMC. However, this is not the case, no doubt because the process of redrafting produces complexity and variety in a printed (especially a published) text. Despite the fact that electronic text provides opportunities for greater variety in the texts produced by individuals, it appears that these opportunities are not taken up in most cases.

Moreover, it is writing that demonstrates the greatest variation around the mean level of vocabulary use, as compared to speech and CMC which have comparable variances. The implication of this result is that factors other than simply the mechanical aspects of the medium are at work in determining the production of utterances.

Vocabulary use is dependent on a large number of sociolinguistic issues, and despite having a clear relationship to the production and consumption of a text, it is not the only measure of the textuality of an utterance.

3.3. The lexical density of CMC

Though type/token ratios are initially revealing, such a measure leaves out a number of more interesting and important linguistic issues. In order to incorporate these issues within an empirical measure we need to consider the issue of lexical density. Halliday (1985:61) begins his explanation of lexical density with the following examples:

(1) If you invest in a rail facility, this implies that you are going to be committed for a long time. ***[lexical density = 0.35]***

(2) Investment in a rail facility implies a long term commitment. ***[lexical density = 0.7]***

Halliday argues that the first of these sentences appears much more like the record of spoken communication than written. The first of these sentences has 7 lexical items and 13 grammatical ones. The lexical items are: *invest; rail; facility; implies; committed; long;* and *term.* In the second sentence there are 7 lexical items and 3 grammatical ones. The lexical items are: *investment; rail; facility; implies; long; term* and *commitment.*

There is therefore a quantitative difference between spoken and written utterances. The ratio of lexical items to grammatical ones is lower for spoken language than it is for written. In the above example the first sentence has a ratio of 7 to 13 while the second sentence has a ratio of 7 to 3. These can be better represented as a ratio or percentage of the number of lexical items to the number of total items within an utterance. According to this measure, the first sentence would score 7 out of 20 or 0.35 (35%). The second sentence would score 7 out of 10 or 0.7 (70%). These types of score Halliday describes as *lexical density* scores (Halliday 1985:61-63).

Ure (1971) conducted a study of the lexical density of texts representing 34 spoken and 30 written registers or genres. Ure used a similar method to that described above, counting the total number of words for each text and then counting the number of words with "lexical properties". From these values she calculated the percentage of the total words with "lexical properties" (Ure 1971:445). Using this method, Ure noted a clear difference across two factors. First, all written texts were found to have a higher lexical density; second, texts containing "feedback" from the listener/reader had lower lexical densities (Ure 1971:445-452).

A similar test was conducted using the London-Lund and Lancaster-Oslo/Bergen corpora, while for CMC the CoSy:Full corpus of interactions and the CoSy:50 corpus of interactions were used, as this measure is not sensitive to text length. A one-way analysis of variance produced the results given in Table 2 and the interaction plot in Figure 2. Once again the results of this analysis were significant ($F=238.439$, $df=810$, $p<0.0001$). A post-hoc Tukey-Honestly-Significant-Difference test indicated these individual differences were all significant at the 0.05 level.

Table 2. Mean unweighted lexical densities for three corpora

Corpus:	CoSy:50 and CoSy:Full (CMC)	LOB (Writing)	London-Lund (Speech)
Mean Lexical Density (Unweighted) [%]:	49.258	50.316	42.292

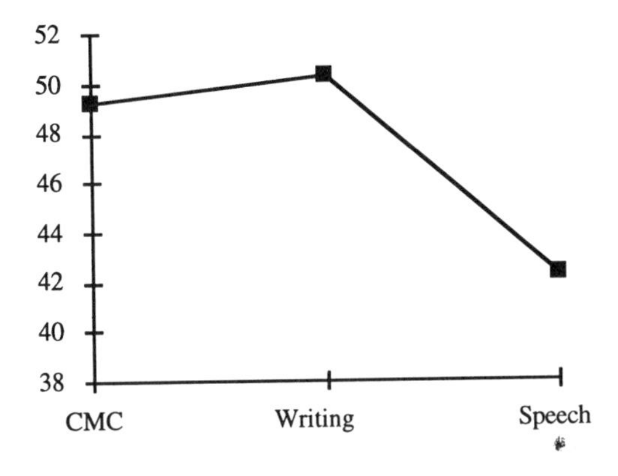

Figure 2. Interaction plot of unweighted lexical densities for three corpora

Some further issues need to be considered here. Lexical density can be crudely described as a measure of the information density within a text. In this sense it measures the ease or difficulty with which a text can be processed by an individual reading it in a specific social context: that is, the cognitive effort required to process a text. Specific styles, genres and/or registers have their own distinctive structure and vocabulary use which limit the variety of language used and generally cause certain words and phrases to be repeated.[2] Repetition of lexical items sets up expectations of the recurrence of lexical items; this includes repetition of the same lexical item in differing forms. In addition, use of more generically common lexical items (e.g., *cat* vs. *feline*) makes processing easier. Last, there are a number of items which serve semi-grammatical functions and structure the text (most often written texts) at a level greater than the clause or sentence (e.g., coordinating and subordinating connectives), and are therefore more common.

To get around these issues, Halliday (1985:65) suggests that more common lexical items be given a lower "score" than others; in fact he suggests a half value. Through this *weighting* the repetition of words within a text, their frequency within the language, and therefore the higher-frequency borderline cases between lexis and grammar are dealt with. Such a half-value weighting is indeed a starting point and was used in earlier versions of this analysis (Yates 1993a), but raises several methodological problems. First, it is not clear at what stage a word becomes a "high frequency item". Nor does Halliday make it clear whether he is referring to high frequency in the text itself, in the genre, or in the language. In fact all these factors may affect lexical density. In practical terms such a method also requires pre-analysis of the data to determine word frequencies in individual texts and then re-analysis of those texts with specifically constructed lists of "high frequency items". What is clearly needed therefore is some definable method which can take into account difficulties associated with high frequency items.

A second problem in creating such a weighting concerns another form of repetition, this being the occurrence of the same lexical item, or lexeme, in several forms (e.g., *differ* and *different*). There is no full solution to this problem although one general and rough measure of the phenomenon is provided by the specifically designed software tools. By taking note of such variants as plurals and other readily identifiable forms of a lexeme, a lexemes-to-lexicals ratio can be calculated.

Following the work of Zipf (1935) on the linear relationship in a given text between word frequency, number of occurrences, and word rank—the word's relative position in a ranking of word frequencies—it is possible to provide a mathematical formula based on rank through which we "weight" each item in an analyzed text. To calculate the lexical density of a text, we need only sum the weights for each word and divide this by the total number of words in the text. This calculation is given in the following equation:

$$L_w = \frac{\sum_{x=1}^{r_{\max}} n_x l^{\ln(r_{\max} - r_x)}}{T}$$

Equation 1

In this formula, L_W is the weighted lexical density, l is the lexeme/lexicals ratio for the text, r_{max} is the rank of the least frequent word and r_x is the present word. n_x is the number of words in the text with rank x and T is the total number of words in the text. Given that the lexeme/lexical ratio is sensitive to text length, as is the number of ranks, this calculation is also sensitive to text length. Weighted lexical density scores were calculated from word frequency listings produced by the software. This required the writing of a further set of software tools and spreadsheet macros in order to transform the output into a statistically analyzable form.

Once again the London-Lund and Lancaster-Oslo/Bergen corpora were used to provide the spoken and written data sets. As with the Type/Token analysis, the set of 61 CoSy conference samples was used to offset text length effects. A one-way analysis of variance was conducted to examine the differences between the three media. The results of this analysis were again significant ($F=193.320$, $df=658$, $p<0.0001$). Table 3 gives the mean values for the different corpora; Figure 3 is an interaction plot of the same. A post-hoc Tukey-Honestly-Significant-Difference test confirmed that the differences were significant at the 0.05 level for the comparisons between CMC and speech and speech and writing.

Table 3. Mean weighted lexical densities for three corpora

Corpus:	CoSy:Full (CMC)	LOB (Writing)	London-Lund (Speech)
Mean Weighted Lexical Density [%]:	44.996	46.076	35.994

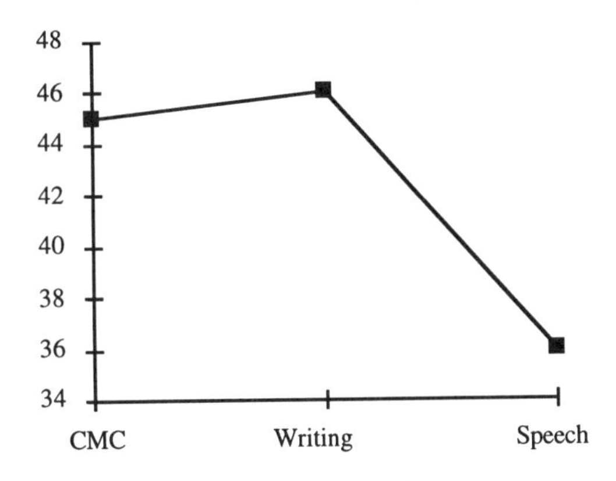

Figure 3. Interaction plot of weighted lexical densities for three corpora

Having considered further the question of vocabulary use in CMC, we have returned to a similar result. CMC users package information in text in ways that are more written- than speech-like. Rather than the making of literate texts into oral ones, we are possibly seeing here what Zuboff (1988) describes as the "textualization of sociality" through CMC. That is, users of CMC systems may be bringing their literate production practices to an interactive, social and orally-oriented interaction.

4. Modality of CMC

4.1. Personal reference

One of the main differences between speech and writing which many researchers focus upon is reference to self and other. Chafe (1982) and Chafe and Danielewicz (1987) have considered differences in the relationship between writer/reader and speaker/listener as encoded within speech and writing. They examine these issues linguistically through considering pronoun use in various genres representing formal written, informal written, formal spoken, and informal spoken varieties of American English. Chafe (1982:45) describes the differences as being formed by levels of *involvement* and *detachment*. He argues that the involvement of speakers with their audiences arises from the fact that

> [i]t is typically the case that a speaker has face to face contact with the person to whom he or she is speaking. That means, for one thing, that the speaker and listener share a considerable amount of knowledge concerning the environment of the conversation. It also means that the speaker can monitor the effect of what he or she is saying on the listener, and that the listener is able to signal the understanding and ask for clarification ... to have less concern for consistency than for experiential involvement. (Chafe 1982:45)

Fowler and Kress (1979) also consider these issues through examining the usage of pronouns in general. In contrast with Chafe, they see the omission of subjectivity from written texts in terms of conventional social practices rather than effects of the medium. They claim that

> [r]emoval of the pronoun associated with personal speech is felt to be appropriate to the impersonal, generalising tone of newspapers, textbooks, scientific articles. (Fowler and Kress 1979:201)

It is not the medium of writing that creates the impersonality but rather the "appropriate" attendant social practices. Fowler and Kress note that the use of *I* is rare in the text of the *Observer* newspaper. It appears most frequently in self-centered articles by people of note, in investigative reporting and in eye-witness accounts (Fowler and Kress 1979:201).

One would expect from such theorizing to see higher levels of first and second person pronoun use in spoken discourse as compared to writing. This is indeed the case, as Figure 4 indicates. Once again a one-way analysis of variance was conducted and CMC, speech and writing were found to be statistically different for all three forms of pronoun use (first person, F=250.6355, p=0.0000; second person, F=218.5472, p=0.0000; third person, F=49.8842, p=0.0000; df=814 in all three cases).

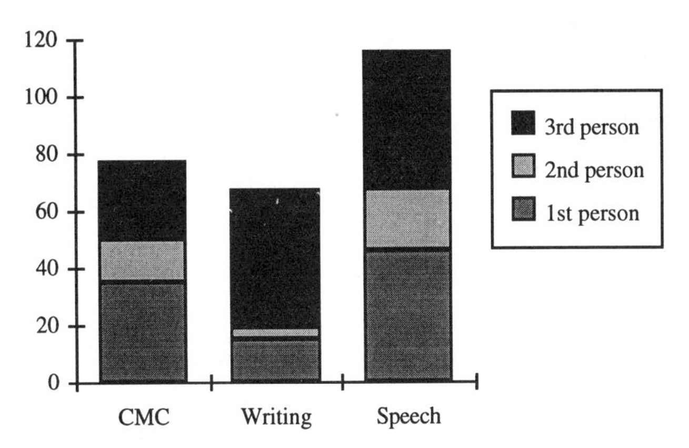

Figure 4. 1st, 2nd and 3rd person pronoun use as a proportion of total pronoun use (Actual values)

Where CMC differs markedly from speech and especially writing is in its lower use of third person reference. In terms of percentage of first and second person reference, it is closer to speech in overall usage, as indicated in Figure 5.

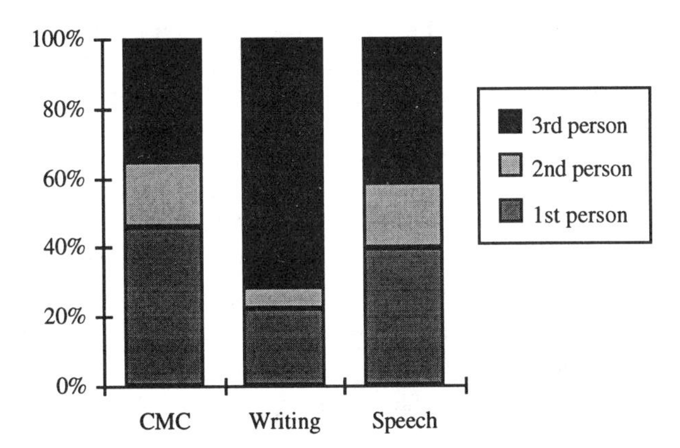

Figure 5. 1st, 2nd and 3rd person pronoun use as a proportion of total pronoun use (Percentage of total)

This provides us with a very interesting result. Despite its similarity to writing in terms of overall frequency of pronoun use (Figure 4), CMC is quite different from writing in how pronouns of each type are distributed. As Figure 5 indicates, in terms of relative proportional usage of each type of pronoun, CMC is more similar to spoken language. However, looking more closely at Figure 5, we can see that CMC makes greater proportional use of first and second person pronouns than either speech or writing. First and second person pronoun use takes up 64% of all pronoun use for CMC, compared to 58% for speech and 27% for writing.

5. Ideational aspects of CMC

Hodge and Kress (1988) begin their discussion of modality in language by noting that:

> In everyday communication it manifestly matters a great deal what weight we attach to an utterance. A statement may be said emphatically, without qualifications, and we know that we are being asked to believe that it is true. Or it may be hedged with 'I think', 'it may be that'. Perhaps it is spoken with rising intonation like a question, and we know that the speaker is offering the statement more tentatively. Or it may be said with a laugh or an ironic sarcastic tone, and we know the speaker does not believe the statement at all. (Hodge and Kress 1988:121)

These methods of encoding attitude towards a statement or the content of an utterance are described by Hodge and Kress as the *modality system of language*. Though Hodge and Kress use this term to cover many aspects of communication, they note that the system manifests itself most notably in the use of *modal auxiliaries* (e.g., words such as 'may' or 'might') (1988:121).

Coates (1983:27-29) conducted two card sorting tests with a group of subjects. Each card indicated the name of a modal auxiliary or modal paraphrase. From the results of these experiments, Coates conducted a statistical clustering analysis. The results of this analysis confirmed Coates' theoretical claim that the modal auxiliaries form and function within semantic clusters (Coates 1983:27-28). Coates' analysis revealed that the modal auxiliaries form five semantic groups, these being:

- Modals of Obligation and Necessity: Must, Need, Should, Ought
- Modals of Ability and Possibility: Can, Could
- Modals of Epistemic Possibility: May, Might
- Modals of Volition and Prediction: Will, Shall
- Hypothetical Modals: Would, Should

(Adapted from Coates 1983:28-29)

Let us first consider modal use in general. The corpora used were the LOB, London-Lund, CoSy:Full and CoSy:50 corpora, and the results were normalized to occurrences per 1000 words. A one-way analysis of variance was conducted and proved significant (F=42.4702, df=809, p=0.0000). An interaction plot of this result is given in Figure 6, and the means are presented in Table 4. Last, a Tukey-Honestly-Significant-Difference post hoc analysis revealed that only CMC texts were statistically different from the other two groups at the p<0.05 level.

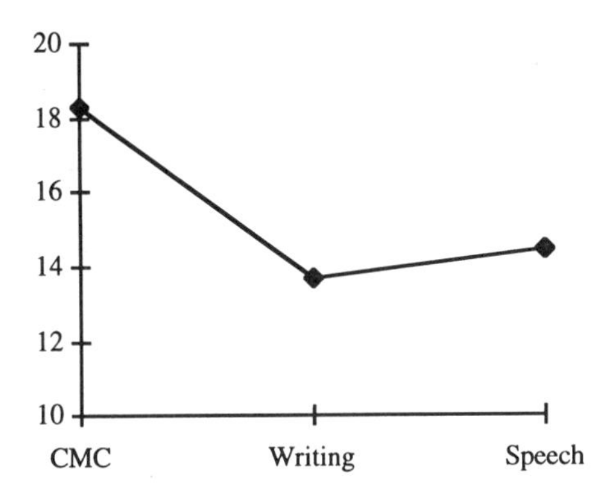

Figure 6. Interaction plot of normalized modal auxiliary use for three corpora

Table 4. Mean normalized modal auxiliary use for three corpora

Corpus:	CoSy:Full CoSy:50 (CMC)	LOB (Writing)	London-Lund (Speech)
Mean overall modal use:	18.2925	13.7042	14.4853

This provides us with an interesting initial result. The usage of modals in CMC is significantly higher than that of either speech or writing, with writing having the lowest usage of all three. As with our overall pronoun use result, however, we need to look further than the basic overall result. The same analyses were conducted for all five of Coates' modal semantic categories. All but one of the five analyses proved significant (Obligation and Necessity, F=6.3622, p=0.0018; Ability and Possibility, F=94.7623, p=0.000; Epistemic Possibility, F=4.1871, p=0.155; Volition and Prediction, F=18.7561, p=0.000; Hypothetical Modals, F=11.0037, p=0.000; df=814 in all cases). Tukey-Honestly-Significant-Difference tests were conducted in all cases and Table 5 indicates those comparisons which produced statistically significant differences at the p<0.05 level.

Table 5. Tukey HSD results for 3 media over 5 modal categories (Letters indicate which comparisons are significantly different)

Modal Group	CMC (C)	Writing (W)	Speech (S)
Modals of Obligation and Necessity	W,S	C	C
Modals of Ability and Possibility	W,S	C,S	C,W
Modals of Epistemic Possibility	S	S	C,W
Modals of Volition and Prediction	W,S	C	C
Hypothetical Modals	W,S	C	C

Our statistical results show that CMC differs from both speech and writing in all cases except modals of epistemic possibility. All of the other results indicate clear differences in the usage of modal auxiliaries within spoken, written and CMC utterances, with CMC making the greatest use in all cases. Figures 7 and 8 collate these results and indicate the relative proportional use of modal auxiliaries in all three media.

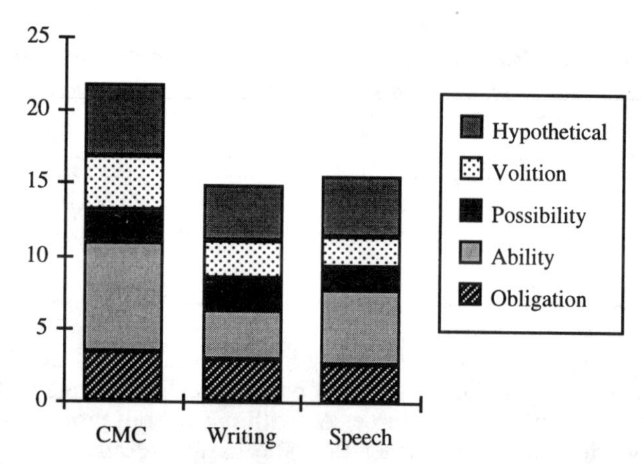

Figure 7. Use of 5 semantic modal groups as a proportion of total modal use (Actual values)

As was the case with pronoun use, the overall relative frequencies of modal usage across the five semantic groups are most similar between speech and CMC.

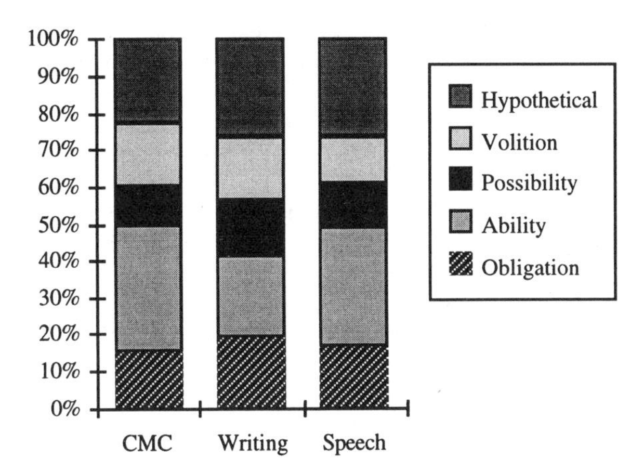

Figure 8. Use of 5 semantic modal groups as a proportion of total modal use (Percentage of total)

Though all of the other groups indicated a significant difference between CMC, speech and writing, the modals of *ability and possibility* (abbreviated 'possibility' in Figures 7 and 8) indicate the greatest differences in use across all three media.

Such results would seem to indicate that the CMC corpus contains a considerable degree of discussion in which statements are modalized in one form or another. Qualitative results obtained by Yates (1993b:134-136) indicate that the contextual use of modal auxiliaries within CMC is comparable to that of speech.

5. Conclusion

At the level of methodology, this paper has demonstrated the usefulness of corpus-based empirical research in assessing and developing theoretical models of language use. The results have raised questions over the factors which define or effect differences in language use across media. In order to consider these issues further, let us return to the work of Halliday. Halliday (1978) makes the argument that an important difference between genres and modes of communication lies in the semiotic *field* in which the communication takes place. An example of such a field would be that of a doctor-patient interview where the field is defined by the situation, as a social structure and as a physical location with discursively available material objects, and by the topic of the interview, as the main discursive object. In the case of CMC discourse, there is no such field beyond the focus of the interaction, which may be quite diverse and without a singly-defined discursive object. In fact the text of the CMC interaction is the field. Such lack of a defined semiotic field may be the explanation for the high levels of modality within CMC discourse. Not only must the text carry the social situation, it must also carry the participants' relationship to the situation, their perception of the relationships between the knowledge and objects under discussion.

Halliday considers next the semiotic *tenor* of the communication; this is essentially defined by social roles, often made clear by the social situation in which the participants are placed. The tenor of CMC interactions may not be as limited as some researchers, especially those concerned with the issue of network anonymity and psychological accounts of de-individuation processes, indicate; it is limited, by the lack of a clear semiotic field, to those presentations of self which take place within and through the CMC text. The necessity to present oneself may be one factor behind the high levels of first and second person pronoun use within CMC discourse.

Finally, the *mode* of CMC, as a communications medium, is neither simply speech-like nor simply written-like. Though CMC bears similarities in its textual aspects (e.g., type/token ratio and lexical density) to written discourse, it differs greatly in others, namely pronoun and modal auxiliary use. Taken together, these similarities and differences make clear the complexity of CMC as a mode of communication. As with both written and spoken discourse, CMC is affected by the numerous social structural and social situational factors which surround and define the communication taking place. What is yet to be made fully clear is the extent to which human beings in specific social and cultural settings can develop and enhance their communication through the use of CMC.

NOTES

1. The DT200 data from 1989 are lost forever as they had been erased from the CoSy system before they could be downloaded.

2. For a full discussion of the psychological aspects of information processing, see Just and Carpenter 1980; Pollatsek and Rayner 1989; Rayner 1977, 1978; Rayner and Duffy 1986; and for their effects on lexical density, see Yates 1993b.

Linguistic and Interactional Features of Internet Relay Chat

Christopher C. Werry
Carnegie Mellon University

1. Introduction

Increasingly, forms of computer-mediated communication are emerging that enable "conversations" to take place in real time through the medium of written language. Synchronous exchanges are becoming popular on bulletin boards, server communities and across much of the Internet. In their simplest form, such exchanges consist of two people in different rooms sitting in front of computer screens that each display a window split into two parts. Everything that either person types will be simultaneously displayed both on their own screen and on the screen of the other person, in either the top or bottom half of the window. In its more complex forms, synchronous computer-mediated communication can involve people from all over the world communicating in sophisticated and highly conventionalized ways within electronic zones that can be said to constitute "virtual communities" (Rheingold 1993).

While different modes, technologies and social spaces inflect this form of communication in significantly different ways, all have in common that they involve the production of writing via computer such that synchronous textual dialogue takes place between spatially distant interlocutors. Such communication, which following Ferrara et al. (1991) I term "interactive written discourse",[1] provides fertile ground for analysis since it makes possible interesting forms of social and linguistic interaction, brings into play a unique set of temporal, spatial and social dimensions, reconfigures many of the parameters that determine important aspects of how communicative acts are structured, and provides a clear instance of how forms of writing made possible by the computer exhibit properties that converge with those typically associated with spoken discourse.

This paper examines a particular form of interactive written discourse known as Internet Relay Chat, or IRC. I begin by providing a brief sketch of

IRC and its relationship to other forms of interactive written discourse. I then describe some of the characteristic discursive properties of IRC in terms of addressivity, abbreviation, prosody and gesture, arguing that the conventions that are emerging are a direct reflection of the physical constraints on the medium combined with a desire to create language that is as "speech-like" as possible.

2. Interactive written discourse and IRC: A brief sketch

While there are a multitude of forms of interactive written discourse, it is possible to classify them roughly into three main types. To begin with, there are those modes of textual communication that are relatively simple, such as TALK (which runs on UNIX systems) and PHONE (which runs on VMS systems).[2] These types of interactive written discourse are generally used by individuals to speak to one another privately, and are often directed towards carrying out workaday tasks. They provide few commands with which one can manage communication, and because they are generally used by only two people at once, limit the range of social and linguistic interaction that is possible.

A second, more complex kind of interactive written discourse involves groups of people engaging in role-playing adventure games. Within electronic environments, labyrinthine textual worlds full of goblins, dragons, swordfights and science fiction cities have been built. These worlds are essentially verbal in nature, constituted through typed conversation and the language of computer programming. Such activities have been alternately dubbed "text only virtual environments" (Carlstrom 1992) or "text based virtual reality" (Hardy 1993). The primary examples of this genre are MUDs ("Multiple User Dungeons" and "Multiple User Dialogue" are two of the many derivations for this acronym that circulate on the net) and their various offshoots.[3] MUDs have become so popular that many computer sites have been forced to limit their use due to the strain imposed on computer systems (cf. Deuel, This volume).

A third form of interactive written discourse consists of what are often called "Chat" systems. These are social spaces made available on bulletin boards, servers and on sites across much of the Internet in which people converse and interact. Chat systems have become the locus of all manner of social interaction, from café style conversation, to the political discussions of members of expatriate communities, to live reports by computer users in countries in which crises are taking place (as was the case during the Gulf war[4] and the attempted coup in Moscow in September 1993). While members of business and academic institutions are increasingly using this mode of communication to conduct meetings, organize serious discussions, hold classes, and stage conferences,[5] most Chat communication is currently recreational in character.

On bulletin boards around the world, areas for chatting are often created in the form of "rooms" where members can "meet". The nature of these areas reflects the general character of a given bulletin board. Thus for example Mark Poster (1990:118) cites a bulletin board in California called the "French Connection" designed to function along the lines of an electronic singles bar. The zones for communicating interactively there are the "Locker Room", where men congregate and speak together (although gender on such systems is usually difficult to ascertain), the "Powder Room", where women collect and converse, and the "Public" area where all gather.

One of the largest chat systems, and that which constitutes the focus of the present study, is called IRC.[6] On IRC, hundreds of thousands of "internauts" from over 70 countries, speaking a variety of different languages, gather to discuss all manner of topics. People congregate in areas called "channels", of which somewhere around 5000 currently exist. These channels are essentially small-scale electronic communities that individuals can join and participate in. The excerpt in Figure 1 below shows a list of some channel names as they appear to an IRC user. The left hand column displays the channel name, the middle column displays how many people are currently on the channel, and the right hand column indicates the theme of the channel or the current topic of conversation:

*** #hottub	18	Come on in..
*** #malaysia	36	SELAMAT PAGI MALAYSIA....
*** #espanol	18	Si quieres jugar ping_pong entra a #espanol
*** #india	10	Namaskar
*** #muenster	15	the friendly german channel
*** #lesbian	7	For women only...No exception.
*** #HipHop	5	It is kinda different....
*** #gblf	12	Gays, Bisexuals, Lesbians & Friends
*** #francais	15	Le soleil vient de se lever, encore une belle jour
*** #viet	13	you have a problem? Ask DesCartes for help.
*** #christian	10	happy, horney Wiccans for a better tonite. }:)
*** #asians	10	Asians' connection :)
*** #Twilight_	35	Abode of the Self-Proclaimed Management :)
*** #hotsex	21	Want to have sex? /msg beastie
*** #amiga	15	Cottleston, Cottleston, Cottleston Pie.
*** #talk	16	WEIRD/CRAZY/KINKY PARTY OCCURRING HERE
*** #cricket	7	T3D3:STUMPS:Eng-321, 122/4(GG-12*,Cad-0*):Aus 373
*** #aussies	10	Ah.. look at all the lonely people.
*** #Crossdres	13	Crossdressers, Transsexuals and friends!

Figure 1. Sample list of IRC channel names

To join a channel, one enters "/join" followed by a # sign and the channel name (all commands are preceded by a slash, and tend to follow simple English. For example "/leave" is the command for leaving a channel).[7] As soon as one joins a channel, any conversation that is taking place there becomes visible on one's screen and people already on that channel are notified of the presence and "nickname" of the new arrival. Everyone on IRC assumes an alias (called a "nickname") so in most cases one has little idea of the gender, race, age or any other such personal details of the person one is talking to.[8] This alias is entirely provisional, and can be changed at any time. To assume or change a nickname, one simply enters "/nick" followed by the name one wants to be known by.

IRC affords each user a large array of commands with which they can perform a number of communicative actions, some of which have close analogues in face-to-face conversation. For example, there is an "ignore" command that makes any communication by whomever one wishes to ignore invisible. One can also speak privately to a person on a channel so that no one else can hear, set the topic for the channel, and send and receive invitations to join other channels.

As with many other forms of computer-mediated communication, IRC has a general code of conduct that one is required to observe. All of the various manuals that exist for IRC have fully detailed sections on "netiquette", as does the IRC on-line help facility.[9] Such texts might be said to perform a function akin to Castiglione's *Book of the Courtier*, providing as they do a handbook of cyberspace conduct. Some of the most important things to avoid doing are: forcing one's way into a conversation, harassing people in various ways, stealing a person's nickname, and "dumping" large amounts of unwanted text (e.g., storing large chunks of pre-composed text which are then "dumped" into a conversation). An example of a more subtle indiscretion is using an "autogreet". This involves automatically sending a 'hello' message to everyone on a channel whenever you join (the *IRC Primer* warns against creating an autogreet, stating that "even if you think you are being polite, you are actually sounding insincere and also interfering with the personal environment of the recipient" (Pioch 1993:2)).

As the existence of a code of conduct suggests, IRC provides a social space where intense personal relationships can be formed and maintained. A number of IRC relationships are reported to have culminated in marriage. It can also become an addictive form of social interchange.[10] Many Usenet newsgroups are devoted to discussions of IRC, and one of these, called *irc.recovery*, is a forum in which people who feel they are or have been addicted to IRC can discuss their experiences and problems. These behaviors suggest that IRC interaction is psychologically real to many users.

3. Some discursive properties of IRC

IRC allows its users to record their sessions in the form of a "log" which saves all on-screen activity to a text file. The extracts used for this study were taken from the log files of two ten-minute sessions on IRC. The extracts are from one

English-speaking channel and one French-speaking channel. In what follows I describe some of the discursive properties of IRC discourse as exemplified in these channels.

One feature of the language produced on IRC that is immediately noticeable is the organization of conversational sequences and exchange structures. On IRC, overlaps and interruptions are impossible. Each utterance is simply displayed in the chronological order in which it is received by the IRC system. This means that disparate strands of conversation are juxtaposed, forming sequences that intertwine to form a multidimensional text. The resulting dialogues scroll up (and then off) each person's computer screen at a pace directly proportional to the tempo of the overall conversation.[11] Until one acquires a sense of how to read such conversational sequences, the experience is rather like trying to follow the text of a play in which the characters' lines have been jumbled up. The extract below shows an example of such a sequence:

(1) <amya> catch you all in about 10 mins :)
<Keels> booooooo
<ariadnne> k e e l s !!! you in and out today?
<bubi> keels, don't scare me!!!
<Keels> you mean youre
<Shaquille> ariadnne-what the hell is your problem?
<Keels> who are you bubi
<Alvin> bubi: What does your friend want to do in Australia... work
<Alvin> Shaquile: Your the problem,
<ariadnne> shaq: i have no problem..you were the "asshole"
<bubi> al, he wants to live and work, i guess...
<Alvin> bubi: depends what sort of qualifications, experience, intentions, area
<Shaquille> Alvin-spell the name right!!!!!!!!
<Alvin> GRRR
<Keels> has anybody seen a pomme called daco?

Successive, independent speech acts are simply juxtaposed, and different topics interwoven. The kind of sequencing evident contrasts significantly with that of oral discourse, as well as most forms of written discourse.[12] As can be seen in the extract above, this leads to rapid shifts in topic, and also to a greater chance of separate conversations intertwining (for example in the extract above, Alvin's first turn responds to two speakers at the same time). For novice users, such complexity may at first prove very confusing and lead to breakdowns in communication. (It is no doubt only because utterances have a longer half-life on the screen than they do in oral discourse that users are able to keep track of the separate IRC conversations going on around them at all.) However, experienced IRC users appear to have internalized a loose set of conventions that enable them to manage and follow the complex structure of conversational sequences that occur on IRC. Some of these conventions are described in the following sections.

3.1. Addressivity

A number of properties of IRC discourse are the result of attempts to avoid ambiguity and discontinuity in structures of exchange or turn-taking, which in face-to-face encounters would typically be negotiated by paralinguistic cues such as intonation, pauses, gesture and gaze (Coulthard 1983). Thus for example it has become entirely conventional for speakers to indicate the intended addressee by putting that person's name at the start of an utterance, followed by a colon:

(2) <Franck> diva: ou t'as mis le "c" ?
<DIVA> franck: oh oh.. je mexcuse :-)

[<Franck> diva: where'd ya put the "c"?]
[<DIVA> franck: oh oh..excuse me :-)]

(3) <boot> frank : voila une fille
<Franck> boot: ou ca? ou ca?

[<boot> frank : there's a girl]
[<Franck> boot: where? where?]

(4) <Shaquille> ariadnne: what the hell does that mean?
<ariadnne> shaq: what are you yapping your lips about?

Such a high degree of addressivity is imperative on IRC, since the addressee's attention must be recaptured anew with each utterance. A contributing factor to the emergence of this convention may be that the role of the "listener" becomes more passive on IRC than in spoken dialogue. On IRC the receiver is usually unable to supply the minimal responses (both nonverbal forms, such as nodding, and verbal forms, such as 'uh huh', 'mm hm', etc.) which signal active attention and may be used to indicate understanding. Addressing the addressee by name and other such conventions can be partly explained in terms of a general tendency to communicate in a way that compensates for the weakened link between sender and receiver.

While a marked tendency toward addressivity appears pervasive across many different channels and languages on IRC, there are several contexts in which it is omitted. One such context is when a statement is being directed to all listeners, as in the following:

(5) <ariadnne> mornin in OZ!!!!

(6) <Agagax> champagne tous
[<Agagax> champagne for all]

(7) <Alvin> He's on the auto kick list now.. LOSER !!!!

Similarly, expressions of greeting and farewell are usually directed to all people on a channel and so are not prefaced by reference to a specific person's nickname. Sometimes the content of a message provides sufficient cohesive force such that it is clear who a statement is intended for without them needing to be explicitly named. Alternatively, when there are not many people on a channel (5 or fewer interlocutors), or if there is a lull in the conversation, this convention may be dropped.

3.2. Abbreviation

In *De Oratore*, Cicero argues that physical constraints such as the amount of breath available to human speakers influence the length and form of written and spoken discourse.[13] On IRC, a combination of spatial, temporal and social constraints act as important limiting conditions that influence the size and shape of communication in roughly analogous ways. Factors such as screen size, average typing speed, minimal response times, competition for attention, channel population and the pace of channel conversations all contribute to the emergence of certain characteristic properties. Some of the most obvious of these properties involve a tendency toward brevity which manifests itself in speaking turns of very short length, various forms of abbreviation, and the use of stored linguistic formulas.

With respect to the length of communicative acts, messages in the extracts I examined averaged around six words in length. Such brevity is in some small part due to spatial restrictions in that many interfaces provide a relatively shallow window in which to compose, and so composing a long message means that the first part of one's message will scroll out of sight before one has finished. More important in this regard however is the fact that in order to keep up with the flow of conversation it is often necessary to respond quickly and this means that unless one can type very rapidly, messages must be kept short. On channels with few people on them, messages will often increase significantly in size. Nonetheless, it is rare to see messages of more than four or five lines in length since the receiver cannot maintain verbal contact with the sender of a message and effectively hangs in limbo while the process of producing a message goes on. Since typing is significantly slower than speech, messages of extended length create time delays that may be unacceptable for communication which attempts to work in a conversational mode. (Work done in conversational analysis that looks at the average period of silence between conversational turns would seem to indicate that delays of no more than a few seconds are usual in oral discourse.[14]) Perhaps just as important on many channels is the fact that speakers are competing for attention. A potential respondent may get drawn into another conversational thread if too much time is spent producing a message. The fact that messages tend to be longer when there are fewer participants competing for attention also supports this view. Thus the tendency toward abbreviation in general, and toward the production of messages of around six words in length, may emerge from the fact that three important conditions are being satisfied. First, messages of around six words give rise to acceptably short gaps between conversational turns, gaps that are reasonably close to those found in spoken conversation. Second, while smaller utterances could in theory also fulfill this requirement, expressiveness might be sacrificed; thus an average message size of six words effectively integrates an acceptable interval between exchanges with the minimum amount of words needed to convey the requisite expressivity and meaning. Third, such a length may be optimal given the amount of competition for attention that tends to occur on IRC channels.

As well as being produced in relatively short bursts, language on IRC tends to be heavily abbreviated. One commonly sees syntactically-reduced forms, the use of acronyms and symbols, the clipping of words, and various other strategies which function to reduce the time and effort necessary to communicate. Subject pronouns are often deleted (or phonologically reduced) to a considerable degree, as can be seen in the examples below:

(8) <Franck> t pardonnee Diva. 8-) [cf. tu es pardonee > t'es pardonee]
[<Franck> Yr excused Diva. 8-)]

(9) <Keels> goodby gonna try and do somthing smart for once

(10) <Smooge> ari: in a bad mood :(

While this deletion of subject pronouns is largely caused by the strong drive towards abbreviation and brevity that shapes communication on IRC at so many different levels, the frequency with which this occurs is no doubt increased by several characteristics of communication on IRC. To begin with, on IRC channels both addresser and addressee are typically already signaled in advance of the body of a speaker's utterance, and so explicit pronominal reference can be deleted without causing confusion. This is especially true for the first person singular pronoun 'I', since the IRC system automatically prefaces each line with the speaker's nickname, as in the example below:

(11) <Keels> got to go for a sec

Furthermore, additional conventions have emerged on many IRC channels that reduce the need for the first person pronoun to be used. For example, some speakers employ arrow symbols that point back to their IRC nickname:

(12) <ariadnne> <-- is fine and dandy thank you!!
<Alvin> <-- is fine and studly thank you!!

Last, since it is conventional to put the intended receiver's name at the start of a message, the second person pronoun 'you' can be omitted in some cases. This is evident in the example below, in which not only the subject but an auxiliary verb 'can' or 'would' is omitted:

(13) <bubi> aargh, al: recommend australia for a finnish friend o' mine?

The omission of subject pronouns and auxiaries is associated in non-virtual modes with an informal spoken style, further lending an air of spontaneous orality to IRC exchanges.

Acronyms common to net culture such as ROFL (rolling on the floor laughing) and IMHO (In My Humble Opinion) are also widely used on IRC, as are "emoticons",[15] both of which function as forms of abbreviation. Participants' nicknames are also frequently abbreviated, especially when they are long or hard to spell or if a certain familiarity exists between speakers. Thus a name like Shaquille may be abbreviated to 'Shaq', Ariadnne to 'Ari' or 'Ar', and Morkelub to 'Mork'. In general, one can observe a tendency on IRC for words to be stripped down to the fewest possible letters that will enable them to be meaningfully recognized. Thus the vowels of some words will commonly be left out, as when participants leaving a channel use expressions such as 'bb ppls' ('Bye bye peoples'). In the following example the word 'please' is abbreviated to 'pls':

(14) <hari> can you get rid of the auto kick pls alvi?

Analogous forms of abbreviation occur regularly on the French channel also (as in 'qqn' for 'quelqu'un' and 'qqes' for 'quelques'). In this incessant drive to reduce the number of required keystrokes to the absolute minimum, some words get truncated especially often, especially those that resemble the sound of a single letter when pronounced. Thus in French 'c'est' is commonly reduced to 'c', both pronounced /se/ ('<Franck> c pas sofie' [that's not sofie]). Some other commonly-seen single letter forms are shown below:

(15) <bomber> ari: where r u from?

(16) <bubi> well i gotta go....c u

(17) <Franck> t pardonnee Diva. 8-)
[<Franck> Yr excused Diva. 8-)]

As with the tendency toward brevity of sentence length, such forms of abbreviation are largely due to the temporal, spatial and social strictures imposed by IRC, specifically, the requirement that messages be typed as quickly and efficiently as possible.

At least partly in recognition of this strong impetus towards condensation and abbreviation, IRC makes it possible to store frequently used phrases or formulas through the use of "key bindings"; that is, a phrase or image that a speaker uses often can be stored so that whenever a function or control key is pressed, the phrase will be instantly displayed. Thus for example people will often have a formulaic message automatically displayed when they leave a channel, as in example (18) below:

(18) <Lune> la lune disparait
<Agagax> salut lune
*** Signoff: Lune (Part dans une nuee de poussieres d'etoiles)

[<Lune> the moon disappears]
[<Agagax> bye moon]
[*** Signoff: Moon (Leaves in a cloud of stardust)

Although it is not always possible to tell with certainty whether a phrase has been produced in this way, the unlikely speed with which some people produce phrases, and the frequent repetition of identically formed expressions, can enable one to make an educated guess.

Certain forms of abbreviation have emerged that are native to particular IRC communities. An interesting example is the word 're'. It is short for 'hello again', and is used to greet someone for a second time, usually after they have recently left a channel and then rejoined. It was first used on various English-speaking channels. Its usage has since declined on English-speaking channels (although variant forms such as 'rehi' occur reasonably often), but it has been taken up and at the time of my observation was extremely common on one French-speaking channel in particular, as the examples below illustrate:

(33) *** StarNet (person@disun47.epfl.ch) has joined channel #francais
<Zola> ding dong !! L'horloge vient d'annoncer la nouvelle heure !
<Sofie> Ta gueule Zola!
<StarNet> salut le monde!
<Bruno> re salut Starnet
<Prosty> re star

[*** StarNet (person@disun47.epfl.ch) has joined channel #francais
<Zola> ding dong !! The clock has just struck the hour!
<Sofie> Shut up Zola!
<StarNet> Hi everybody!
<Bruno> hi again Starnet
<Prosty> hi again star]

(34) *** Alesi (person@147.210.18.8) has joined channel #francais
<Alesi> bang
<Alesi> re
<Sofie> Re Alesi !

Thus features of abbreviation hasten the speed with which messages can be exchanged, making the pace of the exchange more like that of face-to-face conversation. Orthographic reduction and omission of pronouns, etc. also resembles phonological reduction and elipsis in rapid, informal speech, rendering Chat exchanges "speech-like" in their degree of informality as well.

3.3. Paralinguistic and prosodic cues

Some of the most characteristic and interesting features of the language used on IRC are the result of a complex set of orthographic strategies designed to compensate for the lack of intonation and paralinguistic cues that interactive written discourse imposes on its users. An innovative set of linguistic devices has evolved that functions to create the effects of voice, gesture and tone through the creative use of capitalization, spelling and punctuation. For example, reduplicated letters are used to represent drawn-out or expressive intonation:

(19) <Lilus> bomber: deutschland? cooolll

(20) <Lilus> baaaad joke bomber...hehehe

(21) <Smooge> Lilus: awwww, cool :)

Punctuation is also used to create the effects of spoken delivery. Thus periods and hyphens are employed to create pauses and to indicate tempo, as in the examples below:

(22) <Keels> what a peculiar name...cw7r

(23) <Bruno> Avec tout ces saluts .... j'ai pas dit Sabatier because fired

(24) <bomber> ari: hahaha - One of the questions of LARRY - Where do
<bomber> most vergins live ? a) Virginia.... hahahhaha

Other non-standard forms of orthography are endemic on IRC and are appropriated to serve as alternative systems of signification. For example, capitalization is almost never used for proper nouns or at the start of sentences. Instead, it is employed as a convention for expressing emphasis:[16]

(25) <genevieve> re agagaz
<Agagax> non pas agagaZ - agagaX

[<genevieve> hello again agagaz]
[<Agagax> no not agagaZ - agagaX]

(26) <Lilus> cw7r: I cant less than go WOOOOW

In the above examples, Lilus uses capitalization to add impact to her/his exclamation, while Agagax uses capital letters to make it clear to genevieve how her/his name is spelled.

In line with the tendency to produce discursive forms that approximate speech, language use on IRC tends to be highly colloquial. Most interchanges will typically be dense with informal discourse particles such as ‘nope’, ‘nup’, ‘yup’, and ‘hiya’. Colloquial verbalizations and non-standard spellings appear to be self-consciously selected in preference to “standard” linguistic expressions, as in the examples below:

(27) <ari> smooch: wot wuz dat fo?

(28) <Deck> ouais ho hein

(29) <Franck> oyoyoyoy

The style of written discourse produced may mimic that of particular discourse communities. For example, on the channel "aussies" the language produced often reflects the speech habits of Australian speakers of English:

(30) <Alvin> bubi: wotz da question

(31) <Keels> ar...how ya doon

(35) <bomber> ari: ME CUTE??? hahahahahahahaha (how cute!)
<ari> hee hee just wanking yas

However language on IRC rarely stays in one form or register for long. Participants tend to play with language, to produce hybrid, heteroglossic forms that incorporate all manner of communicative styles. A salient property of IRC discourse involves what one might call the written equivalent of speaking in tongues. Participants produce a bricolage of discursive fragments drawn from songs, tv characters, and a variety of different social speech types. The example below captures, to some small extent, this tendency:

(32) <ari> whutta dowk
<ari> hewwo?
<bomber> Lilus: No worries... ;-)
<ari> vewy intewestin
<bomber> ari ????
<ari> rosanne roseannadanna hea
<ari> yup yup?
<ari> <-- in a goofy mood
*** Action: Lilus grins evilly.
<bomber> ari: dwou you haphe annnny pwoblewms???
*** Action: ari removes the laffing gas for a sec to respond
<ari> nup nup!!!
*** Action: bomber breaks out laughing

Throughout the textual dialogues that occur on IRC, one can identify a common impulse: an almost manic tendency to produce auditory and visual effects in writing, a straining to make written words simulate speech. When examining the language produced on IRC, one is reminded of the efforts various writers in the eighteenth century made to produce written language that captured the "music" of speech, its distinctive tones, timbres and patterns of intonation. Indeed, IRC users appear occasionally to be experimenting with written text in a way that is in the spirit of Joshua Steele's 1779 book, *Prosodia Rationalis; or, an Essay towards establishing the Melody and Measure of Speech, to be expressed and perpetuated by peculiar Symbols*, which elaborates a system of notation for transcribing patterns of stress, pitch and intonation in spoken English. Interlocutors frequently construct graphic simulations of sounds such as laughter, exclamations, snarls, barks, singing, the sound of racing cars, and various other noises:

(35) <bomber> ari: ME CUTE??? hahahahahahahaha (how cute!)
<ari> hee hee just wanking yas [laughter]

(36) <Fakir> aaaahhhh....un mordu de PIF ! [exclamation]
[<Fakir> aaaahhhh....a PIF fan!]

(37) <DieuEstLa> WOUARFFFFFFF [dog barking]

(38) <Alesi> mmmmmmmmmmmmmmmMMMMMMMMMMMMMM poc poc poc poc *pouf* [racing car noises]

(39) <ari> kiwis and their sheep!!!! mmmwwwhhahahahaha [sheep sounds]

As the above examples illustrate, one can identify in many of the communicative acts performed on IRC a tendency to foreground the phonetic qualities of language. The language produced by users of IRC demands to be read with the simultaneous involvement of the ear and eye. One can discern an intensified engagement with the sounds of language, with the auditory and iconographic potential of words.

There are no doubt several factors animating this tendency toward verbal play. There is the newness of the medium, the release from any determinate context that it allows, the anonymity it affords, and the transitory character of language produced within its sphere. Also of significance may be the altered relationship to language that IRC promotes. When communicating on IRC there is a different sense of connection to the word; it does not belong to the speaker in the sense that a spoken word does. On IRC the word is distanced from the speaker in that it stands apart from her/him, available to inspection (and revision) in a way that speech is not. Through being embodied in electronic text, the speaker's words are depersonalized, stripped of all of the material qualities that individualize them and connect them to a particular speaker. Yet at the same time, words exist in a temporal framework which approximates oral discourse, which requires interactivity and involvement, and which invites the fabrication of the texture and signature of an individual speaker's voice. The process of self-consciously constructing the paralinguistic dimensions of communication may heighten the sense of their artificiality, and lead to an increased tendency to experiment and play with them. Also important in this regard is the malleability of the roles that IRC users can adopt in the process of social interaction. The roles available to speakers tend to influence the kinds of language they produce. The greater ability to experiment with a range of different roles on IRC may contribute to the increased verbal play observed.

3.4. Actions and gestures

Last but not least, the IRC community also employs a set of codes and conventions whereby words and visual images are used to symbolize gestural qualities of face-to-face communication. The symbolic enactment of physical actions is a particularly distinctive and fascinating discursive property of this genre. Hugs, kisses, offers of coffee, yawns, shaking hands, and the popping of champagne are all enacted symbolically. The convention for doing this is to precede or enclose the dramatized action in asterisks in a manner that resembles stage directions. On the channel "francais", much of this seems to revolve around offers of coffee and the opening of bottles of wine and champagne:

(40) *** Action: Sofie passe un verre a tous et attend que les autres bots apportent le champagne...
*** Action: Zola remplit une flute de champagne a tous
*** Action: frans trouve Sofie tres humaine

[*** Action: Sofie passes a glass to everyone and waits for the other bots to bring the champagne...
*** Action: Zola fills a flute of champagne for all
*** Action: frans finds Sofie to be very humane]

On the channel "aussies", hugging and hand shaking are two of the most commonly enacted activities:

(41) <ariadnne> A N N E M A R I E!!!! *hugs*
<amya> *hugs* :)

<Alvin> *aussie voice* G'day keels *shakes hand*
*** Action: Keels shakes alvins hand a little too vigorousley
*** Action: Alvin shakes up and down... Woah... steady on there

This mode of creating actions is similar to what is called "Posing" or "Emoting" on MUDs. It is largely through such feats of creative ventriloquism that a physical context (often surprisingly sophisticated) for communicative acts is constructed.

Many of the channels on IRC also provide a repository of additional symbols that can be used to enact virtual actions. These can be automatically generated by entering a command while on that channel. Thus one can symbolize the action of a frown, a hug, a smile or a wink. The full range of such commands available on one channel is shown below:

ALL	BLINDFOLD	CANDY	CARESS	CHAINS	CUDDLE
CUFF	EYE	FONDLE	FROWN	FUZZY	GAG
GDNT	HELP	HIT	HUG	ICECUBE	KISS
KNEEL	LOVE	LS	NECK	PICKLE	POKE
POUT	ROSE	ROSEWHIP	SMILE	SMOOCH	SNUGGLE
SORRY	SPANK	SPECIAL	SUBMIT	TICKLE	WAX
WINK	WOOGA				

Some of these commands produce graphical images. For example the user below would have used the "ROSE" command to produce this replica of a rose (rotated 90 degrees):

(42) - Juliet sends thee a rose... @}-'-,-'---

Other channels provide commands that will cause a fictional character, or "bot", to emerge and offer channel members alcohol, food or the recitation of poetry. "Bots" (short for robots) are essentially programs that enable people to produce various effects on a channel. In the example below, a command is used to have a bot called 'Zola' quote poetry by Blake:

(43) <Zola> As God is love: every Kindness to another is a little Death
<Zola> In the Divine Image....
<Zola> --- William Blake (Then Jesus appeared)

Bots are more common on MUDs than on IRC, however. On IRC, there is a general antipathy toward them since they are felt to divert attention away from conversation.

By joining physical actions to words, users compensate in part for the lack of physical and contextual cues. This property of the genre makes Chat more than simply speech-like: it takes on properties of direct face-to-face interaction, thereby distinguishing itself from other technologically-mediated forms of communication such as telephone conversations.

4. Conclusion

This chapter has examined a kind of interactive written discourse known as IRC, detailing some of its distinctive linguistic and interactional features. An analysis of this type of computer-mediated communication was carried out on two IRC channels, focusing on exchange structures, forms of addressivity, abbreviation, prosody and gesture. The chapter proposes that the formal properties and patterns of communicative interaction identifiable emerge out of a complex set of temporal, spatial, contextual and social constraints. It indicates how participants have evolved a number of innovative linguistic strategies which function to both compensate for and adapt to these constraints. It also indicates that communication on IRC is shaped at many different levels by the drive to reproduce or simulate the discursive style of face-to-face spoken language. From conveying patterns of intonation, to supplying paralinguistic cues, to the collaborative construction of a shared contextual frame, language on IRC is crucially inflected by the practice of naturalistic interpersonal exchange, and the tendency to create forms of expression that enable or are appropriate to such exchange.

NOTES

1. I employ Ferrara (1991) et al.'s useful phrase "interactive written discourse" rather than other names (such as "text-only virtual environment" or "Chat system") currently in circulation, since it provides the most generic and all-encompassing description.

2. One can usually access these programs by typing TALK or PHONE (depending on whether the system you are using runs UNIX or VMS) followed by the username and address of the person you wish to contact.

3. Detailed descriptions of MUDs are given in Hardy (1993) and Carlstrom (1992). Rheinhold (1993) also devotes a chapter to MUDs and IRC. Bartle (1990) provides the most comprehensive and detailed description available of the genealogy, typology and operation of MUDs. MOOs are a particular kind of MUD that allows users wide scope in altering the environment.

4. Log files of the discussions held on the Chat system IRC during the Gulf war are available on numerous ftp sites, including the English Server at Carnegie Mellon University. The English Server can be reached via gopher or ftp at english-server.hss.cmu.edu, or via the World Wide Web at http://english-www.hss.cmu.edu.

5. Some of the best-known sites for conducting teaching, research and conferences via such technology are MediaMOO, Diversity University and BioMOO. MediaMOO, founded by Amy Bruckman at MIT, provides a place for researchers in media and communications to hold meetings, share information and convene conferences. The 10th Computers and Writing Conference held in Missouri in May 1994 used MediaMOO to stage its "Online Forum", in which a significant number of conferencees delivered papers in a special room within the MOO to a virtual audience. Both Diversity University and the English Server make available "virtual classrooms" in which courses are presently taught. Bennahum (1994) provides a lively and useful discussion of MediaMOO, Diversity University and BioMOO.

6. IRC is public domain software written by Jarkko Oikarinen in 1988 and first used in Finland. Many large and medium-sized computer sites run IRC. (Entering "IRC" at your local operating system prompt may give you an idea as to whether your site has it—however check with a system administrator if you have no luck). If your system does not have IRC, you can telnet to public access systems such as sci.dixie.edu 6677. This will take you directly into IRC, prompting you for your nickname. (This site also has instructions for installing your own IRC server). Another public access IRC server is obelix.wu-wien.ac.at 6677.

7. IRC commands may vary slightly depending on the system the client runs on (UNIX, VMS, etc). Recently, a user-friendly IRC client called "Homer" that enables one to construct collaborative drawings across the net on IRC has been produced for the Macintosh.

8. Two qualifications need to be made here. First, IRC users can display the login name of people using IRC and thus can in some instances ascertain their identity, although much of the time this login name itself tells one very little, and users can manipulate their login names so that little or nothing can be known of them. Second, the IRC population itself is not terribly diverse. It is still largely composed of males working in universities

or high-tech corporations, although this is changing as commercial on-line providers make Internet access available to a more diverse group of people.

9. A number of on-line and print manuals exist for IRC. *A Short IRC Primer* by Pioch (1993) is perhaps the best print guide. IRC itself has on-line help that includes a section on netiquette. Other electronic guides are regularly updated and circulated on the newsgroup *alt.irc*. Those by Trillian-Rose and Viljanen & Hari (see references) are especially good.

10. Reid (1991, 1995) performs a fine cultural analysis of IRC, and describes many of the forms of social interchange that occur.

11. It should be noted that reproducing the conversations on the static printed page sacrifices the crucial dimensions of pace and tempo that occur as IRC dialogues unfold in time.

12. For example, turn-taking does not function as a means of managing interaction as it does in spoken discourse, and a degree of discontinuity in structures of exchange can be identified which would be unlikely to occur in spoken communication due to the transitoriness of speech and the tendency for overlaps to occur. The closest analogues in terms of structural organization are found in other forms of computer-mediated communication such as MUDs, and on bboards such as Usenet News (on News, messages that treat similar topics are known as "threads" and arrange themselves in a fashion roughly comparable to that described above).

13. Thus Cicero notes: "It happens likewise in all parts of language, that a certain agreeableness and grace are attendant on utility, and, I may say, on necessity; for the stoppage of the breath, and the confined play of the lungs, introduced periods and the pointing of words" (1986:245).

14. For example, in data collected by Zimmerman and West (1975:116), the average silence in single-sex conversations was found to be 1.35 seconds, and in mixed-sex conversations 3.21 seconds.

15. Emoticons are graphical representations of facial expressions designed to indicate the speaker's tone and emotional state. The following is an example of an emoticon: (:-) It is a smiley face rotated 90 degrees.

16. In Netiquette guides, using uppercase characters is referred to as "shouting", an expression that is suggestive of the oral character of much computer-mediated communication.

Functional Comparison of Face–to–Face and Computer–Mediated Decision Making Interactions

Sherri L. Condon and Claude G. Čech
University of Southwestern Louisiana
(Université des Acadiens)

1. Introduction*

Are conversations over computers like face–to–face conversations? Although quite a few studies have directly compared oral and written modes of communication (Olson 1977; Ong 1982; Tannen 1982) and yet other studies have investigated computer interactions in various contexts (Peyton 1989; Seu et al. 1991; Sproull & Kiesler 1991; Li et al. 1992), not much is currently known about how synchronous computer–mediated interaction resembles oral or written interaction. The issue is an important one for several reasons. One is that synchronous interaction increasingly characterizes many large systems in which characters typed by one user may appear simultaneously on the monitors of several users. Thus, an understanding of the dynamics of this type of interaction may be of use in assessing the operation of such systems. Of greater relevance, however, is that the resultant communicative event, though undeniably written, has features typically associated with speech. Indexical features of the context such as speakers, hearers, and times are more fully specified than they can be in most written discourses. As in speech, the linguistic signal is not usually permanent: it will not be reread at another time. Most important, synchronous interaction introduces features such as turn–taking (Sacks, Schegloff, & Jefferson 1974) and repair (Schegloff, Jefferson, & Sacks 1977) that have attracted attention in conversation analysis. The term *synchronous machine–mediated interaction*, abbreviated as *s–interaction*, will be used to refer to interactions with these properties.

S–interactions (including use of telephone devices for the deaf) provide a potentially rich source of materials for linguistic and psycholinguistic studies. Because participants in s–interactions do not share the same physical environment, all understandings they achieve must be established in the linguistic forms they enter on their keyboards, together with the interpretive strategies that they apply to those forms. Thus, s–interactions make a powerful tool available for discourse and conversation analysis, particularly for researchers interested in how speakers determine which information to encode and which interpretive strategies to apply. For example, with software that captures interactants' messages prior to delivering them, researchers can alter messages to test hypotheses about discourse processing. Full utilization of this methodology, however, requires that we understand the similarities and differences between s–interactions and face–to–face interactions. In this chapter, therefore, we present an initial comparison of the two types of interactions. To verify that participants apply the same discourse processes in both, we focus our comparison on discourse–level properties and functions.

In the present study, a simple decision–making task is used to provide a discourse–level comparison of the two types of interaction. We can be certain that participants who successfully complete the task accomplish those functions necessary for making decisions. By focusing on the understandings that participants must achieve in order to perform appropriately in the task, we establish a framework for a systematic comparison of the two types of interaction. In previous work, Condon (1986) observed that families engaged in a similar task produce highly structured discourses, but rarely verbalized the understandings achieved as the talk progressed. Based on this corpus, Condon argued that participants engaged in these discourses must rely on a system of expectations and understandings that is reliable enough to accomplish the task using a minimum of linguistic forms, yet flexible enough to allow for an enormous amount of variation in form and content. The system she identified resembles a schema (Schank & Abelson 1977) or frame (Goffman 1974, 1981; Tannen 1979), and makes crucial use of the notion of markedness. The system has been used to devise a coding scheme of mostly functional categories for utterance–unit analysis of decision–making interactions (Condon, Cooper, & Grotevant 1984).

In the present study, a modified version of the coding scheme is used to compare face–to–face interactions with s–interactions. Each utterance is associated with a MOVE function such as suggesting or requesting action, a RESPONSE function such as agreeing or complying with a request, and an OTHER function such as orienting a suggestion or functioning as a discourse marker. By comparing the relative frequencies of 14 functions, we obtain a fine–grained comparison of the two types of interaction.

2. Data collection

Sixty native English speakers at the University of Southwestern Louisiana participated in the study in exchange for bonus credit in Introductory

Psychology classes. Speakers' conversations were recorded while they engaged in a problem–solving task requiring mutual planning. To facilitate discrimination of voices on audio recordings, the students interacted in pairs consisting of one male and one female. The dyads who interacted face–to–face performed the tasks while sitting together at a table with a tape recorder. The participants read written instructions for the decision–making tasks assigned to them, and then completed two tasks.

The dyads who interacted electronically were seated at microcomputers in separate rooms. They received additional instruction about sending messages on the system, and practiced using the system before they began the tasks. At all times during the interactions, a portion of each participant's screen displayed the commands (function keys) accepted by the system and their functions, and the problem to be solved.

Participants in s–interactions communicated by typing messages on their keyboards. The message appeared on the sender's monitor as it was typed, but appeared on the receiver's monitor only when the sender pressed a designated key. The software was designed in this way to provide well–defined turns and to capture and change messages in future studies. However, the design has the consequence that participants sometimes waited for relatively long periods of time to receive a response to their messages. To reassure them that their partners had begun to respond, their computers beeped when their partners initiated or sent a message. The software kept a record of the source of the message (identified as **P**[articipant]**1** and **P**[articipant]**2**), the time that the message was initiated, the time that the message was sent, and the text of the message. The message text included all keys typed (including backspaces to provide data for future studies of encoding strategy shifts), but for the current project, coders worked with files in which the message text is identical to the final form of the transmitted message.

A decision that arose in designing the software involved allowing participants to interrupt one another (see also Li et al. 1992). In the system devised for the present study, interruption replaced an unsent message with the interrupting message. However, the incomplete message remained in the 1024–character buffer to be transmitted when the SEND key was pressed. Some participants thought that the interrupted message was lost, and so repeated the message. Fortunately, there were few interruptions in the data we collected, though our interpretation of the data must take into account the presence of metalanguage that results when participants discuss these problems.

Previous work had used a task in which families planned a two–week vacation, requiring many decisions, and, therefore, containing a high density of functions essential for decision making. The task elicited interactions that were about 20 minutes and, in most cases, over 1000 utterances long. Cooper, Grotevant, and Condon (1982) demonstrate that if the family interactions are coded with the system described in Condon et al. (1984), the relative frequencies of code categories in the first 300 utterances adequately represent the rest. Consequently, for the present study, we designed tasks that could be completed in about 300 utterances.

We devised four tasks to be used as the basis for mutual decision making. For all tasks, participants were told to assume that they had unlimited funds. In two of the tasks, they planned an itinerary for a weekend, one for a getaway anywhere in the world, and the other for a friend visiting southern Louisiana. As in the family study, participants completed answer sheets to ensure that they made a minimum number of decisions. The answer sheets provided space to record locations and activities for the mornings, afternoons, and evenings of two days. The other two tasks required planning a social event (a party in one case; a barbecue in the other). For these tasks, the answer sheets provided spaces designated *time, location, food, beverages, activities,* and *entertainment.*

Each of the 30 dyads was assigned one of the weekend tasks and one of the social event tasks, and each participant was assigned to record the decisions for one of the two tasks on an answer sheet. The tasks and the order in which the tasks were completed were assigned in a way that balanced the four tasks and their order for each type of interaction. We recorded 32 tasks from 16 dyads engaged in face–to–face interactions (henceforth the *oral condition),* and 27 tasks from 14 dyads engaged in s–interactions (henceforth the *electronic condition*). Only 27 tasks were completed by the 14 dyads because one dyad skipped the first task due to computer error. To maintain comparability, the results below are based on 16 oral–condition and 16 electronic–condition conversations selected to represent four conversations for each problem type, two in which that task was the first task attempted, and two in which it was the second task attempted. We additionally constrained our selection of electronic conversations to those in which there were no problems due to misunderstood instructions or attempts to type in messages longer than the buffer. Where we had a choice of interactions in this condition, we generally selected the longer ones to reduce variability and maximize the number of utterances in the corpus.

Transcriptions of face–to–face interactions and records of s–interactions were divided into utterance units defined as single clauses with all complements and adjuncts, including sentential complements and subordinate clauses (Condon et al. 1984). Therefore, clauses connected by *and* or *but* were separated, while clauses connected by *if* or *when* were marked as one utterance. In addition, interjections such as *yeah, now, well,* and *ok* were considered to be separate utterances due to the salience of their interactional, as opposed to propositional, content. Consequently, for coding purposes, a single message in the s–interaction or a single turn at talk in the face–to–face interactions might be divided into several utterances. When presented below as examples, these records will include a reference of the form [e] or [o], where *e*[lectronic] identifies an s–interaction and *o*[ral] identifies a face–to–face interaction.

It is useful to establish some terminology for discussion of the data. The term *adjacency pair* has been used (Goffman 1981; Schegloff & Sacks 1973) to label sequences such as question and answer or request and compliance in which one function, the first pair part, anticipates a particular kind of response, the second pair part. The terms RESPONSE and *response function* are used here to refer to the functions of second pair parts, while the terms MOVE and *move function* are used to refer to the functions of first pair parts. The term *continuation* is used more generally to refer to an utterance (first or second pair part) produced by one participant in response to a previous utterance produced by another participant.

3. Data analysis

The data were transcribed, if necessary, separated into utterance units, and coded by students who received academic credit for their involvement in the project. Coders' training manuals included conventions for transcription as well as conventions for utterance units, along with an analysis of decision–making interaction and a dictionary of the code categories. Reliability tests were administered frequently during coding to preserve reliability. Reliability scores were high (80–100%) for frequently occurring MOVE and RESPONSE functions, discourse markers, and the two categories designed to identify affective functions. Scores for infrequent MOVE and RESPONSE functions, metalanguage, and orientations were often high, but were not as reliably so. Consequently, to increase coding reliability, each interaction was coded by two coders, and disagreements were resolved by the first author.

3.1. The structure of decision–making interactions

Decision–making interactions require participants to generate suggestions for a decision, evaluate the suggestions, recognize when a decision has been agreed on, and move on to the next decision. Since participants achieve these understandings with very few linguistic forms, they seem to rely on a system of expectations that exerts powerful constraints on the interpretation of linguistic forms in decision–making contexts. Condon (1986) suggests that the principles which are active in decision–making interactions establish a structure of expected or unmarked continuations for the talk. The structure can be represented in schematic form as in Figure 1.

GOAL →→	INPUT →→	EVALUATION →→	CRITERIA →→	OUTPUT →→	NEXT GOAL
orientation	suggestion	agreement	(consensus)	[writing]	

Figure 1. The decision structure

The functions represented in block capitals in Figure 1 are intended to suggest that the structure observed in the interactions instantiates a more general schema. Every decision satisfies a goal or need, every proposal must be evaluated, and there must be criteria for determining, from the evaluations, whether the proposal has been accepted or rejected. Finally, all decisions generate minimal output in the sense that subsequent behavior must reflect the understanding that the proposal has been accepted or rejected. Parliamentary procedure can be viewed as a complex elaboration of the general schema, while the interactions in our data optimize the simplicity and efficiency of the structure.

The terms *orientation, suggestion,* and *agreement* in Figure 1 are terms used in coding to identify utterances that function as indicated in the decision structure. In the family interactions examined in Condon (1986), participants adopted a consensual approach to making decisions, but suggestions did not require positive evaluations from every participant. Instead, suggestions became decisions if they received at least one positive evaluation and no negative evaluations. More specifically, a single unmarked continuation of a suggestion counted as a positive evaluation leading to consensus and adoption. Departures from this sequence (e.g., negative evaluations of suggestions or utterances serving other functions such as requesting) were less frequent and encoded by more linguistic material.

The sequence becomes especially streamlined in dyads, because there is only one participant to evaluate the suggestion. If that person fails to evaluate the suggestion negatively, then a positive evaluation becomes redundant, and we can anticipate that suggestions might be adopted without any forms that function as evaluations. However, in our data there are few instances in which a suggestion is not continued by an utterance that can be interpreted as a positive evaluation of the suggestion, though these evaluations are often expressed using minimal forms such as *yeah, ok, alright,* and *cool.*

The term *consensus* has been placed in parentheses and is not used in coding because, although participants clearly adopted a consensual approach to the tasks, it is extremely rare for them to comment on the establishment of a consensus. In fact, there are no utterances in the 32 interactions analyzed for the present study that occur immediately after consensus has been established and express content of the sort expressed in (1).

(1) a. so we agree
b. so we're going to Hawaii

The corpus includes utterances like (1b), but these function to orient the talk. Often they occur when dyads in the oral condition are recording their plans on the answer forms, as in (2).

(2) a. ok
b. we are going to the French Quarter about...[writing]
c. French quarter after...after eating...[writing] [o]

(2b,c) illustrate utterances produced while the speaker is writing, and when these occur, the speakers are usually pronouncing the words they are writing. The term *writing talk* is used in the coding manual to refer to utterances like (2b,c), as well as utterances in which participants who are not recording the plans repeat decisions to remind or direct the partner who is writing. As (2) illustrates, the notation *[writing]* marks all writing talk, and the same notation appears under OUTPUT in Figure 1 to represent writing talk in the decision sequence. Sequences like (2) do not occur in the s–interactions of our corpus. Instead, decisions were recorded as they were established by whichever student was assigned the answer sheet for the current task. Accordingly, we did not use a separate code category for writing talk. While no messages like (2b,c) were produced, most s–interactions contained one (and only one) utterance concerned with writing. (3) provides a few examples:

(3) a. do you have the paper [e]
b. you write down the details [e]
c. I wrote everything down [e]
d. give me a minute to write this down [e]

Consequently, without talk that reflects consensus or writing, the decision structure reduces to orientation, suggestion, and evaluation. (4) demonstrates how smoothly and minimally the decision structures can be formulated, by annotating each utterance with functions. Orientation is usually accomplished in questions, such as (4a) and (4i), and by incorporating the orientation into the suggesting utterance, as in (4d) and (4f). In (4d) and (4f), the phrases *in the afternoon* and *at night* reflect an answer sheet that orients activities into morning, afternoon, and evening sections. The suggestions can be interpreted as satisfying the goals of something to do in the afternoon and something to do at night in the same way that (4a) establishes the goal of something "to do in the morning." Once a goal has been established for the suggestion, the suggestion is recognizable based on its content alone. If the suggestion can be interpreted as a proposal that satisfies the goal, then it will be, and may consequently be communicated by a minimal amount of linguistic material. The suggestion *sleep* in (4b) is an example. Similarly, the minimal responses to suggestions in (4c,e,g) are typical of the interactions we have analyzed.

(4) a. P2: what do you want to do in the morning *[orientation]*
b. P1: sleep *[suggestion]*
c. P2: cool *[agreement]*
d. P2: I say we lay out in the afternoon *[suggestion, orientation]*
e. P1: ok *[agreement]*
f. P1: and at night we party *[suggestion, orientation]*
g. P2: yea *[agreement]*
h. P1: ?
i. P1: whats next? *[orientation]* [e]

3.2. *The role of markedness in decision structures*

While Figure 1 establishes structural relations among functions in decision making, the relations must be more carefully defined in order to account for the variation in form and content observed in the data. When a relation is represented by x →→ y in Figure 1, we will say that y is an *unmarked continuation* of x. Therefore, suggestions are unmarked continuations of orientations and agreements are unmarked continuations of suggestions. Furthermore, writing talk and orienting the next decision are unmarked continuations of agreements. At least three properties are associated with unmarked continuations. First, any utterance that continues x will be interpreted as y even if the form and content of the utterance are not obviously associated with y. The interpretation y is the default, allowing utterances to be extremely *indirect* (Searle 1975) or *off record* (Brown & Levinson 1987). Second, as a consequence, unmarked continuations can be encoded in a minimal amount of linguistic form (4c,e,g), whereas marked continuations such as disagreements will require additional form. For example, a disagreement following (4b) would require more content than the simple form *no*. Finally, we expect higher frequencies of utterances that conform to the unmarked structure. For example, in utterances responding to a previous suggestion, we would expect higher frequencies of forms signaling agreement than disagreement.

The term *default* is usually associated with these three properties, but the term *unmarked* is used here to call attention to the similarity between the manner in which the system operates and ideas associated with the notion of markedness in linguistics. In the distinctive feature theory of phonology, a natural or unmarked class requires fewer features to define. Similarly, an unmarked continuation requires fewer linguistic signals to encode its function. Finally, we expect unmarked phonological classes to occur more frequently in the languages of the world, as we expect unmarked decision structures to occur more frequently in decision–making interactions.

3.3. *Functional categories and the organization of the coding system*

Each utterance was classified in one of 6 MOVE functions, one of 5 RESPONSE functions, and one of 6 OTHER functions. When coders found utterances that could be classified in more than one category of MOVE, RESPONSE, or OTHER functions, they were instructed to select the highest category (Table 1 presents these categories in order of importance). In this hierarchy, *suggests action* (SA) is the highest MOVE function and it corresponds to the suggestion/input function in the decision structure. The highest response function is *agrees with suggestion* (AS), which corresponds to the agreement/positive evaluation function in the decision structure. The *disagrees with suggestion* (DS) category includes negative evaluations of suggestions as well as refusals to comply with requests and utterances that deny the truth of a previous utterance.

Three types of requests are distinguished in the MOVE functions. *Requests action* (RA) identifies utterances that attempt to influence the hearer's behavior in the speech event, as opposed to suggestions about behavior during the hypothetical weekend or social event. Requests for action frequently arise in the context of writing in both types of interaction, as in (3b,d) and (5a,b).

(5)
a. just put Sunday [o]
b. write it in activities [o]
c. remember we have un—unlimited funds [o]
d. We need to decide on somewhere to have it. [e]
e. You may decide [e]
f. where did you go to school? [o]
g. What city is Destin beach in? [e]
h. I must be messing you up. Correct? [e]
i. just Lafayette? [o]
j. Christmas–Comes–Alive used to be there [o]
k. I heard they are good [e]
l. It's been nice talking with you. [e]
m. jungle fever [e]

Requests for action that orient and manage the talk as in (5c,d,e) are also coded as metalanguage (ML). *Requests for information* (RI) seek information not already provided in the discourse as in (5f,g), while *requests for validation* (RV) seek confirmation or verification of information already provided in the discourse as *Correct?* does in (5h). The request for validation in (5i) occurs in response to the partner's assertion that the task requires them to confine their plans to Lafayette. Also included as requests for validation are utterances that seek agreement with a suggestion. The final MOVE category *elaborates, repeats* (ER) serves as a catch–all for utterances with comprehensible content that do not serve any other MOVE or RESPONSE functions. The category includes writing talk, repetitions, and utterances that support or comment on suggestions as in (5j,k).

The RESPONSE category *complies with request* (CR) identifies utterances that reflect compliance with any of the three types of requests, and the category *acknowledges only* (AO) identifies utterances that acknowledge a previous utterance. Since most continuations acknowledge previous utterances in some sense, we restricted utterances in the AO category to utterances like *yeah* when they seemed to function exclusively to acknowledge an ER utterance such as (5j,k) and to utterances like (5i) which assess whether a message was received and understood accurately.

Two categories in the OTHER functions were designed to assess affective functions. *Requests/offers personal information* (PI) identifies utterances in which participants discuss personal information or make other personal comments not required to complete the task as in (5f,l), while the *jokes, exaggerates* (JE) category includes utterances that inject humor as in (5m).

Discourse markers (DM) identify forms such as *well, so, ok, let's see, now,* and *anyway* when they occur at the beginning of an utterance. Functional and syntactic criteria are also used to discriminate among multifunctional forms to exclude those forms that serve other functions, such as the agreeing function of *ok* or the use of *so* as a subordinating conjunction. The most frequent form of discourse marker is *ok*, and (2a) provides an example of the form functioning in this manner. The *metalanguage* (ML) category includes utterances that manage or direct the talk as in (5d,e) as well as utterances about the task itself as in (5c,i) and (6a), or about what speakers meant or said as in (6b). Metalanguage also includes utterances such as (6c) that focus on the transmission of the message.

(6) a. I think we are finished [e]
b. sorry i meant to type saturday [e]
c. Are you there? [e]
d. Day one...morning [o]

The category *orients suggestion* (OS) identifies utterances in which suggestions begin with an orienting phrase (4f). Included are orientations expressed in a request for information (4a,i), or in a short phrase (6d).

Table 1. Organization of code categories

MOVE FUNCTIONS		*RESPONSE FUNCTIONS*		*OTHER FUNCTIONS*	
SA	Suggests Action	AS	Agrees with Suggestion	DM	Discourse Marker
RA	Requests Action	DS	Disagrees with Suggestion	ML	Metalanguage
RV	Requests Validation	CR	Complies with Request	OS	Orients Suggestion
RI	Requests Information	AO	Acknowledges Only	PI	Personal Information
ER	Elaborates, Repeats	NC	No clear response	JE	Jokes, Exaggerates
NC	No clear move			NC	No clear other

4. Results

Given the additional effort required to type messages, it is not surprising that face–to–face interactions were considerably longer than s–interactions (259 versus 57 utterances averaged over interaction; see also Seu et al. 1991). We establish comparability across interaction type by analyzing *proportion* of times per discourse a given function was used. This has the advantage of normalizing function use not only across interaction type, but also across problem type, and most important, across dyads. Thus, in the analyses below, we need not be concerned with whether one dyad was more talkative than another.

We will start with the question of whether second conversations systematically differ from first conversations. Second conversations might shorten and become more schematic as participants become familiar with one another's background or linguistic and problem–solving styles. However, the use of the abstract decision structure schema presented in Figure 1 should remain substantially unaltered. Regardless of familiarity, such a schema ought still to determine the discourse structure at an abstract level, and thus, the relative proportions of the functions listed in Table 1. In fact, our results collapsed over communicative modality exhibited remarkable agreement in function usage from first to second discourse. This is shown in Figure 2 (diamonds in Figure 2 present the data for first conversations; rectangles present the data for second conversations). In separate repeated–measures analyses of variance on the three function classes that treated discourse (dyad) as the random variable, we failed to find any evidence of a main effect of order, or of an interaction of order with function (all *F* s < 1). In these and subsequent analyses, we did not include the no clear move (NC) functions, as inclusion would have forced levels of the between–discourse factor to the same value.

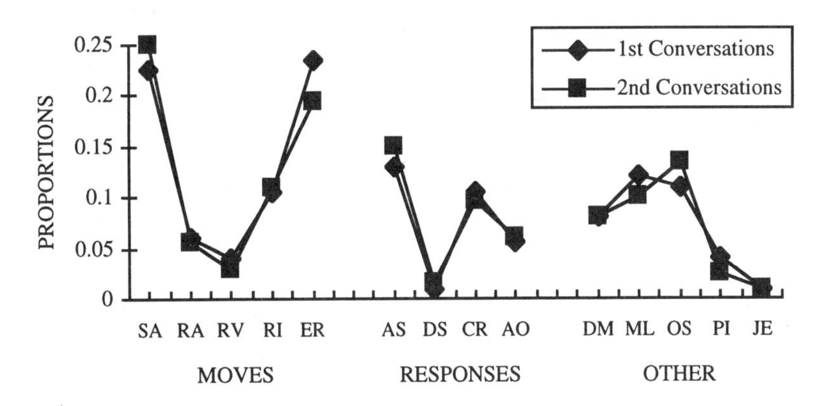

Figure 2. Effects of first versus second conversation on the three function classes

We can also look at the effects of problem type. Undoubtedly, each problem type establishes its own constraints on the discourse, but from our theoretical perspective, the same decision schema should still apply at an abstract level across these different types of problems. Hence, the effectiveness of this abstract representation may be assessed, at some level, by the similarity of results across problem type.

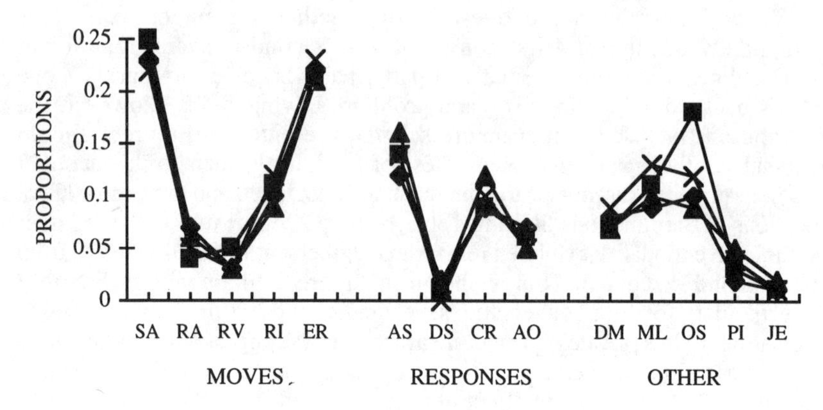

Figure 3. Effects of problem type on the three function classes

As may be seen from Figure 3, there was again substantial agreement in proportionate category usage. In this figure, the two weekend problems are represented by the rectangle and cross symbols; the social visit problems are represented by the diamond and triangle symbols. No effect of problem type was found in the analyses of variance including this variable. In particular, although the data for OTHER functions were a bit noisy, the apparent main effect of problem type was not reliable, $F\,(3,28) = 1.654$, $p > .10$, nor was there any interaction of problem type with function ($F < 1$).

Finally, given the comparability of results across problem type and order, we may examine function usage to see whether there are systematic differences in s–interactions and face–to–face interactions. The data of interest here appear in Figure 4.

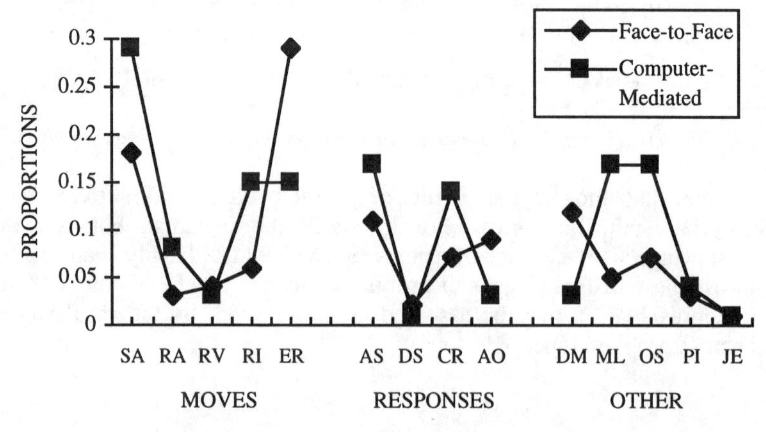

Figure 4. Face-to-face versus s-interactions

At a quantitative level, the data of Figure 4 provide yet further support for the claim that the decision sequence operates across modality. Thus, although the proportions of suggestions and agreements differ in our two conditions, the ratio of suggestions (SA) to agreements (AS) in each is nearly identical: 1.64 in the oral interaction, and 1.71 in the s–interaction. Another adjacency relation not unique to decision sequences is the relation between requests and compliance with requests. There are three types of requests in the MOVES category (RA, RV, and RI). The ratio of these to the compliance function (CR) in the RESPONSES category is 1.86 in each interaction condition.

We may also examine the relation between orientations and suggestions. This relation is more difficult to assess because orientations can be accomplished by three types of utterances. OS codes identify orientations incorporated into suggestions (4f) or questions (4a,i), or accomplished by short phrases such as (6d). However, orientations may also be accomplished through metalanguage statements (ML). Moreover, discourse markers (DM) such as *ok* or *so* serve an orienting function (Condon 1986). Thus, as a rough approximation of frequency of orientation, we combined the three code categories of OS, DM, and ML. The ratio of these functions to suggestions was 1.33 in the s–interactions, and 1.27 in the oral interactions.

The general decision schema suggests that some continuations are more likely than others. While departures from the expected do occur, we would nevertheless argue that across a large enough sample of tasks and dyads, the frequency of continuations for certain adjacent functions should be reasonably constant. As the ratios above illustrate, there is some compelling evidence that the same expectations operate in both face–to–face and electronic discourses. The model also anticipates that functions in the decision sequence should be the most frequent in the discourse. In accord with this prediction, suggestions (SA) and agreements (AS) were quite frequent in both modes, although the ER category was actually more frequent than the SA category in the oral condition. Of course, this category includes functions (orientation, writing talk) which do play a significant role in the decision schema, especially in oral interactions (see below). In fact, the model predicts that as interactions are reduced to essential functions, the proportion of utterances functioning in the decision structure should increase, which is exactly what we observe in the proportion of suggestions from the two conditions.

Although the general model applies to each type of interaction, there are nevertheless differences in the two conditions. In analyses of variance on these data, the interaction of function type with discourse modality was significant for all three categories of function: $F\,(4,120) = 24.1, p < .001$ for MOVES; $F\,(3,90) = 20.2, p < .001$ for RESPONSES; $F\,(4,120) = 22.9, p < .001$ for OTHER. Subsequent tests of simple effects of modality type at each function indicated that only the RV function in the MOVES category, the DS function in the RESPONSES category, and the PI and JE functions in the OTHER category were identical in the s–interactions and face–to–face interactions (see Figure 4). What, then, do the obtained differences signify?

A first generalization we may make concerns the efficiency of decision making in s–interactions. If we operationalize efficiency through the proportion of decision sequences and measure the latter by proportion of suggestions, then s–interactions appear to be more efficient than face–to–face interactions (29% versus 18%). This conclusion appears to contradict Kiesler et al. (1985). However, they measured efficiency by absolute numbers of prepared questions addressed by dyads. Had we measured absolute numbers of suggestions, we might also have been tempted to claim greater efficiency for oral discourses. Alternatively, we might have made the *opposite* claim that s–interactions are more efficient precisely *because* they produced fewer utterances: they achieved the required goal with less linguistically–encoded discussion! Obviously, at issue here is how to measure efficiency in a way that maintains comparability between conditions that will systematically differ in length for not–terribly–important reasons (e.g., relative difficulty of typing versus speaking). As pointed out above, we chose to establish comparability in terms of proportion of functions per discourse. And on this approach, the proportion of suggestions is the more appropriate measure of efficiency.

Of course, the face–to–face discourses also tended to produce more detailed and elaborate plans. Thus, much of the increase in the electronic condition in proportion of suggestions may be explained by a corresponding decrease in the proportion of elaborations, repetitions, and writing talk. In a nearly perfect reversal, the oral condition displayed 29% usage of ER functions whereas the electronic condition displayed only 15% usage.

We also found that requests for information (RI) and requests for action (RA) were more common in the s–interactions (15% versus 6%, and 8% versus 3%, respectively). This result may be due in part to different orientation strategies adopted in the two conditions (see below). However, part of this difference is undoubtedly due to the effectiveness of questions for turn management in electronic discourses. We discussed briefly in Section 2 the problems that s–interaction participants experienced in turn taking; by orienting the talk with a specific context of presuppositions and implicatures (and given the demand that the adjacency relation creates for an answer), question forms and utterances with questioning functions help structure discourse into manageable sequences.

MOVE and RESPONSE functions are related in adjacency pairings; hence it will not be surprising that the differences we obtain in response functions mirror the differences we have just examined in MOVE functions. That is, the electronic discourses also exhibited more agreements (AS) and more compliances with requests (CR). However, one difference in proportions that did not exactly mirror the earlier differences involved the acknowledgment (AO) function: The ratio of elaborative or writing talk comments (ER) to acknowledgments was 5 in the electronic discourses, but only 3.2 in the face–to–face discourses. This result probably reflects the fact that this relation is not a typical adjacency relation: acknowledgments do not seem to be obligatory continuations of utterances in the same way that answers and evaluations are obligatory continuations of questions and suggestions. Because unnecessary talk tends to be omitted in s–interactions, a smaller proportion of acknowledgments appears likely. At the same time, the non–obligatory nature of acknowledgments suggests that they might be a useful category to investigate the influence of social and affective factors in discourse.

Two OTHER functions coded affective qualities of the interaction: PI which involved personal information, and JE which captured joking or exaggeration. Contrary to Kiesler et al. (1985), we found no differences in affective consequences between electronic and oral interactions. However, we did exclude laughter from the JE category in the latter interactions, as we could not track laughter in the former. In addition, the discourses in Kiesler et al. involved quite different situations, in which the goal included unacquainted participants learning about one another.

The use of discourse markers (DM) and orientation (OS) also differed in the two modalities. These differences seem to reflect differing orientation strategies. Dyads in the electronic condition were twice as likely to orient suggestions using a request for information (4a,i) and to produce suggestions with incorporated orientations (4f). In contrast, dyads in the oral condition were four times as likely to use discourse markers. Assuming that most discourse markers served an orientation function (see Condon 1986 for evidence supporting this claim), we are struck by the fact that the proportion of orientations is nearly identical for both conditions when orientations are tracked by combining the DM and OS categories (20% in s–interactions; 19% in face–to–face interactions).

Finally, we note the threefold increase in the use of metalanguage (ML) in the electronic condition. Since metalanguage includes orientations formulated as direct or indirect requests, the greater proportion of metalanguage in the electronic condition along with the greater proportion of utterances in the orientation (OS) category seems to reflect a tendency to express orientations more overtly in s–interactions. Whereas dyads in face–to–face interactions used more short orienting phrases and discourse markers, dyads in s–interactions used more requests for information and requests for action to determine the structure of decision sequences. (Of course, other factors contributed to the large difference in the metalanguage category as well, since participants in s–interactions engaged in metalanguage when they discussed problems they were experiencing with the electronic modality.)

5. Conclusions

Analysis of the individual code categories suggests that two major factors influence differences observed between face–to–face interactions and s–interactions. First, participants in s-interactions tend to omit unnecessary linguistic material, which makes what they do say more efficient and more likely to accomplish more than one function. Thus we find a preference for forms that accomplish both orienting and turn management functions. Second, while participants seem to rely on lower level adjacency relations in much the same way in both types of interactions, the higher level functions that organize and orient the structure and sequence of decisions are accomplished using different encoding strategies. In this case, participants in s–interactions seem to be willing to use more linguistic material in order to accomplish the functions.

There is still much to be learned about the strategies participants employ to satisfy their cognitive, interactional, and affective goals in the two types of interaction. We have not discussed, for example, the predictions that could be made concerning such effects as mean utterance length, structuring of turns in the discourse, and markedness. Clearly, this paradigm provides a rich source of information that goes well beyond the boundaries of electronic discourse.

Despite the differences we found between electronic and oral interactions, both types of discourse fit a generic decision–making schema that determines, at an abstract level, the flow of conversation. The stability of the decision sequence across problem order, problem type, and medium of communication provides strong motivation to continue exploration of s–interactions. We are excited by the promise of new tools and increased methodological precision inherent in the prospect of using electronically–mediated discourse to investigate discourse processes.

ACKNOWLEDGMENTS

* This project was supported by a Faculty Research Award at the University of Southwestern Louisiana. For their help with data analysis, we gratefully acknowledge Ryan Aubert, Eileen Barton, Cathy Landry, Joyce Lane, Tom Petitjean, Traci Smrcka, and John Strawn.

Two Variants of an Electronic Message Schema

Susan C. Herring
University of Texas at Arlington

1. Introduction*

An emergent stereotype about computer-mediated communication (henceforth, CMC) is that male users are concerned primarily with the exchange of information, while female users send e-mail primarily to promote and maintain interpersonal relationships. This stereotype is consistent with Tannen's (1990) claim that men prefer to use language in the "report" function and women in the "rapport" function in face-to-face communication, a claim she explicitly extends to CMC (Tannen 1994). The stereotype takes on new significance, however, in the context of the current "Information Age", where it is typically evoked to represent women's use of computer networks as marked or deviant relative to the "normal" (male) use of computer networks as a tool for information exchange. Thus Yates (1993:22-23), in a study of female participation in computer-mediated distance education courses, hypothesizes that "women [...] are more likely to exploit the opportunity to engage in interactive interpersonal communication than men", and a high school computer lab director was quoted in *Newsweek* as stating that girls "see [sending e-mail] as high-tech note-passing" (Kantrowitz 1994:52). However, no empirical basis for the stereotype of the informative male and the interactive female computer user has yet been established.

The kind of evidence that would support or refute such a stereotype depends on how the stereotype itself is interpreted. According to one interpretation, men and women use CMC in different functional domains, with men posting more (information-oriented) electronic messages to public discussion groups, and women sending more (personally-oriented) private e-mail. Unfortunately, no one has yet collected a representative corpus of private e-mail messages that would make it possible to confirm or disprove this hypothesis. The second interpretation is that women and men participate in the same domains, but their communication is oriented differently, such that men's messages to, e.g., public discussion groups are more information oriented, while women's messages to the same groups are more socially oriented. In this chapter, I bring empirical evidence to bear on this latter hypothesis.

I do so by analyzing the schematic structure of electronic messages posted publicly by women and men to two listserve discussion groups. The results of my investigation reveal that both men and women structure their messages in interactive ways, and that for both, the pure exchange of information takes second place to the exchange of views. Significant gender differences are found in how electronic messages are oriented, but the differences are not those predicted by the stereotype. Although messages posted by women contain somewhat more interactional features, they are also more informative, in contrast with male messages which most often express (critical) views. The evidence further suggests that members of the minority gender on each list shift their style in the direction of majority gender norms. These results provide no support whatsoever for the stereotype that women are less interested in the electronic exchange of information than men, or that men do not use computer networks for social interaction; rather, they show that women and men negotiate information exchange and social interaction in gendered ways.

The chapter is organized as follows. Section 2 describes the data and methodology employed in the investigation. Section 3 presents evidence for a basic electronic message schema, and section 4 describes gender variation within the basic schema. Finally, section 5 reinterprets the stereotype of the informative male and the interactive female in light of these findings.

2. Data and methodology

2.1. Data

Two Internet mailing lists were analyzed for the purposes of this study: the LINGUIST list and the WMST (Women's Studies) list. Both are large lists (several thousand subscribers) which generate an average of 30-80 public postings per week and have a strict academic focus. Participants on both lists are mostly academic professionals, graduate students, and other professionals associated with the list's field of study.

The two lists contrast in one important respect: their gender makeup. WMST, which focuses on women's studies teaching and the establishment and administration of women's studies programs, is 88% female, and women participate in discussion at a rate about equal to their numerical presence (Korenman & Wyatt, This volume). LINGUIST, which describes itself as a forum for discussion of issues of interest to academic linguists, has only 64% male subscribers, but men regularly contribute 85% or more in LINGUIST discussions (Herring 1992, 1993a, 1993c).

For the purposes of this investigation, I analyzed all of the messages posted in two extended discussions, one from each list. The primary criterion for selecting the discussions was that they attracted large numbers of participants relative to other discussions on the same list, and thus presumably represent the interests and interactional norms of list subscribers. The LINGUIST discussion took place after the list had been in existence for several months, and concerned the use of the label "cognitive linguistics" to describe different (and competing) schools of linguistic thought. The WMST discussion took place after the list had been in existence for about a year, and concerned a television documentary that was airing at the time entitled "Brain Sex", as well as the broader question of whether there are differences between the brains of women and men. Summary data about the two discussions are given in Table 1.

Table 1. Discussions selected for analysis

List	Topic	Dates	# Participants (M)	# Participants (F)	# Messages (M)	# Messages (F)	# Words (M)	# Words (F)
LINGUIST	"cognitive linguistics"	2/2-4/20, 1991	30	5	53	18	21,469	3,789
WMST	"brain sex"	9/14-9/21, 1992[1]	3	26	3	62	472	13,037
total			33	31	56	80	21,941	16,826

In all, 136 individual messages totalling 38,767 words were analyzed. These represent the total contributions of 33 male and 31 female participants.

2.2. *Methodology*

A basic assumption underlying this investigation is that individual electronic messages are internally-organized texts. As such, insights about their structure can be gleaned using methods of linguistic text analysis. Text linguists such as Longacre (1992) and Swales (1990) have observed that informational texts tend to be organized as expository essays or reports (usually written), while interactive texts tend to be organized as conversational turns (in speaking) or personal notes (in writing). Moreover, each of these text types has a distinctive schematic organization, or conventional sequence of functional "moves" into which the text can be chunked. By comparing the schematic organization of messages posted by women and men in similar electronic groups, we can evaluate the claim that these messages function in different ways, e.g., as exposition or interaction.

Our basic unit of analysis is the *macrosegment*, a functional constituent of the text at a macro- or global level of organization (Longacre 1992). Macrosegments are identified according to their notional coherence and their surface cohesion. Surface cohesion refers to consistent linguistic choices a writer makes with regard to e.g., person reference, tense usage, or sentence structure; a macrosegment can also be set off from other macrosegments by a skipped line before or after, paragraph indentation, or use of formulae which explicitly introduce macro-level ideas, such as "My point is this:". However, while linguistic signals often provide useful cues, they are not sufficient to identify macrosegments: a macrosegment may be said to exist solely on the grounds of its notional coherence, without any explicit signals of its boundaries, and shifts in person reference, tense, etc. do not always correspond to the boundaries of macrosegments.

Notional coherence refers to the ability of a macrosegment to fulfill a higher-order function in the schematic organization of a text. A scientific essay or other information-oriented exposition, for example, will typically be constructed of macrosegments of the following four functional types, each constituting a higher-order move in the *informational expository* schema:[2]

1. Identification of problem
2. Proposal of solution
3. Evidence in support of solution
4. Evaluation of solution

Figure 1. The informational expository schema (adapted from Longacre 1992)

Another common exposition type aims not so much to inform as to effect a change in the addressees' beliefs or opinions; this type Longacre terms *persuasive*. The persuasive schema is similar to the informational one except that in place of "evaluation of the solution", the persuasive schema has as its fourth move an "appeal to give credence, or to adopt certain values" (Longacre 1992:111).

The insight that text types are associated with conventional sequences of moves can be extended to include more interactionally-oriented texts such as personal notes and conversational turns. These interactional text types have in common a basic three-part structure made up of a contentful message that is framed before and after by moves which link the message to the larger interactive context. Personal notes (a sub-type of letters) also have an additional external frame of opening and closing epistolary conventions. The generalized interactive schema is represented in Figure 2.

(Opening epistolary conventions)
1. Link to previous discourse
2. Contentful message
3. Link to following discourse

(Closing epistolary conventions)

Figure 2. The interactive schema

Letters typically realize this schema with the aid of fixed and semi-fixed linguistic formulae. *Opening epistolary conventions* include date and salutation, the latter often made up of a vocative form of address plus a title or name ("Dear Madam"; "Hi Sally!", etc.). *Links to the previous discourse* introduce the purpose of the letter ("I am writing in response to...") or seek to establish common ground between the letter writer and the addressee ("I hope this letter finds you well"). *Links to the following discourse* allude to future correspondence, and include offers ("Do not hesitate to contact me if I can provide any further assistance") and appeals ("Write soon"). *Closing epistolary conventions* are highly formulaic, and include complimentary closes ("sincerely yours", "love", etc.) followed by the signature of the letter writer, and an optional postscript conventionally preceded by the abbreviation "p.s.". At the center of this chiastic or mirror-image structure, the *contentful message* contains new information that is the ostensible reason for which the letter was written. Reasons for writing letters vary widely, and thus the contentful message is the most structurally and functionally heterogeneous move in the schema.[3]

Conversational turns lack epistolary conventions but otherwise have analogous structure. A prototypical, maximally-specified conversational turn acknowledges the previous speaker's contribution, e.g., by means of discourse markers such as "oh", "yeah", and "well" (Schiffrin 1987), before contributing new information to the conversation, and concludes by allocating the turn to a next speaker, e.g., by means of gaze or directed questioning ("What do *you* think?") (McLaughlin 1984). Thus in turns as in letters, a contentful message is bracketed by moves that situate the contribution in the ongoing interpersonal interaction. In contrast, the informational and persuasive expository schemata contain no overtly interactional moves; rather their moves present and develop a solution to a problem.

Drawing on these observations, in order to evaluate the gender stereotype, I hypothesized that the messages posted by men on LINGUIST and the WMST list would be organized like (i.e., illustrate the schematic moves of) expository texts, while the messages posted by women on both lists would be organized more like personal notes or conversational turns. That is, I hypothesized that there would be a Gender Effect which groups together men on both lists and women on both lists. I further hypothesized that messages posted to the male-predominant list would be more expository than those posted to the female-predominant list, and that messages posted to the female-predominant list would be more interactional, regardless of the gender of the sender. That is, I also expected to find evidence of a List Effect, whereby the communicative practices of the majority of active participants become normative for the group as a whole.

In order to test these hypotheses, I chunked each of the 136 messages in the corpus into macrosegments according to the criteria described above. In what follows, the resulting sequences of moves are presented and discussed.

3. The basic electronic message schema

3.1. Recurrent macrosegments

The most immediate result of chunking the messages into macrosegments was the discovery of a limited set of recurrent textual-pragmatic functions. These are listed in Table 2, along with their frequencies in the two discussions. The order of presentation of functions in Table 2 corresponds roughly to the linear order in which they appear in the messages in the corpus, although no single message contains all of the functions listed.

Table 2. Functions and frequencies (% of total messages) of macrosegments

Function	Brain Sex (N=65)		Cog Lincs (N=71)		Combined (N=136)	
	%	N	%	N	%	N
Epistolary Convention						
salutation	6%	4	19%	14	13%	17
Introduction						
preamble	2%	1	3%	2	2%	3
metacomment	9%	6	10%	7	10%	13
prospective introduction	8%	5	7%	5	7%	10
link to previous message	68%	44	66%	47	67%	91
Total	87%	56	86%	61	86%	117
Body						
express views	52%	34	80%	57	67%	91
request information	9%	6	1%	1	5%	7
provide information	31%	20	24%	17	27%	37
express feelings	17%	11	3%	2	10%	13
suggest solution	17%	11	6%	4	11%	15
offer	9%	6	0%	0	4%	6
Total	135%	88	114%	81	124%	169
Close						
apology	28%	*18	15%	**11	21%	29
appeal to others	28%	18	20%	14	24%	32
chastisement	2%	1	1%	1	1%	2
Total	58%	37	36%	26	46%	63
Epistolary Conventions						
complimentary close	2%	1	3%	2	2%	3
signature	91%	59	70%	50	80%	109
postscript	0%	0	1%	1	1%	1
Total	93%	60	74%	53	83%	113

* 3 in Introduction, 8 in Body
** 4 in Introduction, 5 in Body

Note that the total percentages for each category in Table 2 do not add up to 100%. This is because not all messages contain epistolary, introduction, and close macrosegments, and some messages contain more than one body macrosegment. Four categories of macrosegment are discussed below.

3.1.1. Epistolary conventions

The first and last rows of Table 2 show the frequency of epistolary conventions in the electronic messages in the two discussions. Surprisingly few messages are preceded by a salutation (only 13% on average), and fewer yet are followed by a complimentary close or a postscript. Of those salutations that occur, most are in the Cognitive Linguistics discussion, and most are of the form "To: [Name]". The relative lack of epistolary conventions can be explained in part by the fact that a header is added automatically to each message by the electronic mailer, including a separate line for who the message is "from", who it is addressed "to" (in these data, the entire mailing list), and the date and time of posting.

The existence of "from" lines in headers leads us to predict that signatures will be redundant as well, and hence infrequent. However, as Table 2 shows, signatures are the *most* frequent feature of the electronic messages in the corpus (80% of all messages). A possible explanation for this is that some people's electronic mail systems omit sender information in the header; thus WMST users are regularly reminded through the "user's guide" (Korenman & Wyatt, This volume) to sign their messages, a fact which may account for the higher incidence of signed messages in the Brain Sex discussion. However this cannot be the reason users sign their messages on LINGUIST, as header information including date, subject line, and sender is preserved with all LINGUIST postings, because of the format in which they are packaged and distributed by the moderators. The general tendency of users to sign their names at the end of messages suggests that they view them as more similar to print correspondence than to expository treatises (or, for that matter, conversational turns).[4]

3.1.2. Introductions

After signatures, two macrosegments vie for highest frequency in that both are found in 67% of all messages. The first *links* the current message to a previous message or messages. The high frequency of textual links reflects participants' need to establish and maintain coherence across messages. This is especially important in CMC, in that any given discussion is apt to be interwoven with discussions on different topics, and subject headers alone often do not provide sufficient information to identify which discussion the message is responding to. Several examples of linking macrosegments, each of them the opening line of a message, are given in (1). (All names cited in messages are pseudonyms assigned by the author.)

(1) a. I would like to respond on the question of [sic] Kathy Trager.
b. Sharon Thompson's letter raises two important questions:
c. In view of the several lengthy and unanswered dissertations that have been posted to this list about the merits or demerits of the appropriation of the name Cognitive Linguistics, I would like to put in my little grain of sand, for whatever it's worth.
d. Three bits' worth on autonomy/cognitive linguistics:

Such links characteristically constitute the opening move, or *introduction*, of an electronic message. Other types of introduction include a *prospective introduction* which introduces the message to follow, e.g., by providing a summary abstract ("This is not the reply to Larry I promised—just a couple of quick comments to Koch and Wisniewski"). A third type of introduction is a *metacomment* on the discussion as a whole ("I am glad to have generated such a storm of protest"; "Everyone is probably tired of this argument by now..."). Finally, a few messages start off with a *preamble*, which neither links nor summarizes but rather provides background information against which to evaluate the content that follows. (For example, one message begins: "I have a pet beagle named Fred who thinks he's a linguist and who sometimes reads my e-mail. After sniffing around for a while yesterday, he left me the following note.") However, none of these latter types is very frequent (7%, 11%, and 2% of messages, respectively), and textual links clearly predominate as the most prototypical form of electronic message introduction in the corpus. The roughly equal presence of such links on the two mailing lists suggests that participants of both genders view their messages as contributions to an ongoing discussion, rather than as isolated pronouncements. Further, to the extent that introduction involves mentioning another participant by name (68% of all introductions in the LINGUIST discussion, and 58% of introductions in the WMST discussion), it is also interpersonal. Interpersonal introductions in electronic messages recall the openings of conversational turns and the lead-ins of letters.

3.1.3. Body

The second high-frequency function expressed by a single macrosegment is *expressing views*, a term I use to refer to statements of ideational content evaluated implicitly or explicitly with respect to the speaker's commitment to their truthfulness. This category includes expressions of opinion, belief, understanding or judgment associated with some aspect of the topic under discussion. Expressing views differs from *providing information* (such as bibliographic references, conference announcements, or announcements of software availability) in that the author's commitment to the truthfulness of the content is part of the communication in the former, whereas in providing information the content is merely reported. Despite the popular belief that electronic mailing lists are used mainly for information exchange, expressions of views are more than twice as frequent as purely information-oriented messages (both requesting and providing information) in both discussions combined, with the difference being greatest in the Cognitive Linguistics discussion. Note that this finding runs counter to the hypothesis that the primarily male discussion would be more information-focused than the discussion in which most of the participants are women. Indeed the opposite is true: the Brain Sex discussion has more messages in which information is requested and provided (31%) than the Cognitive Linguistics discussion (24%), and fewer messages in which participants express or argue their views (52%, as compared with 80% in the Cognitive Linguistics discussion). This is consistent with previous findings that male computer network users are more assertive and argumentative than female users (Herring 1993a). Nevertheless, expression of views appears to be the most important function of e-mail messages in both extended discussions.

Expression of views ranges from forcefully-worded assertions (including assertions of alleged "fact") to opinions presented as such, e.g., through the use of hedged evidential phrases such as "I think" and "It seems to me". The following examples are portions of views statements from the corpus.

(2) a. Perhaps this is the only forum where such a discussion could take place across the cognitivist-generativist divide. It is impossible at the LSA, which has a conservative, generatively-oriented program committee and which has refused to permit paper sessions devoted to results in cognitive linguistics.

[statement of "fact" about the LSA ('It is impossible...'); embedded statements of "fact" ('[the LSA] has a conservative...program committee' [and] has refused...cognitive linguistics']

b. It seems to me that what is so dangerous and insidious about the "biological" approach to understanding gender is the usually IMPLICIT, UNSPOKEN message that if there are genetic or brain-based differences, that these determine male and female life trajectories, ...

[statement expressing writer's understanding, ('it seems to me') with embedded judgment ('dangerous and insidious') and embedded statements of "fact" about the biological approach to gender]

Expression of views typically constitutes, in whole or in part, the *body* of the electronic message; it transmits the message's primary ideational content. The message body may also include one or more of a variety of functions, including *suggestions* ("Let's all subscribe to "Cognitive Linguistics" and read it"), *expression of feelings* ("I, too, am concerned with the current wave of determinism ... It angers me, a great deal") and/or *offers* ("If you have any questions or criticisms that you would like him to see, I would be happy to pass them on"). In the present corpus, messages in which the body is something other than an expression of views or information are found primarily in the (mostly-female) Brain Sex discussion. Conversely, there is a possible correlation between expressions of views and information and the expository schema (hypothesized to be associated with male users), in that "information" is often provided as a solution to a problem raised in a previous message (see example 3). Statements of views also sometimes contain embedded exposition (see example 4) and persuasion.

3.1.4. Close

A third type of macrosegment, the *close*, follows the message body, although it does not occur as predictably as the first two types. Electronic messages may close with an *appeal* for discussion or action, with an *apology* (e.g., for a misstatement posted earlier, or for a longer than usual message), an offer, a chastisement ("So let's not be too quick to make generalizations about what various 'Xists' do or do not believe, ok guys?"), or some other interactional speech act. Of these, the appeal function is most common (24% of messages), and is the only one which regularly occupies the position at the end of a message. Apologies are almost as frequent (21%), but they are distributed across introductions and message bodies as well. For this reason, I consider *appeals to other participants* to be the most prototypical electronic message closing in the discussions analyzed in this study.

Appeals are of two types: appeals for action (e.g., "Subscribe to our journal at the bargain rate of $18"), and appeals for participation—or the cessation of participation—in the discussion itself ("Can we have some discussion and suggestions on this issue?"; "Let's stop bickering and get back to work"). Appeals are interpersonal, in that they invoke the other subscribers to the list in their role as addressees; in some cases they invite others to take over the conversational floor, and thus faciliate turn-taking. Explicit message closings are significantly more common in the mostly-female Brain Sex discussion (59% of all messages) than in the mostly-male Cognitive Linguistics discussion (35% of messages), lending support to the hypothesis that women are more oriented toward the interpersonal aspects of e-mail communication than are men.

3.2. The basic electronic message schema

Despite the richness of functional possibilities listed in Table 2, most messages in the corpus contain only two or three of the 17 types of macrosegments listed, and few messages contain more than four. This distribution suggests that participants are aiming at an ideal message schema comprised of three functional moves: an introduction, a contentful message body, and a close. (The horizontal gray lines dividing Table 2 into three categories are intended to classify functions, roughly speaking, into one or the other of these types.) Of the three basic moves, the message body is the core or dominant move of the schema.

This accords with the common intuition that a well-formed electronic message should minimally contribute some new information or perspective—one can do without an appeal to the audience, and under some circumstances, get by without an explicit link to the previous discussion, but a message with no ideational content is likely to be dismissed as pointless and a "waste of bandwidth".[5]

We may thus posit a three-part schema for electronic messages, based on the preferred realization of the three moves, as in Figure 3.

1. link to an earlier message
2. expression of views
3. appeal to other participants

Figure 3. The basic electronic message schema

I will henceforth refer to this sequence as the basic electronic message schema. Note that it constitutes a balanced communicative unit, comprising all three of Halliday's (1978) primary language functions: a textual link, an ideational body, and an interpersonal close.

The actual percentages of all macrosegments manifesting the moves of the basic schema are shown in Figure 4. Percentages were calculated out of the total number of macrosegments which realize each of the three basic moves: the percentage of linkers out of all openings, expressions of views out of all message bodies, and appeals out of all closes. (The numbers correspond to those in Table 2, except that apologies found in introductions and bodies have been subtracted from the total number of macrosegments in the "closes" category.)

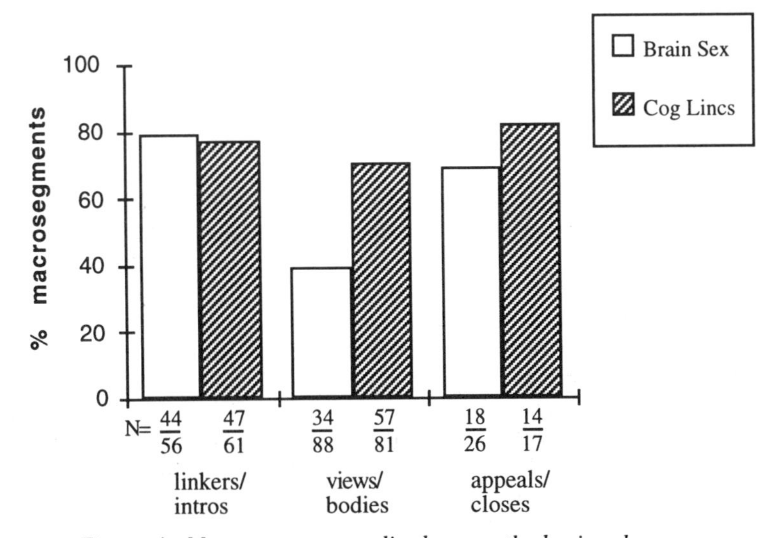

Figure 4. Macrosegments realized as per the basic schema

Figure 4 shows that the basic schema is a good characterization of the macro-organization of the majority of electronic messages in the corpus, especially those in the Cognitive Linguistics discussion. In other words, most participants, regardless of whether male or female, incorporate interactive features into their electronic messages (via the linker and appeal), as well as contributing their views. The pure exchange of information, narrowly defined, is of secondary importance in both discussions. The basic electronic message schema thus more closely resembles that of interactional text types such as personal letters and conversational turns than that of expository text, although moves of the expository schema are sometimes found in the message body. These results are perhaps not surprising, given the widespread perception among users that electronic exchanges are "discussions" or "conversations" rather than monologues in sequence. At the same time, the results provide *prima facie* counterevidence to the stereotype that there is a fundamental difference in what motivates male and female messages, at least insofar as such difference is reflected in their basic organizational structure.

4. Gendered variants of the basic schema

Thus far I have identified a schematic organization that is characteristic of messages posted in both discussions. However, the basic electronic message schema as described above is considerably idealized; actual instantiations of it vary along gender lines. Two variants within the basic schema can be identified, according to the stance taken by the message sender vis à vis the addressee.

4.1. The aligned variant

The first variant, which I term the *aligned variant*, represents the writer's stance as aligned with and supportive of that of the addressee. This variant is characteristic of messages in the Brain Sex discussion. According to this variant, the first schematic move is prototypically realized as a link to a previous message accompanied by an expression of agreement or appreciation. The second move is a non-critical expression of the writer's views (often presented as opinion rather than fact) or, more commonly, something other than a views statement: a question, an answer to someone else's question, a reference, a suggestion, an offer, or an expression of feelings about the topic at hand. The closing move is an appeal to other participants to engage further in the discussion.

The following message illustrates the aligned variant of the electronic message schema. The writer of the message, whom I will call Miriam Hillyard, had earlier put out a call for someone to write a feminist textbook on genetics. In this message, Miriam responds to a message from a younger woman, Penelope, expressing tentative interest in authoring such a textbook, and asking Miriam to clarify what it should contain.

(3) This is wonderful...exactly what I had hoped would happen! Thanks to Penelope. I would like to keep the discussion going on this in the network so that she and I might hear from others about what they think is needed. I will also write to Penelope, and if anyone wants to be involved, please let me know. I hope this is all right with Penelope.

1. I mean a feminist perspective of genetics in general...this would mean a discussion of the history of the study of genetics and its societal context in regard to its use in derogating different populations according to "race" and women.

2. I think it would require a clear statement about what "genes" are, what they do, and what is known and not known about how they function.

3. It would require a review of the literature in both animal and human research in which the relationship between genes and morphology, physiology, and behavior would be critically reviewed and stated. (Twin; "race"; "sex difference"..in both humans and nonhuman animals.)

4. It would have to deal with developmental processes and the relevance of individual and group differences, etc.

This is just for starters. Anybody else? As ever, Miriam Hillyard

The first macrosegment of this message is an *appreciative response* to Penelope's offer of possible authorship. This is followed by an attempt to mitigate the potential burden on Penelope if Miriam accepts Penelope's offer.[6] Linguistically, this section contains the only politeness markers in the text ("thanks", "please"), and is characterized by a first-person orientation. It is set off graphically from the following text by a blank line.

The second macrosegment is the list of desiderata for a feminist textbook on genetics. In this section, Miriam answers Penelope's question, and thus *provides information.*[7] (In an expository schema, this would be the solution to the problem, but note that the message itself contains no statement of the problem or evidence in support of the solution). The linguistic devices that characterize this segment include repetition of the conditional "would", as well as a third-person orientation (i.e., on the proposed textbook). Vocabulary and grammar are somewhat formal and academic; there are learned terms such as "derogation" and "morphology", numerous agentless nominalizations ("discussion", "statement", "review") and several passives (e.g., "would be critically reviewed and stated"). A further distinguishing characteristic of this segment is that its propositions are sequentially numbered.

The third macrosegment is made up of the last line of the message, minus the complimentary close and the writer's signature. This line functions as an *appeal to others to participate* in the joint planning of the textbook by responding with other ideas of what it should contain. (The same appeal, only worded less directly, can be found in the first macrosegment of the message.) Linguistically, the cohesive features of this segment include informal vocabulary ("just for starters") and informal grammar (elipsis in "Anybody else?"), and an implicit second person orientation in the appeal question to the other members of the list.

The basic moves of the aligned variant are summarized in Figure 5.

1. linker agrees with or appreciates a previous message
2. body questions, answers, makes a suggestion, offer, etc. (body is other than an expression of views)
3. appeal to continue the discussion

Figure 5. The aligned variant of the electronic message schema

Figure 6 shows the percentage of macrosegments in each move that are realized according to the aligned variant. The first pair of bars in the graph shows the percentages of all linkers that are agreeing linkers, the middle bars show percentages of all message body macrosegments that are other than expressions of views,[8] and the third bars show percentages of all appeals that are appeals to continue the discussion.

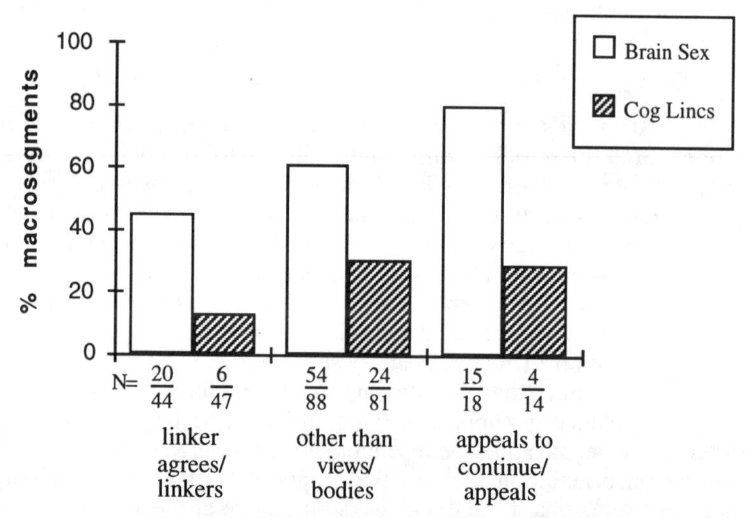

Figure 6. The aligned variant by discussion

Note that the moves of the aligned variant are more than twice as frequent in the Brain Sex discussion as in the Cognitive Linguistics discussion. Since 95% of the messages in the Brain Sex discussion were posted by women, this suggests that the aligned variant represents a female style of message presentation.

4.2. *The opposed variant*

The functional complement of the aligned variant is the *opposed variant*, in which the writer takes a stance directly opposed to and in conflict with the views of the addressee. This realization of the basic schema, which characterizes many messages in the Cognitive Linguistics discussion, also follows the three-move sequence in Figure 3. However, instead of linking to a previous message and agreeing with it, the writer disagrees;[9] instead of building supportively on the ongoing discussion, the writer expresses a critical view; and instead of appealing for continued discussion, the writer proposes that the discussion come to an end. An example of a message illustrating the three schematic moves according to this variant is given below.

(4) This list has seen two recent postings expressing outrage at the *name* ("Cognitive Linguistics") of a theoretical framework (or set of related frameworks). The first time I took to be an idiosyncrasy, but the recurrence alternately bothers and amuses me. I thought this list was a forum for more substantive discussions than grousing about what someone else's name is.

The *mode* of objection is curious. Its logic seems to be:

1. The name A of some approach implies they study B;
2. Other (perhaps contrary) approaches also study B;
3. Therefore use of name A is a usurpation and derogation of others who study B.

On its face, this seems plausible, but in light of the past 80 years or so of the history of linguistics, it is a strange turnabout in standards of naming. Examples of "violations" of the same sort would have to include "Structuralism", "Functionalism", "Transformational Grammar", "Relational Grammar", "Lexical-Functional Grammar", "Government-Binding Theory", and many many more. Note that it would be circular to claim exemption by assigning the pseudo-descriptive label the particular technical interpretation that practitioners of the approach so named wish it to have -- the same defense would suffice, as previous posters have indeed indicated, for "Cognitive Linguistics".

At best, such pseudo-descriptive brand names indicate that the approaches so named give (or at least see themselves as giving?) greater centrality to something their names indicate than do other/most contemporaries. By that criterion, "Cognitive Linguistics" (in the broad construal indicated in the charter of the ICLA, for example) is in the tradition, since the approaches using that name give greater prominence to (general) cognition in linguistics.

I hasten to add that the long history of libertarian naming of theoretical approaches includes acceptance of more evaluative labels such as "Natural...", "Standard Theory" (and its etymological heirs), etc.

> Not to mention, by the obsessively picayune sensibilities recently shown, such out and out misnomers as "Generative Phonology" (since most practitioners regard phonology as *interpretive*). About the *only* names that might not be objected to on the grounds recently unearthed would be those of geographic or personal origins (e.g. "Prague School" or "Bloomfieldian"), although even these are usually based on stereotypes; or those derived from a technical term that has no homonyms in other approaches (e.g. "Tagmemics").
>
> So why not let's get back to doing some *linguistics* instead of prescriptive metametalinguistics?

The first segment of this message situates the writer with respect to the previous discussion, which involved disagreement as to which of two rival schools of linguistic thought can be said to do “cognitive linguistics”. This writer’s position is that participants on both sides are wrong to be concerned with the issue. He thus sets himself off as unique in the discussion, *not aligned with either side* but rather opposed to both. Linguistically, this segment has an overall first person orientation, and is relatively formal in its vocabulary and grammar. It states, indirectly, the thesis of the message as a whole: “grousing” about someone else’s name is not a legitimate activity.

The body of the message is a lengthy expression of *critical views*, in which the writer elaborates his opinion that it is “curious” and “obsessively picayune” of others to be concerned with the name of a theoretical approach in linguistics. The body itself is arguably expository in structure: the “mode of objection” of others may be said to contain the problem (how to resolve the naming conflict), and the following two paragraphs the writer’s solution (inferred: it’s not worth worrying about), followed in the third paragraph by a supporting argument (even more problematic labels have been accepted in the past).[10] Like the body of the previous message, this segment contains numbered propositions, formal vocabulary and grammar, and third person reference (to naming and names of theories).

The closing appeal is again encoded as a single line at the end of the text: let’s stop discussing the use of the term “cognitive linguistics”. This *appeal discourages response*, or at least appears to. Note, however, the use of inclusive “let’s”, and the fact that the appeal is framed as a question, both features that invoke the audience as discursive participants.

Figure 7 summarizes the moves of the opposed variant.

1. linker disagrees with a previous message
2. views challenge or criticize others
3. appeal to end the discussion

Figure 7. The opposed variant of the electronic message schema

The percentage of macrosegments from each discussion which realize the opposed variant of each of the three moves is shown graphically in Figure 8. The first pair of bars in the graph shows the percentages of all linkers that are disagreeing linkers, the middle bars show percentages of all expression of views that challenge or criticize others, and the third bars show percentages of all appeals that are appeals to end the discussion.

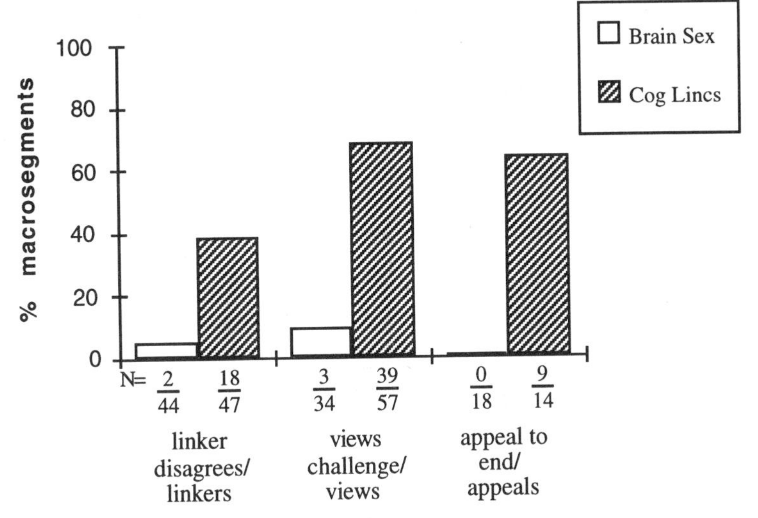

Figure 8. The opposed variant by discussion

The opposed variant is overwhelmingly more frequent in the Cognitive Linguistics discussion than in the Brain Sex discussion. Since 75% of the messages in the Cognitive Linguistics discussion were posted by men, the opposed variant would appear to represent a male style of message presentation.

4.3. Gender vs. list norms

Thus far, I have identified two different realizations of the basic electronic message schema, the first of which characterizes the WMST discussion and the second of which characterizes the LINGUIST discussion. Further, I have suggested that these variants represent preferred female and male styles of schematic organization. However, there is an alternative explanation to this distribution, namely that the two styles simply reflect the different norms of each mailing list. That is, it is possible that messages posted to WMST tend to take an aligned form, regardless of the gender of the one who posts them; similarly, messages posted to LINGUIST may tend to follow the opposed model, regardless of whether they are posted by men or women.

To address this possibility, I broke the data down by gender of message poster, male or female. Since most messages in the discussion were signed, it was not difficult to determine the writer's gender in the majority of cases. (For unsigned messages, if I did not recognize the sender's address from personal knowledge or from their previous participation, I consulted the list of subscribers to each mailing list.) Figure 9 (for women) and Figure 10 (for men) display the results of the analysis for use of the aligned variant. The percentages were calculated as for Figure 6, with the exception that Figure 9 considers only messages posted by women, and Figure 10 only messages posted by men.

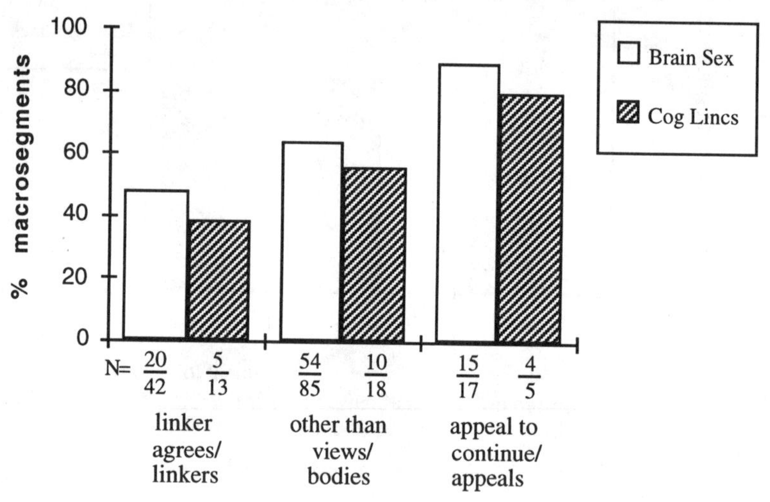

Figure 9. The aligned variant: Messages posted by women

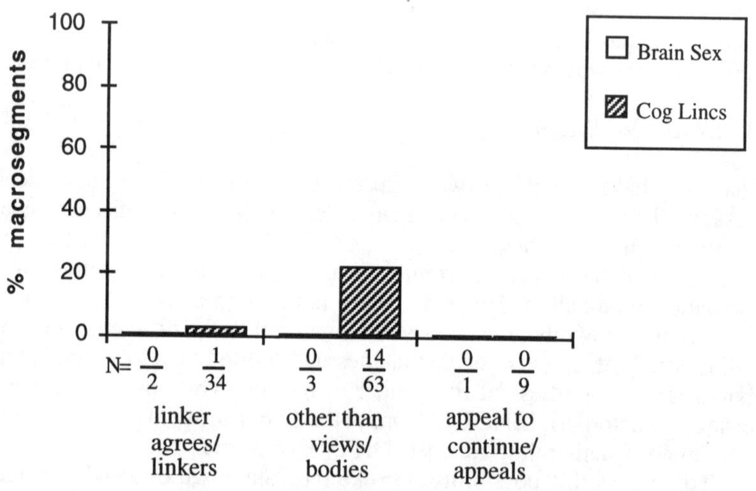

Figure 10. The aligned variant: Messages posted by men

Figures 9 and 10 show that use of the aligned variant is strongly gender-linked: women on both lists employ it often, while men do not employ it at all. The only apparent exception is the use by LINGUIST men of "other than views" segments in the message body; most of these provide information (such as references) and co-occur with expression of views.

Figures 11 and 12 display the results of analyzing male and female messages separately for use of the opposed variant. These percentages were calculated as described for Figure 8, except that Figure 11 considers only messages posted by men, and Figure 12 only messages posted by women.

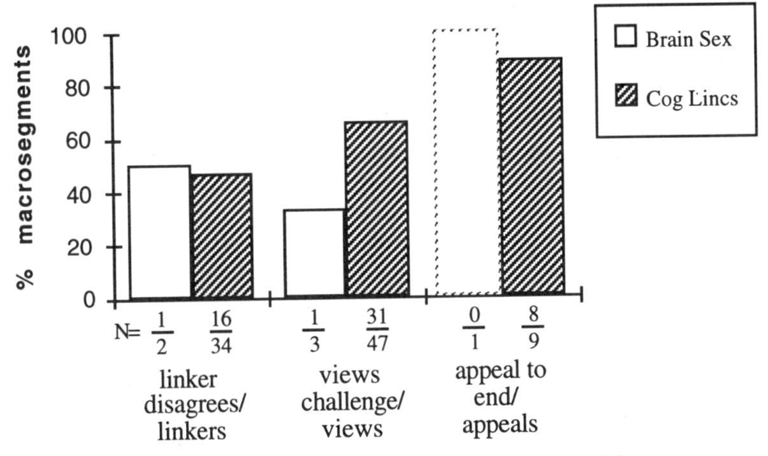

Figure 11. The opposed variant: Messages posted by men

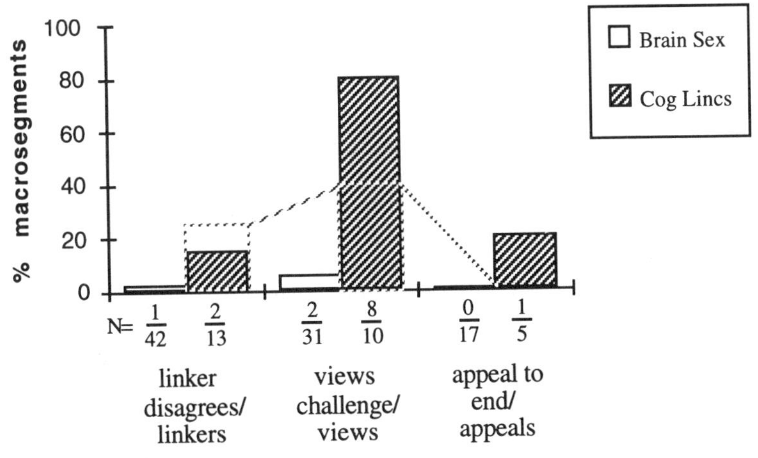

Figure 12. The opposed variant: Messages posted by women

The overall predicted pattern is again evident: men on both lists favor the opposed variant, while women, especially in the Brain Sex discussion, make less use of it. There are two exceptions to this pattern, however. In Figure 11, no men from the Brain Sex discussion make an appeal to end the discussion, in contrast with men in the Cognitive Linguistics discussion. This is however not a significant exception, in that only one message contributed by a man in the Brain Sex discussion contains an appeal of any kind. Although this appeal was critical in its content (it was a "nag" to a previous poster to include her name at the end of her message; see example (6) below), it did not call for the end of the discussion, and thus was not counted in this category. (Had it been counted, it would have put the value in the appeal category for the Brain Sex discussion at 100%. This is indicated by the dotted line in Figure 11.)

A more troublesome exception is the high percentage of women in the Cognitive Linguistics discussion whose messages express critical or challenging views. In part, this is an artefact of the posting behavior of one high-status woman, who contributed 13 of the 18 messages posted in the discussion by women, and who has an adversarial style (see Herring 1992 for further discussion of this individual's posting behavior). If her contributions are excluded, the percentage of disagreeing linkers rises slightly to 25%, challenging views decrease by half to 40%, and appeals to end the discussion are reduced to 0%, as indicated by the dotted lines in Figure 12. Nevertheless, these percentages are still considerably higher than for women in the WMST discussion. This finding constitutes evidence for a List Effect. That is, women on the male-predominant list, where the norms of interaction are oppositional, are more oppositional than are women on the female-predominant list, where the norms of interaction are aligned. Correspondingly, women on the male-predominant list express less alignment than women on the female-predominant list, as Figure 9 illustrates.

Interestingly, there is less evidence in these data of a List Effect for men—men on LINGUIST exhibit slightly more alignment features in their message organization than do men on WMST, which is the reverse of what we would predict. Does this mean that men in the Brain Sex discussion did not adapt their discursive style to reflect the female norms of interaction on the list? In fact they did, although not with respect to discourse-level schematic organization.[11] Rather they modified local features of their style, e.g., by hedging and posing their assertions as questions. In others words, they adopted the *attenuated* features of women's on-line style, rather than its *personal/interpersonal* orientation (Herring 1992, 1993a).

As a consequence of their attempts to adapt to dominant list norms, minority gender participants incorporate features of usage of both genders in their messages, resulting in style mixing. This is illustrated by the two messages below, the first from a female contributor to the Cognitive Linguistics discussion, and the second from a male contributor to the Brain Sex discussion.

(5) Thank you for your information. I do think you should be aware that there are many linguists who consider themselves cognitive scientists who do not share your particular views as to the relations between language and other cognitive structures. It is interesting to note that more and more neurologists and neuropsychologists are of the opinion that the brain and mind is indeed modular in structure and function and that language is not derivative of non-linguistic cognition but that it is one among many cognitive sructures. That is, I take issue with you and your usurping the title of 'cognitive linguistics' since I, and others with whom I work in the cognitive psychology, neuropsychology, neurolinguistics, neurology, brain anatomy, philosophy fields, support the view that the formal structures of language are "autonomous" (and not) "reflective of general conceptual organization, categorization principles, and processing mechanisms" as your statements below claim. I would be happy to provide evidence, citations, references, quotes, results of mri scans + linguistic/non-linguistic cognitive texts etc.

As to this issue, it is clearly an empirical question, and we do need to exchange views among ourselves and in an interdisciplinary atmosphere.

Sally Psycholinguist

This example is made up of three functional macrosegments, the first and the last of which express an aligned orientation, while the second expresses an opposed orientation. The first sentence, an aligned linker, constitutes the opening macrosegment. The last sentence of the message, an appeal for further participation in the discussion, is the closing macrosegment. The message body, however, is an expression of disagreeing views ("I take issue with you and your usurping the title of 'cognitive linguistics'"), as befits the opposed variant. The body also contains self-promotion (by informing us that the author is well-connected with researchers in other fields), a feature found elsewhere to be more characteristic of male than female messages (Herring 1992, 1993c). Style-mixing is characteristic of female participation on LINGUIST more generally. In a larger corpus of LINGUIST data (described in Herring 1993c), 46% of all messages posted by women mix features of male and female styles, as compared with only 14% of messages posted by men.

Men on WMST also mix gendered features, as illustrated in the following message posted to the Brain Sex discussion.

(6) Someone ... who? wrote ...

"I am somewhat puzzled by the seemingly unanimous view that it is dangerous/reprehensible to even consider the possibility that some sex differences are biologically based. This seems to take for granted that if there are, this would be a compelling argument for an anti-feminism, anti-woman, anti-gay agenda."

> The "positions" didn't seem that uniform to me, but it did sound like a lot of people with answers rather than questions. I was *very* surprised at the reaction to [David Carpenter's] original post which seemed (to me) to raise alternatives rather than provide answers/conclusions ... perhaps it's an example of (pretty good) science training focused on manager-type problems, where we (trainers) *hammer* on "look for alternatives" ... don't reject options too soon, etc.
>
> Now, please! (I'll "nag" for [the listowner]) signature lines *in the message* ... who wrote the posting?
>
> Jack Shearin, School of Business, Northern Michigan University
> xxxxxxxxx, MI 49xxx (xxx) xxx-xxxx shearin@xx.nmich.edu

This message also has a three-part organization, realized predominantly as per the opposed variant. A previous contributor is cited (a common type of linking introduction), only to be disagreed with in the message body ("The positions didn't seem that uniform to me"). The last orthographic paragraph ("Now, please!...") appeals to the previous contributor to state her identity, but in a way that is critical of her. At the same time, the message body reveals a concession to stereotypical female style in its liberal use of hedges ("seem", "seemed (to me)", "perhaps", "(pretty good)") and overall indirectness, such that the writer's point (that "alternatives" should be valued) is partially obscured. Presumably, this is because the "alternative" he mentions reflects a male perspective that women on the list might be unwilling to accept.

Ironically, this male writer is concerned not to offend the women on the list by his differing views, which he hedges, yet he seems unaware that the oppositional structure of his message itself might be viewed as offensive or inappropriate. This observation suggests that discourse-level macro-organization is relatively less accessible to conscious reflection than other kinds of linguistic behavior. A consequence of this is that if one wishes to "pass" or fit in on a list dominated by the opposite gender, one must make adjustments not just at the level of conscious expression, but at the deeper level of schematic organization, reflecting the socialization of one's communicative aims.[12]

These results affirm both of the predictions advanced in section 2.2. That is, the data show a strong Gender Effect which determines the schematic orientation of electronic messages, as well as a secondary List Effect which leads members of the minority gender to modify their schematic orientation (in the case of women) and surface style (in the case of both women and men) to resemble that of the dominant gender on the list.

4.4. Gender vs. discussion topic

A final consideration concerns the effect of the topic of discussion on the linguistic and organizational strategies used by participants. The Cognitive Linguistics discussion involved a clash of views on a controversial topic, while the Brain Sex discussion was largely uncontroversial. To what extent does the choice of the opposed or the aligned schema fall out from the topic of the discussion itself? To address this question, I briefly examined two additional discussions from each list, one on a controversial topic related to societal sexism, and the other on a "just-for-fun" topic on the origin and meaning of certain taboo words. Despite a higher incidence of oppositional messages in the controversial discussions on both lists, LINGUIST participants more often than WMST participants represented themselves as opposed, even on the uncontroversial topic, and WMST subscribers more often than LINGUIST subscribers represented themselves as aligned with other participants, even when their views differed. Thus the schematic orientations described above appear to hold more generally for each list.

Additional support for this conclusion comes from a consideration of all messages posted to each list during a randomly-selected 2-week period. Out of 139 messages posted to LINGUIST (114 by men, and 25 by women), 29% were critical or challenging of another participant, as compared with only 1% of the 79 messages posted to WMST (74 by women, and 5 by men). Also revealing is the breakdown of message function during the two-week period:

Table 4. Functions of messages posted during a random two-week period

	express views	query	provide info
LINGUIST (N=139)	42%	19%	19%
WMST (N=79)	10%	23%	55%

In this sample, the most frequent functions conveyed through the message body were expressions of views, queries, and providing information. Two observations regarding their distribution are relevant here. First, expression of views, the vehicle through which disagreement and conflict are most likely to arise, occurs four times as often on LINGUIST as on WMST. Second, the women's list posted roughly three times as much information as the men's list. To the extent that the two-week periods are indicative of the day-to-day activity of the lists, these additional observations not only support the findings for the two extended discussions, they go further and partially reverse the stereotype about gender and information: female users are more interested in the exchange of pure information, while male users are more interested in debating their views, regardless of the topic being discussed.

5. Summary and conclusion

In this chapter, I have brought empirical evidence to bear on the stereotypes of the informative male and the interactive female computer network user. By analyzing the schematic organization of publicly-posted messages to two Internet mailing lists, I have shown that these stereotypes miss the mark in important respects. My results suggest that *both* women and men participate in discussions on electronic mailing lists to exchange opinions, beliefs, understandings, and judgments in social interaction with other human beings, with the pure exchange of information taking second place. Indeed, the era since the advent of computer networks might better be termed the "Interaction Age" rather than the "Information Age", since it is in the potential for interaction with others that the primary appeal of computer networks appears to lie.

At the same time, my investigation uncovered significant gender differences. Women's messages on both lists tend to be aligned and supportive in orientation, while men's messages tend to oppose and criticize others. Further, the lists themselves exhibit an overall aligned or opposed orientation, depending on whether the majority of participants are women or men. However, this is not the same as claiming that men are not interactive, nor women interested in the exchange of information. Rather men and women present different styles of interaction and information exchange.

At this point, the question naturally arises as to what relationship, if any, these differences bear to the stereotypes of the interactive female and the informative male. Let us first consider the female stereotype. By aligning themselves with and expressing support for others, women create solidarity and promote harmonious on-line interaction. This characterization is compatible with the claim that women value interpersonal relations and seek to develop them on-line. At the same time, the stereotype is misleading to the extent that interactivity is taken to exclude informativity. In fact, the female-predominant list is *more* informative than the male-predominant list as regards the pure, unevaluated exchange of information. This suggests that far from being "uninterested", women are important purveyors of information on the Internet.

The stereotype of the informative male is harder to explain. By challenging and criticizing others, men attract attention to themselves and engage in "contests" as a result of which they gain or lose in status (Tannen 1990). However, this characterization bears no evident relation to the claim that men are information oriented. One might argue that information of a different sort is involved in oppositional exchanges; certainly new understandings can be forged through heated debate. However this explanation overlooks the important role played by linguistic expression. Men are more likely than women to express their views as assertions of "fact", e.g., through the use of strengtheners such as "obviously" and "of course", and the avoidance of hedges such as "perhaps" and "it seems to me" (Coates 1993; Herring 1992, 1993c; Lakoff 1975; Popkin 1992). As a consequence, male users may appear to be exchanging information even when in reality they are exchanging opinions and evaluations.

A second explanation is that men discursively construct a reality in which their primary on-line activity is the exchange of "information". In response to an electronic survey on network etiquette (Herring 1994, 1996), men complained far more than women about messages with "a low signal to noise ratio" (i.e., which do not contain much information), or which do not document their assertions with references. Proscriptions against messages with low information content are also found in many male-authored netiquette guides. In practice, however, accusations of insufficient informativity are often levelled against participants with whom the message poster disagrees, independent of the actual degree of informativity of their messages. In such discussions, what passes for "information" is often the expression of highly subjective views. In short, the concept of "informativity" figures prominently in the way men talk about—if not how they actually write—electronic messages.

Finally, the stereotype that men are more interested than women in information exchange must be interpreted against a socio-cultural backdrop according to which men are expected to be knowledgeable, rational, and dispassionate, and in which information is highly valued. These expectations are, if anything, exaggerated in the "Information Age", in which computer technology and computer use are disproportionately male domains (Wajcman 1991). Cultural ideals of femaleness, in contrast, include expectations that women will be caring, sociable, and hence interactive. Stereotypes of gender differences in e-mail use directly mirror these cultural expectations, and are partially explained by them: we interpret male communication as informative and female communication as interactive in part because we expect men and women to behave in those ways. As a consequence, male informativity is inflated and promoted above that of women, an illusion further abetted by the linguistic and metadiscursive practices of men.

These findings have practical consequences, in that stereotypes about computer use influence the attitudes and behavior of users. Given that the stereotypes glorify men's role in and exclude women by definition from the "Information Age", it is not surprising that women are more reluctant to go on-line, less confident of their abilities when they do so, less participatory in on-line group discussions, and less represented among computer network policy makers and designers than men (Herring 1993a; Spender 1992). These trends are cause for concern no matter what their source, but they are all the more egregious if underlying them are stereotypes about gender and computer use that are demonstrably false.

ACKNOWLEDGMENTS

* The research described in this chapter was first presented at the 1993 Georgetown University Round Table on Languages and Linguistics, presession on Discourse Analysis: Written Texts. The author wishes to thank Brett Benham, Pam Echerd, Suzanne Fleischman, Britt-Louise Gunnarsson, Shin Ja Hwang, Robin Lombard, and John Paolillo for their valuable comments on the current version.

NOTES

1. The discrepancy in the duration of the two discussions can be explained in part by the fact that LINGUIST messages are sent out by the moderators at intervals, resulting in a slower rate of message exchange than on WMST, which is not moderated.

2. This use of the term 'schema' differs from that of psychologists and computational linguists, for whom a schema is a theoretical construct representing an idealized knowledge structure in the minds of language users (e.g., Rumelhart 1980; Shank and Abelson 1977). While the view presented here and in Longacre's work does not rule out the possibility that schemata exist as mental structures, they are arrived at empirically, as idealizations of recurrent textual patterns (cf. van Dijk's (1980) *superstructures*).

3. For further discussion of the letter schema, see Mann, Matthiessen and Thompson (1992).

4. This finding shows that the anonymity potential of CMC is underutilized by computer users. A similar finding is reported by Selfe and Meyer (1991).

5. 98% of the messages in the combined corpus have a contentful message body, 80% have an introductory macrosegment, and 24% have a closing macrosegment.

6. In a more fine-grained analysis, this could be considered a separate functional move, but as it is integrated with and dependent on the larger function of appreciative back-reference, I treat both as parts of a single macrosegment.

7. Miriam's list is arguably also an expression of her views, but it was classified as providing information in that it includes conventional criteria for textbook writing, and was clearly intended as a response to Penelope's information-seeking question.

8. This proved to be a more revealing measure for the middle move than the percentage of all expressions of views that are not critical. An absence of criticism does not indicate alignment as explicitly as do suggestions, offers, questions, etc.

9. This category includes "I agree with X, but" linkers, which account for slightly less than half of the disagreeing linkers in the Cognitive Linguistics discussion.

10. Note however that the writer's position on the naming problem is not explicitly stated; rather the engagement of others in the discussion is simply mocked. This practice deviates from the expository ideal of providing a clear solution to a problem. An alternative characterization of messages of this type, which are frequent on LINGUIST, might be as functional insults. Insults, including flames, merit study as a separate text type for evidence of organizational regularities.

11. Recall however that the number of men who posted messages in the Brain Sex discussion is very small (N=3). It would be unwarranted to generalize from this that male subscribers to female-dominated lists never modify their schematic orientation.

12. In light of these observations, it is not surprising to learn that recent male-to-female transsexuals attempt to pass as women on-line by adopting stereotypical surface features of "women's language" (Lakoff 1975), especially hedges and gendered vocabulary ('adorable', 'charming', etc.). In contrast, those who have been women for a longer time manifest more subtle female discourse patterns (Erich Trapp, personal communication).

II: Social and Ethical Perspectives

Managing the Virtual Commons:
Cooperation and Conflict in Computer Communities

Peter Kollock and Marc Smith
University of California, Los Angeles

1. The problem of cooperation*

Computer-mediated communication systems are believed to have powerful effects on social relationships. Many claim that this new form of social interaction encourages wider participation, greater candor, and an emphasis on merit over status. In short, the belief is that social hierarchies are dissolved and that flatter, more egalitarian social organizations emerge. Networked communications, it is argued, will usher in a renewed era of democratic participation and revitalized community. But as with earlier technologies that promised freedom and power, the central problems of social relationships remain, although in new and possibly more challenging forms.

One of the most basic questions in the social sciences is the problem of cooperation. In the face of temptations to behave selfishly, how might a group of people ever manage to establish or maintain cooperative relations? The character and qualities of this problem are different when groups use computer-mediated communication to interact, but the differences do not guarantee a uniformly positive effect or resolve many of the long-standing problems of cooperation. Indeed, we will show that there is a double edge to computer-mediated interaction: many of its central qualities make it easier both to cooperate and to behave selfishly. Thus, computer-mediated interaction raises political, practical, and sociological problems in new ways and with new stakes.

At the root of the problem of cooperation is the fact that there is often a tension between individual and collective rationality. This is to say that in many situations, behavior that is reasonable and justifiable for the individual leads to a poorer outcome for all. Such situations are termed *social dilemmas* and underlie many of the most serious social problems we face.[1] One of the most famous models of social dilemmas is the "tragedy of the commons" (Hardin 1968). Hardin described a group of herders having open access to a common parcel of land on which they could let their cows graze. It is in each herder's interest to put as many cows as possible onto the land, even if the commons is damaged as a result. The herder receives all the benefits from the additional cows, and the damage to the commons is shared by the entire group. Yet if all herders make this individually reasonable decision, the commons is destroyed and all will suffer.

A related model of the tension between individual and collective rationality is the challenge of providing public goods. A public good is a resource from which all may benefit, regardless of whether they have helped create the good (e.g., public television or a community improvement project).[2] The temptation is to enjoy a public good without contributing to its production, but if all reach this decision, the good is never created and all suffer.

The tragedy of the commons and the challenge of providing public goods share a common feature:

> At the heart of each of these models in the free-rider problem. Whenever one person cannot be excluded from the benefits that others provide, each person is motivated not to contribute to the joint effort, but to free-ride on the efforts of others. If all participants choose to free-ride, the collective benefit will not be produced. The temptation to free-ride, however, may dominate the decision process and thus all will end up where no one wanted to be. (Ostrom 1990:6)

In the face of the free-rider problem, how is cooperation possible? The pessimistic conclusion of many researchers (e.g., Hardin 1968, 1974) is that coercion by a strong external authority is necessary in order to insure cooperation. But other researchers (e.g., Fox 1985) have argued that an external authority may not be necessary and may even make the situation worse. The question becomes, to what extent can group members regulate themselves, providing collective goods and managing common resources without recourse to external authorities? Given the new possibilities that emerge in computer-mediated interaction, cyberspace provides an important research site to explore this fundamental question of social order.

Thus, the free-rider problem and the ability of a group to overcome it is our focus for this chapter. We apply the logic of social dilemmas to a portion of cyberspace known as the Usenet—a collection of several thousand discussion groups that is distributed and maintained in a decentralized fashion. In sections 2 and 3, we describe the Usenet and discuss the major social dilemmas that members of the Usenet face. In order to explore how these problems might be solved in the Usenet, in section 4 we make use of the innovative work by Ostrom (1990), who studied a wide variety of communities in order to determine what features of a group contribute to its success or failure in managing collective goods. The set of cases she examined include common forest and grazing grounds in Swiss and Japanese villages, fisheries in Canada and Sri Lanka, and irrigation systems in Spain and the Philippines. She identified a set of design principles that are features of communities which have successfully met the challenge of producing and maintaining collective goods despite the temptation to free-ride, and without recourse to an external authority. We discuss each of these principles and ask to what extent they are present in the Usenet and whether their relevance changes when groups interact via computer networks. Thus, our goal is to contribute both to the study of computer-mediated interaction and to research on cooperation and social dilemmas.[3]

2. The Usenet

The Usenet is one of the largest computer-mediated communication systems in existence. Developed in 1981 as an alternative to services available through the ARPANET (the Advanced Research Projects Agency Network, developed and funded by the Department of Defense), the Usenet has grown exponentially and currently consists of several thousand discussion groups (termed *newsgroups*). Recent estimates suggest that roughly two million people from all around the world participate in some way, with further increases expected (Quarterman 1990). The Usenet is similar in many ways to *conferencing systems*, often referred to as a *Bulletin Board System* (BBS), and compared to *e-mail distribution lists*. It shares many qualities with these forms of computer-mediated communication, but differs in significant ways. No central authority manages the Usenet, although considerable cooperation exists around the definition of standards that determine the technical organization of the distribution system. It is distributed in the sense that there is no central repository for Usenet postings; each contribution is passed throughout the system of interconnected *hosts*—systems that receive and pass along each contribution they receive. The Usenet is not a commercial product; it is distributed through connections that are often informally maintained.

The Usenet is accessed via a variety of tools that alter the way in which groups and messages can be selected and read. However, a theme common to most of the tools used is that one or more *newsgroups* are selected or "subscribed" to, each of which contain one or more *threads*, or series of *postings* and responses (and the responses to responses) on a common subject. Postings are normally stored for a short time, ranging from a day to a few weeks. There are several thousand newsgroups in current wide circulation, covering a diverse range of topics. The topics of newsgroups are displayed in the name of the group and are designed to advertise the focus of the group. For example, *comp.sys.mac.hardware* focuses on issues concerning the Macintosh computer's hardware. The Usenet has institutionalized eight general thematic categories[4] and has developed a range of conventions to describe and delineate the kinds of activity and contributions that group considers desirable and appropriate.[5] The names serve not only to identify what is desired in a group, but what is inappropriate as well. Thus, discussion of IBM PCs, foreign affairs, film, or even Macintosh software is not welcome in *comp.sys.mac.hardware*. Newsgroups provide a forum for individuals with esoteric interests to find one another, thus providing the service of a "Schelling point".[6]

A number of newsgroups are centered around technical subjects, such as programming languages, operating systems, and kinds of computer hardware. However, less technical subjects are the basis for many newsgroups as well. For example, *sci.lang.japan* contains discussions about the Japanese language, and a collection of groups starting with the name *alt.current-events* have focused on issues ranging from the World Trade Center bombing to the Los Angeles earthquake. Many newsgroups focus on cultural or recreational activities, such as *soc.culture.bangladesh* and *rec.arts.movies.* There are newsgroups, such as *alt.barney.die.die.die* or *alt.swedish.chef.bork.bork.bork*, that are intended to provide a venue for a humorous and whimsical discussion. Other newsgroups cover subjects that rarely get candid public discussion in any other forum, such as the *alt.sex* groups. There are also newsgroups, such as *alt.sexual.abuse.recovery*, that are specifically created to provide support for its members.

Newsgroups typically contain requests for information, replies to requests, discussions of the validity and accuracy of replies, and further questions prompted by the discussion. Newsgroups can and often do have dozens of threads running simultaneously, some referring to one another, some cross-posted to other newsgroups.[7]

Figure 1 illustrates how a collection of threads is displayed in *comp.org.eff.talk*, a newsgroup sponsored by the Electronic Frontier Foundation (EFF), an organization dedicated to the discussion of legal, political, and economic issues raised by new information technologies. This newsgroup is a forum used to provide information and news about issues of relevance to the EFF, and hosts extended discussions and debates.

```
comp.org.eff.talk    117 articles
a Tom Miller         1  >NET system
b Joe Cipale         4  >A chance to repeal the DAT tax
  John Henders
  Don Reid
  John A Sigmon      1  >Where can I find HI FI World in S.Bay
d J Heitkoetter      1  Big Dummy's Guide in Texinfo, etc....
e Bob Smart          1  *FLASH* Moby SUBPOENA served
f Stephen Savitzky   1  NSA, meet NRA -- If s/w is a munition...

(Mail) -- Select threads -- 47% [>Z] --
```

Figure 1. Display of threads in a sample Usenet newsgroup

The first column in Figure 1 provides a menu letter for each thread (typing this letter selects the thread listed next to it), the next column lists the authors' names (or usernames)[8] for each response in that thread. The third column indicates the number of messages in each thread (which can be as many as hundreds of messages), and the final column displays the thread's subject. The ">" character indicates that this is a reply to a message with the same subject. Selecting a thread causes the messages stored within it to be displayed. Figure 2 illustrates an excerpt from one of the postings listed in Figure 1.

```
comp.org.eff.talk #16743 (52 + 61 more) +-( )+-( )+-(1)--(2)
Newsgroups:comp.org.eff.talk,sci.crypt, |     |     \-[1]+-[1]+
alt.security.pgp,talk.politics.crypto   |     |          \-[1][1]
Re: *FLASH* Moby SUBPOENA served        |     \-( )--[1]
From: bsmart@bsmart.TTI.COM (Bob Smart) |-( )--[1]
Date: Mon Sep 20 8:00:08 PDT 1993       \-[1]+-[1]
Distribution: inet
Organization: Citicorp+TTI
Nntp-Posting-Host: bsmart.tti.com
Lines: 30

In article <TED.93Sep18104722@lole.crl.nmsu.edu>,
ted@crl.nmsu.edu (TedDunning) writes:

> no. ecpa-86 only prohibits recordings made without the
> permission of either party.  if one party to the conversation
> consents, then the tap is legal.  thus you can record your
> own conversations.

That's not necessarily the whole story, though: some states
require that ALL parties to a conversation must consent to any
recording.  At a minimum, you need to know whether you're in a
two-party or a one-party state before you proceed.
[...]
---------
A fanatic is someone who does what he knows that God would do
if God knew the facts of the case.

Some mailers apparently munge my address; you might have to use
bsmart@bsmart.tti.com -- or if that fails, fall back to
72027.3210@compuserve.com.  Ain't UNIX grand?
```

Figure 2. A sample posting to a Usenet newsgroup

This post is typical of many found in the Usenet. First, the top block of lines contains header information, such as the names of the newsgroups to which the message should be added, the subject line (which is used to construct threads), the date and author of the post, and information concerning each of the machines that passed along the message. Opposite the header is a *thread tree*, generated by some newsreaders, that provides a graphical representation of where in the numerous turns in a thread this message is located. Messages that copy the subject line from this message are represented as branches below this message. Below both the header and thread tree is the body of the message. The body of this message is typical of many Usenet messages in that it contains "quoted" material, often from a message posted earlier in the thread. Here, for example, the quoted text is preceded by ">" characters with a line attributing the source of the quote above it. This cycle of quoting and then commenting can go on for many rounds, and sometimes results in postings that are several pages long, but contain very little new text. Finally, the last few lines are a signature, often referred to as a *sig*. *Sigs* frequently serve a combination of the functions of bumper stickers and business cards; quotes and jokes are common, along with return addresses and phone numbers.

Contributing to a Usenet newsgroup is a relatively simple matter. Using a text editor, a post can be written immediately after reading another post, and many editors allow the contents of any previous post to be copied into the reply. Sending the post is similar to sending e-mail; however, the message sent is copied to the newsgroup(s) specified by the sender, and so will be read by all participants of the newsgroup rather than by just a single person.

Having described the Usenet, we turn in the next two sections to a discussion of the free-rider problem in this part of cyberspace, and the design principles of successful communities. We base the analysis that follows on extended observations of the daily workings of the Usenet. It is important to note that Usenet postings, like audio recordings of telephone conversations, have the advantage of capturing everything that was publicly available to the participants in that setting. The copies of postings we drew from the Usenet are exact copies of what others who read them saw. Usenet postings also have the advantage that one can observe patterns of interactions without affecting those patterns. But as with telephone conversations, there is much that is beyond the spoken word or string of ASCII; Usenet postings cannot capture the private meanings people may intend or take from messages. Further, even more than records of spoken interaction, postings have an ambiguous tone. While a variety of textual practices have been developed to convey the subtleties of communication that are normally carried by tone, posture, gesture, and a host of other indicators of nuance, this medium remains particularly open to multiple interpretations. In addition, members of the Usenet have a multitude of alternative channels of communication that often escape our examination. Participants in the Usenet may e-mail each other directly, avoiding the public arena of a newsgroup, or may even telephone, write, or meet each other without evidence of this appearing in a newsgroup. While these limitations should caution against over-ambitious claims, similar constraints exist for all forms of observation. The fact that the postings we use to ground our claims are available for examination by others provides a useful check on distorted interpretations.

3. Social dilemmas in cyberspace

There is a layer of cooperation and coordination in the details of communication, conversation, and interaction that is unacknowledged by most researchers. An important exception is work by ethnomethodologists and conversational analysts, who have shown how orderly processes of interaction are founded upon an immense amount of collaborative work which is ordinarily taken for granted (Heritage 1984). The tension between individual and group outcomes can be seen here as well. There is a sense, for example, in which the conversational "floor" constitutes a commons: if access to the floor is allocated in an ordered way by speakers exchanging "turns", each has the opportunity to accomplish his or her interactional goals, but if all crowd in, the communication breaks down. Similarly, the interactional work that is necessary to keep a conversation going is a kind of public good in the sense that it is possible to free-ride on others' efforts, using and abusing the conversation without contributing to its maintenance. While there are many important ways in which spoken conversation differs from interaction on the Usenet, similar challenges exist there as well.

Despite the great potential of the Usenet to provide collective goods, it is often the case that this potential is not realized. The endemic tension between individual and collective rationality is as present in Usenet newsgroups as it is in shared pasture lands. On the Usenet, the key common resource is not an open pasture, but *bandwidth*. The term refers to "the volume of information per unit time that a computer, person, or transmission medium can handle" (Raymond 1993). Thus, bandwidth refers to both the limited capacity of the Usenet in terms of its technical capacity to carry and store information, and the capacity of its members to attend to and consume that information. A great concern on the Usenet is using the available bandwidth wisely, which is to say, refraining from posting unnecessary information. Among the actions that are usually considered an inappropriate use of bandwidth are: posting extremely long articles, reproducing long sections of text from a previous post rather than summarizing or excerpting only the relevant passages, including long signatures full of comments and diagrams at the end of a post, and posting the same message to many newsgroups instead of one or a small, well-chosen set.

If members exhibit restraint in their use of bandwidth, the Usenet benefits everyone by being an effective and efficient means of exchanging information and carrying on discussions. Unfortunately, an individual member looking out on the huge capacity of the Usenet can reason (with some justification) that his or her individual use of bandwidth does not appreciably affect what is available for others, and so use this common resource without restraint. The collective outcome of too many people reaching this individually rational decision is, of course, disaster. Here then is a crucial way in which a participant on the Usenet might free-ride on the efforts of other members: using the available bandwidth without restraint, while others regulate their own behavior.

Overusing bandwidth is not the only social dilemma members of the Usenet face. Whatever the goal of the newsgroup, its success depends on the active and ongoing contributions of those who choose to participate in it. If the goal of the newsgroup is to exchange information and answer questions about a particular topic (e.g., *alt.comp.sys.gateway-2000*), participants must be willing to answer questions raised by others, summarize and post replies to queries they have made themselves, and pass along information that is relevant to the group. If the goal of the newsgroup is to discuss a current event or social issue (e.g., *soc.veterans*), participants need to contribute to the discussion and encourage its development. Once again there is the temptation to free-ride: asking questions but not answering them; gathering information but not distributing it; or reading ongoing discussions without contributing to them (termed *lurking*). Some newsgroups successfully meet these challenges, others start well and then degrade, and still other newsgroups fail at the beginning of their existence, never managing to attract a critical mass of participants.

Wise use of bandwidth and the active participation of its members are not enough to ensure the success of a newsgroup. One of the most important collective goods that the Usenet provides is a system for coordinating the exchange of information. By providing the means for maintaining a set of several thousand topics, as well as more specific threads within each topic, the Usenet allows individuals with common interests to find and interact with each other. Given the huge amount of information that is transferred through the Usenet, it is critical that members respect the focus of a newsgroup and of the various threads within a newsgroup by sticking to the topic that is being discussed. Being off-topic threatens the coordination of discussion that the Usenet rests on. The logic of social dilemmas is present here as well. If no one worried about being on-topic, meaningful interaction would be impossible in the Usenet, but as long as most people are careful to make comments that are relevant to the newsgroup and thread, others can free-ride on this restraint by posting their opinions widely and indiscriminately to many groups. Users who do post to many newsgroups without regard to the topic are said to be *grandstanding*, a violation that highlights both the erosion of the organizational boundaries that enable the Usenet to remain a coherent place, and the moral and practical limits on the use of another's attention.

Finally, a successful newsgroup depends on its members following rules of decorum. What counts as acceptable behavior can, of course, vary tremendously from newsgroup to newsgroup: a hostile, provocative post (termed *flaming*) is an etiquette breach in most newsgroups, but not in *alt.flaming*, where violating decorum would mean engaging in a sober, restrained discussion. Often the cultural rules that define what is and is not appropriate are implicit or poorly understood and articulated, which can itself lead to conflict as participants with different expectations attempt to interact. Whatever the local rules of decorum, it is important that most participants follow them. However, there is the temptation to free-ride on others' efforts to maintain norms of civility while violating those norms oneself, saying whatever one wants to without any self-regulation.

Ideally, members of the Usenet would make efficient use of bandwidth, participate actively in newsgroups, insure that their comments are posted only to relevant newsgroups, and abide by the local norms and culture that govern decorum. Everyone is better off if all behave in such a manner, but there is the temptation to free-ride on the efforts of others. Thus, some participants post articles that are unnecessarily long, or lurk rather than contributing to the give and take that is the essential feature of any newsgroup, or post articles that are off-topic, or violate the local rules of decorum. The more people free-ride, the more difficult it is to produce useful information and interaction. In the language of the Usenet, the *signal-to-noise ratio* deteriorates. The challenge becomes how a group of individuals can "organize and govern themselves to obtain collective benefits in situations where the temptations to free-ride and to break commitments are substantial" (Ostrom 1990:27).

4. Managing the virtual commons

To address this issue, Ostrom (1990) studied a wide range of face-to-face communities which had a long history of successfully producing and maintaining collective goods. She also studied a number of communities which had failed partially or completely in meeting this challenge. In comparing the communities, Ostrom found that groups which are able to organize and govern themselves are marked by the following design principles:

1. Group boundaries are clearly defined
2. Rules governing the use of collective goods are well matched to local needs and conditions
3. Most individuals affected by these rules can participate in modifying the rules
4. The rights of community members to devise their own rules is respected by external authorities
5. A system for monitoring members' behavior exists; this monitoring is undertaken by the community members themselves
6. A graduated system of sanctions is used
7. Community members have access to low-cost conflict resolution mechanisms[9]

We use these design principles as a way of organizing our discussion of the Usenet. Our analysis extends Ostrom's original points and applies them to the kinds of organization found in the Usenet. We have grouped the various design principles under three general headings: group size and boundaries (in which we discuss the first principle and the related issue of group size); rules and institutions (in which we discuss the second, third and fourth principles); and monitoring and sanctioning (in which the last three principles are discussed). In each case, we ask to what extent these design principles can be found in the Usenet, and whether the relevance and costs and benefits of these design principles change in this new form of social interaction.

4.1. Group size and boundaries

One of the most common and accepted tenets in the literature on cooperation is that "the larger the group, the less it will further its common interests" (Olson 1965:36). Researchers have identified a number of reasons why cooperation may be more difficult as group size increases. First, as the group becomes larger, the costs of an individual's decision to free-ride are spread over a greater number of people (Dawes 1980). If an individual's action does not appreciably affect others, the temptation to free-ride increases. More generally, the larger the group, the more difficult it may be to affect others' outcomes by one's own actions. Thus, an individual may be discouraged from cooperating if his or her actions do not affect others in a noticeable way. Second, it is often the case that as group size increases, anonymity becomes increasingly possible and an individual can free-ride without others noticing his or her actions (Dawes 1980). Third, the costs of organizing are likely to increase (Olson 1965), i.e., it becomes more difficult to communicate with others and coordinate the activities of members in order to provide collective goods and discourage free-riding.

Does this logic hold in the Usenet? In many ways it does not, because the costs and benefits of free-riding, social control, and coordination in the Usenet are very different than for groups that interact without computer-mediated communication. A key difference is that one's behavior in a newsgroup is visible to every other participant of the newsgroup, whether there are 10 participants or 10,000. Thus, the costs of free-riding by, for example, being off-topic, posting huge articles, or violating decorum, are not diffused as the number of participants in the newsgroup increases. Indeed, one could argue that the effects of free-riding increase as newsgroup membership increases, because there are a greater number of participants to be inconvenienced or angered by such actions. This characteristic of the Usenet creates new challenges for those wishing to establish cooperative communities, but also new possibilities. The fact that every individual's behavior is visible and identifiable discourages free-riding among those who only free-ride when they can do so anonymously. This same visibility can make monitoring people's actions easier.

Another important difference is that the Usenet can reduce the costs of coordination and communication, in some cases allowing groups to produce and maintain collective goods that would otherwise be too expensive. In particular, the challenge of finding people with similar interests is greatly reduced, and the usual problems of meeting at a common time and place are eliminated. There are other advantages as well: communicating with a thousand people involves essentially the same personal costs as sending a message to a single individual; a great number of members can participate in discussions involving numerous topics without overloading participants; and an historical record of members' interactions is automatically produced. Thus, there may be the potential to sustain cooperation in much larger groups than is possible without computer-mediated communication. For example, the *comp.sys.ibm.pc.games.action* newsgroup provides several thousand people scattered around the planet with access to each other, detailed information about where to find games for the IBM PC, strategies for playing those games, and reports of problems and patches for fixing bugs. While this group could exist by meeting face-to-face, or could publish a paper newsletter, by interacting via the Usenet participants can interact more frequently, at less cost, and among a larger and more wide-spread group than could be sustained otherwise.

However, these features of the Usenet do not by themselves guarantee a cooperative community, as is readily apparent to any participant on the Usenet. There are other design principles that also seem to be necessary if a community is to work well.

Ostrom found that one of the most important features of successful communities is that they have clearly defined boundaries: "Without defining the boundaries of the [collective good] and closing it to 'outsiders', local appropriators face the risk that any benefits they produce by their efforts will be reaped by others who have not contributed to those efforts. At the least, those who invest in the [collective good] may not receive as high a return as they expected. At the worst, the actions of others could destroy the resource itself" (Ostrom 1990:91). Boundaries are also important in that they encourage frequent, ongoing interaction among group members, if only by limiting interaction with others. This is critical because repeated interaction is perhaps the single most important factor in encouraging cooperation (Axelrod 1984). If individuals are not likely to interact in the future, there is a huge temptation to behave selfishly and free-ride. On the other hand, knowing that one will be interacting with others on a continual basis can lead to the creation of reputations, and serve as a powerful deterrent to short-run, selfish behavior.

One of the greatest challenges to cooperation on the Usenet is that its boundaries are often both undefendable and undefined, and cannot sufficiently ward off those who would exploit the collective goods produced by others. While there are many resources to construct boundaries in the Usenet, many of these boundaries exist only by voluntary compliance and are easily violated.[10]

In many ways, a newsgroup's name is one of its most effective means of defining a boundary: by announcing its contents, it attracts the interested and repels the disinterested. But within this boundary, a newsgroup's membership can be extremely fluid. Some newsgroups do attract and hold a fairly stable group, but many do not. To the extent that membership in a newsgroup is not stable and its boundaries are not clearly defined, cooperation will be more difficult.

One way of increasing the stability of a group is by actively restricting its membership. The overwhelming majority of newsgroups in the Usenet are potentially open to anyone.[11] However, there is no technological reason why restricted newsgroups cannot be created, just as there are e-mail distribution lists that one must ask to join or private conferences on bulletin board systems.[12] On the Usenet, there are two broad types of boundaries that are relevant: barriers to access to the content of the newsgroup, and barriers to posting to the newsgroup. Thus, one possible type of restricted newsgroup might allow anyone to read a discussion but permit only admitted members to contribute to it. Alternatively, both reading and posting could be limited to group members.

There is, however, a technical device already in place, known as a *kill file* or *bozo filter*, that an individual can use to create a kind of customized personal boundary. If someone's actions in the Usenet are considered objectionable, an individual can put this person in his or her kill file, which filters out any future posting by this person. In some ways a kill file reduces a member's reliance on the larger group's ability to define and defend a boundary. This offers both individuals and groups greater flexibility—the effects of some sorts of violations of the commons can be minimized without the costs of restraining the offending activity. It also illustrates the kinds of powerful interaction tools that can be built in cyberspace—imagine a conversation in which one could make invisible any objectionable person. While this capacity might be longed for in many situations, it has some practical problems: even though the person using the filter will not see the offending party's postings, other participants in the newsgroup will see future postings and comment on them. Thus, one must continue to deal with the reactions to the posting, even if the original postings are kept from one's eyes.

Although it does not yet exist on the Usenet, one way of addressing this limitation would be to create a community kill file. In other words, members of a newsgroup could decide (via majority voting, consensus, etc.) to place an offending individual in a shared, newsgroup-specific kill file such that the individual would be prevented from posting to the newsgroup in the future. Note that this is a different approach to group boundaries than the idea of a private, restricted newsgroup discussed above. A community kill file allows anyone to join a newsgroup but provides a mechanism for banishing people. In contrast, the emphasis in a private newsgroup is making it difficult to join in the first place.

4.2. Rules and institutions

Any successful community will have a set of rules—whether they are implicit or explicit—that govern how common resources should be used and who is responsible for producing and maintaining collective goods. However, it is important that the rules are tailored to the specific needs and circumstances of the group. Ostrom identifies this as another design principle that is a feature of cooperative communities: there is a good match between the goals and local conditions of a group, and the rules that govern the actions of the group's members. Her research indicates that there is often great variation from community to community in the details of the rules for managing collective goods. One lesson is that it is dangerous to take the specific rules of a successful group and apply them blindly to other groups.

Ostrom also found that an additional characteristic of successful communities is that most of the individuals affected by the rules governing the use of common resources can participate in modifying those rules. She argued that this feature results in better-designed rules, because the individuals with the knowledge of the day-to-day workings of the group and the challenges the group faces could modify the rules over time to better fit local conditions. In contrast, rules that were created and forced upon a community by outside authorities often failed miserably because the rules did not take into account knowledge of local conditions, or because the same set of rules was applied in a procrustean fashion to many communities despite important differences between them. Indeed, another design principle that marked successful communities was that external government authorities recognized (at least to some extent) the rights of communities to devise their own rules, and respected those rules as legitimate.

Are these features present, and are the issues underlying them relevant on the Usenet? A well-crafted set of rules for managing collective resources is certainly important for newsgroups, and some progress has been made in defining those rules. Rules and institutions exist on a global and local level throughout the Usenet.[13] At the global level, there are some concerns that are common to all newsgroups, and a set of documents exist which chart out rules that should govern participation. Six key documents have been grouped together in what is described as a "mandatory course" for new users.[14] These documents discuss rules of etiquette, suggestions for using the Usenet efficiently, cautions against wasting bandwidth or being off-topic, and many other issues.

On the local level, and consistent with the principle that rules should be tailored to local conditions, many newsgroups have also established a body of information about the newsgroup, complete with prescriptions and proscriptions, that is know as a Frequently-Asked Questions file, or FAQ. However, there are problems: not every newsgroup has a FAQ (indeed, the creation of a FAQ is often the first sign that a group has resolved some of the hurdles of collective organization); some FAQs do not addresses critical issues or do so ambiguously; some newsgroups do not have a clear sense of their goals or the challenges they face; and many participants in the Usenet (especially new members) do not bother reading FAQs and other related documents. Finally, these documents contain no specific recommendations for dealing with violations of their rules; all enforcement on the Usenet remains an informal process (this is discussed further in the following section).

These points raise the issue of socialization. Even if a community has developed a good set of rules, there is the task of teaching new members about those rules. The logic of social dilemmas exists here as well. All benefit if all members have learned the information and rules necessary to carry on interaction in a newsgroup, but long-time members are tempted to ignore questions from neophytes (termed *newbies*) and not contribute to the creation or maintenance of FAQ files. New members are tempted to wade into a newsgroup without first learning the local culture by reading the documents that have been prepared by other members or by observing the group for a period of time before attempting to participate.

The production of FAQs illustrates the ways in which local rules are produced and modified endogenously, by the members themselves. However, participation in creating and modifying the rules that govern a community does not necessarily mean that every member is involved in every decision. A FAQ may be produced by a single entrepreneurial member of a newsgroup, or may be the product of many individual contributions.[15]

Even in newsgroups that have produced a FAQ, many of the rules and institutions that are present remain informal, undocumented and difficult to enforce. As a result, there are certain chronic problems that are difficult to resolve through these informal means. For example, groups routinely wander off of their declared topics, and are frequently invaded by those who are either ignorant of the goals of the group or who actively seek to disrupt them. In some of these cases, groups have decided to deal with a social dilemma by turning over authority for the management of a collective good to a particular member or group of members, trusting these leaders to manage the resource well. This is, in a broad sense, Hobbes' classic solution of Leviathan: people give up part of their personal freedom to an authority in exchange for some measure of social order. While Leviathan conjures up visions of a fascist, totalitarian state, a milder version of this solution can be found on the Usenet in the form of moderated groups. "These are groups which usually have one or more individuals ... who must approve articles before they are published to the net. ... [Moderated groups are often] derived from regular groups with such a high volume that it is hard for the average reader to keep up, ... [or] from regular groups that have often been abused" (Spafford et al. 1993b). Since each contribution is evaluated for its appropriateness to the newsgroup, a moderated group avoids many of the problems of unrestrained participation. But it resolves the problem of collective organization by depending on the willingness of a moderator to invest significant time and effort in managing the newsgroup. And for the majority of newsgroups that cannot find someone to make such a contribution or oppose ceding control to a central authority, the problem of self-organization remains. Moderated groups are one of the rare examples of a formal and enforceable institution on the Usenet.

Finally, in its present state, the Usenet is not subject to much interference from external authorities. This has the advantage of allowing newsgroups to fashion their own rules and institutions. However, increased government regulation is a possibility in the future. There are political pressures to regulate cyberspace, and external interference, despite its dangers and limitations, is sometimes necessary if communities are unable to solve their own social dilemmas. To the extent the Usenet successfully manages its collective resources, and retains its distributed, decentralized structure, it can avoid the need for external regulation and resist outside pressures encouraging external regulation.

4.3. Monitoring and sanctioning

Each of the successful communities studied by Ostrom was marked by clearly defined group boundaries and a set of well-designed rules. Because community members participated in refining the rules and the rules were well-matched to local conditions, most members believed in the rules and were committed to following them. However, this does not seem to be enough to insure cooperative relations. Some type of system to monitor and sanction members' actions was a feature of every successful community.

Monitoring and sanctioning is important not simply as a way of punishing rule-breakers, but also as a way of assuring members that others are doing their part in using common resources wisely. Ostrom and other researchers (Levi 1988) have argued that many individuals are willing to comply with a set of rules governing collective goods if they believe the rules are efficacious and if they believe most others are complying with the rules. That is, many people are contingent cooperators, willing to cooperate as long as most others do. Thus, monitoring and sanctioning serves the important function of providing information about other persons' actions.

In every successful community studied, the monitoring and sanctioning of peoples' behavior was undertaken by the community members themselves rather than by external authorities. Another common pattern was that cooperative communities employed a graduated system of sanctions. While sanctions could be as severe as banishment from the group, the initial sanction for breaking a rule was often very low. Community members realized that even a well-intentioned person might break the rules when facing an unusual situation or extreme hardship. Severely punishing such a person might alienate him or her from the community, causing greater problems.

Interaction in the Usenet makes monitoring much easier, but poses special problems for sanctioning others. Because of the nature of computer-mediated communication, it becomes possible to monitor others more thoroughly and more cheaply than has heretofore been possible in groups. Most forms of free-riding in the Usenet, such as using the bandwidth unwisely, being off-topic, or violating norms of decorum, are seen by all other participants of the newsgroup, and one's actions are usually identifiable because each posting is accompanied by the person's e-mail address.[16] Further, because an exact record of every participant's actions is kept (at least for a few weeks), it is possible to "go back into history" and recover a sequence of interaction. On the Usenet, unlike most interactional settings, the claim "I didn't say that" had better be truthful, because anyone can call up the exact words.

While monitoring can be accomplished at a very low cost (almost as a side effect of regular interaction), sanctioning participants' behavior on the Usenet is more of a challenge. There are some types of sanctions that are simply impossible: threats of physical violence are necessarily empty threats,[17] and no system exists to levy and collect monetary fines (though such a system is technically possible). Indeed, it is very difficult to force anyone to do anything—this is both the charm and frustration of the Usenet.

What participants can do is use a variety of informal sanctions to try to shape behavior. Free-riders might be insulted, parodied, or simply informed that their actions are undesirable. Often the response is both intense and voluminous, in part because of the effortlessness with which one can comment on other's actions.[18] In this sense, informal sanctions are easier to carry out in the Usenet than in many other settings. However, enforcing social order is made more difficult by the fact that many newsgroups have no clear common understanding of what should and should not occur in their interactions.

Nonetheless, some actions step clearly out of the bounds of acceptability. For example, recent discussions of cruel acts to cats in the *rec.pets.cats* newsgroup were recognized as a clear violation of decorum. A post with the subject "****MAKE MONEY FAST****" containing an invitation to participate in a classic pyramid scheme was recently widely cross-posted throughout the Usenet and also drew widespread sanctions. Responses ranged from cautions against participating to expressions of extreme irritation and personal insults directed to the poster. In addition, there were some calls for a coordinated collective response: "Remember people -- Just ignore it and it will go away. If you have to write something, do it via e-mail. ... Behavior modification in action: Don't bother flaming them -- attention is their reward. Just ignore them. They'll get bored and go away."[19] These kinds of informal social control mechanisms depend upon moral suasion to have an effect—they lack any capacity to actually restrict deviant behavior, they can only discourage it. Nevertheless, many people report that informal sanctions do have a significant effect on their behavior.

More severe sanctions are possible but rarely carried out. In extreme situations, a participant might have his or her computer account revoked by the institution that controls the physical hardware. This occurs rarely, can provoke widespread outrage, and is ultimately not a fool-proof way of banishing someone from the Usenet because of the many alternate routes for getting access.

No set of rules is perfectly designed, and there will always be ambiguity in applying a particular rule. Consequently, it is important to have some method to resolve the conflicts that will inevitably arise. This is the final design principle Ostrom identifies as common to successful communities: access to low-cost conflict resolution mechanisms. The need for these mechanisms in the Usenet is clear: for the reasons already discussed, conflicts in newsgroups are fairly common. In fact, some newsgroups seem to be dedicated entirely to on-going conflicts. However, formal methods for dealing with these conflicts have yet to develop—there is no Usenet court system or even a place to engage in arbitration. While the Usenet has survived without these institutions for many years, as the size and diversity of the Usenet population increases, these institutions may become increasingly necessary. Other forms of social organization in cyberspace have already developed such institutions. For example, some MOOs and MUDs have developed councils and judiciary systems to resolve conflicts.[20] In contrast, the Usenet relies on the principle that most conflicts die out after a period of time, if for no other reason than the combatants become exhausted.

5. Conclusions

As computer-mediated communication increasingly becomes the medium through which public discourse takes place, the ways in which that discourse is socially organized become more consequential. While systems like the Usenet are continuously changing, their present form has implications for the future nature of a society increasingly woven together by these technologies. "Computers are being used, in effect, to manage networks of relationships between people" (Applegate 1993:A9), thus changing the costs and benefits of cooperation.

Cooperation is an accomplishment, and on the Usenet, cooperation must occur without recourse to external authorities. That it occurs at all is somewhat amazing. As Olson (1965:1) observed in his classic work on collective action, "if the members of some group have a common interest or objective, and if they would all be better off if that objective were achieved, it [does not necessarily follow] that the individuals in that group would ... act to achieve that objective."

For all its declared faults, the Usenet has developed into a remarkably robust institution. It has endured more than a decade, and grown exponentially to include millions of participants.

Yet, for all of this cooperation, there remain significant shortcomings. Many newsgroups remain relatively uncooperative places, filled with noise and argument. The Usenet may not need to resolve these problems, it may simply become the public space in cyberspace where the balance between order and autonomy is decided in favor of the latter. Other institutions in cyberspace may, however, learn the lessons the Usenet can teach and provide alternatives that satisfy a wide range of desires.

One of the broad lessons that we draw from the social organization of the Usenet is that cyberspace has a double edge: monitoring the behavior of others becomes easier while sanctioning undesirable behavior becomes more difficult; the costs of communication between members of a large group are decreased while the effects of free-riding are often amplified; and the existence of several thousand newsgroups makes it easy for individuals to find others who share specific interests and goals, but also makes those who want to disrupt those groups able to find them. Thus, there is no simple conclusion to this story, and one-note predictions of either a utopian or dystopic future must be considered suspect. This double edge makes it imperative that we deepen our knowledge of the ways in which computer-mediated communication alters the economies of cooperation.

ACKNOWLEDGMENTS

* Direct correspondence to Peter Kollock, Department of Sociology, University of California, Los Angeles, CA 90095 (e-mail: kollock@ucla.edu; smithm@nicco.sscnet.ucla.edu). Order of authorship is alphabetical to indicate equal contributions. We wish to thank Ronald Obvious for comments on an earlier draft of this paper.

NOTES

1. For general reviews of the research on social dilemmas, see Messick and Brewer (1983); Dawes (1980).

2. *Public good* is sometimes defined in a more restricted sense (see Taylor 1987:5-8). Here we use the term public good (or collective good) simply to refer to resources that are in some degree non-excludable.

3. Given the space constraints here, we are restricted in the amount of detail and number of examples we can present. In a forthcoming study we go into much greater depth in our analysis of social interaction and order in cyberspace (Kollock and Smith, forthcoming).

4. Usenet newsgroups are named according to a loose convention. Groups are to start with one of eight main hierarchy names, and then add words separated by periods that increasingly narrow the scope of the group. There are seven broad official classifications of Usenet newsgroups: "news", "soc", "talk", "misc", "sci", "comp", and "rec" (Spafford et al. 1993a). An additional classification, the "alt" hierarchy, contains "alternative" newsgroups that are less regulated.

5. For example, newsgroups with suffixes of ".d" are intended as places for meta-commentary on the antecedent newsgroup.

6. In *The Strategy of Conflict,* Schelling (1960) wrote of features on a landscape that permit tacit coordination. For example, there are points in a city that provide natural spaces for finding others, such as the clock in Grand Central Station.

7. *Cross-posting* is the practice of posting the same message to multiple newsgroups. This is intended to allow items of interest to be easily shared by more than one group. In practice, it is often the source of annoyance and conflict as items of limited relevance are cross-posted to a number of groups.

8. *Usernames* are labels that identify the machine and user from which a message originates. "Real" identity is sometimes difficult to determine from usernames. This is due in part to usernames like izzy3046. But even a username like smithm@nicco.sscnet.ucla.edu conveys a minimum amount of information about its owner.

9. Ostrom identified an eighth design principle that is relevant in complex social systems: monitoring, sanctioning, and other governance activities are organized in multiple layers of nested enterprises. Ostrom considers this list to be a first, speculative attempt to isolate what is required to manage a common resource successfully. She and her colleagues are currently involved in a large research project to develop and refine this list further.

10. Social boundaries are never hermetic; their value to a group is often based on what they let in and let out as much as they keep in and keep out. Further, it is a mistake to conceive of boundaries as singular forces. Instead, boundaries are erected and maintained by a variety of practices and tools, some of which have conflicting effects.

11. Note, however, that there are *de facto* barriers that can keep people out of the Usenet in general. Some people do not have access to or cannot afford the hardware necessary to connect to the Usenet. Others may have access to the hardware, but do not have the necessary knowledge in order to participate—they may not know how to use newsreading software, or may not even be aware of the Usenet's existence. These barriers are likely to decrease in the future as access becomes both simpler and cheaper.

12. There has been limited experimentation with restricted newsgroups through the use of coded messages that can only be decoded by members who have been provided with a key. Another example is the Clarinet newsgroups, which provide information from commercial news providers to paying subscribers only. Legal recourse provides Clarinet with a major element of its boundary.

13. By *institutions* we mean "...the sets of working rules that are used to determine who is eligible to make decisions in some arena [and] what actions are allowed or constrained..." (Ostrom 1990:51)

14. The course consists of: "A Primer on How to Work With the Usenet Community" (Von Rospach et al. 1993), "Answers to Frequently Asked Questions about Usenet" (Schwarz et al. 1993), "Emily Postnews Answers Your Questions on Netiquette" (Templeton 1991), "Hints on writing style for Usenet" (Offutt et al. 1992), "Rules for posting to Usenet" (Horton et al. 1993), and "What is Usenet?" (Salzenberg et al. 1992).

15. Note that boundaries and rules are interrelated. Having members of a group participate in the design of rules to govern the group makes sense if the members all have experience in the group, knowledge about the challenges the group faces, and an investment in the group (i.e., they intend to stay in the group and value their membership in the group). But if the boundaries of a group are not well defined, such that there are many participants who have little knowledge about the group or little investment in it, involving all affected participants in the modification of rules can result in poorly-designed institutions.

16. However, there has been increasing use of services that provide a form of anonymity or pseudo-anonymity for users of e-mail and the Usenet. *Anonymous name servers* accept e-mail or Usenet postings, strip all identifying information from them, assign a pseudonym (such as an3209@anon.penet.fi), and redirect them to the person or newsgroup to which they are addressed. The effects anonymity has on the social organization of groups based on computer-mediated communication bears close investigation, but goes beyond the scope of this chapter.

17. Although the very real instances of stalking that have been accomplished through the use of networks highlights the fact that the Usenet can become a means by which real violence is carried out.

18. Ironically, the sanction itself can consume more bandwidth than the original violation, but the sanction may still make sense if it encourages wiser use of this common resource in the future. A similar logic can be seen in the action of the agents of the I.R.S., who sometimes spend more finding and prosecuting a tax offender than they collect in back taxes and fines.

19. From: *alt.best.of.internet*, message id# 3211, 23 January 1994.

20. MUDs and MOOs are real-time text-based social worlds. For a detailed description of MUDs and MOOs see Curtis (1991).

Our Passionate Response to Virtual Reality

Nancy R. Deuel
University of Maryland, College Park

> Our passionate response to VR [virtual reality] mirrors the nature of the medium itself. By inviting the body and the senses into our dance with our tools, it has extended the landscape of interaction, to new topologies of pleasure, emotion and passion.
>
> Brenda Laurel, *Computers as Theatre*

1. Introduction*

In daily life in the spaces of "post-virtual reality" (Laurel 1991b) known as MUDs (Multi-User Dungeons, or Dimensions), people are frequently confronted with evidence, direct as well as indirect, of the practice of sex in cyberspace (virtual sex, or VSex). However, such practices are rarely discussed openly even among MUD participants, and certainly not in a critical, scholarly forum. The present essay is intended as a first step toward a critical understanding of virtual sex.[1]

First, some basic definitions of text-based virtual environments and of VSex activities are provided. Second, I consider how sexual activities unfold in this environment, based on information gleaned from interviews with virtual reality (VR) participants, personal observations, and references to current research in the field. I illustrate the evolving etiquette and mores of virtual sexual behavior and demonstrate the range of real life (RL) sexual practice and fantasy that is mirrored and recreated in a virtual environment. After discussing the rich variety of interactions, behavioral norms, and enhancements of which players avail themselves, I conclude by considering some human implications of VSex, related political issues, and ways in which it may develop in the future.

The activities described herein constitute one important facet of what Rheingold, using a metaphor of disease, describes as a "text-based cyberspace phenomenon that seems to have broken out all over the Internet" (1991:308).

However, far from sounding "alarm bells about this artificial world that we're buying into" (Rheingold, quoted in Bright 1992:64), I maintain that VSex practices are consonant with what Laurel describes as the theatrics and mimesis of "human-computer activities" (1991b:43-48). I feel, with Leary, that VSex has the potential to offer people "a tool for expanding the power of their minds.... The screen is where minds of tomorrow will mirror themselves, meet each other, enter the universe of information and knowledge" (Leary 1990:230-232). The computer screen opens a pathway where, to echo the opening epigraph, minds of today may enter a universe of pleasure, emotion, and passion. As such, VSex activity requires the same rigorous protections of freedom of expression and privacy as other communications methods utilized by society.

1.1. MUDs and MOOs

Multi-User Dimensions, or MUDs, are programmable text-based environments wherein participants may interact in virtual spaces. MOOs (MUDs, Object-Oriented) are variants of MUDs which employ a programming approach based on creation of "objects" which may include virtual rooms, things, and even the player characters themselves. LambdaMOO (internet address lambda.parc.xerox.com, port 8888), developed by Pavel Curtis (1992), was announced in January 1991 as the first publicly accessible MOO. In five years it has grown into a mature self-governing community of over 8500 citizens (Bruckman 1994; Reid 1995), and forms the basis for much of the present analysis and commentary .

People connect to a MOO via Internet or World Wide Web links and are logged in as individual characters. Participants set all characteristics of their character's persona including its name, gender, and appearance as viewed by other participants. Participants may expand the environment by the creation and description of virtual rooms and programmable objects of an infinite variety. Conversations and interactions take place within virtual rooms, ideally in real time, but actually with some degree of system-generated delay (known as "lag"). The objects created may be fixed within a room, or carried by the character and transported between rooms. It is also possible for characters to communicate between rooms by means of paging protocols (Marvin 1995).

1.2. Virtual sex

VSex may be defined as a series of communications protocols and virtual actions occurring in real-time between two (or more) participants that establish explicitly sexual stimulation as the focus of the interaction. VSex is distinguished from other forms of computer sex (compusex, cybersex, or netsex) which provide few, if any, virtual spatial constructs, in that VSex is a form which utilizes the unique characteristics of VR systems "organized around the metaphor of physical space" (Bruckman 1993).

Immediately upon consideration of these practices, fundamental questions arise: What can possibly be the attraction of sexual activities taking place on a computer? Is it simply some strange perversion? How often does VSex activity occur, and by what proportion of players? If it occurs frequently, why is it not more openly discussed?

The question of attraction and interest in virtual sex has one obvious response. Sexual drives are fundamental to human existence in real life (IRL, in net acronym). Sexual activity transfers over quite naturally to the virtual environment. Use of the term "natural" is deliberate, in contrast to the condescending and even moralistic tone taken by Rheingold to characterize such activities on MUDs as "sophomoric" and "dirty" and practitioners as "offenders" (1993:150). "Computers, it seems, have intensified, not diminished, our culture's fascination with sexuality" (Springer 1993:714).

VSex constitutes a creative sexual outlet in the form of interactive personalized erotica, providing a mental (and no doubt physical) stimulation. Unlike RL sex, however, in the anonymity of cyberspace there is little pressure or stress of the sort imposed on an individual by another's physical presence. Kadrey explains, "If we go to some nice hotel to have sex, you still need to provide your physical body, the physical body of the other person and the given surroundings. With VR, nothing in that scenario is locked in. Using VR, there is no reason you have to be you" (Bright 1992:64-65). Branwyn (1993:780) explains, "Compu-sex enthusiasts say it's the ultimate safe sex for the 1990s, with no exchange of bodily fluids, no loud smoke-filled clubs, and no morning after."

Moreover, there is a sense among practicing virtual eroticists that such experiences are actually no less "real" than RL. Carlstrom (1992:7) concludes: "The ways in which interaction[s] on a textual interactive system are different from real-life interactions should not be seen as flaws or signs of inferiority, but as indications of a different kind of reality." There is always the tantalizing possibility, if only in fantasy, that such interactions may serve as an entree to RL relationships. However, the bridge to RL does not constitute a *necessary* component for ongoing interest in VSex activities. "These encounters rarely carry over into face-to-face meetings. Rather, the participants are content to return night after night to explore this odd brand of interactive and sexually explicit storytelling" (Branwyn 1993:780).

What is the frequency of VSex? What proportion of MOO participants engage in sex in cyberspace? While exact numbers are difficult to assess, by all indications VSex is immensely popular and pervasive in virtual communities. "Pioneered by computer hobbyists, the exchange of explicit and personal sexual material has taken on international proportions" (Springer 1993:715). "Every computer information service, large or small, has lurking within its bits and bytes an active subculture of users engaged in text-based sexual exchanges" (Branwyn 1993:780).

The concomitant question posed—why discussion of VSex has occurred, for the most part, behind the scenes—relates to the private, personal nature of such interactions, the implicit but vigorous process of self-censorship among participants of behavior deemed inappropriate such as open exchange on VSex practices, and the political ramifications of such activities. Nevertheless, on various discussion lists within MOO sites (similar to computer bulletin boards), ongoing debates address various "dangers". These relate to individual participants' affective relationship to such interactive exchanges (e.g., loss of boundaries between RL and VR; net-addiction (Rheingold 1993:33)), to the potential for deception between participants, and even to issues of sexual harassment and "virtual rape" (Dibbel 1993b). Related to all of these topics is the need to balance freedom of expression, on one hand, with participants' responsibility to their virtual communities, on the other. These observations lead the discussion to the edge of the protocols of VSex, which I now address in greater detail.

2. What happens in VSex? Protocols of sex in the virtual environment

Communications protocols on MOOs include a large array of tools and methods that are readily available to all participants. These include the basic elements of self-description, the communications commands that enable participants to engage in VSex interactions with a diversity of sexual orientations and interests, and participants' use of the programming environment to create objects and stimulate activities for increased erotic enhancement. Each set of protocols illuminates VSex practices and provides examples of the creative use of the virtual environment to enhance sexual encounters.

2.1. Descriptions

The first decision one faces when logging onto a MUD (usually via a telnet connection to the site's Internet address) is whether to remain generic, with a Guest name assigned randomly, or to create a character, selecting a name to which one can assign different aliases. MUD registration requires that one provide a real name and electronic mail address in order to receive a password. One's identity and site connection information is usually maintained confidential by "wizards", i.e., the site administrators.

The next decisions one is faced with are the selection of a name and gender, and providing the public with a description of one's appearance. One can choose any characteristics and style of description one wants, from realistic to fantastic, from alluring to repulsive. These include "names from or inspired by myth, fantasy, or literature, common names from real life, names of concepts, animals, and everyday objects that have representative connotations ...

[although] no such category includes a majority of the names" (Curtis 1992).

As for gender, Curtis (1992) maintains that this choice is "one of great consequence and forethought." One count I made in January 1994 on LambdaMOO revealed 4857 different registered characters that had logged in within the previous 6 months (at that time usually between 80 and 150 individuals were logged on at any particular moment). Out of those, 2423 (50%) had elected to represent their character's gender as male, 920 (19%) had elected gender female, while 1514 (31%) had elected another gender. The male-presenting characters therefore outnumber the female-presenting characters by a ratio of 2.6 to 1. Players may also creatively designate other genders, including neuter, Spivak, plural, royal, alien, stud, and dude.

Evidence suggests that most MOO participants represent themselves as their true gender or as neuter, with only a small percentage of players actually attempting to conceal or intentionally misrepresent their gender. Since the majority of participants on MUDs are male, some gender-swap, presenting themselves as female in order to gain attention as part of a sought-after minority group. Female participants, on the other hand, sometimes present themselves as male or neuter to avoid harassment and special treatment, a practice which suggests that societal sexism carries over into the virtual domain. As Bruckman (1993) notes, this practice highlights "the ways in which gender structures human interactions, ... the ways in which MUDs help people to understand these phenomena by experiencing them."

When one "enters" a room on a MOO (by typing the appropriate directional command), one generally sees a list of players "located" within the same virtual space. Some of the names encountered immediately present sexual overtones, functioning as obvious encouragement for potential partners: female_nudist, Fantasy, KYJELLY, Penis_Envy, Big_Dick, Won_Hung_Low, Horny_Homo, femmefatale. There is no censorship of name choices.

The virtual appearance of a participant in the same room may be displayed by typing the command "look <playername>". There are as many descriptions as there are players registered on a given MUD, so a limited number of examples cannot do justice to this multiplicity. The character descriptions are utilized by participants to provide clues to personality, interests, mode of dress, age, gender, sexual availability, and sexual preference.

In the realistic genre, the description of Infinity is typical: "In his late teens and ready to find excitement, wherever it may lead him. He has blonde hair, blue eyes, and stands about 6 feet tall. He has a good sense of humor and likes to make others feel good. Talk to him; he loves to talk to anyone about anything." For Quentin, who describes himself as "wearing a tweed jacket, grey shirt, a colorful yet subdued tie, and khaki pants", an appended detail provides a clue to sexual orientation: "He's wearing a pink triangle on the lapel of his jacket."

For female-presenting descriptions, rare are aggressive statements like Autumn's, apparently meant to repel all but the most eager interlocutor: "21 y/o, obnoxious, bites, nasty temper, evil laugh, impatient, sarcastic, quite rude at times, long auburn hair that's curly, grey eyes. A complete bitch. Just ask her." More commonly a female wishing to avoid eager suitors will present as a relatively nondescript male.

More typical, especially in sexually explicit allure, is Silverheel, "a petite, sultry red-head, with a cigarette in hand and a ready smile on her lips. She wears a black, silky dress trimmed with silver that clings to her body. Beware! she has the mouth of a trooper", or Morgana, "a funny and warm person. You see large breasts and shapely legs, but other than that, she's a little overweight. This is made up for by her beautiful reddish brown hair and starry gray blue eyes. Always wearing blood red nail polish to show off her small, soft hands. Generally sweet and very sexual."

More problematic for determining sexual orientation are descriptions that are either extremely explicit sexually or deliberately neutral. Lemi's description (gendered Spivak) is intentionally ambiguous, "A tall and muscular person with broad shoulders. A slight swelling in the chest and a lilt to this character's walk suggests breasts and hips, but you can't quite tell." Moreover, Lemi creates confusion not only for gender, but also for age, another detail in many descriptions: "A few crinkles around the eyes suggest age, but the floating, bouncing, weightless quality of Lemi's movements are child-like."

A creatively explicit description like Betty's implicates the viewer, and even demands that one explore her body: "Your orbs feast themselves on Betty's radiant sexuality. Greedily, they flow from her perfect face, down to her ample bosom, and rove over her curvaceous hips. Onward they travel down her legs, your ocular journey nearly at an end...." BlackOrchid's inviting description employs a touch of hyperbole: "The most beautiful sight you've ever seen ... a woman with flesh of swirling violet and eyes that could hold an army in thrall ... her movements entrance you ... you want to have her ... she knows you're staring at her ... she can feel you ... your will is slowly becoming hers..." As Curtis (1992) points out, sexually explicit enticement has been commonly associated with male characters who gender-swap, leading the savvy participant "to assume that any flirtatious female-presenting players are, IRL, males. Such players are often subject to ostracism based on this assumption." Sexual aggression is stereotypically assumed to be a male trait, and one participant notes: "It seems to me that if a female character shows any bit of intelligence and sexual recognition, people will think she's a male IRL. If she flirts shamelessly and has a 'smutty' description, people will think she's a male IRL."

The descriptive methods emphasized here reveal the most fundamental form of representation available on MUDs for establishing one's persona, affirming identity and, by extension, intentions and interests. Just as IRL, an individual's appearance determines one's first impression of their character. Later conversations and interactions serve to substantiate or refute initial impressions. Developing a creative description and inspecting the descriptions of others constitutes the first mode of approach in the gradual acquaintanceship process leading to virtual intimacy.

2.2. *Behavior and "netiquette"*

Most people logging on to a MOO spend the majority of their time in social conversation with others in groups of varying sizes, in public or private rooms, although time may also be spent in exploring the environment, reading mail and announcements, and programming new rooms and objects. All participants are referred to a "help manners" scroll which clearly defines the basics of acceptable social behavior. Certain modes of behavior deemed inappropriate by the majority are quickly and vehemently criticized. Offending players are verbally rebuked, and if that proves unsuccessful, they may be ostracized in MOO society and subject to punitive actions. One infamous example on LambdaMOO resulted after a participant named Mr. Bungle had treated several others in sexually abusive ways. His behavior prompted the evolution of a whole process of mediation within the community as a means of addressing socially unacceptable behavior and banning repeat offenders (Dibbell 1993b).

Peer group pressure, reinforced by this formal disputation procedure, effectively enforces most behavioral standards on LambdaMOO. Some participants volunteer to serve the community officially as mediators of interpersonal disputes, or voluntarily choose a designation as Official Helpful Persons. Many others simply observe an implicit law of MOO karma in helping newbies (new registrants) as well as guests, demonstrating a helpful respect and patience with fundamental questions. In the fluid MOO society, the person guesting today may be a familiar member of the community next month. One apparent convention among many participants is to observe age standards in protecting anyone, new or veteran alike, who confides that he or she is a minor IRL. However, other participants abuse guests particularly, and some consider newbies as fair prey for harassment and sexual advances.

While sexual innuendoes and jokes about sexual issues are common, established participants and guests are occasionally urged to respect implicit taboos in the public sites (particularly the Living Room). The effective societal taboos are open to individual interpretation, but may be considered to include those against sexual harassment, overt public sexual activity and undress, defamatory gossip, and publicly revealing details of participants' real lives without their permission. Peer group pressure discourages open sexual advances in public spaces, as for example when participants tell an openly demonstrative couple to "get a room" and take their pursuits to a private, enclosed space. (Most registrants are easily able to create such spaces by employing simple building commands such as @dig). Similarly, guests who demonstrate ignorance of MOO basics are often urged to declare themselves, for example, to "get a character" (i.e. register as a participant), "get a gender" and "get a description".

2.3. Privacy

Although often socializing in "public" spaces on a MOO, participants are also interested in maintaining private, secure spaces for discussion and other intimate interactions, including VSex. Hence, a group of commands has evolved offering degrees of anonymity and privacy, but also providing access to information about the registered participants with whom one is likely to associate. Identifying information such as home town, time zone, electronic mail address, and even age may be supplied voluntarily in a participant's public @dossier. However, in most cases, such personal information is kept private and provided only to close confidants. As the range of such commands is enormous, I limit this discussion to questions of privacy that relate directly to VSex practices and that fundamentally contribute to the development of trust between participants.

Although public spaces on MUDs (such as the Living Room or the Hot Tub on LambdaMOO) are most frequently the sites in which the flirtation and seduction process commences, participants quickly learn that to obtain real privacy for conversations and other pursuits, it is necessary to create one's own private room. Once the basic room is created via the @dig command, a participant may assure its security for the occupants through a set of commands that provides access only to selected participants (on @accept status) or that can close the room entirely to any uninvited entry.

Privacy is a complex issue, however, when abuses occur. Having accepted an invitation from two more experienced players to visit in a private room, one newly registered participant reported being unable to teleport from the space, then was stripped of her property objects, including her clothes, and was forced to appear naked under the scrutiny of all other participants. This occurred through deliberate and clever program manipulation on the part of the more experienced players involved, and only the intervention of a wizard could halt this abuse of the new participant's trust.

There is no doubt a capability for identity shifting and deception (gender and other) on MUDs. However, while "boundary stories" of VR exist (Stone 1991, 1992), they are not as extreme as Rheingold suggests (1993:164-166). Moreover, intentional misrepresentation of gender can be maintained for extended periods of time in intense relationships, but not without consequence. One long-term female-presenting participant finally posted a confessional, not only revealing that he was actually male, but also "outing" another female-presenting character, a RL male.

Password security also becomes an issue. One female participant discovered that a RL male acquaintance had "borrowed" her character (and password) only after she subsequently received an intimate message (via intraMOO "page") from another male-presenting participant, who had apparently enjoyed VSex with her character the previous evening. In another instance, a participant's password and MOO identity were appropriated by a group of drunken fraternity brothers whose offensive behavior in the Living Room resulted in a dispute and sanctions against the careless MOO registrant.

There are, however, means one may employ to help determine the trustworthiness of a particular participant. A typical initial step is to consult the participant's list of @pals, if any. Second, one may observe with whom a participant has extended and especially sequestered encounters on the MOO, and then contact that other person. In case of doubt about a participant with whom one comes into contact, one can often find a third party who knows this participant better, even IRL, and obtain assurances about the participant's identity, circumstances, and motives. Some participants have a policy of not engaging in VSex with anyone prior to conversing with them on the phone and reassuring themselves that the voice on the other end is the desired gender.

2.4. *Sexual interactions and orientations*

In any situation on the MOO, use of the basic communication commands—say and emote (readable by all in a room), and whisper, page, and remote-emote (readable only by the recipient)—is the key to any successful communicative interaction. Moreover, a whole range of "social verbs" (such as nod, smile, grin, hug, kiss, and even lick and fondle) is available for frequently-used quick statements and responses. Any participant can learn to program a set of personalized verbs, some of which extend to long series of sequential statements and can be quite explicit sexually. Besides these verbs, pre-programmed @features that are available optionally to all participants offer amusing social interactions that often function as elements of courtship and seduction. These include creative virtual on-line activities such as dance steps, pizza delivery, flower delivery, keg parties, and games like Scrabble and Twister.

In all of these forms of communication, the skill level of the participant facilitates (or hinders) the ease of interchange and enhances (or destroys) the level of trust between two individuals. Accidents occur in communications in VR, even as they do IRL. Some of these are unique to the MUD environment, such as when one errs in designating the correct recipient of an explicit whisper or page, and thus sends a message intended to be received by someone else.

Once a couple (or even a group) accedes to the suggestion, implied or expressed, to "go somewhere more quiet", basic communication skills (most often utilizing the say, emote, and whisper functions) become crucial for engaging in conversation and especially in intimate expression and contact. Here, the range of activities available for VSex play is limited only by the participants' imagination in command manipulation and by their typing skills. Besides standard heterosexual intercourse, participants have reported engaging in oral sex, group sex, bondage and discipline, same-sex activities, and even secretive sex undertaken (via private emote and whispers) in public places (Woodland 1995).

However exciting these activities may be inherently, for some participants they constitute mere play with little if any RL emotional engagement or physical involvement. For many others, however, VSex activity is more than text on a screen, for there is quite often some form of RL involvement. The physical aspect might be described simply (if cynically) as mere cyberwanking, or what Davis more generously describes as "the on-line world's curious and surprisingly moist blend of phone sex and raunchy pen-pal letters" (1994:43-44). Whether or not the interactive VSex fantasy inspires one or more participants to engage in manual self-stimulation IRL, the potential for such RL engagement adds a dimension to the "consensual hallucination" (Gibson 1984:51) of VR. Concomitant planes of reality intermesh when the participant with whom one is interacting in VR declares and describes RL masturbatory activity occurring simultaneously with VSex.

For participants who are emotionally invested in such activities, a number of additional factors come into play to enhance the experience: the slow development of real-time interaction and mutual stimulation between the two participants, the tempo inherent to this process, and the gradually unfolding expression as participants react to each successive response. Most experienced participants describe a point at which the screen disappears, when one is no longer sitting at a terminal but is perceptually in another space and the imagination has taken over entirely. Someone just logging on occasionally gains little sense of the participatory experience with familiar people that a regular knows well. Branwyn's glib summary, that "compu-sex is a curious blend of phone sex, computer dating, and high-tech voyeurism" (1993:784), remains at the surface of what is, for many members of virtual communities, a significant part of a deeper interpersonal experience.

Branwyn (1993:790) notes that "sexual interaction in current text-based compu-sex almost exclusively mirrors...real-world intercourse", i.e., a progression from foreplay to "usually simultaneous" on-line orgasm. Anecdotal evidence substantiates Branwyn's observations. Although it is possible in the virtual environment to practice virtual sex in an infinite variety of environments (e.g., under the sea, in weightless outer space, inside the sun) and with an infinite variety of partners (including those presenting characters described as aliens, animals, vegetables, and so on), the actual expression of sexual acts is generally confined to the realistic genre. Participants have also described variants of the "fantasy" variety of virtual sex, but these are relatively rare and generally attempted experimentally. The most peculiar of this sort is between the indeterminately gendered Spivaks. One player who adopted this gender reported that VSex between Spivaks has its own particular excitement since each participant is free to create organs and modes of excitation and consummation as the spirit and imagination move "em".

Another participant described the experience of having two alternate characters, one a mature predatory mammal (such as a wolf, lynx, or leopard), and one an immature domestic mammal (such as a kitten, bunny, or puppy). While both characters were gendered male, he found it much easier to attract partners in the predatory guise. Interestingly, though, he related that none of his sexual partners had seemed to interact in their imagination with an animal possessing paws, claws, and teeth, but rather mentally anthropomorphized the character to be relatively human-presenting, complete with clothing, hands, lips, and human sexual organs. These anecdotes seem to confirm that, contrary to the potential for creating a totally amoral society, human taboos against bestiality and sex with immature or helpless beings carry over into behavior in the virtual environment.

2.5. Erotic enhancement

One distinct advantage of a manipulable VR environment over other forms of computer-mediated communications is that participants may make accessory use of the programming environment (beyond basic descriptions of their own character and use of communications commands) to enhance their experience. Predominant forms of enhancement are room descriptions that promote a sensual mood, erotic objects, clothing objects, and pre-programmed clothing stripping functions. The creation and use of these forms reflect the level of participants' programming abilities, and their imaginative engagement in virtual activities.

The most prevalent practice in this regard is the creation of private rooms, lockable by the creator to prevent unwanted entry. Like player descriptions, private rooms may take on an infinite variety of forms, and sophistication in describing, furnishing, and accessorizing them contributes to creating an atmosphere favorable to more intimate activities.

A bedroom of a female-presenting bisexual character is attractively described as "gently lit by candlelight [which] flickers and you feel very relaxed, leaving all your troubles and worries behind you." Another bedroom "is hung with many silks and fabrics. There are a number of mirrors in the room. In the north-west corner you see a large four-poster bed. On a cabinet by the bed there is a pair of handcuffs and a leather riding crop. You may wonder if you *really* want to come any further?" Two participants have a sign in their Nudist Trailer requesting, "If you have clothes please leave them by the door!" In another lovely room called Nocturne, "Moonlight pours through an open window, as rain beats a steady patter on the balcony to the west. The floor is a patchwork of dark-coloured stones, the walls a solid ebon rock, gleaming with a lunar glow. The large bed lies unmade, soft pearl duvets shimmering with a chill draught, making it seem all the more seductive."

Simple objects may be easily created and then placed in a room or carried. Virtual contents of a "tube of lube" may be applied at appropriate moments, and a virtual "loofah" can be useful in a bathing scenario. More experienced participants can program objects to respond to a variety of simple typed commands, even to be remote controlled from other rooms, or to move independently according to a programmer's design. A whip wielded in dominance situations by one participant on another transmits the message, "<name> cracks her whip and you wince in ecstatic pain, begging for more." A feather duster, as one informant explained, was used for spankings in a master-servant role-play. Objects that are carried by a player are readily viewable in their description and may add to the allure of a description. A character carrying a battleaxe and an electric guitar would have a different sort of attraction than a character carrying daisies and granola.

Love gifts in VR usually imitate those proffered IRL, but vary in levels of creative sophistication. Objects such as flowers, bottles of wine, teddy bears, and jewelry are common since they are simple to create and to describe. Objects bearing personal messages (such as cards, books, or lockets) may be slightly more sophisticated and encoded so that only the giver and the bearer can read the inscription. One couple went to great lengths to program sophisticated devices not merely for exchange, but for increased togetherness. A "Magick Ring" presented as a birthday gift functioned as a communication device that allowed the lovers to view each other and remain in touch no matter where they were located on the MOO.

Another erotic enhancement is the capability of participants to undress during VSex foreplay. One mode of "performance" is simply to type out the gradual changes of dress to undress. Alternatively, some partners are more aroused by inquiring what each is wearing IRL, and then stripping the other textually and mentally, and sometimes themselves physically as well. Individuals may also adopt a particular character class "parentage", which provides programmed sets of characteristics and abilities. The most popular character classes are those which provide the ability of the player to be stripped of clothing. One character class allows players to strip themselves (progressively altering the description to depict street clothes, intimate attire, or fully naked conditions) or allows a list of certain characters to strip them, or even all players of a particular gender. Another character class allows the ability to engage in bondage and discipline activities with other players. For example, this permits another player to blindfold a character, preventing him or her from seeing the room description or observing actions made by others present in the room, such that he or she can only "hear" spoken statements.

However, our informants suggest that the use of clothing objects or canned messages for VSex gradually loses its charm. It would seem that as VSex encounters become more "real" and developed, the textual and mental description of each partner's actual setting IRL, including reported dress (and undress), gains increasing importance. Laurel argues, "As an activity becomes less artifactual (like painting or literature) and more ephemeral (like conversation or dancing), sensory immediacy and the prosody of experience gain primacy over structural elegance in the realtime stream of events" (1991b:208).

3. On-line sexual issues

3.1. Examination of gender roles and preferences

Bruckman (1992) highlighted the possibilities MOOs provide for examining one's values and pursuits, as well as their educational value. This potential stands in sharp contrast to Rheingold's (1993:150) depiction of activities in MUD sites as sophomoric. Exploration of one's sexual pursuits and identity is likely to be fulfilling throughout life, and the creative possibilities for this process of discovery are maximized in a role-playing environment such as a MUD.

There are numerous in-house mailing lists on LambdaMOO which, like Listservs on the Internet, provide a forum for anonymous discussion and peer education on the broadest range of topics imaginable. The most popular lists such as *queers, *smut, *bisexuals, and *gender-issues focus on sexual concerns and preferences in cyberspace as well as IRL. In contrast to many of the Listservs, however, the language on MOO-lists is frank and comprehensible. Moreover, even if "flaming" (direct, sometimes gratuitous criticism of another's opinion) is common, the key to such MOO-lists is free and open access to read and to express oneself regardless of gender.

MOOs provide an on-line experiential laboratory for examination of gender roles. "Many women find that gender follows them into the online community, and sets a tone for their public and private interactions there—to such an extent that some women purposefully choose gender-neutral identities, or refrain from expressing their opinions ... a case where the false denial of the body requires the defensive denial of the body in order to communicate. For some women, it is simply not worth the effort. For most men, it is never noticed" (Balsamo 1993:698). Springer notes: "Gender, rather than disappearing, is often emphasized after cybernetic transformation." In contrast to some views that "gender will become obsolete once human minds have been transferred to software, cyberpunk points instead to a future in which gender and sex not only exist but have become magnified" (Springer 1993:727).

An obvious benefit of such discussion, and of eventual personal connections and exchanges, is the possibility of learning about sex, and even mentally experiencing it, without actually practicing it IRL. It is not uncommon for individuals who are sexually active on MOOs to confess to being RL virgins. It is also not uncommon to encounter postings, verbs, or descriptions of a sexual nature that demonstrate the author's profound ignorance of RL sexual practices. "In a time where sexual contact with other humans carries the risk of AIDS, computer sex can pose an attractive alternative" (Springer 1993:717). "One Atlanta-based sex expert goes so far as to say that VR will be a mainstream sex aid by the end of the decade, stimulating yet pathogenically prudent" (Balsamo 1993:694).

In the safety of anonymity, participants have the opportunity for education in a way which does not threaten their sense of personal worth. Springer (1993:715-718) contends: "Computers have seduced some users away from face-to-face romantic interactions altogether", becoming "all-consuming for young men who perpetuate the caricature of the solitary social misfit who prefers to commune with his terminal rather than with actual people, especially with actual women." However, characterizing sexual activities on MUDs as a manifestation of the obsessive sexual fantasies of college-age males not only trivializes it but is sexist and ageist. MOOs offer an environment for exploration of one's sexual pursuits and identity which is intrinsically rewarding throughout various stages of life.

3.2. Increasing awareness and compassion on gender-related issues

Discussions occurring regularly on the in-house MOO mailing lists suggest that the process of consciousness-raising straddles the VR and RL divide. One example, i.e., on-line "virtual rape", arose from the unfortunate Mr. Bungle affair mentioned earlier. One participant noted, "Rarely have I heard that the physical part of rape is what makes it so monstrous. Usually the emotions are the most important part of a rape case, and emotions are definitely real on VR, even if nothing else is." As Dibbell (1993b:42) concludes, "Where before [the virtual rape controversy] I'd found it hard to take virtual rape seriously, I now was finding it difficult to remember how I could ever *not* have taken it seriously." Others questioned passionately the appropriateness of even using the term "rape" to refer to explicit on-line sexual aggression. The focal issue was whether one could employ arguments from "tangible reality" within a virtual, i.e., intangible space. The incident resulted in the development of one of the first formal mediation systems in cyberspace, to which victims of any form of harassment on LambdaMOO now have recourse.

The heated discussions on various online mailing lists and the dynamics of public disputes within MOOs prove that such episodes are taken seriously in virtual communities. Moreover, these discussions offer opportunities for reflection and exchange not often available IRL. Dibbell extends his own process of reflection beyond the aforementioned Mr. Bungle affair: "For whatever else these thoughts tell me, I have come to believe that they announce the final stages of our decades-long passage into the Information Age, a paradigm shift that the classic liberal firewall between word and deed (itself a product of an earlier paradigm shift commonly known as the Enlightenment) is not likely to survive intact" (1993b:42). These words echo Leary's aforementioned assertion of the "undreamed-of changes in the consciousness of people" (1990:230) that experiences through the human-computer interface, including VSex, can precipitate.

3.3. Examination of the mechanics of individual attraction and love

The virtual environment permits one to enjoy numerous personal interactions in a relatively short time span with individuals who are known only by their words and actions. This allows participants a valuable personal exploration of the dynamics of personal attraction and love. The opportunity to transcend the physical and to scrutinize the qualities that attract someone to another can be of enormous personal benefit. One father of a MUD enthusiast said of his son: "He was using his character to explore social interactions, to learn to be funny, charming, direct. He was using the net...to work out his life" (Schwartz 1994:F4).

Many individuals relate that through the use of the virtual environment they have learned to look at people IRL differently (Kerr 1993). As one participant commented, on MOOs "you meet everyone that you pass on the street without speaking to." Dibbell (1993b:42) noted that his experiences on-line had "unsettling effects on the way that [he] looked at the rest of the world." The preconceptions and prejudices based on gender, skin color, body weight, and age that are invariably brought to RL personal encounters may be transcended in the virtual environment, where individuals are evaluated on the basis of their minds and not their bodies. "Concepts of physical beauty are holdovers from 'MEAT' space. On the net, they don't apply. We are all just bits and bytes blowing in the phosphor stream" (Balsamo 1993:696; cf. Nakamura 1995).

While intimate sexual encounters in VR entail the risk of deception and betrayal of trust, this is also true IRL. In VR, however, the screening out of physical distractions by the interface permits the development of what some participants feel are attractions in the purest form, and even love in the truest sense. A conscious choice is made in VR relationships "to stay in cyberspace—where there is no pain, no separation—or to renounce [it] ... and return to the real world, where such love is impossible" (Balsamo 1993:692).

3.4. Freedom of expression issues

Debates revolving around practices of VSex relate directly to larger political questions of access, regulation and censorship (Godwin 1994a, 1994b, 1995a, 1995b, 1995c, 1995d, 1995e). It seems that text-based uses of computer media are often regarded with disdain as social, soft research, as opposed to serious, hard research (to employ the familiar gendered sexual metaphor) (Krol 1992:259). If exploration of sexuality in cyberspace can be so beneficial, one might well ask why MUDding has been trivialized in certain sectors.

Why are there not yet straightforward "sex MUDs" or "matchmaker MUDs"? The French experience of developing *messageries roses,* i.e., sex-chat services, on the national network shows that even when heavily taxed, these services remain extremely popular (89% of French people were against banning them, in a 1989 Harris poll), and the messages transmitted are considered sacrosanct, private communications (Rheingold 1993:233; Stenger 1991:56; Vantses 1991).

The creation and existence of a "sex MUD" would depend, at the very least, on the local site (i.e., computer) from which it were running, on the funding sources for its operation, and on the local political implications that such a purpose might pose to administrators. Rheingold reports, "the combination of the potential for addiction and the drain on local computer system resources led to a ban on MUDding at Amherst University in 1992. The increase in telecommunications traffic was the official reason for the Australian ban on MUDs" (1993:163; Maslen 1993, 1994).

More broadly, the subversive potential of Internet access lies in the public's direct "power to broadcast" (Cook and Lehrer 1993:62). Articles continue to pour forth on the struggle over access to the so-called "Information Superhighway" (DeLoughery 1993; Wilson 1993a, 1993b) and the role that government and private corporations will play in this struggle (Auferheide 1994; Cook and Lehrer 1993; Dibbell 1993a; Erhard 1994). The battle-ground over access will be the courts, as in the case of a University of Texas graduate student who sued the university for barring him from the Internet and the campus network (Wilson 1993c), and the Jake Baker case at the University of Michigan in 1995, dismissed by a federal judge in June of that year (Godwin 1995f). Rheingold (1993:164) points out that in the Australian case, "MUDs were an extremely low priority on the network administration's list of 'acceptable uses' for Internet." Yet the question of blocking access in public institutions is a thorny one, as the Texas and Michigan cases suggest.

MUDs are valuable for understanding the intersection of social interactions and the development of a new technological medium. It is no exaggeration to assert that this form of *global* community and interaction has never existed before in human history. Thus, censorship and administrative limitation, for whatever reason, serve to block public access to capabilities of a new technology without reasonable justification. Such censorship is all the more egregious in an age when educators and officials in all commercial and government sectors decry the limitation of students' knowledge of higher technical skills. MUDs constitute an interactive community spanning the globe. Nevertheless, it would seem that students and educators at certain institutions, in America and abroad, have less access and fewer rights than even hate-mongering groups whose freedom of expression on electronic bulletin boards remains guaranteed.

Clearly, this essay reflects an American perspective on an issue that is global in scope. In terms of VSex, the limitations on access and the dangers of censorship are all too clear in the case of a second-year university student in Great Britain, John_K (pseudonym). John_K reported a startling experience he had while logged onto a MOO in a university computer terminal room: "I was engaged in VSex with a friend of mine, in RL terms it would be at the foreplay stage. I got a request on my screen for a talk window [and accepted it]. I got a bit of a shock. I saw a copy of my screen. Some bastard had grabbed my screen and stored it. I didn't even know that it WAS possible. They'd posted an encoded copy to our sysadmin [who] sent me a message via our internal mail that he wanted to see me.... He just went on about how it was a misuse of University resources, about how it might even be illegal (obscene phone-calls and all that). I tried to say that it had been on a Sunday, when there's almost no net-traffic, but he just said that I was wrong. Anyway, I've had my access cut for a week. If I try to logon, it tells me that I've been banned." John_K described an atmosphere of disapproval and surveillance: "To be frank, MUDding, in any form, is frowned on by the staff. But they say that it's OK outside of office hours, when traffic from the University is low. If the sysadmin sees you MUDing during normal hours, you get a severe telling-off. I don't know who grabbed my screen. It's not the banning that gets me, it was the spying." The justification for such censorship and limitation comes from those who point to VSex as the "only" activity that interests students logging on to MUDs.

However, sexuality is a fundamental part of human growth and interaction, on the Net or off. Stigmatizing MUD activities as dirty and participants as offenders can only have destructive consequences in terms of civil rights to expression and access, driving participation underground without dampening the interest in such potential growth.

4. Conclusions

In this essay, I acknowledge VSex as *a phenomenon of social interaction*, without claiming that it is the only activity or even the most important one occurring on the Net or in the MUDs. While media accounts have portrayed VSex as the Net's most sensational activity (Elmer-Dewitt 1995; Godwin 1995g), it may also be the most personal for participants. It may not be "productive" in the sense that objects of consumption will be made out of such activities, but participants insist that it contributes to individualized learning, development, and exploration. Further, pursuit of VSex activities constitutes a distinct form of personal expression, and until a new civil order is imposed in society, Americans are guaranteed freedom of expression under their constitutional rights. The biggest potential danger to individual exploration of VR in general, and of VSex in particular, comes from outside regulation and has little to do with actions within these sites. On the contrary, one discovers within MOOs an increasing concern for respect, self-regulation, and equitable and creative access to resources, as developments within MOOs toward dispute adjudication and virtual governments attest.

Attention to net security, encryption, and individual identification will remain at the forefront of discussions of CMC. The opening screen upon connecting to LambdaMOO reflects this concern: "LambdaMOO is a new kind of society, where thousands of people voluntarily come together from all over the world. What these people say or do may not always be to your liking; as when visiting any international city, it is wise to be careful who you associate with and what you say.... you must assume responsibility if you permit minors or others to access LambdaMOO through your facilities."

The future of sex in VR? We approach "a world where new technologies are immediately adapted to provide sexual pleasure in even its most extreme forms" (Springer 1993:722). Depending on the sources one reads, this future will tend to be more "real" as technology becomes more sophisticated. Sensationalized descriptions of "teledildonics" (Rheingold 1991:345-352) continue to fill media discussion of VR. As Tierney (1994:18) describes it, "With future virtual-reality technology, [people engaged in computer VSex] could presumably alter their screen appearance. They could project screen images—of Daniel Day-Lewis, say, or Julia Roberts—that would mimic every move and noise they made in their living rooms. Eventually viewers might be able to indulge other senses...[through the use of] 3-D glasses, headphones and lightweight body suits with a mesh of tiny tactile detectors coupled to stimulators." In the MUD environment, experiments are underway to create "multimedia MUDs" (WebMUDs, or WOOs) that would generate visual models and sound to complement, and possibly to supplant, the text-based environment (Curtis and Nichols 1993).

Many eagerly await future technological developments in the human-computer interface. In the meantime, the present textual activity of computer-mediated communication occupies current users. The focal issue that VSex brings forth most clearly is the human potential for growth through personal, intimate exchange. Wherever there are people engaged in private conversations, the possibility exists for flirtation and beyond, particularly in on-line anonymity. Only by shutting down access to Internet sites themselves can VSex be stopped. It is not in the interest of participants nor of regulatory bodies to monitor and attempt to control and censor the enlightening interpersonal interactions carried out daily in cyberspace.

ACKNOWLEDGMENTS

* Charles J. Stivale, Department of Romance Languages and Literatures, Wayne State University, is gratefully acknowledged for substantial contributions to this essay.

NOTES

1. A number of studies have recently developed complementary perspectives on VSex (Barrett and Wallace 1994; Bennahum 1994; Grindstaff and Nideffer 1995; Sagan 1995; Savetz 1993; Smolowe 1995; Van Der Leun 1995).

Cyberfeminism

Kira Hall
Rutgers University, Camden

1. Introduction*

In her now classic "A Manifesto for Cyborgs", Donna Haraway ([1985]1990) brings together a number of disparate philosophical responses to the increasing sophistication of technology, and identifies a new feminism. Arguing that the blurring of the boundaries between human and machine will eventually make the categories of female and male obsolete, she contemplates the "utopian dream for the hope of a monstrous world without gender" (610). Her futuristic vision, inspired in part by the gender-free utopias of feminist science fiction,[1] is an extension of the postmodern interest in challenging essentialist and dualistic understandings of gender. With her concluding pronunciation "I would rather be a cyborg than a goddess", Haraway urges feminists to give up their gender-emphasizing icons in favor of gender-neutralizing ones. "This is a dream not of a common language," she explains, "but of a powerful infidel heteroglossia" (610).

Haraway's dream of heteroglossia is born from the theoretical tenets of postmodernism, which Jacquelyn Zita (1992) claims "make[s] possible the transmutation of male to female as a matter of shifting contextual locations that 'reinvent' the body" (110). The most recent realization of this emphasis in American academia has been the development of queer theory (e.g., Butler 1993; Sedgewick 1993). Although the field is rapidly changing and expanding, proponents generally argue that since it is an unyielding, dichotomous notion of gender that has rendered people of alternative sexual persuasions invisible, a cultural conceptualization of variability is necessary before visibility can occur. It is no coincidence that many queer organizations and social groups have embraced the computer as a cultural icon, theorizing it as a utopian medium which neutralizes physical distinctions of gender, race, and sexual orientation.[2] Less often addressed, however, are the ways in which these utopian theories correspond to the reality of gender in cyberspace.

In this essay, I attempt to reconcile two conflicting feminist responses to computer-mediated communication in the early 1990's. Since both responses reflect the intersection of computer technology with subversive feminist counterculture, I refer to them collectively as *cyberfeminism.*[3] The first, influenced by postmodern discussions on gender fluidity by feminist and queer theorists, imagines the computer as a liberating utopia that does not recognize the social dichotomies of male/female and heterosexual/homosexual. Because of its similarity to what is often referred to as "liberal feminism" in the non-virtual world, I identify this perspective as *liberal cyberfeminism*. The opposing perspective, grounded in a reality of male-initiated harassment on the Internet, has resulted in the separatist development of numerous lists and bulletin board systems which self-identify as "women only". Although this on-line *radical cyberfeminism* has developed alongside the utopian predictions of liberal cyberfeminism, their mutual incompatibility reflects the often irreconcilable differences between theory-based and practice-based feminisms in the non-virtual world. It is doubtful that Haraway envisioned either of these feminist developments when she wrote her cyborg manifesto, yet both serve as logical extensions of their real-world counterparts.

My essay focuses on the discursive styles that characterize each of these feminisms, revealing the complexities of what might be referred to as bodyless pragmatics. While it may seem that body-free interaction would foster the kind of gender neutrality proposed by liberal cyberfeminists, in fact it brings about radical creations of gender which exaggerate cultural conceptions of femininity and masculinity. In support of this claim, I compare the theoretical position taken by the women editors of the cyberporn magazine *Future Sex* with the actual computer-mediated interaction of women participants on a separatist discussion list called SAPPHO. Participants on SAPPHO, which is sometimes frequented by as many as 400 subscribers, collaboratively construct a female-gendered discourse in opposition to the textual and sexual harassment found elsewhere on the net. Gender is not erased in the virtual world as the editors of *Future Sex* would claim, but intensified discursively. The gendered exchange that results is often so unsettling for its female participants that increasing numbers of self-proclaimed cyborgs are unsubscribing from the heteroglossia in search of a common *cyborgess* language.

2. Liberal cyberfeminism

The magazine *Future Sex* is one of the more extreme contributions to liberal cyberfeminism. It embraces the tenets of Haraway's cyborg feminism in order to advance *sexual liberation theory*—a political ideology which developed out of the feminist debates on sexuality in the 1980's, and which continues to influence today's feminist politics. Proponents of the theory argue that women's sexual liberation is necessary before gender equality can occur, and oppose the claim of radical feminists that pornography is inherently harmful to women and should be made illegal.[4] The unyielding antagonism between these two views is said to have divided American feminism into the misleadingly labeled camps of "anti-pornography" radicalism and "pro-sex" liberalism, a split represented in the 1990's by anti-porn activist Catherine MacKinnon on one side and pro-porn activist Suzy Bright on the other.[5]

A number of women self-identifying with the latter branch of feminists—feminists who place primary importance on freedom of expression—have now embraced cyberculture as a new frontier of sexual activism and rebellion. Their most recent efforts have culminated in a successful infiltration of what is often referred to as the *cybermag scene*, a male-dominated pro-computer subculture which is characterized by slick, high-tech magazines like *Mondo 2000* and *Wired.* Framing their enterprise within a discourse of sexual liberation, the feminist-identified editor Lisa Palac and her supporters produced a magazine that the editors of these male-oriented magazines would have never dared to publish: its name *Future Sex*, its subject cyberporn, its goal virtual utopia.

The creators of *Future Sex*, together with other women uncomfortable with the similarities between Jesse Helms's and Catherine MacKinnon's anti-pornography activism, are developing a feminist discourse strikingly different from those that have preceded it—a discourse that, by denying the social existence of gender and sexual hierarchies, assumes a futuristic equality. In the magazine's 1992 premiere issue, Palac welcomes her readers to "the sexual evolution" and invites them to "explore the guilt-free zone of erotic infinity". The essay, entitled "Crystal Ball Persuasion", frames a photograph of the red-lipped editor holding the earth in her hand as a crystal ball. It is only electronic erotica, Palac suggests, that will "promote the evolution of sexual intelligence", allowing women and men to come together in a virtual world where gender identities and sexual persuasions are crystal ball fantasies instead of physically grounded categories. The magazine instigates this evolution through visual and verbal challenges to constructions of race, gender, and sexual orientation, among them transsexuality, interracial coupling, cross-dressing, role-playing, bisexuality, butch/femme, and sado-masochism.

The notion that futuristic technology will free its users from the limitations of the physical world, thereby allowing for a more democratic society, has been bandied about for decades, long before Haraway wrote her cyborg manifesto. When the growing sophistication of computer technology in the early 1980's added new fuel to the claim, fiction writers began to theorize on the instability of the physical body, and, subsequently, on the inappropriateness of physical categorizations. Central to the science fiction of those associated with the 1980's *cyberpunk movement*,[6] for instance, is what Bruce Sterling (1986:xiii) calls "the theme of body invasion". Paralleling Haraway, cyberpunk writers imagine an electronically-mediated world where the mental is no longer limited by the physical. When Sterling argues that "the technological revolution reshaping our society is based not in hierarchy but in decentralization, not in rigidity but in fluidity" (1986:xii), he imagines a utopia that will free its inhabitants from the rigid nature of physically based hierarchies.[7]

The extension of this utopian notion to sexuality is a more recent development, influenced by the growing affinity between liberal feminism, postmodernism, and queer theory. In Arthur and Marilouise Kroker's collection *The Last Sex: Feminism and Outlaw Bodies*, theorists from all three groups offer diverse perspectives on what the Krokers call the "virtual sex"—a third sex (non)identity which personifies the intersection of virtual reality with postmodern thought. Asserting that electronic communication will encourage the evolution of "intersex states", the editors argue that body-free interaction will liberate participants from the binary oppositions of female/male and homosexual/heterosexual:

> Neither male (physically) nor female (genetically) nor their simple reversal, but something else: a virtual sex floating in an elliptical orbit around the planet of gender that it has left behind, finally free of the powerful gravitational pull of the binary signs of the male/female antinomies in the crowded earth scene of gender. A virtual sex that is not limited to gays and lesbians but which is open to members of the heterosexual club as well and one that privileges sexual reconciliation rather than sexual victimization. (Kroker & Kroker 1993:18)

For the Krokers, as well as for the editors of *Future Sex*, the absence of the physical invites infinite sexual possibilities—possibilites which will "reconcile" the two sexes "rather than victimize". Like the cyberpunks before him, Arthur Kroker (1993) inundates his experimental text *Spasm: Virtual Reality, Android Music, Electric Flesh* with discursive images of physical disintegration and confusion;[8] chapter headings include "Organs Without Bodies", "Floating Tongue", "Severed Heads", "Transistorized Face", "Nose Spasms", "The Transsexual Voice", "Liquid Self", "Displaced Ear", and even "The Eye Has a Penis". With these severed and disjointed images, Kroker suggests that virtual interactants will be able to achieve conversational utopia only when they are freed from the physical aspects of speech production—e.g., the tongue, face, nose, voice, and ear.

The idea that computer-mediated communication is bringing about a new "in-between" gender awareness has also influenced the fiction of Kate Bornstein, a transsexual playwright and performer from San Francisco who considers herself to have a "fluid identity" rather than a male or female one (see Bornstein 1994). Her most recent play *Virtual Love*, which opened in New York City and San Francisco in 1994, focuses on a futuristic virtual reality game. By creating seven differently oriented selves through the aid of the computer, the main character, a male-to-female transsexual lesbian, attempts to come to terms with the fact that her female lover has suddenly decided to become a female-to-male transsexual heterosexual. In a similar vein, the third issue of *Future Sex* carries a feature story on a post-operative transsexual named Max, entitled "From Dyke to Dude: How Does a Gay Girl Transform Herself into a Straight Boy?" Max, who used to be a feminist lesbian but now identifies as a straight man, is nothing short of a liberal cyberfeminist success story. With the help of modern technology, Max was able to evolve beyond the limiting categorization "lesbian feminist" and appropriate a more powerful and all-encompassing position in society. "I lost the queer subculture," Max exclaims at the end of the interview. "But, god, I've got the whole world!"

The logical extension of this sort of optimism is a de-emphasis on gender oppression, a stance recently articulated by Trudy Barber, a London-based virtual reality artist and active member of the Feminist Anti-Censorship Taskforce. Barber criticized the British government for its failure to support virtual sex technology by arguing that the feminist emphasis on oppression is not only old-fashioned, but irrelevant. "I like sex. I like men. I like women," she proclaimed. "I don't care about what language you use. I don't think I'm being oppressed by any male. I think that people should try and explore their sexualities, and virtual reality is one of those tools which they can use."[9] A similar reasoning is perhaps behind the growing popularity of the identification "humanist, not feminist; queer, not lesbian", an e-mail signature sported by a number of female Internet surfers. By negating the two categorizations which entail gender ("not" feminist, "not" lesbian) and replacing them with non-gendered terms denoting unity and sexual plurality ("humanist", "queer"), e-mail correspondents assert that gender is irrelevant to self-identification. Liberal cyberfeminism, in short, is identified by an insistence on equality rather than oppression, plurality rather than binarism, fluidity rather than categorization, unity rather than separatism—a vision inspired by the increasing sophistication of technology and the advent of body-free communication.

2.1. Liberal cyberfeminism on the Internet

Liberal cyberfeminism has not been the exclusive property of cybertheorists and feminist pro-porn activists; its tenets have also been embraced by a number of participants in actual computer-mediated interaction. The on-line practice of this theoretical position is evidenced by the growing number of women who dabble in *cross-expressing*, a term I used in an earlier article on the conversational styles of telephone sex workers (Hall 1995) to refer to the practice of "verbal" gender-shifting. Cross-expressers exploit the potentially anonymous nature of the technology in order to perform other personas. Since the success of their encounters is dependent on their ability to "pass" textually, they must learn to appropriate discursive fields which are normally foreign to them.

When I posted a query to several women's lists with the subject heading "cross-expressing", I received over thirty enthusiastic responses from self-identified gender-shifters. One woman, whose posting is reproduced below, explains that she frequently shifts personas electronically in order to test her own limits—appropriating categories which, for obvious physical reasons, are inaccessible to her in the non-virtual world:[10]

(1) Heh heh heh heh heh!!!...
Yeah, I've done cross-expressing, a couple of different ways. I used to play on a couple of MUDs (Multi-User Dungeon), which is basically interactive, on-line dungeons&dragons (more or less). I've played a couple of different male characters, a bi woman (i'm lesbian), and also an asexual seal named Selkie (well, she wasn't exactly asexual, but she flirted with women and loved to be stroked.) Yes, sex was included some of the time -- I was in an LDR [=long distance relationship] with a woman in San Diego, and she had a female character that took my male character as a consort, so we could get away with getting "caught" having sex on-line without her blowing her cover of being straight. ::grin::

Well, near as I can tell, there are plenty of identities I would shift to. In my D&D days, I played a prudish virgin (str8 [=straight]), a bi woman, men of different characters (one was truly evil -- boy, THAT was a stretch for me!). I had one femme character on-line, but she was a great deal like I would be if I were in that universe (another medieval MUD), so it wasn't nearly as much role-play as just being myself.

I'm not entirely certain that I *have* any limitations, truth be told. I'm still exploring my boundaries...I think I want to look into my submissive side next...I tend to get a bit dominating in bed...

The anonymous nature of the medium, as this MUD-user goes on to state, has enabled her to change not only her gender (female to male), but also her sexual persuasion (lesbian to bisexual to asexual), her in-group orientation (butch to femme), her sexual behavior (dominant to submissive), and even, albeit fantastically, her animacy (woman to seal).

Intrigued by these gender-shifting possibilities, a number of feminist artists have turned to computer-mediated communication as a new form of artistic expression.[11] Helen Cadwallader, a freelance curator in England, is currently producing an exhibition of computer-inspired aesthetics entitled "Simulated Identities". One of the pieces in the exhibition, jointly produced by artists Pat Naldi and Wendy Kerkup, is a collection of on-line conversations created through the Citizen Band simulation option of Compuserve. Under the pseudonym *SIS*, the artists engage in experimental conversation with participants on Compuserve's *alternative lifestyles* and *alternative genders* chat lines, recording their dialogue in an exploration of gender identity and sexuality. According to Cadwallader, it is the ephemeral nature of computer-mediated communication—or more specifically, "the absence of the material body"—which allows these participants to construct what she calls a "multiply locatable" identity. No longer restricted by physical limitations or categorizations, users can cross-express into other identities successfully, or in Cadwallader's words, they can "enter into and explore a constantly shifting, almost fictional world of assumed identities".[12]

These assumed identities, for many cross-expressers, include those of sexual orientation as well as gender. A number of women who responded to my query, both heterosexual and lesbian, reported that they had cross-expressed as gay men, appropriating what they referred to as a "gay conversational style". One of them offered the following electronic example of conventions she might use in her "gay mail" persona:

(2) I guess with e-mail we are what we write and I could *easily* impersonate a gay mail. "Hi hon. How are you today? I saw so-and-so and sister did he look *bad*. A *serious* fasion no-no. Throw *that* boy back to the straights..." etc.

The subject matter of her impersonation, with its emphasis on "so-and-so's" fashion sense, is a recognizable stereotype of gay male conversation; moreover, her insulting remarks recall an in-group verbal behavior identified as *dishing* by members of the gay community.[13] Not only does the author employ a number of address terms and vocabulary items associated with gay conversation (e.g. "hon", "sister", "fashion no-no", "the straights"), she decorates the adjectives, adverbs, and demonstratives that modify them with double astericks for added emphasis (e.g., *easily*, *bad*, *serious*, *that*)—perhaps to suggest the greater pitch variation and flamboyancy stereotypically associated with the speech of gay men.[14] A second cross-expresser identified these exaggerations as flaming "in the original sense of the word", drawing a contrast between the emasculated meaning of "flaming" in the non-virtual world (where it is used to refer to extremely effeminate men) and the hypermasculine meaning of "flaming" in cyberspace. "In the real world," she explained, "a 'flamer' is a man who talks like a girl; in the electronic world a 'flamer' is a man who talks like an asshole."

2.2. *Cybermasculinity meets liberal cyberfeminism*

The physical anonymity that fosters attempts at cross-expressing, however, also encourages a certain on-line hostility. Researchers have studied the expression of "affect" in computer-mediated communication for some time, with Kiesler, Zubrow, Moses, and Geller (1985) claiming nearly a decade ago that electronic mail has a more emotional structure than other types of written discourse. Indeed, Niko Besnier (1990) finds the stylistics of on-line affect so compelling that he includes a discussion of it in his review of research on "language and affect" for the *Annual Review of American Anthropology*. Pointing to the development of electronic discourse as "an interesting case of emergent tensions among affect displays, their folk accounts, and normative control" (433),

Besnier explains that while folk models account for the frequent occurrence of emoticons and flames on public electronic forums as "a natural adaptation to the technological characteristics of the medium", normative discourse "targets them as disruptive of academic social order" (433).

What Besnier does not say, however, is that the employment of these verbal features, whether discussed as adaptive or disruptive, differs markedly across gender lines. Recent linguistic studies of computer-mediated discourse have illustrated, both statistically and pragmatically, that women and men have different ways of displaying affect electronically. Male interactants have not only been shown to dominate mixed-sex electronic conversation, they have also been identified as frequent instigators of on-line sexual harassment—observations difficult to reconcile with the liberal cyberfeminist notion of a gender-neutral utopia. What might be viewed as "disruptive of the academic social order" by male participants is being perceived by an increasing number of female participants as gender-based verbal abuse.

2.2.1. *Conversational dominance*

The majority of linguistic studies on gender differentiation in computer-mediated communication have paralleled the results of early feminist studies on face-to-face conversation in mixed-sex groups. Linguists Susan Herring (1993a; Herring, Johnson and DiBenedetto 1992, 1995) and Laurel Sutton (1994) both found that male participants, even when in cyberspaces overtly formed for the discussion of feminism, silence their female conversational partners by employing electronic versions of the same techniques they have been shown to employ in everyday face-to-face interaction (Lakoff 1975; Edelsky 1981; Fishman 1983)—ignoring the topics which women introduce, producing conversational floors based on hierarchy instead of collaboration, dismissing women's responses as irrelevant, and contributing a much higher percentage of the total number of postings and text produced. Similar gender differences have been noted by CMC researchers in a variety of disciplines, among them Selfe and Meyer (1991), Taylor, Kramarae, and Ebben (1993), Turkle and Papert (1990), and We (1994).

2.2.2. *Textual harassment*

While the linguistic evidence for on-line conversational dominance is impressive, still more research is needed on the qualitative differences between women's and men's electronic contributions—differences realized in choice of imagery, lexical items, and metaphor. The linguistic observation that men "talk more" in mixed-sex electronic discussions, or that men regularly ignore women's topics in favor of their own discursive threads, does not account for the misogynist nature of many of the flames posted to public lists, nor does it explain ongoing reports of aggressive sexual harassment over private e-mail and bulletin board systems. The masculine discursive style witnessed on the Internet is a kind of verbal violence that only rarely occurs between strangers in the non-virtual world, where its employment in casual interaction would be perceived as the exception and not the rule.

Indeed, the incident of sexual harassment on Multi-User Dimensions (or MUDs) has occurred often enough to have acquired the electronic designation "MUD-rape". Julian Dibbell (1993) exposes an extreme case of such harassment in his discussion of a disturbing interaction on the LambdaMOO, where a character sporting the pseudonym "Mr. Bungle" exploited the tools of the medium in order to slander women interactants and force them to perform sexual acts.[15] Using the "voodoodoll", a program which allows users to attribute actions to other characters without their permission, Mr. Bungle created a series of violent textual images: "As if against her will, Starsinger jabs a steak knife up her ass, causing immense joy. You hear Mr. Bungle laughing evilly in the distance"; "KISS ME UNDER THIS, BITCH" [a belt buckle inscription]. Electronic interactants like Mr. Bungle have become so common, both on multi-user dimensions and on personal e-mail, that the *National Law Journal* (Weidlich 1994) and the *New York Times* (Lewis 1994) recently came out with articles on electronic "stalking", reporting in particular on the legal aspects of an e-mail stalking case, via America Online, in Michigan. Similar instances of sexual harassment have been reported by participants on a variety of interactive databases, among them Prodigy, Compuserve, and the Well.[16] The computer lab at the University of Illinois' College of Engineering went so far as to issue a sexual harassment policy for its computer users, after the university's Center for Advanced Study found that a significant number of women had been victimized by sexist jokes, obscene limericks, and unsolicited pornographic pictures.[17]

2.2.3. Heterosexism

An important sub-genre of cybermasculinity is what might be called *heterosexism*, a prejudice realized on the Internet through the proliferation of "anti-homosexual" discursive threads. Frequently instigated by male participants in mixed-sex interaction as a means of sexualizing the discourse, homophobic hate-mail on public forums has escalated dramatically during the past two years. One of its realizations, promoted by anti-homosexual agitator Ben Phelps, is an ongoing invasion of lesbian and gay discussion lists. For example, shortly after the lesbian and gay celebration of the 25th anniversary of Stonewall in New York City, a string of hate messages such as the following were sent to the QSTUDY-L ('queer studies') list:

(3) So, did you filthy sodomites see us picketing at your parade? Just in case anyone is wondering, I was the one holding the "SHAME" part of the "FAG SHAME" signs. The other side of mine said "2 GAY RIGHTS: AIDS AND HELL." A few other of my personal favorite signs said "GOD HATES FAGS", "FAG GOD = RECTUM," and "FEAR GOD NOT FAGS." It is interesting how you lying, filthy, vile murderers pretend to ignore us, but we always seem to become the center of your fag parades. I like all the attention we get.

GOD HATES FAGS.

Other examples of homophobic commentary are readily available in the personal profiles of *America Online*, where over fifty subscribers during the spring of 1993 mentioned "gay bashing" as a favorite pasttime. Hiding behind pseudonyms like "Hetro", "Pyro Slug", "SpeedKiller", and "NeoNazi1", *AOL* subscribers identified themselves as having "hobbies" such as: "Fag bashing, being an asshole"; "Burning things, killing innocent animals, and gay bashing"; "It's not how many fags you bash, its how hard you bash them"; "Gay bashing, offending feminists, defacing environmentalists"; "Gassing jews, blacks, spicks, fags, etc."; "Killing, torturing fags, murdering and raping women". These examples bind together homophobia, misogyny, and racism—a connection which merits further research.

2.2.4. Physical hierarchies and the "talking penis"

In the shelter of physical anonymity, a significant number of male users have adopted this new discursive medium as an electronic "carnival" in the Bakhtinian sense (Bakhtin 1968), viewing it as a kind of institutionalized outlet for violence and vulgarity. Masked behind a medium that is exclusively textual, interactants find themselves freed not only from the politeness expectations of face-to-face interaction, but also from the more identifying physical characteristics of vocality. According to cybertheorist Mark Dery (1994), this separation of word from body serves to promote the acceleration of electronic hostility: "The wraithlike nature of electronic communication—the flesh become word, the sender reincarnated as letters floating on a terminal screen—accelerates the escalation of hostilities when tempers flare; disembodied, sometimes pseudonymous combatants tend to feel that they can hurl insults with impunity" (559). In keeping with Dery's claim, male conversants in public forums may fail to take responsibility for the words they create, drawing a distinction between computer-mediated communication and face-to-face communication. Mr. Bungle's demand for impunity with respect to his MUD-rape because it was not "real life existence" (Dibbell 1993) is typical in this regard. "I engaged in a bit of a psychological device that is called thought-polarization," Mr. Bungle explained to his MOO community; "The fact that this is not RL [=real life] simply added to heighten the effect of the device. It was purely a sequence of events with no consequence on my RL existence."

Dery's interest in the disembodied nature of on-line discourse is shared by a number of male cyberphilosophers, who frequently wax poetic on the physical disintegration of self. In their discussions, the electronic loss of the physical self ultimately leads to a violent and sexualized verbal compensation. Kroker (1993), when theorizing "the tongue in virtual reality", identifies this compensation overtly when he calls it "the talking penis":

What is the fate of the tongue in virtual reality? No longer the old sentient tongue trapped in the mouth's cavity, but now an improved digital tongue. A nomadic tongue that suddenly exits the dark cavity of oral secretions, to finally make its appearance in the daylight [...] The tongue might begin by curling back in the mouth with all the accompanying nasal sounds, but then it migrates out of the mouth, travelling down the chest, out of the toes, and even taking libidinal root in the talking penis. Not a surrealistic penis where objects lose their originary sign-referent, and float in an endless sign-slide, but a tongue referent that has actually lost its sound object. (23)

It is illuminating to compare Kroker's statement with an actual cyberspace posting which appeared in the feminist newsgroup *alt.feminism* studied by Sutton (1994), in which the author countered another subscriber's opinion through the creation of a rape scenario. The electronic discussion, a portion of which is reproduced below, concerns the controversial subject of gay men in the military. When a woman participant takes the more liberal position in the debate, she is met with a retort that, I would argue, is uniquely cybermasculine:

(4) >What disharmony will they cause? The people that are worried that a
>member of the same sex will be looking at them in the shower or
>coming on to them in the barracks should stop flattering themselves
>and start thinking about what their jobs really entail.

Really "entail"! Quite a punny lady aren't you. Of course I would consider true social justice to be when you get assaulted by a bulldyke named Bertha. Twice as big as you, she laughs as you suddenly realize how aggressive female homosexuals can be if they think they have an easy lay like a white liberal. Especially when the liberal no longer recognizes right from wrong or the implications of having to live in the amoral world she has tacitly created.

With this response, the male participant subordinates his conversational partner through the verbal creation of a sexual assault, projecting his own aggression onto what he names "a bulldyke named Bertha". He sets the scene by subverting and sexualizing her own use of the word "entail", thereby reducing her comments to a mere homophobic pun. Moreover, perhaps to compensate for his own physical anonymity, the speaker constructs hierarchies of size and race, creating a Bertha who is "twice as big" as her "white liberal" opponent.[18] Bodyless communication, then, for many men at least, is characterized not by a genderless exchange, but rather by an exaggeration of cultural conceptions of masculinity—one realized through the textual construction of conversational dominance, sexual harassment, heterosexism, and physical hierarchies.

3. Radical cyberfeminism

In response to this cybermasculinity, increasing numbers of women have organized their own lists and bulletin board systems, creating women-only spaces where participants can collaboratively construct an oppositional gender. One of the largest such spaces is SAPPHO, a women-only list dedicated primarily to the discussion of lesbian and bisexual issues. This electronic discussion group, according to a recent survey conducted by one of its subscribers,[19] is made up of women associated with three major professional groups: university students and professors (27%); women working in computer-related fields (22%); and women employed by universities in non-academic positions (21%). The e-mail postings reproduced in this portion of the study are drawn from exchanges which occurred on SAPPHO between January and June 1993.

It is important to mention at the outset that the aggressive stylistics which characterize cybermasculinity have also been reported on a number of gay lists. Many of the women on SAPPHO complained that they had received hostile and insulting messages from men on GAYNET and QSTUDY-L—messages that occurred with such regularity that the women were ultimately compelled to unsubscribe. In the posting reproduced below, a lesbian-identified subscriber to SAPPHO points out the need for separatist cyberspaces, or in her own vocabulary, a net where women can go to avoid "gwm [=gay white male] cybermogs" who "egofill on flaming to an fro":

(5) SOME gwm cybermogs egofill on flaming to an fro on gaynet. I've lurked around gaynet for a time and many of the participants speak a queer language i don't EVEN want to interact with-let alone read. My subscription didn't last long ... due to the moderately high level of toxic banterings filling my mailbox.

I prefer to dedicate my lurking and scripting time to a net where those who subscribe know how to respect other netter's opinions and not do ad hominims, which take up bandwidths. I am grateful for having the option of SAPPHO. I want SAPPHO to maintain its lesbi [=lesbian and bisexual] only protocol.

In contrast to the "toxic bantering" identified by this contributor as characteristic of gay male lists, the discursive environment which characterizes SAPPHO could be described as aggressively collaborative, as women participants, most of them lesbian or bisexual, jointly create a way of cyberspeaking that opposes the type of talk encountered elsewhere on the Internet.

Although it would seem that maintaining a "women-only" status on an anonymous e-mail list would be a difficult, if not an impossible undertaking, subscribers to SAPPHO have devised a number of methods for determining the gender of new participants. Essential to what might be called the *on-line screening process* is the new subscriber's ability to meet the list's discursive standards, with list veterans becoming quickly suspicious of anyone who does not conform to their idea of discursive femininity. The elements which constitute this collaborative women-only cyberspeak are numerous and complex; taken together, they impose a female/male dichotomy instead of obscuring it. Among the elements discussed below are an expectation of name conformity, an aggressive "anti-flaming" policy, a demand for conversational support and respect, a "politically correct" politeness strategy rarely found elsewhere on the net, repeated discussion of overtly "female" topics, a pro-separatist and pro-woman attitude, and the employment of feminist signatures.

3.1. Name conformity

The screening process begins with an examination of the subscriber's name. In spite of the potentially superficial nature of electronic pseudonyms, participants are expected to bear a feminine-sounding e-mail title. The importance of name conformity is spelled out by the author of the response in excerpt (6) below, who answers the doubt expressed by two newcomers with a succinct explanation of how the on-line test works:

(6) >In this virtual world how do we determine the gender of another? [...]
>Unless you can physically see the person, then women-only space on
>the internet is a farce and impossible.

>But now I'm confused by the "women only". Have you had this
>discussion before and are all bored with it? What is the collective
>definition that is being used to allow access to SAPPHO? Do you use
>self-definition?

As I recall, we use the old McCarthyist definition: If it looks like a duck, and it quacks like a duck, well then its a duck. (Looks on e-mail result in things like questions about atypical names.)

While most of the subscribers to the list carry overtly female names, a few members have what this veteran calls "atypical names", or rather, ambiguously gendered names like "Lou" or "ibu6tys"—hence the veteran's statement, "If it looks like a duck, and it quacks like a duck, well then it's a duck." New subscribers who "look" like ducks (i.e., who carry more masculine-sounding names) require greater scrutiny, and the on-line veterans watch to see if any "quacks" will betray maleness. One woman subscriber sporting the name "James", for example, ultimately had to justify her name choice in a public posting after receiving a flood of questioning messages through private e-mail. "I'm a female who has a traditionally male first name," she explained. "I am quite definitely female, at least that's what they told me when they handed me those books on the 'birds, bees, and puberty' [...] I chose 'james' because I _like_ the name! It's cool, and men shouldn't have a monopoly on it."

3.2. Anti-flaming policy

Even if a participant joins the list bearing an overtly feminine name, she is still expected to conform to the list's idea of discursive femininity. Essential to this femininity is the avoidance of any verbal behavior which could be perceived as adversarial. Although electronic insults certainly appear now and then, particularly around the discussion of political issues, the majority of SAPPHO participants adamantly oppose the practice of flaming. In excerpt (7), for instance, a list member, disturbed by an aggressive exchange on the list between two participants, criticizes their behavior with ironic reference to the John Wayne Bobbitt affair.

(7) It appears we should prepare ourselves for another bonfire in sappho. I'm donning my asbestos suit, gloves, boots and helmet and am taking refuge underground. Let me know when the flames die down a little. Me and John Wayne Bobbitt will bring the hotdogs - I'll carve! Oh, and S'mores [20] would be good too!

-L., who now knows how Campfire girls got started.

For this subscriber, aggressive flaming is equivalent to an undesirable Bobbitt-like masculinity, and as such, should not occur in women-only space. The visual image she constructs of John Wayne Bobbitt, the hotdogs, and the carving knife, certainly offers a different interpretation of Kroker's "penis talk"—one that is unabashedly cyberfeminist. In a similar vein, another participant reprimands a fellow subscriber for overreacting to a posting on the virtues of internet spying:

(8) Hey! Lighten up on E.! Her post was primarily about the "finger" command, which makes one feel like somewhat of a spy, but certainly does not constitute breaking into private files. I thought it was humorous, and think the heat from the current flame wars is getting to some people's brains. Abusive responses like telling E. to "eat shit" are unacceptable, no matter how strong one's opinion.

Although this author's posting is much more direct than the previous one, her intent is the same: verbal abuse is simply not acceptable on a women-only list.

A different realization of the same anti-flame mentality is illustrated in the posting reproduced in (9), in which a veteran subscriber criticizes a new participant for her violent discursive behavior. The messages in question were sent privately to one of the older sapphites, who had in a public posting expressed the need for a "committed, monogamous, loving relationship with a woman", even though she was currently in a relationship with a man. "I'm available," the new subscriber said. "But I might as well warn you that I intend to kill the next bitch that leaves me. I should have killed the last one who, like you, left me for a man." The highly aggressive nature of this and other responses, which the recipient subsequently posted to SAPPHO, shocked the other members of the group and provoked a thread entitled "Despair".

(9) When I see such despair, hatred and anger as is reflected in the note below I get scared. This is the pivotal point, women... are we going to follow the poor example of the white male patriarchal system... or are we going to set our own example?! Such self-centeredness and poor sense of self that is the cause of the posts that K. shared is going to be our challenge. We must hold on to our identity and improve and apply our values and world views. Do you think this is possible? What can we do to support this kind of focus and introspection in others? It is so disturbing to hear a woman "talk like a man". I was amazed that the posters who responded to K. were women. That is not a high-and-mighty judgementalism ... but a real and deep concern.

I am scared by the world and alot of what is in it... and when I see those specters reflected in the eyes of my sisters... I AM TERRIFIED!

This response, influenced by the reality of a male-dominated cyberspace, is indicative of the commitedly collaborative techniques in cyberfeminist practice. The author's perspective is notably different from the liberal interpretation of computer discourse as gender-free, particularly since she argues that there is gender differentiation in electronic talk and that women participants should not "talk like a man". Like many messages appearing on this women-only list, this participant's response emphasizes that cyberspace *is* a form of reality—an emphasis very different from male claims that on-line interaction is nothing but fantasy. The author suggests that the computer can become a very real tool for battling gender oppression, or, in her own words, a place where women can set their own example in opposition to "the white patriarchal system".

Occasionally, however, the list's demand for discursive conformity will lead to an incorrect gender diagnosis. The author of the posting in (6) above continues her explanation of the on-line screening process by telling the story of a verbally dissonant subscriber who challenged the list's anti-flaming policy:

(10) The funniest version of this I remember was when J. first joined sappho. She upset and offended so many people, there was concern that she was really a man. *Lots* of concern. (This may have been near the first discussion I remember about transexuals on the list.) Anyway, it finally calmed down when someone from So. Cal. posted saying that while they found her offensive too, they had met her and she was a woman.

The member in question, who I have abbreviated as "J." in order to preserve her anonymity, launched participants into a number of angry discussions on whether her aggressive interactional style demonstrated femaleness or maleness. In this particular case, the matter was resolved only when the subscriber was identified in a real-world interaction as a woman. As an interesting reversal of this situation, another subscriber mistook one of her e-mail correspondents to be female, only to find out weeks later that "shade" was male: "There was no overtly 'male' stuff in his notes, in terms of stereotypical gay male phrases, descriptions of behavior, etc. Now, I know not all men (or gay men) or even all those who are gendered male act like assholes. But usually, someone will say something that can be taken in our society as a gender marker."

3.3. Support and respect

Perhaps to avoid the fate of subscribers like J., participants quickly learn the rules of a supportive and respectful cyberfeminist discourse. When the author of the posting in (11) criticizes a contributor's insulting remarks by emphasizing the importance of respect, she pinpoints the list's first and foremost rule of netiquette, a rule usually taught to new subscribers at the appearance of the first wayward message: *Respect your e-neighbor as your self.*

(11) i think the "jargon/cant/gibberish" and "most unintelligible academic rambling of the year" comments were a little out of lin[e], especially since [k.] was making a perfectly valid point about respecting other's spaces. perhaps we not only need to respect each other's spaces [...] but each others ideas and opinions as well."

The author's interest in keeping the list a safe space for its participants is rather different from the male 'if you can't take the e-mail heat, unsubscribe' perspective which often appears on mixed-sex lists. A male member of the gay list *gl-asb* for instance, recently explained, "NO mailing list is 'safe space'... If an issue is so delicate, so close to one's heart, so much 'the soft underbelly' that a flame would cause you psychic damage, DON'T expect e-mail to give you a safe forum for it." These conflicting approaches to what constitutes appropriate behavior on the net support the results of Herring's (1994) research on gendered attitudes toward netiquette, in which she found that "women and men differ not only in net behavior, but in the values they assign to such behaviors." Sapphites overwhelmingly favor what Herring calls a "politeness-based communicative ethic", showing overt contempt for the "ethic of self-determination and vigorous debate" favored by male participants in her study.

3.4. Political correctness

The list's desire for discursive conformity is so strong that one subscriber satirized it in a public posting of netiquette rules entitled "How to be Politically

Correct on Sappho; or, How to Answer Posts Without Starting Flame Wars." Some of these rules are reproduced in (12) below:

(12) a. Only politically correct language is allowed (wimmin, herstory, etc.)

b. No words that imply racism, sexism, republicanism, or any other ism for that matter will be tolerated.

c. Only people with correct political views will be allowed to post. What are these correct political views? Well if you have to ask, then you don't have them.

d. People from outside of the good ole U.S. of A. are nice to have on the list, but don't talk too much. Your views tend to differ from the right ones, and we'd prefer to not take up valuable bandwidth with propoganda.

e. Sometimes, some new rookie on the list will post something that is unacceptable. If you should happen to agree with it, post to them personally that you agree, but by no means let any other sapphite know you support this radical.

"All of these rules are set in stone," the message concludes, "so please respect them if you wish to maintain your subscription. Any lurkers felt to be unfriendly are subject to be searched by the PC police." The self-imposed conformity that this message satirizes—e.g., the list's expectation of feminist orthography, "correct" political views, and uniform agreement on all topics of conversation—points to an ethic of collaboration even more severe than that discussed by Herring in her articles on computer-mediated ethics and politeness (1994, 1996). The rules which constitute this netiquette are not only *characteristic* of the postings on the list, they are *required* as proof of one's femaleness.

3.5. Separatism and the creation of a cyberculture

Corresponding to this female-gendered netiquette is a separatist attitude that, in the words of one subscriber, "will not tolerate the discussion of anyone's bf [=boyfriend], or any other men for that matter." A transsexual subscriber to SAPPHO, after migrating to another list in disgust, identified this attitude as "the lesbian rhetoric that shoves Goddess overworship and intolerance of men down our throats." But in the message reproduced below, a SAPPHO subscriber outlines the reasons behind this intolerance, pointing to the necessity of separatist cyberspaces:

(13) SO- When women get together to create women's space (or virtual space)...we do it to strengthen ourselves and other women, to learn from and with other women, to share resources with eachother and affirm our experiences, create culture with eachother, etc. Exclusion of men from this context is a precondition...not the purpose itself...of creating women's space. When we ask men to respect women's space, we ask

> them to let it happen WITHOUT making a fuss, WITHOUT trying to convince us that "really I'm very sensitive and aware, not like other men, so you should let ME in", WITHOUT accusing us of being man-haters, and WITHOUT imposing upon us the arrogant posture that they are entitled to be included in everything and allowed access to every part of women's lives. Women's space is simply not FOR men, and a man with a clue about what it means to be respectful will simply say to himself "oh, that's not FOR me...I guess I'll go do something else".

The above post was written in response to a male-initiated anti-separatist thread on GAYNET, where a number of participants condemned SAPPHO for its exclusion of men. When a woman subscriber to GAYNET posted a poem by the Native American poet Chrystos in an effort to explain the need for women-only lists like SAPPHO, she was quickly silenced with the following retort :[21]

(14) It seems to me in my humble opinion,
That La Femme Chrysto, is Satan's minion!
Stirrin up trouble whenever she can,
Against whites, heteros, and sensitive men
Who want to commune with their love and pain,
But who just get kicked out, into the rain.
Pardon me for all my white male confusion?
I thought we were against this kind of exclusion?
Segregation is hate, like it or not,
Even when it's the hate that "hate begot."

Needless to say, the poem was not found amusing by sapphites, who began their own *anti-* anti-separatist thread on SAPPHO. "This is *our* list," one of the participants wrote. "We do not need to justify our existence, nor do we need to apologize for running the list the way we choose. And we are most emphatically not answerable to the aforementioned twerp... harumph!"

The "creation of culture" alluded to by the author of the posting in (13) is accomplished exclusively through textual practice. One of the primary ways that subscribers participate in this creation is through the collaborative development of lengthy threads on women's topics, as well as through the overt discussion of what it means to be female, and more specifically, a sapphite. In the month of February 1993—a typical month for sapphite exchange—major threads of discussion involved femininity ("Learning to be Female", "Women in Non-traditional Careers", "Butch vs. Bitch"), feminine appearance ("Fat Oppression", "Long Hair", "Getting Dressed"), lesbianism ("Lesbian Sex", "Class A Lesbian", "Lesbians on Emergency 911"), gender-bending women in the news ("Lily Tomlin", "Nancy Kerrigan is Gay", "K.D. Lang Video", "Roseanne's Kiss", "Truth Behind Bobbitt Case"), and patriarchy ("Male Doctors", "Violent Men"). More personal contributions included intimate references to difficult experiences in the non-virtual world ("Rape", "Positive Coming Out Experience", "One Woman's Longing") and affirming experiences on SAPPHO ("I Wuv Sappho", "Family"). "I LOVE SAPPHO," one enthusiastic subscriber exclaims;

(15) I think this is a most unique, peaceful, joyful and beautiful place. Every day, all of us women gather together and discuss *whatever*, we share our thoughts, feelings, and days with each other cross country and overseas. The fact that I have this place to talk, share, listen is one of the more joyous and special things in my life... I value all of your opinions (even if I don't agree) and feel the knowlege and perspective I gain through all you lovely women is priceless. I think this group of women is unique, special and *blessed*... I am very fortunate to have met you all!

Also instrumental to the creation of culture is the assertion of a pro-woman attitude; participants frequently set up womanhood in opposition to manhood, exaggerating the qualities stereotypically associated with each gender. The author of the posting reproduced in (16), for instance, is responding to a discussion of gender identity by James, who, perhaps influenced by the utopian imaginings of liberal cyberfeminism, had mentioned that she preferred to adopt a male persona in cyberspace. In stark contrast to the other women on the list, James had explained that she felt more comfortable talking with gay men on the internet than with lesbians, claiming that the men's talk was "more real and interesting".

(16) James, James, James,.... Girl... <sigh> where to begin? [...] Women are more caring, compassionate, holistic, introspective, accepting, beautiful, centered, earth/cycle centered, natural and basically are the pivot of our species (er... IMHO).

If you look at the biological basis of behaviour theories... men were simply created to guard or "serve" the child bearing ones (women!) I see a different plane of conscience, emotionability and pacifism that is absent in many men... no matter how "progressive". For the emotions, the perspective, the beauty, the sensativity, the intelligence, the nurturing, and the UNDERSTANDING of the world... I would never trade my gender... no matter what the cost.

The exaggerated nature of this response (e.g., "women are more caring, compassionate, holistic, introspective, accepting, beautiful, centered, earth/cycle centered, natural, and basically are the pivot of our species") illustrates how some of the list's subscribers, in order to develop a gender for themselves on the Internet, take cultural conceptions of womanhood and femininity to the extreme in their postings.[22]

3.6. Signatures

Finally, participants on SAPPHO create a female gender overtly in their e-mail signatures, which many of them regularly attach to the end of their messages. These signatures are almost always pro-female, representing each subscriber's take on being a woman:

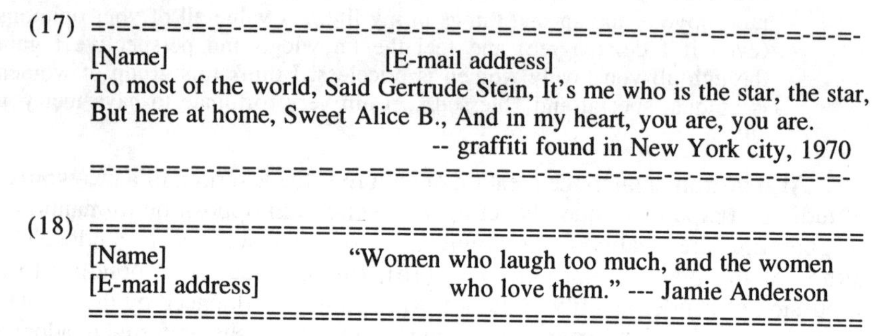

(17) =-

[Name] [E-mail address]
To most of the world, Said Gertrude Stein, It's me who is the star, the star,
But here at home, Sweet Alice B., And in my heart, you are, you are.
-- graffiti found in New York city, 1970

=-

(18) ==

[Name] "Women who laugh too much, and the women
[E-mail address] who love them." --- Jamie Anderson

==

The strategies employed in the signatures reproduced in (17) and (18) are frequently seen on SAPPHO; both authors have taken quotations from other discursive spheres and subverted them for a woman-oriented electronic distribution. The quotation about Gertrude Stein and Alice B. Toklas is taken from graffiti, a medium which is similar to electronic communication in that it serves as an outlet for anonymous and underground forms of resistance (Leap Forthcoming; Moonwoman 1995; Nwoyi 1993)—in this case lesbianism. The quotation in the second signature is a conflation of the titles of two popular psychology books on heterosexual relationships: *Women Who Love Too Much* and *Men Who Hate Women and the Women Who Love Them.* With the subversion "Women who laugh too much and the women who love them", the subscriber projects a lesbianism that is sane and happy, and which thereby opposes the pop psychology image of the tortured heterosexual.

A third signature, although less typical, reveals much about the nature of gendered discourse on-line. There is a small number of male-to-female transsexuals on SAPPHO, some of whom have joined the list as a means of learning more about women's conversational patterns. One of these participants regularly tags the following signature to her messages:

(19) ==

I am Woman, hear me Roa....oh, sorry, was I interrupting.. no no, it
wasn't important... no, really; it's fine. // [Name] <[e-mail address]>

==

Her signature says it all. What more would a man-who-became-a-woman want to do than to assert her newfound womanhood: "I am Woman! Hear me Roar!" Yet in the end she realizes that in order to pass electronically, she has to appropriate the corresponding conversational style and cater to a cultural expectation of discursive femininity: "Oh, sorry, was I interrupting... no, no, it wasn't important... no, really, it's fine."

4. Conclusion

In this article, I have identified two varieties of cyberfeminism—one inspired by the utopian imaginings of Haraway's cyborg feminism, the other by the reality of male harassment on the Internet. Rosi Braidotti, a pioneer in virtual studies, recently made the observation:[23]

> One of the great contradictions of cyber-images is that they titillate the imagination, promising marvels and wonders of a gender-free world or a multi-gender world; and yet, such images not only reproduce some of the most banal, flat images of gender behaviour imaginable, they intensify the differences between the sexes.

The same is true of computer-mediated communication; rather than neutralizing gender, the electronic medium encourages its intensification. In the absence of the physical, network users exaggerate societal notions of femininity and masculinity in an attempt to gender themselves. Gender may well be an unfortunate dichotomy, as postmodern virtual theorists argue, but cyberspace is generating goddesses and ogres, not cyborgs.

ACKNOWLEDGMENTS

* I presented an earlier version of this paper (Hall, 1996) at the 1994 Women and Language Conference, University of California, Berkeley. Many thanks to Anna Livia and Susan Herring for discussing this article with me during its various stages of development. I would also like to thank a number of friends and computer-mediated acquaintances who provided me with invaluable information and references, among them Virginia Barret, Mary Bucholtz, Kate Burns, Margaret Chon, Julian Dibbell, Regis M. Donovan, Chris Hall, Jeanne Hall, Lisa Haskel, Dorsie Hathaway, Deena Hill, James Kythe, Wendy Minkoff, Pamela Morgan, Veronica O'Donovan, Julie Petersen, Sadie Plant, Kate Remlinger, Leslie Shade, Laurel Sutton, Kris Shanks, Eugene Volokh, and Nina Wakeford. Above all, I want to express my gratitude to the members of the women-only list under study, whose sapphic wanderings in cyberspace made this project possible.

NOTES

1. In her manifesto, Haraway explicitly mentions the science fiction of Octavia Butler, Suzy McKee Charnas, Samuel Delaney, Anne McCaffrey, Vonda McIntyre, Joanna Russ, James Tiptree, Jr., and John Varley.

2. In addition to real-world organizations such as the San Francisco-based *Digital Queers*, there are over 150 active lists and bulletin board systems in the U.S.A. devoted to the discussion of queer issues, some of which have as many as 2,000 subscribers. In response to this development, the new electronic quarterly *Queer-e*, an interdisciplinary journal for research in "lesbian, gay, bisexual, transgender, and queer" studies, is devoting one of its special issues to a theoretical exploration of the notion *cyberqueer*. For an overview of lesbian electronic culture and activism, see Haskel's (Forthcoming) article "Cyberdyke".

3. After arriving at the term independently, I noticed that some participants in the 1994 London conference "Seduced and Abandoned: The Body in the Virtual World" spoke of "cyberfeminism" as a derivative of Haraway's "cyborg feminism". Virginia Barret of the VNS Matrix (an electronic art project) in Adelaide, Australia, and Sadie Plant at Birmingham University, England, have been influential in popularizing this use of the term. The VNS Matrix first employed the term in their 1991 billboard manifesto *A Cyberfeminist Manifesto for the 21st Century*. Plant has discussed cyberfeminism from both a philosophical and activist standpoint in a number of short articles (1993a, 1993b), and is currently expanding her ideas in *Beyond the Spectacle* (Forthcoming).

4. In employing the labels "liberal feminism" and "radical feminism", I do not mean to suggest that all politically self-identified liberals are "pro-porn" or that all politically self-identified radical feminists are "anti-porn"; the many different opinions expressed in the works cited in this article speak to the inaccuracy of such a generalization. Many thanks to Margaret Chon for her thoughts on this issue.

5. I have considerably simplified the history and import of this theoretical division; see Bacchi (1990) for an illuminating and thorough portrayal of these two strands. Interesting discussions of sexual liberation theory include Echols's (1983) and Rubin's (1984) early essays, and more recent articles by Butler (1990), Valverde (1989), and Freccero (1990). Discussions of radical feminism (often referred to as "cultural feminism" by its opponents) include Dworkin (1981, 1988), Jeffreys (1990), and MacKinnon (1987, 1993).

6. The *cyberpunk movement* developed in the mid-1980's when a San Francisco-based group of diverse social activists (rumored to have been composed of computer revolutionaries, anarchists, and Deadheads) adopted computer-mediated interaction as a tool of resistance, using it to bring elements of underground counterculture to the fore of technological advance. The movement's more celebrated science fiction writers include William Gibson, Bruce Sterling, and Pat Cadigan. See Sterling (1986) and Springer (1994) for an interesting in-group and out-group analysis, respectively.

7. The characterization of the computer as a democratic medium also figures prominently in the discourses of popular CMC analysts, e.g., Rheingold (1993).

8. Sterling (1986) summarizes the two central themes of the movement in the following manner: "The theme of body invasion: prosthetic limbs, implanted circuitry, cosmetic surgery, genetic alteration. The even more powerful theme of mind invasion: brain-computer interfaces, artificial intelligence, neurochemistry—techniques radically

redefining the nature of humanity, the nature of self" (xiii).

9. From the transcripts of an untitled paper first presented as part of an Institute of Contemporary Art/Arts Council of England conference, "Seduced and Abandoned: The Body in the Virtual World", London, March 1994.

10. I have maintained the original punctuation and spelling in these electronic excerpts, but not the original formatting (unless clearly used to emphasize a textual point).

11. One of the more extreme examples of this trend is the work of the French artist Orlan, who periodically alters her appearance with cosmetic surgery so as to reflect computer-created self-portraits. To date she has undergone nine operations, which were recorded and distributed by video, telephone, modem, and/or other technology media as part of a performance piece. Her goal is not only to illustrate that "the body is obsolete", but also "to bring out the internal image towards the external image", thus blurring the boundaries between the physical and the mental. Since her operations challenge the feminine ideal (e.g., in one of her operations she had cheekbone implants placed above her eyebrows; in a forthcoming operation she will have her nose dramatically lengthened), Orlan refers to herself as a "woman to woman transsexual". (From the transcripts of an untitled paper first presented as part of the Institute of Contemporary Art/Arts Council of England conference, "Seduced and Abandoned: The Body in the Virtual World," London, March 1994.)

12. From the transcripts of an untitled paper first presented as part of the Institute of Contemporary Art/Arts Council of England conference, "Seduced and Abandoned: The Body in the Virtual World", London, March 1994.

13. The term *dishing*, short for "dishing the dirt", refers to the gay male custom of gossiping about other members of the gay community who are not present, either acquaintances known to all participants or celebrities known to be gay. Participants in the discourse jointly reveal information about a third party, particularly of a sexual nature, that would otherwise be kept hidden.

14. For an interesting article on stereotypes of gay male pitch variation, see Gaudio (1994).

15. A "MOO" (short for MUD, Object Oriented) is a kind of Multi-User Dimension designed to give users the impression that they are moving through a physical space. Users may be given brief textual descriptions of various "rooms" in the database's mansion, for instance, replete with a listing of all the objects available in the room. Users interact with each other under pseudonyms, employing the various objects available to them. See also Deuel (This volume).

16. Recent articles and personal accounts of on-line harassment include Armstrong (1994), Brail (1994), Burns (ms.), Campbell (1994), Holderness (1993), Jerome (1994), Lewis (1994), Magid (1994), and Petersen (1994).

17. The full text of the University of Illinois' code on electronic harassment can be found in *The University Code on Campus Affiars and Handbook of Policies and Regulations Applying to All Students*, University of Illinois.

18. "Bigness" becomes a pervasive metaphor through many of these postings, and in cyberphilosophy in general. One of my male colleagues recently joked with me about "the ultimate in computer-sex". His futuristic vision? "Eliminating the people completely," he explained, "so you could have this cute little Mac getting it on with some big hefty mainframe." For my colleague, as with many network users, the absence

of a physical body leads to the creation of a verbal one, and suddenly, "this cute little Mac" has sex with "some big hefty mainframe".

19. Many thanks to sapphite Kris Shanks for these percentages, which are based on responses from 198 list subscribers. Questions in her survey addressed a number of areas, among them age, lifestyle, occupation, relationship status, dependents, and reasons for joining SAPPHO. As a complement to Shanks' survey, I analyzed the actual postings that occurred between January and June in order to see how list participants chose to self-identity: 74% self-identified as lesbian, 14% as bisexual, 8% as heterosexual, and 4% as transsexual.

20. *S'mores* are a campfire sandwich made of graham crackers, marshmallows, and chocolate; they are especially popular on Girl Scout and Campfire Girl outings.

21. One GAYNET subscriber who had secretly joined SAPPHO in order to "gain insights into lesbian thinking" contributed his own personal experience to this thread, explaining how he had suffered "verbal abuse" at the hands of separatist women: "Most women in our society are conditioned to 'let the man speak' and will stop talking if you interrupt them. But just try interrupting a woman who has learned to recognize this behavior! When I first entered into lesbian discussions, I brought with me this behavior. And when I tried interrupting one of them, they ignored me (rejecting my male priviledge), verbally rolled right over me and finished their thought."

22. Unless, of course, they are engaging in parody.

23. From the transcripts of an untitled paper first presented as part of the Institute of Contemporary Art/Arts Council of England conference, "Seduced and Abandoned: The Body in the Virtual World", London, March 1994.

III: Cross-Cultural Perspectives

Computer-Mediated Conversations as a New Dimension of Intercultural Communication between East Asian and North American College Students

Ringo Ma
State University of New York, Fredonia

1. Introduction

As a result of modern technology and global interdependence, communication between individuals from different cultures is occurring more and more frequently. Most recent studies of intercultural communication focus on face-to-face (FTF) interactions; interpersonal communication via electronic media in intercultural contexts is largely ignored. Although mediated interpersonal communication has been introduced in previous studies (e.g., Cathcart & Gumpert 1983; Walther 1992; Walther & Burgoon 1992), its role as a new dimension of intercultural communication has been addressed in only a few unpublished studies (e.g., Chung 1992; Olaniran 1992).

Over the past few decades, cultural differences between East Asians and North Americans as reflected in their communication behaviors have been extensively explored. These differences constitute the backbone of many current theories of intercultural communication. Intercultural communication via computer networks, however, seems to have modified, if not drastically changed, some previously identified characteristics of FTF intercultural communication. The purpose of this study is to examine the differences between the two versions of intercultural communication and claim that some current theories of intercultural communication, when applied to communication via computer networks, are subject to modification.

Among various forms of mediated interpersonal communication, computer-mediated communication (CMC) through international networks has been extensively applied at institutions of higher education in many parts of the world. CMC refers to interactive computer messages (e-messages), electronic mail (e-mail), forums, computer conferencing, etc. (Murray 1988). CMC through international networks is, as Dern (1992) writes, "convenient and...less expensive than establishing...wide-area networks" (111). Dern estimates that more than 5,000 networks with 500,000 computers in 33 countries, or more than 3 million users, are linked through the computer network Internet. It would be much more costly and inefficient if the communication currently performed via computer networks were replaced by phone talk or facsimile transmission. In comparing e-mail with other communication systems in organizational settings, Booth (1988) writes that e-mail "is the facility that has been much written about and of which the most serious attempts at evaluation have been made" (38). He also reports a case in which the number of e-mail users through an organization providing network access services rose from zero in 1982 to approaching 80,000 in 1987 (38).

According to Garnsey and Garton (1992), CMC offers "a solution to the constraints posed by time and space on geographically dispersed organisations seeking to communicate with each other." This statement also applies to many college students who are exposed to the idea of multiculturalism and yet unable to experience it directly. Computer networks connecting campuses in different countries provide students with an opportunity to communicate with their culturally dissimilar counterparts.

Although emotional support through CMC is reported for elderly users in previous research (Furlong 1989), Steinfield (1986) discovered in an organizational study that newer and younger employees were more likely to use CMC for social purposes. The finding seems to suggest that CMC can be easily adopted by college students.

College students can use "synchronous" as well as "asynchronous" computer programs to engage in CMC within and between college campuses. E-mail and some conferencing systems, such as COnferencing SYstem (COSY), are "asynchronous", because "users need not be on-line simultaneously" (Walther & Burgoon 1992). The Relay program on Bitnet, the Internet Relay Chat (IRC) program on Internet, and the "interactive talk" on bulletin board systems (BBSs) are, on the other hand, examples of "synchronous" CMC. They are real-time "chat" systems for on-line users that replicate "everyone's input to the others whose computers are 'tuned' to the same topical 'channel'" (Dern 1992:118). Computer users can also engage in synchronous conversations by sending interactive e-messages. However, e-messages are usually exchanged between previously acquainted users who know each other's computer usercode. Only relay and BBS talk programs facilitate conversations between previously unacquainted users.

Most institutions of higher education in Canada and the United States are connected through Internet and Bitnet. Institutions in Hong Kong, Japan, South Korea, and Taiwan are also linked through these two networks. In Taiwan, for example, all major universities and colleges are currently connected to both Internet and Bitnet through six regional service centers of the Taiwan Academic Network (TANet).[1] A notable number of students from Hong Kong, Japan, and Taiwan can be identified on IRC. In other words, "relay" programs are accessible to students on many campuses in East Asia and North America.

The approach adopted in the present study is as follows: (a) Five propositions on intercultural communication between East Asian and North American college students were generated on the basis of a review of the current literature on CMC and intercultural communication, and (b) these propositions were empirically tested through real-life CMC experiences reported by college students from both cultures.

2. CMC and interpersonal relationships

Computer networks have changed the traditional view of communication environments. In her discussion of a case of an "electronic lover", Van Gelder (1990) writes that "Computer networks connect people of common interests through text-based interaction" (128). Furlong (1989) states that an "electronic community" has been created via on-line networks (149). Gumpert and Drucker (1992) also note that the traditional notion of physical space co-occupied by communicators is replaced by "electronic space", which is "an associational construct *without place* between two or more persons..." (189).

Closely related to the concept of text-based communication is the absence of nonverbal cues in computer-mediated conversations. Nonverbal behavior is traditionally regarded as carrying more weight than are verbal codes for the relational function of communication. In a "virtual classroom", the lack of nonverbal cues to regulate interactions was sometimes found to cause awkwardness or difficulty in communicating (Hiltz 1986). That relational development in CMC is inhibited by the paucity of nonverbal cues, however, has not been reported consistently. Both the social presence theory (Short et al. 1976), and media richness theory (e.g., Daft & Lengel 1984, 1986) propose that communication is affected by the quality of the medium (the level of "social presence" or information "richness"). Due to its lack of nonverbal cues, CMC is expected to be extremely low in social presence and is perceived to be a very "lean" channel in comparison to FTF communication. Sproull and Kiesler (1986) also indicate that CMC lacks the social context cues exchanged in FTF communication. These cues are transmitted through the physical environment, nonverbal behaviors, and each participant's social status. This "cues-filtered-out" characteristic makes CMC "appropriate for the kinds of tasks requiring less social interaction and social intimacy" (Rice & Case 1983:137). Overall, CMC is regarded as being more impersonal than FTF communication (for a detailed review, see Walther 1992). Durlak (1987), nevertheless, notes that one of the three dimensions of social presence is "the potential of immediate, two-way exchange"; the remaining two are the ability to convey nonverbal cues and the context (746). On the basis of Durlak's criteria, synchronous CMC is not necessarily low in social presence. Perse et al. (1992) also suggest that perceptions of social presence in CMC vary by user.

Walther and his associates (Walther 1992; Walther & Burgoon 1992) argue that, in spite of its limitation in the transmission of nonverbal cues, CMC allows relational development. A recent study on relational communication in task-oriented group contexts indicates that the depersonalizing effects of the medium (CMC) are limited to initial interactions and that changes in relational communication will occur as a result of extended interactions (Walther & Burgoon 1992).

Although nonverbal cues are inaccessible in CMC, alternative relational cues are available to its participants. Relational cues can be transmitted in the absence of nonverbal cues in two ways. First, verbal messages are capable of conveying relational meanings (Rice & Love 1987; Walther & Burgoon 1992). In other words, relational tones can be incorporated in verbal messages. For example, the choice of topics, words, syntax, and punctuation marks can all serve as relational cues. Second, relational messages can be transmitted through "electronic paralanguage" (Gumpert 1990:151). "Electronic paralanguage" is also referred to as "emoticons", which is a hybrid name derived from the words "emotive icons" (Metz 1992). According to Metz (1992), there are four different forms of "emoticons": those used to verbalize physical cues, such as "hehehe" (laughter); those used to describe physical actions, such as "*hug* and *kiss*"; those used for emphasis, such as "no, I *won't* go"; and those used as a "shorthand" form for the description of a physical condition, such as ":-)" for a smiling face.

In the absence of visual cues, CMC tends to promote egalitarian and uninhibited behaviors. Kiesler et al. (1984) found that "group members using computers participated more equally than they did when they talked face to face" (1129). According to Van Gelder (1990), since some barriers common to FTF communication, such as race, physical appearance and language accent, are non-existent in computer-mediated interactions, a more egalitarian situation is created (130). The most important criterion by which we judge each other in computer-mediated conversations is one's mind rather than appearance, race, accent, etc. (130). CMC users also tend to be more uninhibited than they are in FTF situations. Reid (1991) notes that in CMC it is not immediately apparent what forms of social etiquette are appropriate at any given time. The practice of expressing oneself more strongly on the computer than one would in other communication settings, such as "flaming", has been reported in various studies. For example, Kiesler et al. (1984) discovered uninhibited verbal behavior in computer-mediated decision-making groups. Kim and Raja (1991) identified the frequent occurrence of extreme verbal disinhibition (aggression and self-disclosure) in computer BBSs.

3. CMC between East Asians and North Americans

Communication between students in East Asia and North America is increasing in both quantity and quality as the access to synchronous CMC programs on both sides increases. A large amount of information can be exchanged in a short "relay" or BBS "talk" session, in which more than two persons can participate. The instant feedback allowed in the process decreases the chance for misinterpreting messages received from others. Information about the other culture that students formerly acquired through mass media can now be obtained through talking directly to people in that culture. The direct interaction tends to demystify some distorted mass media reports. For example, while a media program in East Asia may positively or negatively exaggerate the educational system in the United States, viewers who have access to information on the same topic through computer-mediated conversations as an alternative channel are less likely to be misled by the distorted report than those who do not have such access. Based on this reasoning, the following difference between those who participate in intercultural computer-mediated conversations regularly and those who do not is proposed:

Proposition 1:

Those who engage in intercultural computer-mediated conversations regularly are better informed about the culture of their communication partners than are those who do not about the same culture.

The concept of "stranger" has been developed by Gudykunst and Kim (1984) to characterize FTF intercultural communication situations, since "strangers represent both the idea of nearness in that they are physically close and the idea of remoteness in that they have different values and ways of doing things" (19). The concept also implies that there is a host/guest distinction. However, because the host/guest distinction disappears in computer-mediated conversations and the participants are not physically close, the concept does not apply. Either all are "strangers" or none is a "stranger". The cultural variation in the degree to which communication is influenced by context also seems to be reduced. Those from different cultures engaging in computer-mediated conversations do not occupy a common physical place, so they are not bound by any particular set of cultural rules. Although each participant's communication behavior is expected to reflect his or her own culture to a certain degree, the context in which they communicate is not overshadowed by either participant's culture. Therefore, the following difference between computer-mediated and FTF conversations in intercultural contexts is proposed:

Proposition 2:

Those who engage in computer-mediated intercultural communication are less likely to adapt to each other's cultural rules than those who engage in FTF communication.

Previous research indicates that a major difference between East Asian and North American communication is the "indirect" versus "direct" mode of communication (e.g., Ting-Toomey 1985, 1988; Yum 1988). Ma (1992), based on a literature review, summarizes "indirectness" as underplaying all matters of the heart, being non-assertive and non-argumentative, releasing very little information via coded, explicit, transmitted parts of the message, assuming a nonconfrontational attitude toward conflicts, performing two types of illocutionary act at the same time, adopting avoidance styles in face negotiations, etc. (269). "Directness", on the other hand, denotes displaying strong emotionality, vesting the mass of the information in explicit code, adopting confrontational styles in conflict management, etc. (Ma 1992:269). Given the previously mentioned differences between face-to-face and computer-mediated communication, East Asians are expected to be more direct in computer-mediated conversations than in FTF conversations while North Americans are expected to be even more direct than East Asians. This is so because indirect communication relies heavily on context for creating meanings (Hall 1976).

The relative "low context" associated with computer-mediated conversations does not seem to foster many forms of indirect communication. For example, to avoid direct confrontation in FTF conversations, East Asians do not always verbalize "no" to turn down another's proposal. The "yes" or "no" message can be encoded and decoded by varying the level of enthusiasm associated with an ambiguous "yes" message (Ma 1993). It would be much more difficult to create such a variation in computer-mediated conversations. Second, indirect communication is largely a result of face-saving concerns (Gudykunst & Ting-Toomey 1988), or more specifically, a way to "prevent the embarrassment of rejection by the other person or disagreement among partners..." (Yum 1988: 383). The risk involved in intercultural computer-mediated conversations is significantly lower than in intercultural FTF situations because participants usually do not share a common social network and because the chance to meet their communication partner in FTF situations is slim. A content analysis of computer BBSs by Kim and Raja (1991), for example, has disclosed a high frequency of face threatening acts and a reduced inclination to protect others' faces. The low risk of CMC may promote a more direct mode of communication for East Asians as well. Finally, the CMC-related uninhibited behavior identified in previous studies suggests that people from all cultures will tend to be more direct in computer-mediated than in FTF conversations. The preceding discussion leads to the following proposition:

Proposition 3:

Both East Asians and North Americans tend to be more direct in computer-mediated conversations than in FTF conversations.

Berger and Calabrese (1975) propose in their uncertainty reduction theory that "As the relationship develops, persons are more willing to proffer information about themselves without specifically being asked for it" (109). In explaining why we need to disclose ourselves, Jourard (1971) writes that "mutual ignorance seems to be at the root of all problems between family members or between citizens of different nations" (5). According to him, self-disclosure is a yardstick for the development of intercultural and intracultural relationships, though research has not always supported this value (for a detailed discussion, see Bochner 1984). East Asians have been found to self-disclose at a lower level than North Americans (e.g., Gudykunst & Nishida 1984; Okabe 1983; Ting-Toomey 1987). Chinese, for instance, "express less emotion than Americans...and are less likely to express emotions with strangers or acquaintances than with close friends in the context of their communication system" (Schneider 1985:275). No systematic cross-cultural study on self-disclosure in CMC has yet been reported. However, a higher level of self-disclosure has been identified in a content analysis of computer BBSs, as compared to FTF communication (Kim & Raja 1991). Like verbal aggression, high-level self-disclosure is considered to be associated with the general tendency toward verbal disinhibition in CMC (Kim & Raja 1991). Based on these research reports, the following is proposed:

Proposition 4:

Both East Asians and North Americans tend to show greater self-disclosure in computer-mediated conversations than in FTF conversations.

Fewer barriers and greater equality have been associated with computer-mediated conversations than with FTF conversations as a result of the lack of visual/social cues in the former (e.g., Van Gelder 1990; Kiesler et al. 1984). Two common barriers in intercultural FTF encounters, accent and physical appearance, are non-existent in computer-mediated conversations. Lack of security, or anxiety, as usually experienced by a "stranger" interacting with members of the ingroup (Gudykunst 1988:125-126), is not likely to occur in computer-mediated conversations either. The focusing-on-mind computer-mediated conversations should thus provide a better opportunity for information exchange between participants from different cultures. The lack of a host/guest distinction also tends not to put anyone in a one-up or one-down position in the communication process. Therefore, the following difference between computer-mediated and FTF conversations is proposed:

Proposition 5:

Both East Asians and North Americans perceive computer-mediated intercultural communication as a more egalitarian and information-oriented experience than FTF intercultural communication.

4. An empirical study

4.1. Method

Twenty U.S. students taking junior-level communication courses at a state university in the northern United States chose to fulfill a class project requirement by participating in relay chats and writing a report based on their relay chats. Twelve of them were female and eight were male. Each student was requested to complete 15 "natural conversation" sessions with East Asian students from China, Japan, Hong Kong, Korea, and/or Taiwan within a two month period. The duration of each session ranged from 20 minutes to several hours. At least five different East Asian communication partners were included in the sessions reported by each student. They were also instructed to engage in relay chats with North American students, so a comparison could be made between their East Asian and North American partners. At the completion of these sessions, they were requested to write a report. The report included the following two parts: (a) a detailed tabulation of the date and time of each session, and the nickname, gender, and culture of each communication partner; and (b) an essay addressing the issues associated with the five propositions. A total of 286 relay sessions with East Asian communication partners were reported.

Fifteen East Asian students from China, South Korea, and Taiwan attending universities in the United States and 10 attending universities in Taiwan were initially interviewed through synchronous CMC (IRC, Bitnet Relay, or the "interactive talk" on BBSs). Follow-up inquiries were conducted through e-mail. They were all asked to address the five propositions. Ten of those in the U.S. and five attending school in Taiwan were female; the remaining 10 were male. Two females in Taiwan were master-level graduate students; all others were undergraduates. All 25 of the East Asian students had been engaging in relay chats frequently. Notes were taken while they were interviewed.

U.S. students' written reports and notes from the interviews with East Asian students were analyzed and recurring themes were identified. The analysis yielded the following results pertaining to the five propositions:

4.2. Results

4.2.1. Responses pertaining to Proposition 1

First, most (18) U.S. students stated in their reports that intercultural computer-mediated conversations helped them understand the culture of their communication partner. For example, a female student reported the following learning experience:

> I learned that Canton [Guangzhou] is the largest and most important metropolis of South China. ... Canton has the most important educational and research resources available to them. I also learned that Chinese people do not celebrate Christmas. During the celebration of the New Year they receive a lot of new clothes and lucky money.

A male student learned from his Chinese communication partner that modesty is a strong Chinese value. Another male student made the following statement:

> I personally learned a lot about other cultures as well as about people in other parts of the U.S. during these talks. By just conversing about everyday things such as school work, social lives and hobbies I was able to infer what type of person I was talking to and what type of influence their culture had on their opinions and outlooks.

Increased cultural understanding was reported by 16 of the 25 East Asian students, though 19 emphasized that improving their English, rather than cultural understanding, was the most important advantage. One noted that in FTF situations she would not feel comfortable asking so many questions about the U.S. culture to Americans. She also indicated that she had learned many idiomatic expressions from her on-line American friends. Another male student in Taiwan made the following remark:

> Now I know in the U.S. the difference between big cities and small towns is very large. Like us, family ties can be strong in some areas of the U.S.

A female Korean student in the U.S., while agreeing with the proposition in general, cautioned against over-generalization:

> Whether relay chats can increase cultural understanding largely depends on what the topic is and who the communication partner is. It's always possible, but not guaranteed, to learn something about my partner's culture.

4.2.2. Responses pertaining to Proposition 2

In response to the question whether they were less likely to adapt to each other's cultural rules in computer-mediated conversations than in FTF conversations, a total of 16 U.S. students did not think that they had to adapt to each other in their relay chats with East Asian students. Nevertheless, in one of these reports, “no adaptation” is attributed partially to the nature of the conversations that the student had on relay. She reported the following:

> Conversations stayed primarily on a superficial level, so there weren't any ways I had to curb my ways of speaking.

Another student indicated the existence of a “relay culture”:

> I don't feel as though I had to adapt to anyone's culture, if anything, I had to adapt to the “relay culture”.

Two other students identified a trend of mutual adaptation in their conversations with East Asians. The remaining two felt that they had to make a lot of effort adapting to their partner, because of either their partner's different communication style or their partner's poor English.

East Asian students' responses were quite consistent. No adaptation was reported in any but one female in the U.S.

4.2.3. Responses pertaining to Proposition 3

Students in both cultural groups reported unanimously that people in relay conversations are more direct than people usually are in face-to-face conversations. For instance, one U.S. student noted the following:

> When talking to college students from the United States, I have found that they are extremely forward and direct. I think this is because it would be rare that you would ever meet any of these people and no one has to worry about impressions.

A female Taiwanese student mentioned that she tended to be more direct because she did not have to worry about what she would normally do in FTF situations.

Although East Asians thought they were more direct on relay, seven U.S. students did not agree. They judged East Asians to be "polite, reserved, and indirect" in both FTF and relay conversations. A U.S. male's report, for example, included the following description:

> She [a Chinese] in particular always directs our conversations around another person other than herself. Another element of her personality is the way she apologizes for not being an adequate computer user, when in fact she is excellent. ... I have found through our conversations that she is less direct [than I am]. On one occasion when I asked her what she looked like, she responded by saying, "Most people get to know me inside instead of outside."

However, these students also noted that they did not have much experience interacting with East Asians.

4.2.4. Responses pertaining to Proposition 4

Similar to their responses to the question regarding "directness", both East Asian and U.S. students perceived themselves to engage in a higher level of self-disclosure in relay conversations than in FTF conversations. As one U.S. male student stated, "Relay participants acquire a large amount of information about each other in a relatively short period of time." A female student in Taiwan made the following remark:

> People definitely self-disclose more on BBS than in FTF situations. That's the reason why some people even think it's easier to make a boyfriend or girlfriend via BBS. Most people are more reserved in FTF conversations.

Eight U.S. students did not feel that East Asians self-disclose more in relay conversations than in FTF conversations. A female, for example, said that "[East Asians] are extremely nice and polite, but do not initiate self-disclosure." A male student found that East Asians did not talk about themselves. The information disclosed was usually "facts" about their culture instead of personal opinions or feelings.

4.2.5. Responses pertaining to Proposition 5

It was unanimously acknowledged in both cultural groups that status difference was unnoticeable in computer-mediated conversations. The absence of physical appearance and voice, as one American male student noted, did "make us focus on verbal messages". Although three East Asian students (two females and one male) were occasionally dismayed by American students who used slang extensively, they felt that it was still more relaxing to talk to Americans via computer networks than in FTF situations.

Most (18 U.S. and 16 East Asian) students characterized computer-mediated conversations as being more informational than FTF ones. The remaining 11 (2 U.S. and 9 East Asian) students would not endorse this view unconditionally. According to them, whether computer networks nurture information-oriented conversations depends largely on who the communication partner is and what the topic is. A "fantasized tea party" or joking session on relay, for example, would not be more informational than a regular FTF conversation.

5. Discussion and conclusions

Intercultural communication has been recognized as an important area of communication studies for several decades. Among the many reasons why it continues to receive more and more attention is the rapid development of modern technology. Modern technology has shortened the distance between people in different societies and made it increasingly likely that intercultural communication will play a significant part in our lives. The same reason calls us to reconsider some of the previously identified concepts of intercultural communication. Nowadays, instead of traveling to a different society, with a computer and a modem we can stay home communicating interactively and synchronously on a regular basis with culturally dissimilar others on the other side of the globe. In other words, intercultural communication can occur via computer networks as well as in FTF situations. Indeed, it takes place more easily and more frequently than before.

In this study, the influence of computer networks on intercultural communication and the differences between computer-mediated and FTF intercultural communication were addressed. Five propositions were developed on the basis of the current literature on CMC and intercultural communication. The propositions were then examined in an empirical study.

As predicted, the five propositions were largely supported in the empirical data collected for this study. There are, however, two phenomena identified in the empirical study that deserve special attention. First, participants in synchronous CMC do not seem to have as high a commitment as when they engage in FTF communication. They tend to be more direct and self-disclosing, but the reason they do so is not the same as that for similar behavior in FTF situations. In FTF communication, being more direct and self-disclosing usually indicates a more serious commitment to a close relationship, while in synchronous CMC participants self-disclose simply because the chance to meet the other is "rare", or there is little risk involved. The "worry-free" attitude associated with synchronous CMC can facilitate intercultural understanding under many circumstances. It can also serve as an ice-breaker in initial interactions. However, the question of whether self-disclosure without serious commitment can promote close relationships between individuals from different cultures has yet to be answered.

Second, there seemed to be a discrepancy between how U.S. students perceived East Asian students and how East Asian students perceived themselves with regard to directness and self-disclosure. Even though East Asians thought they were more or "much more" direct in relay or BBS chats than in FTF conversations, some U.S. students still perceived them to be "polite" but "reserved", "indirect", and "not talking about themselves". One explanation is that most U.S. students might not have a solid base for comparison between FTF and computer-mediated conversations with East Asians. Although all U.S. students involved in this study had some previous experience interacting with East Asians in FTF situations, their experience was often limited to only a few East Asian acquaintances. It is also possible that what constitutes "directness" is subject to cultural variation. While East Asians perceived a specific behavior to be very direct, North Americans might not agree with them. For example, saying "I can't stay on relay for too long" during a relay chat to turn down an invitation to a private channel could be perceived as being "explicit and rude" to an East Asian, but may mean "beating around the bush" to a North American.

This study has at least two possible limitations. First, the empirical data presented above were not collected under experimentally controlled conditions. Instead, they were detailed reports prepared by real users of synchronous CMC, based on natural conversations occurring over an extended period of time. The validity associated with the data is thus expected to be high. However, since it is a relatively new phenomenon to engage in conversations via computer networks, and not very many people at this point know how to do it, the high validity was obtained at the expense of the unavailability of a large sample. The small sample made control of some variables such as gender and personality impossible.

Second, although some barriers in FTF intercultural communication such as race and accent are non-existent in computer-mediated intercultural communication, social status is usually detectable through the exchange of personal information or the usercode. The question of whether social status can constitute a barrier was not answered in this study. All participants in this study and their CMC partners were students and hence of similar status to start out with; thus their reports regarding egalitarian experience might not be as revealing as these reports would have been if people of different social status, such as students and professors, were interacting.

Finally, there is also a potential obstacle to the realization of intercultural CMC. Current regulations governing participation in these relay programs vary from campus to campus, ranging from no access at all to 24-hour access. For example, a commonly adopted regulation for Bitnet Relay in the United States is to open for access between 5:00 p.m. and 9:00 a.m. local time. Due to time zone differences, it would be very difficult for computer-mediated conversations between East Asian and North American students to occur if the regulation were adopted on both sides of the Pacific Ocean. Then frequent interactions would be likely to occur only between those participants from the same or nearby time zones. As a consequence, the intercultural functions performed by synchronous CMC programs, as proposed in this paper, could be severely hampered.

NOTE

1. Information about TANet is available from the Internet ftp site moers2.edu.tw.

Perceptions of American Culture:
The Impact of an Electronically-Mediated Cultural Exchange Program on Mexican High School Students

Mary Elaine Meagher and Fernando Castaños
Universidad Nacional Autónoma de México

1. Introduction

Much has been made of the potential of computer-mediated communication to facilitate global, cross-cultural communication, yet little empirical research has been conducted in this area. This chapter discusses the impact of a CMC cultural exchange program on Mexican high school students' perceptions of American culture. It is divided in two parts, to report findings of quantitative and qualitative research separately. Quantitative analysis is based on a semantic differential constructed to measure changes in attitude between pretest and post-test. It shows that the students' perceptions were less positive after the CMC exchange program than before. Although no control group was present, triangulation with results from qualitative research substantiates the claim that these changes are due to the exchange. The combined data indicate students selectively criticize the culture of L2 while they reconsider attitudes towards the culture of L1. A lesser trend towards identification with young speakers of L2 was recognized. Positive effects on learning are also mentioned.

1.1. Program objectives

The exchange program is part of a high school English course designed to enable Mexican students to interact with people from other cultures.[1] The course also aimed to teach students how to select the content of their own learning process and use the resources of the information age. Students had to integrate their work with that of others to solve problems.

An important objective was the development of higher-order learning skills such as the ability to recognize and analyze differences, perceive relationships, determine priorities, emit value judgments, organize ideas and synthesize conclusions. These goals were justified by the increasing globalization of the economy and the exponential growth of information world-wide.

1.2. The CMC program

Twenty-six Mexican 10th grade students (11 boys and 15 girls) at *Escuela Nacional Preparatoria No. 6* in Mexico City participated in a bilingual cultural exchange with American students in Spanish classes from Gompers Secondary School in San Diego, California, via Internet during the 1991-1992 school year.

The Mexican students had three 50 minute English classes per week. One of these was usually spent in the school computer lab which has approximately 80 IBM compatible computers. The school was not connected to the Internet at the time, but since it belongs to the *Universidad Nacional Autónoma de México (UNAM)*, students had access to the Internet through the university's Academic Computing Center a few miles away. Each student visited this center on an average of six separate occasions during the project. Usually students worked in their school's computer lab, saving files in ASCII, and the teacher uploaded and downloaded these at the university facility several times a month.

At the beginning of the school year, the students took a twenty hour introductory computing course as an extracurricular activity to prepare them for the program. They learned some basics, word processing skills and the use of electronic mail.

An electronic bulletin board created for the project permitted all participants in both countries automatic access to messages exchanged over the network. Academic personnel from both technical and research areas at collaborating *UNAM* institutions were connected to the bulletin board to facilitate control and evaluation of the project. Besides providing a vehicle for instant communication, the bulletin board also created a mechanism for automatic data collection.

1.3. The study

A parallel research program was initiated to measure participating students' foreign language acquisition as well as changes in learning concepts and attitudes towards different modalities of learning, technology and other cultures.[2] In this study, we address the research question of how an electronically mediated exchange program affects student attitudes towards their own and other cultures. We also consider how confronting the culture of L1 and L2 impacts the learning process. Culture is used here in an anthropological and social sense to include attitudes, values, thought patterns, frames of reference and daily activities.

2. Quantitative research

Our research poses the hypothesis that participation in a bilingual CMC program modifies participating students' attitudes towards members of the culture of L2. It further assumes that the changes are reflected in student descriptions of members of that culture.

2.1. Subjects

Our subjects were the twenty-six 10th grade high school students in group 416B at *Plantel Antonio Caso, Escuela Nacional Preparatoria No. 6* mentioned in 1.2. The students had varying levels of linguistic competency in English upon entering the project.

Although students are generally assigned to groups by random computerized procedures and changes regarding assignment to groups and schools are not permitted, these students were transferred to ENP No. 6 at their own request. (This school is considered by many students and their parents to be the best high school in the *UNAM* system.) However, there was a certain random element in the way they were assigned to this group rather than to one of the other groups held open for transfer students. In no way was their ability for foreign languages or their attitudes towards aspects of this research project a factor in the process. Group 416B was selected for practical purposes because its schedule permitted observation for a two hour block once a week.

2.2. Instrument

The same questionnaire soliciting information (in Spanish) about student concepts of language learning and attitudes towards language learning, cooperative learning, technology and the foreign culture was administered to the experimental group at the beginning (pretest) and end (post-test) of the pilot project. 21 pairs of questionnaires corresponding to those students who filled out both the pretest and post-test surveys were processed.

The questionnaire contained a section (item no. 33) which requested that students select adjectives from a given list to describe Americans in general. Students were free to select as many adjectives as they wished from the list which included, for example, *independiente* (independent), *orgulloso* (proud) and *flojo* (lazy). A complete list of possible adjectives is given in the Appendix.

2.3. Data analysis

2.3.1. First, each adjective on the list was assigned a semantic differential factor. We applied Osgood's thesis that a judgment can be conceived as a point on a bipolar scale (Osgood 1952) and his idea that the associations or connotations of words can, therefore, be plotted in a semantic space[3] defined by antonyms (Osgood *et al.* 1957).

Specifically, we used a short procedure[4] outlined by Díaz Guerrero and Salas (1975) in their book on the semantic differential in Mexico, which discusses one of several coordinated research projects aimed at assessing the universality of Osgood's approach. There, on the basis of factor analysis, they showed that three dimensions (evaluation, potency and activity) were adequate to define the space for the whole of the vocabulary. We considered that, of these, evaluation was the most relevant for our needs. Following Díaz Guerrero's recommendations, in order to ensure reliability, we determined the connotation of our adjectives on this dimension by calculating an average of scores on three bipolar scales.[5] These scales, which potentially range from -3 (most negative) to +3 (most positive), were:

simpático - antipático
odioso - amoroso
bueno - malo

These pairs of antonyms can be roughly translated as:

nice - not nice
hateful - lovable
good - bad.

As can be seen, in two of the scales the positive term was presented first and the negative second, whereas on the other scale the reverse order was followed. This was to guarantee validity: it prevented automatic, irresponsible answers.

The subjects that provided the data necessary to calculate the semantic differential factors were a group of 21 comparable students from the same high school. All factors are listed in the Appendix.

2.3.2. Target students' responses to item 33 on the questionnaire were analyzed using the adjective factors we had obtained by the procedure described in 2.3.1. The total score per subject (TS) was calculated separately for both pretest and post-test. Each time, this was divided by the number of words (W) to obtain the average score per word per subject (AS):

$$AS = \frac{TS}{W}$$

As a result, we obtained 21 related samples. These were graphed and one outlier was discovered. The same subject had obtained both the lowest score on the pretest and the highest score on the post-test. In addition, the movement of her data was in the opposite direction of the tendency. The conclusion was drawn that this was due to adolescent emotional instability, and the pair of observations was removed. The 20 related samples shown in Table 1 were analyzed.

Since we were studying related samples, we decided to apply a paired *t* - test because it was important to compute the difference between the average pretest score (AS_1) and the average post-test score (AS_2) per subject.[6] The result indicates that participation in an electronically-mediated cultural exchange program produced significant changes (mean=-0.5660, $p<.05$) in student attitudes towards members of the culture of L2. Mexican students' perceptions of the American culture were significantly less positive after than before the CMC exchange.

Table 1. Average score per word per subject

	Pretest	Post-test		Pretest	Post-test
1.	0.42	-0.61	11.	1.34	-0.43
2.	1.02	-1.73	12.	0.72	1.55
3.	0.11	-0.69	13.	0.88	-0.49
4.	1.78	1.63	14.	0.14	1.37
5.	1.07	1.36	15.	1.04	0.58
6.	2.12	1.17	16.	0.36	-1.11
7.	1.03	-0.64	17.	1.53	0.51
8.	0.66	0.39	18.	0.08	1.70
9.	-0.14	-0.66	19.	-0.47	-0.37
10.	1.72	-0.11	20.	-0.71	-0.02

2.4. *Conclusions*

The significant change in attitude toward members of the culture of L2 experienced by participants in the pilot project suggests that computer-mediated communication facilitates the perception of cultural values. It is probable that the intercultural exchange via computer network provided students with a contrast between the ideas, values and/or attitudes of L1 and L2 and that the moment in which we measured their perception of American culture corresponds to a stage of culture shock. In any case the results suggest a rejection of the other culture's values by Mexican telecommunications students.

3. Qualitative research

We felt it was important to triangulate the findings of our quantitative study with the results of our qualitative research. The latter poses the hypothesis that participation in an electronically mediated cultural exchange program produces changes in participating students' attitudes towards members of the culture of L2 and towards the culture of L1. We also assume that increased contact with the culture of L2 will have a positive impact on the learning process. Our subjects were the same twenty-six Mexican high school students described in section 2 of this paper.

3.1. Instruments

3.1.1. The questionnaire described in 2.2. contained two open ended questions soliciting a description of a typical young American and value judgments about Americans (items numbers 31 and 32):

> *No. 31.*
> *Descripción: ¿Cómo te imaginas que son los jóvenes norteamericanos? Describe a un joven norteamericano típico.*
> (Description: What do you imagine young Americans are like? Describe a typical young American.)
>
> *No. 32.*
> *¿Qué te molesta de los norteamericanos?*
> (What bothers you about Americans?)

In addition, there were three questions with bipolar scales on similarities between young people in Mexico and the United States, and concerning the ability of Mexican students to understand the interests and aspirations of young Americans and vice versa. The following is an example:

> *No. 18. Los jóvenes de habla inglesa tienen en común con los jóvenes mexicanos.*
> *nada 1 2 3 4 5 mucho*
>
> (No. 18. Young English speaking people have in common with young Mexicans.
> nothing 1 2 3 4 5 a lot)

21 questionnaires corresponding to those students who filled out both the pretest and post-test surveys were processed.

3.1.2. Answers to the questionnaire described in 2.2. were used to select 8 students (4 male and 4 female) with different attitudes towards learning English, technology and the culture of L2. Recorded interviews consisting of open-ended questions concerning these aspects of the CMC program were administered to the 8 students in Spanish before and after the cultural exchange.

Specific questions for each area were designed to elicit opinions about determined aspects in every interview. However, neither the order, nor the wording of the questions was necessarily the same, in order to permit sufficient flexibility for exploring certain aspects of student ideas in depth. Questions evoked descriptive, evaluative and affective responses. These responses were translated by the authors for reporting in this chapter.

In addition, the above were compared with 32 hours of transcribed classroom observations, student work and teacher observations.

3.2. *Data analysis*

3.2.1. *Questionnaire answers*

An analysis of questionnaire answers supports the overall findings reported in section 2. At the same time, they suggest that a complex set of opinions regarding the foreign culture develops during the exchange.

Question 31, soliciting a description of typical young Americans, elicited various answers on both the pretest and the post-test, e.g.,

Pretest
Six statements similar to the following:
(1) White skin, light eyes, blond hair, tall, thin.
(2) Tall, blond, intelligent, friendly.

Post-test
(3) The majority are tall and strong, regarding their color I think there are all kinds.
(4) Intelligent, of different colors with aspirations like all young people.
(5) They come from many different races and places.

We think it is important to highlight that students had learned to recognize diversity in the USA. Pretest responses included at most three critical commentaries in answer to this question whereas post-test responses included 9. The criticisms included the following:

(6) Somewhat arrogant, presumptuous, with feelings of superiority.
(7) Racist.
(8) Mistaken opinions about the rest of the world.
(9) Not agreed with their opinions (about racism).

When asked what bothered them about Americans (question no. 32), many students responded *nada* (nothing). However, pretest questionnaires contained observations by 11 subjects whereas post-test questionnaires contained statements by 16. The responses in the pretest questionnaires included 15 negative elements whereas those in the post-test included 33. Critical comments about arrogance and feelings of superiority increased from 6 to 9. Criticism of racist policies augmented from 2 to 10. Critical comments about mistaken ideas and unfair treatment of other nations went from 3 to 4.

At the same time that answers to question no. 31 reflected what it was Mexican students did not like about the culture of L2, they indicated that feelings of identity with young people from the culture of L2 had increased. Pretest responses included three such statements:

(10) I believe they are like the majority of young people.
(11) For me, they are normal people like all the young people in the world.
(12) Well they are young like everyone else.

By contrast, post-test responses included eight identification statements. Some of these are:

(13) I think they are almost just like us.
(14) I think they are persons like us.
(15) Just like any young person from any other country
(16) Now that I know them, they are like any other person who has aspirations and wants to meet different people and some day live in a world of peace.

Questions number 18, 20 and 21 dealt with identification on bipolar scales from 1 to 5 (nothing—a lot). The average answer for each of these questions increased from pretest to post-test. Although this increase was not statistically significant, there again seems to be a tendency for increased identification with young people from the culture of L2.

3.2.2. Recorded Interviews

The recorded interviews also shed light on student perceptions of American culture. Here is a translation from Spanish of a typical statement:[7]

> I think they were very influenced by their elders and by a very commercial culture. They have mistaken ideas about other countries. In everything else I think they are very much like us. (Luis)

This excerpt from a student's interview reflects how this educational experience provoked thought and a critical attitude towards the foreign culture. Racism stood out as one of the issues that most effected changes in Mexican students' attitudes towards American culture. The teacher states that information they exchanged among themselves as well as what came across over television about the Rodney King case in Los Angeles generated a great deal of curiosity on the part of Mexican students to know more about the American point of view and its causes.

> When we asked them about racism, there were those who didn't want to talk about it, I don't understand why, but Afro-Americans told us that this was a great problem. There in the cafeteria everyone was separated in groups of whites, orientals, Latins and blacks. (Roberto)

3.2.3. Student work

An analysis of student work provides a framework from which to evaluate data mentioned previously. E-mail correspondence with the sister class in San Diego proceeded on two levels: informal communication (pen pal letters) and cooperative projects. Informal communication began with introductory letters followed by a series of questions and answers about life in the other culture. The following letter is typical of this stage of the cultural exchange:[8]

hi! how are you? We are Marcela, Susana, and Roberto.
We'd like to answer some of your questions:
1) What kind of music do you hear?
answer= rap, industrial, house, pop, heavy metal,and reggae.
2) What does our school look like?
answer= it's big, fun, with all kind of persons.It has several buildings, a lot of classrooms, a swimming pool, green areas ,a gym, a theater and a football court.
3) What kind of clothes do you wear?
answer= the same as you.(Jeans, TShirts, Sweaters, Jackets, etc.)
4) What do you do for fun?
answer= All the friends join together for goin' out to the movies, to have dinner, and go shopping.
5) What kind of movies do we like to see?
answer= thrillers, action, suspense, romantics, comics, etc.
6) What are your favorites hobbies?
answer= speak on the phone for hours, go to the movies, eat popcorn, and play some sports.
7) Did you see the Super Bowl?
answer= It was fun.(in fact we didn't understand it)
8) What is the age for driving?
answer= 14 years old, with many requierments.
Well so long. Many kisssssssssses.Bye bye!!!!!!.

This kind of spontaneous correspondence between the two groups of young people included many questions about likes and dislikes in the areas of music, sports, friends, school, clothing and daily activities. There was a great deal of agreement about values as well as interests in these spheres.

In a long list of questions sent to the sister class, one of the Mexican students asked if they had problems with racism in San Diego. The following is the reply they received:[9]

Hola
Do you have problems with racism?

Claro que tenemos problemas con racismo. Hay problemas en todos lugares del mundo. En San Diego, hay muchas culturas differentes.

Es un lugar que muchas personas del mundo vienen. Muchas de las problemas son de pandillas. Hay muchisimos pandillas en San Diego. Hay violencia. Que mas podemos decir? Ya saben acerca de las pandillas.

Nuestras problemas con pandillas son parecidas a suyos.

Adios
Yang Jiu, Joan West, Jim Pack

Tienen mas prguntas? Tienen problemas de racismo tambien?

(Hi
Do you have problems with racism?
Of course we have problems with racism. There are problems everywhere in the world. There are many different cultures in San Diego.
People come here from all over the world. Many of the problems have to do with gangs. There are very many gangs in San Diego. There is violence. What else can we say? You know about gangs.
Our problems with gangs are like yours.
Good bye
Yang Jiu, Joan West, Jim Pack
Do you have any more questions? Do you also have problems with racism?)

This is a very defensive answer. San Diego students state they have problems with racism and gangs like everywhere else in the world. Only at the very end do they ask the Mexican students if they also have problems with racism.

This provoked a lot of correspondence. Here is one of the follow-up letters:[10]

Hi Hu Yie!
My name is Roberto Gonzales Lopez. I read your letter and I found it very interesting. I agree with you, after watching on T.V. the images of Rodney King being beaten by the cops. You think that the USA is not the land of freedom where all people can do what they want without racist problems. I guess you feel disappointed about the government and your judicial system. Here in Mexico we don't have such problems with racism.
What do you think about N.W.A? Do you think that their lyrics are too violent, crude, strong or they are singing the truth about the situation in the streets. Here in Mexico almost nobody knows them. But I like their lyrics, maybe cause they aren't following the normal social rules and they enjoy being differents. You have your own "compton"?
Some other time I'm gonna talk to you about the troubles in my country. They are big and very serious. Sorry I still have a lot of mistakes in my English, I hope you understand what I want to say, and that the problems in your country get solved.
Bye
Roberto
P.D. Please answer the questions

Due to frank discussions about this issue, both groups opened up and began to dialogue freely about other sensitive issues such as their image of the other country. Here is a sample:

Hi!
We received your letter about Mexico,I think that the people of my class weren't so sincere about our country. I think they sent you just information about the good places here,but they didn't talk to you about the real corruption, and misery here. I think this is because maybe they haven't been in places where that is so evident.

> Our contry is so marginal and because of the way that our goverment is acting, the rich people are earning more money while the poor are in real misery. I think that your goverment is acting the same way. Here we have areas like Netzahualcoyotl City where the poor lives and if you go there you can see maybe the most marginal area so if you go to El Pedregal that is where the richest live so you can see the contrast. I want to talk more about this, but I think it's enough for today.
> Sincerly, Luis

This letter also typifies another phenomenon produced by the confrontation of different cultural values—analytical evaluation of the culture of L1. Here Luis not only criticizes Mexico, but also the way in which his fellow students describe their own country to students abroad. The teacher feels that contrasts inherent in the computer-mediated communication project, such as different points of view about racism and value judgments about each others' countries, provide students with a sharper perspective from which to reconsider attitudes towards their own culture.

In general the results of an examination of the correspondence between the two groups of young people parallel the results of an analysis of the questionnaires. The computer-mediated exchange allowed participants to observe many different ideas, attitudes, values and customs as expressed by the members of the culture of L2 at the same time as it permitted them to identify similarities between the culture of L1 and L2.

3.2.4. Cooperative projects

Mexican students worked on cooperative projects from March to June. Students selected the topic they wanted to research and formed teams to carry out their projects. Work was divided into phases: data collection and analysis, focusing objectives, synthesis, and presentation of results via e-mail.

Students were encouraged to organize tasks bearing in mind the strengths of individual team members while sharing all aspects of learning at the group level. The role of the teacher was to facilitate this process.

Teachers in both countries had agreed to this at the beginning of the school year. However, problems of scheduling use of the computer laboratories and logging on to the network in combination with rigid curriculum demands prohibited students in San Diego from contributing to this aspect of the exchange. Nevertheless the presence of a real audience stimulated Mexican students to produce a collection of Mexican legends, descriptions of museums and monuments in Mexico City, an explanation of sports at the ENP No. 6 and an analysis of the Free Trade Agreement.

The teacher in Mexico City was surprised at the quality of student work: not only at their proficiency in language use but also at their commitment to high-level content. This is atypical for 10th grade student production in a foreign language class. Previous courses given by this teacher were curriculum oriented and did not yield anything comparable. The teacher's reaction is congruent with research findings by Riel (1989) that indicate telecommunication student gains in the areas of language mechanics and language expression as measured by standardized tests.

Here is the teacher's description of how the project on the Free Trade Agreement developed:

Stage 1
Students collected newspaper and magazine articles on the Free Trade Agreement both in English and in Spanish. They were a bit overwhelmed by the breadth and depth of information available.
Stage 2
Students elaborated a questionnaire in Spanish on this topic. They decided to interview Luis' father, a professor at the UNAM's School of Economics.
Stage 3
An English version of the interview was elaborated.
Stage 4
A British expert in the field offered them an opportunity to repeat the interview in English. They carried out the interview in English, recorded it and subsequently transcribed most of it with very little help from me.
NOTE:
Not only were Luis and Roberto vital to the carrying out of this research project, but they designed the entire project with their team mates and planned every detail necessary to carrying it out. At no time did the teacher offer any suggestions as to which topics would be acceptable or valid for research. She merely rëinforced students initiatives.

The following is an excerpt from the project the teacher is referring to.

Questionnaire about the Free Trade Agreement
1.Basically what is the Free Trade Agreement?
It is an agreement between three countries to trade goods and services.
2. Why was it created?
For the profit of U.S.A. to create a potential market in the Latin American area, in response to changes in Europe and Asia where US predominance can not be maintained.
3. What are the main advantages of this agreement for Mexico?
To integrate with the changes that the historic moment requieres, because otherwise, maybe Mexico will be relegated to an inferior position vis a vis developed nations.
6. Which sectors of the Mexican economy will gain the most from the Free Trade Agreement?
The textil, automotive and petrochemical sectors.
7. What are the main disadvantages of this agreement for Mexico?
The industrial sector generally will not be as competitive as the US industrial sector.
8. What will be the situation of the labor class as compared with Northamerican and Canada industries?

They will have more employment because Mexican workmanship is cheaper and therefore attractive to the U.S.A.
9. Is the Free Trade Agreement essential for Mexico's Development?
It is not essential, but it is a positive factor in accelerating Mexico role in international competition.
10. Will the Mexican industries be at the same level as Northamerican and Canadian ones?
Just the enterprises that get to compete with international quality.

The most striking feature of this report for the English teacher was its analytical nature and the way students strove to express precise ideas in L2. Often foreign language students limit their efforts to producing grammatically correct statements. Here in contrast the message students wanted to convey to members of the other culture took precedence.

3.3. Conclusions

If we define culture in an anthropological and social sense as including attitudes, values, thought patterns, frames of reference and daily activities, we can say that electronically-mediated exchange programs increase contact with the culture of L2. There is a confrontation between the ideas, values and attitudes of the culture of L1 and L2. The contrast seems to provoke criticism and analysis on behalf of participating students. They selectively criticize the other culture and their own and begin to analyze what is happening in the world around them from the perspective of their newly acquired knowledge. However, they may still be lacking much necessary information about the phenomena they are striving to analyze, and may fail to appreciate and understand fully the data before them. Nevertheless, in engaging in this confrontation of cultures, the students initiated a very worthwhile process in an experiential fashion. It is this process that is most important and not their conclusions which may sometimes be erroneous. Perhaps we could say that this stage at which we are measuring their perception of the culture of L2 corresponds to one of culture shock. In any case it is a form of rejection of different values, attitudes and customs which leads to a rethinking of one's own cultural values. It seems as though concepts of the culture of L1 remain constant, but the point of view from which students view these concepts changes through contrast with the culture of L2. This experience provides students with a wider perspective from which to view their own experiences.

It is also pertinent at this point to evaluate what impact this cultural confrontation and the presence of a real audience had on the learning process. The teacher of the experimental group feels that the process helped develop higher-order thinking skills. It also personalized the learning process and yielded quality student output as well as commitment, to say nothing of introducing students to the benefits of modern telecommunications systems.[11] We also have empirical evidence that language acquisition is positively affected by a structured bilingual cultural exchange.[12]

4. Discussion and further research

The statistical analysis of student answers on the questionnaire indicates their perception of American culture was less positive after than before the CMC cultural exchange. These results are very thought provoking, and it would be worthwhile to repeat the experiment with two variables, a control group and a similar question describing members of the culture of L1.

Other information gathered from the questionnaire was not susceptible to statistical analysis. Nevertheless, it seems to substantiate the findings of the statistical analysis.

Another lesser trend was recognized—identification with American young people. Aspects of the recorded interviews and class observations coincide here, indicating that participants in the electronically-mediated cultural exchange are more aware of both differences and similarities between the culture of L1 and L2. This suggests a model of intercultural dialogue according to which simple, general attitudes towards the foreign culture are replaced by complex, diversified opinions about different aspects as knowledge of the culture increases. The research results also suggest that attitude changes might not be linear, but rather show decreases and increases at different moments.

Developing a complex model useful to describe variable trends would seem to require a typology of positive perceptions, including categories such as admiration, identification, acceptance, and tolerance, because simple notions might miss important subtleties. We believe such a typology could be constructed on the basis of empirical work of the sort reported here. We also think the kind of instruments we have devised can play an important role.

In conclusion, this chapter shows CMC can be valuable in foreign language courses. It also suggests further research on the effects of intensive intercultural dialogue made possible by CMC.

NOTES

1. The course was developed by three institutions of the *Universidad Nacional Autónoma de México* (the *Centro de Enseñanza de Lenguas Extranjeras,* the *Dirección General de Cómputo Académico,* and the *Escuela Nacional Preparatoria*), with the support of grant no. CD702292 from the *Dirección General de Asuntos del Personal Académico.* See Aguilar (1992:617).

2. Our research team also included Anna De Fina, Diana Jenkins and Phyllis Ryan from the Foreign Language Center (CELE) and Ma. Elena Delgado and Marlin Valenzuela from the National Preparatory School (ENP). Federico O'Reilly and Alejandro Reyes from the Institute for Research in Applied Mathematics and Systems (IIMAS) aided us in the statistical analysis of data.

3. See Carter (1987:212-214) for a concise explanation of semantic space and semantic differentials.

4. The procedure was developed on the basis of a suggestion by May (1967).

5. Although the evidence available indicates that the dimension of evaluation is universal, the scales that best represent it could vary from one culture to another. The scales we used have been found by Díaz Guerrero and Salas (1975) to give optimum results in Mexico.

6. The paired *t* - test computes a mean and standard error of the differences and determines whether the absolute value of the mean difference is greater than zero by chance alone (see, e.g., Cody and Smith 1991:131-133).

7. All names used are pseudonyms.

8. Students often wrote their letters in the language they were studying. Neither the grammar nor the spelling and punctuation of the student productions were corrected for presentation in this paper, unless stated explicitly. The English translation of exchanges in Spanish is provided in parentheses.

9. We have written the Spanish text in italics to separate it from the English text, although no typography was indicated in the original version produced by the students. The English text following in parentheses is a translation.

10. We have changed the typography of both Roberto's and Luis' letters for readability. The originals were all in upper case.

11. Delgado *et al.* (1993) assert that cooperative learning via telecommunications provides a flexible educational opportunity without limits where students can achieve their own goals.

12. Quantitative research (Meagher 1993) demonstrates that structured cultural exchange programs via telecommunications facilitate more language acquisition than traditional situations where class time is spent learning grammatical structures.

Appendix

Semantic differential scores for adjectives in question 33

1. *Amigable*	(Friendly)	2.60
2. *Alegre*	(Joyful)	2.41
3. *Sincero*	(Sincere)	2.29
4. *Amable*	(Kind)	2.17
5. *Feliz*	(Happy)	2.10
6. *Generoso*	(Generous)	2.10
7. *Respetuoso*	(Respectful)	2.05
8. *Confiable*	(Trustworthy)	1.95
9. *Interesado por la familia*	(Interested in the family)	1.71
10. *Accesible*	(Open)	1.70
11. *Limpio*	(Clean)	1.65
12. *Util*	(Useful)	1.62
13. *Cómico*	(Funny)	1.54
14. *Laborioso*	(Industrious)	1.52
15. *Paciente*	(Patient)	1.46
16. *Considerado*	(Considerate)	1.44
17. *Emotivo*	(Emotional)	1.43
18. *Trabajador*	(Hard working)	1.42
19. *Emprendedor*	(Enterprising)	1.35
20. *Inteligente*	(Intelligent)	1.21
21. *Independiente*	(Independent)	1.17
22. *Persistente*	(Persistent)	1.14
23. *Competitivo*	(Competitive)	1.13
24. *Comunicativo*	(Communicative)	1.10
25. *Organizado*	(Organized)	0.97
26. *Correcto*	(Proper)	0.79
27. *Religioso*	(Religious)	0.62
28. *Despreocupado*	(Unconcerned)	0.43
29. *Pasivo*	(Passive)	-0.25
30. *Flojo*	(Lazy)	-0.86
31. *Anticuado*	(Old-fashioned)	-0.86
32. *Descuidado*	(Careless))	-0.98
33. *Desconfiado*	(Mistrustful)	-1.22
34. *Autoritario*	(Authoritarian)	-1.30
35. *Orgulloso*	(Proud)	-1.33
36. *Arrogante*	(Arrogant)	-1.51
37. *Insensible*	(Insensitive)	-1.52
38. *Prejuicioso*	(Prejudiced)	-1.97
39. *Hipócrita*	(Hypocritical)	-2.03
40. *Grosero*	(Rude)	-2.11
41. *Creido*	(Presumptuous)	-2.13
42. *Cruel*	(Cruel)	-2.21
43. *Odioso*	(Hateful)	-2.38

Visible Conversation and Academic Inquiry:
CMC in a Culturally Diverse Classroom

Gregory G. Colomb and Joyce A. Simutis
University of Illinois at Urbana-Champaign

1. Introduction

As a tool for teaching writing, computer-mediated communication in a networked classroom has had enthusiastic supporters and mixed reviews. Those reviews, however, have not offered the kind of analysis that might inspire confidence. The reservations expressed about CMC have been chiefly anecdotal, while the support has relied less on cogent argument than on "a visionary image" (Hawisher and Selfe 1990:7; Romano 1993). CMC applications were introduced with claims that they would transform education, claims that computing enthusiasts echoed and then supported with a pastiche of theoretical speculation. The scenario is a familiar one for new computing technologies. Similar arguments about brave new textual worlds marked the early enthusiasm for hypertext among vendors, authors, and scholars (Landow 1989; Bolter 1991). But specific hypertexts have been as varied as their authors, and have fulfilled few visionary promises (Douglas 1994; Clark and Hocks forthcoming). We can expect that, in much the same way, CMC will be shaped by its uses and will be only as valuable for teaching writing as the pedagogical designs which it serves.

For the present, claims about the value of CMC deserve scrutiny. Networked classrooms are costly, and most writing programs are underfunded, which forces them to rely on poorly compensated graduate students and part-time faculty. In such circumstances, both teachers and administrators will be properly reluctant to support an investment of tens of thousands for technology that might give a program cachet without substantially improving instruction. The case for CMC in writing instruction has to be based not on visionary claims about CMC as an all-purpose tool for automatic teaching but on specific accounts of how *and why* the technology has helped teachers and students to achieve specific goals (see, for example, Moran 1991a, 1991b).

In this study, we report on an ongoing investigation of CMC in a writing class for "at risk" students. The class was designed to take advantage of CMC's capacity to support specific kinds of interactions among students, and writing assignments were designed to build on students' experience with CMC. After studying students' evaluations, their papers and drafts, and transcripts of CMC sessions, we conclude that CMC allowed us to orchestrate writing situations that supported and improved students' learning in two ways. First, students encountered the disciplinary demands of academic writing less as a purely external imposition than as an internal dynamic of a developing, "proto-disciplinary" community of inquiry. In their CMC interactions with the teacher, the class materials, and each other, students found the social support needed to build and maintain a community of inquiry the necessary material support they found in CMC transcripts. Second, these situations helped students focus their explicit attention almost exclusively on higher levels of text structure. This proved especially valuable for these particular students because it limited interference by concerns about sentence grammar, interference that normally hampers the learning and performance of so-called "basic writers". In what follows, we explain how CMC supported these outcomes.

2. A pedagogical design for CMC

An investigation involving CMC was conducted in a first-year college writing class, one of four "special options" ("SOP") sections reserved for the lowest-scoring students admitted to the University of Illinois. The class was racially mixed (four students were African-American, four Asian-American, two Hispanic, and three Caucasian), with eight men and five women. The target class was part of an "equal opportunities" ("EOP") rhetoric program, since restructured, whose 28 other sections were reserved for minority students, most with higher scores than those in SOP Rhetoric. All sections ostensibly covered in two semesters the same territory as the standard, one-semester composition class, although the readings and approach were different. In addition to the extra semester, students in the special program received weekly individual tutorials from a teaching assistant assigned to their section.

Data were collected from the target class (taught by Simutis), one section of EOP Rhetoric that also used CMC (also taught by Simutis), and one section of SOP Rhetoric that did not use CMC (taught by June Lyle). Students knew that they were testing a new program, and they specifically asked to be identified by name. The pedagogy had been tested in a pilot class using CMC. All classes used the same pedagogy, largely the same readings, and the same kinds of writing assignments. Both Simutis and Lyle had significant experience with the pedagogy, although Lyle was teaching first-year students for the first time.

For this study, we introduced two new elements in the target class. One was CMC. The class met twice a week for 75 minutes, once in a traditional classroom and once in a networked computer lab outfitted with Daedalus™ InterChange. InterChange sessions are synchronous electronic discussions in which each student has access to two writing spaces: a public discussion space which contains a running, scrollable record of all the messages posted to that session's discussion, and a private word processing space in which a student could compose her message before posting it to the public forum. Students received transcripts of the discussions, which were often used in the traditional classroom. Students also had access to e-mail. There was little class-related e-mail traffic among students; the teacher and tutor each received an average of four messages a week.

The second new element was a pedagogy focused on the social/disciplinary demand that academic texts raise a problem or question worth asking, and respond with a point worth making. This pedagogy had two dimensions. The first was to teach an explicit text grammar for formulating problems and making and supporting points; this aspect, addressed chiefly in the traditional classroom, closely followed a program of instruction developed for first-year courses at the University of Chicago by Colomb, Joseph Williams, and others.[1] The second dimension was to provide the social support students needed to judge what, in the disciplinary context of this class, counted as a question worth asking or a point worth making; this aspect, accomplished chiefly with CMC, was developed specifically to support students in their socialization into an academic mode of discourse. The pedagogy avoided any focus on "basics" at the sentence level, relegating all explicit sentence instruction to the individual tutorial sessions.

3. Some pedagogical effects of CMC

In the period under investigation, the weekly InterChange sessions improved students' learning and engagement in two ways. Through InterChange, we created a forum in which students experienced their learning and writing as growing out of their collective activity. In this forum, the students became a community of inquiry which they recognized as having a substantial, though peripheral, relation to a larger community of scholars. This proto-disciplinary community developed in large part through the dynamics of discussion on InterChange. The second group of effects concerns the specific kinds of writing practice students were able to achieve in the InterChange sessions.

3.1. Sustaining computer-mediated conversations

One of the most common themes in reports of classes using CMC is the problem of keeping students on task (Batson 1988b; Bump 1992; Daisley 1994; DiMatteo 1990; Kremers 1990, 1993; Peyton 1989, 1990; Sirc and Reynolds 1990; Thompson 1988). Sometimes students use the time for chatting, sometimes for serious conversations unrelated to the task at hand, and often for "flaming" and other forms of social aggression. Obscenity and other kinds of outlaw discourse seem to be particularly favored by off-task students—a form of resistance perhaps related to the tasks they were set: to discuss the weather, events in the news, other students' papers, whether they wanted to work for a Japanese or American company, etc.

While some think the lack of control in CMC sessions serious enough to make CMC unusable, others look for its virtues. DiMatteo found "issues as profound as those that had been technically assigned" (1991:17): "Their written violence [obscenity] heralded their entrance into a previously alien zone of education" (1990:80). When students avoided the task of critiquing a colleague's paper, Sirc and Reynolds (1990) valued the lesson it taught the teachers: "the raw materiality of our students' social behavior in seeming to invert or displace the task as we set it in reality showed us the limits of our linguistic conceptualization of texts and writing" (65; also see Sirc 1995; Sirc and Reynolds 1993). These are dubious virtues, hardly enough to justify expensive equipment that encourages students to goof off in class.

However, our experience was different. In the transcripts for three classes, we found no evidence that students used the time inappropriately. There was often a brief period of greeting chatter (usually fewer than six turns), and occasionally a period of idle conversation at the end of sessions. Students routinely made side remarks (one or two turns, sometimes as many as four), but they were not disruptive and were most often pertinent to the task at hand. There were disagreements enough, but they remained on point and within reasonable bounds of classroom decorum. We found no flaming, no disparaging remarks, no obscenity.

The students did not arrive at this ability to focus their efforts by accident. Students have to learn how to conduct a successful CMC discussion (just as they once had to learn how to conduct an oral discussion). They also need topics about which they are knowledgeable and tasks in which they have some stake. It took three or four sessions before students began to assume responsibility for the direction of CMC discussions, six or eight before they assumed control. The first sessions were essentially classroom exercises, with students responding to questions in a collection of two-way conversations between the teacher and individual students. By the third session, students began to comment on each other's responses, which generated short conversational threads. As students began to trust InterChange as a space in which they were safe to put themselves forward, the teacher's influence diminished and the students' grew, but only because the students had begun to develop a body of shared knowledge, to understand how to perform the tasks they were set, and most of all to have a stake in those tasks.

3.2. CMC and the novice learner

Students in this class were new to the university, new to the forms of textual analysis they were learning, and new to the genres they were writing. Given their status as "special options" students, we wanted to provide added measures of the kind of support all novice learners require. InterChange bolstered that support in several ways. One small way was simply its novelty. We wanted students to avoid patterns of behavior learned in earlier situations in which they were treated as basic writers. Since at first they wrote only on InterChange, we hoped that its novelty would keep them from using their earlier writing experiences as rigid templates for this one (Fuhrer 1993:195). This seems to have been the case.

InterChange supported novice learning in a second way, by enabling forms of apprentice teaching (Brown, Collins, and Duguid 1989; Collins, Brown and Newman 1989). On InterChange, students could observe the teacher and their more adventurous colleagues model the activity they were expected to learn. They could study postings that garnered favorable responses and practice privately on their own screen until they were ready to make their efforts public. With this immediate modeling and the "scaffolding" (Rosenshine and Guenther 1992) provided in handouts and other teaching materials, students could begin with as much (or as little) imitation as they needed to be comfortable. As they developed their own practices, students learned through interaction so that the teacher could "fade" from the process, giving only as much help as the group needed to keep on track.

InterChange also supported novice participation in unanticipated ways. Our computer classroom is arranged so that each student faces a wall or post. They are close enough that a student can watch a neighbor's actions, but isolated enough that a student working at a machine does not have to interact with anyone. Both aspects of this physical arrangement proved helpful. Newcomers perform more comfortably and more effectively when they don't feel that they are being watched; they can be especially unnerved when they have to make eye contact at a point of uncertainty about their performance (Fuhrer 1993:201). At the same time, newcomers often derive comfort from unobtrusively watching others perform the task at hand (Fuhrer 1993:198). The arrangement of the room and the mechanics of InterChange supported both kinds of behavior, so that students were at first more comfortable and more interactive in the InterChange sessions than in the traditional classroom. Students could also use e-mail to ask the teacher questions that they were reluctant to share with the class, an opportunity that several used, almost always for questions concerning their final papers.

3.3. A computer-mediated community

Almost all reports note that CMC changes the interpersonal dynamics of the writing classroom. First-time observers are most struck by the strange "look and feel" of a networked classroom, as students center their attention (or even their lounging) on keyboards and screens, the only sound the steady click-click of fingers on keys. It would be easy to assume that such significant changes in the circumstances of classroom conduct must change the nature of that conduct, and there is evidence to support some such assumptions. But the evidence indicates that many such claims are too general and too little analyzed.

3.3.1. The dynamics of computer-mediated conversations

One claim often made for CMC is that its new mechanics of discussion give voice to students silenced in traditional classrooms. For example, Batson notes that in a networked classroom, students do not have to "compete for the floor" (1988a:7; quoted in Peyton 1990:17), a point repeated by Cooper and Selfe in the context of an e-mail conference (1990:848). While we did observe different patterns of participation in the computer classroom and the traditional classroom, such claims proved for our test classes to be only partially accurate (see Moran 1991a).

It is true that CMC gives students easy access to the evolving transcript. They can register their words merely by giving the SEND command. But to do that is not to "gain the floor". In oral discussions, one gains the floor by registering one's words, because classroom convention demands that others listen while the speaker has her say. (Not to mention that the teacher is expected to proffer at least a minimal response.) But in CMC, unless students are forced to respond (as in Moran 1991b), they have no corresponding assurance that what gets sent gets read. Intent on the thread they are following and busy composing their own messages, students often give scant attention to messages not pertinent to their current concern. What counts as "gaining the floor" in CMC is that one's message draws a response and in some way affects the direction of a current thread. Our students recognized this as soon as their discussions developed recognizable threads, as evidenced by the plaintive requests of those who had not gained responses: "Please write me some comments........." (Eun Joo Lee 10/21/93).[2]

In these circumstances, there was significant competition for the floor, and some negotiation over how that process would be managed. A posting was more likely to gain a response if it (i) was controversial because it disagreed with an earlier posting, provoked others to disagree, or had evident consequences unacceptable to someone else, (ii) surprised someone enough to prompt a question,

(iii) raised an issue already on the table because it was part of a currently active thread, had been discussed earlier, or had been given the teacher's imprimatur, or (iv) allowed someone to post something that he or she wanted to say but that otherwise might not have gained the floor. Of course, students could also gain the floor by joining an existing thread, responding in almost any relevant way.

Excluding charity cases in which a kind soul or the teacher responded for the sake of responding, these criteria account for all but a few postings that gained the floor. In one sense, the criteria were the students' own. They evolved without direct intervention, and we did not recognize them explicitly until evaluating the transcripts after the class. In another sense, however, these criteria result from the proto-disciplinary community that the class was designed to foster. They are, for example, not unlike criteria we have observed for gaining and holding the floor in academic e-mail discussion groups, and they contributed importantly, we now believe, to helping students understand both how to recognize an academic question worth asking and how academic fora work.

The longest and most interesting thread arose when Aaron Gordon captured the floor more successfully than any student had or would, by claiming that Martin Luther King Jr.'s "I Have a Dream" speech was inappropriately joyous. Aaron's posting met three criteria for gaining the floor: it raised an issue that was already on the table and had the teacher's imprimatur; it surprised several students, who immediately asked for clarification; it intentionally contradicted the prevailing view that King could do no wrong, provoking immediate disagreement. This thread held the floor because it raised a problem that students *wanted* to see resolved with their newly acquired tools of textual analysis. Aaron was particularly adept at gaining the floor, although he was not always comfortable with the interest he created. In a later session he tried to avoid the objections of Amy Hendricks (a frequent antagonist, but also his self-chosen writing partner): "Amy would you please stay out of my conversations!!!!!!!!!!!!!!!!!!!!!!!!!!!!" But Amy set him straight: "Aaron, That was very rude!! This class is for everyone to discuss. If you and Charles want a private conversation then don't do it on the classes interchange" (11/30/93). Amy's posting met the class's criteria for gaining the floor, and in this public, academic space, those criteria mattered more than Aaron's wish not to have to consider her position.

Thus in our experience CMC does require students to compete for the floor, an observation we must qualify in two ways. First, the competition arose from the specific circumstances of the class. It resulted both from the students' engagement in the academic, proto-disciplinary questions of the class and from their growing command of procedures for creating and responding to such questions. Without such grounds for relevance, we cannot imagine students competing to answer such prompts as, "I most hate to drive in the winter when it's sleeting. Does anyone here work and go to school?" (Thompson 1988:20).

Nor would we expect to see much enthusiasm for gaining the floor to respond to such "class exercise" prompts as to find the main idea or evaluate the evidence in a sample essay.[3] Since many teachers seem to use prompts that involve chat, or personal testimony, or class exercises, it may be that in many CMC classrooms having the floor is of so little moment to students that it is in fact easily gained.

The second qualification concerns the nature of the competition, which differed from that in oral discussions. Some factors relevant to oral discussions had no influence in our CMC sessions: for instance, strength of voice, physical presence, location in the room. Others had some but less influence, such as personal presence and social aggressiveness. Faigley (1990) and Aiken (1992) found that minority and other marginalized students participate more easily on InterChange than in oral discussions. We could not make such a comparison, since all of our students were in one way or another marginalized. Some participated more, some less, but we did note that the students who posted more on InterChange were not always the ones who spoke more in class. In fact, in the pilot class, two of the more frequent participants on InterChange were women who were absolutely silent in the traditional classroom.

Finally, while the mechanics of InterChange prevent interruptions (a student can always finish what she has to say before giving the SEND command), the competition for the floor led to phenomena with some features of verbal interruptions. Since the competition makes timeliness a factor in being heard, a student who composes too slowly faces two risks: that someone will have jumped in with a message that makes hers redundant, or that the thread she wants to join has passed on to something new. One particularly poignant case was the woman in the target class who wrote a lot but posted very little: she would carefully compose responses to earlier postings, only to erase them because the discussion had moved elsewhere, and then she began the cycle again.

In this test, InterChange did help students find an academic voice they might not have achieved otherwise. This can be partly attributed to the reshuffling of conversational practices enforced by the technology. But the voice students achieved—and most of all the value they, their teacher, and the larger community placed on that achievement—was the result of the way the technology was used rather than of any automatic or even likely result of the technology itself.

3.3.2. CMC and distributed authority

As a group, teachers of writing are less easy about their authority than most teachers we know, a concern that has fueled their interest in CMC and related technologies. Influenced by claims that CMC limits social difference by reducing social cues (Kiesler, Siegel, and McGuire 1984), writing teachers have thought that CMC "blurs the social distinctions in the class" (Peyton 1990:17), disrupts "the subject positions assumed by classroom discourse" (Faigley 1990:307), grants students "total freedom of expression" (Kremers 1990:35), "results in the erasure of the teacher's authority" (DiMatteo 1990:76), "diminish[es teachers'] authoritarian status" (Cooper and Selfe 1990:852), and so on. This is not what attracted us to CMC. We saw no evidence that CMC might lead students to forget who has the power to set their assignments and deadlines, require or excuse their attendance, evaluate their work, and select their final grade. We turned to CMC because it made visible for students' inspection some of the processes by which authority and related matters are constituted in academic discourse. Just as the simplified text grammar helped to foreground for students how knowledge and meaning were situated in their texts, so the visible record of their CMC discussions helped to foreground how knowledge and meaning were also situated in the practices of the class, of English studies, and of the academy.

As we used it, CMC was not a means to avoid or pretend to avoid the teacher's power over students but a means to let them share in the teacher's authority. That authority is more like an idea than like a dollar: when shared, it is not lost, diminished, or erased but enhanced. It is already a distributed possession, shared with many others and derived from the teacher's participation in a variety of communal and institutional practices.

> Knowledgeability is routinely in a state of change rather than stasis, in the medium of socially, culturally, and historically ongoing systems of activity, involving people who are related in multiple and heterogeneous ways whose social locations, interests, reasons, and subjective possibilities are different, and who improvise struggles in situated ways with each other over the value of particular definitions of the situation. (Lave 1993:7)

One does not become knowledgeable overnight, and these students began farther than most from having a sense of their authority, of their participation in their teacher's practices. But the teacher foregrounded right from the start the distributed, shared nature of her own authority. By focusing the class on problems/questions worth raising, she highlighted the connection between their papers and the interests of a larger community. Within weeks, the students came to see themselves as "legitimate peripheral participants" (Lave and Wenger 1991), whose status as newcomers was a mark of inclusion rather than exclusion.

The best example of this legitimate peripheral participation can be seen in an InterChange session nine weeks into the semester. The class had read three versions of the Cinderella story, had talked about the cultural differences in the stories, and was preparing to write a paper. The teacher began by using the class's own informal language to pose a problem students had already raised, but now in an unexpected scenario: "Help! I have to give a paper at a conference about the Cinderella stories. I think I want to write about what a wimp Cindy can be--but how do I start? Any suggestions?" (11/11/93). The class cheerfully set about advising their teacher on avenues she might take to develop her conference paper. The students did not expect to be able to write a conference paper themselves, and at several points they had to be told what the larger community would expect from their teacher: "How short should I make a summary of the stories? Literary types would have already read these stories—literary types read everything!" But they clearly believed that they had the knowledge and the standing to participate in a scholarly activity in this peripheral way.

Later, students used the transcript in writing their papers. In the session, the class generated good questions and problems but did not arrive at answers that anyone considered particularly satisfying. So most students used the discussion as a starting point to raise more complex questions, and several argued for positions contrary to those developed in the transcript. This had four advantages. (i) The students had a stake in their arguments; they had something to prove and were motivated to prove it. (ii) They were able to frame their arguments "Most scholars think X, but Y", which is the most common frame for articles in the humanities and a particularly productive way for students to show why their question is worth asking. (iii) They used the transcript as a body of common knowledge on which to build and against which to react. (iv) They saw in the transcript examples of what not to do, what lines of inquiry did not get picked up, which ones were rejected out of hand, and so on.

3.3.3. Authentic tasks

Intimately connected to the need for students to believe in their authority as writers is the need that their tasks be authentic. In most assignments, students write in order to display their knowledge and writing ability. But in order to display themselves successfully, students have to pretend to be accomplishing some other rhetorical task—to *simulate* reporting on research, interpreting a text, evaluating a problem, and so on, often in an environment that supports the simulation poorly. This well-known problem is most serious in first-year composition, since there students face a double burden of disbelief: they are locked in a simulation, with no reason to believe that their texts respond to an authentic need (apart from the need for evaluation); but they are also unable to believe in the simulation itself, since they have little basis for understanding how the task they are simulating might ever be authentic in any circumstances. So they write to please teacher, and, if they are conscientious, work hard to get all the basics right.

Among the several reasons why students feel alienated from the writing tasks they are asked to simulate, one of the more important is their difficulty with conceptual problems (Booth, Colomb and Williams 1995). While most writing outside of the academy grows out of tangible problems or needs, most academic and some professional writing grows out of conceptual problems or needs: we write in response to some state of ignorance, puzzlement, misunderstanding, failure to notice, and so on whose consequences some community of inquiry is unwilling to bear. Even when academics study tangible problems—crime, cancer, student writing—we formulate our research and texts in terms of conceptual problems: what we do not know or understand about crime or cancer or student writing. These problems are defined socially: both the ignorance or misunderstanding and the unwillingness to accept it must be shared by some community of inquiry.

To an academic, an area of ignorance or misunderstanding is like gold to a prospector: we hunt, refine, and cherish such areas, at first for all the goods they can bring, but eventually for themselves. Students do not often understand our love of problems, and the role of problems in academic writing is not explained to them very well. Nothing is more common than for students to write poorly because they have failed to formulate a conceptual problem: they write about a topic rather than on a question or issue. Even when they do formulate a question, it must be a question worth asking, one that identifies an area of ignorance or misunderstanding that matters in that field of study.

In this class, students were taught an explicit means for finding and formulating conceptual problems of the sort they would be expected to build their papers around, for this class as well as others. But they could not be taught an explicit means for identifying worthy problems for the class. That they learned through experience, specifically their experience on InterChange. Although the first writing tasks in the class were not full-fledged papers, students began the work of formulating problems right from the start, finding questions worth asking and sketching responses on InterChange. On paper, which the students mistakenly thought of as their "real" writing, they began with summaries, brief comparisons, and other exercises intended only to build a fund of experience in writing about and manipulating the parts of texts. On InterChange, students carried on the work of creating the fund of good questions and answers that would become one basis of their proto-disciplinary community. This process was not automatic: the first questions were supplied by the teacher, and she had to sort out and occasionally reshape questions offered by students, although students did find good ones right from the start: "Do you think that the people understood what Lincoln was saying the first time he said it [in the "Second Inaugural"]? and if not, once they decoded his address how did they feel about what he said?" (Dorian Green, 9/2/93).

We might think of this as simple imitation or rehearsal for students trying to learn their lines. But the process was more like the "user-testing" that academic writers do all the time, using graduate seminars, e-mail discussion groups, conversations at conferences, and other means to gather reactions to the questions and answers we hope to write about. As the class developed, students' questions began to converge so that they more frequently fell within the range of questions worth asking. More importantly, through the process of problem formulation, the class began to develop its internal standards for what matters would gain and hold the floor. Though the teacher would remain a continuing source of intelligence from the larger community "out there", their own standards became equally important in establishing for the class what was a question worth asking.

We believe that within the protected space of InterChange, the students found a basis for making their writing assignments authentic, as Batson (1988b) had hoped. While their papers were assigned and evaluated, we also believe that the tasks in those assignments, asking and answering questions about texts, were more than just simulations for these students. They had developed in the space of InterChange a body of questions that they knew represented good problems for their proto-disciplinary community—good in the sense that they were "of the approved sort", but also in the sense that they were problems the students believed were worth solving, problems they were glad to have.

Most impressive was how some students learned to reformulate personal concerns into a problem that preserved what was important to them but also spoke to the interests and procedures of the group, as in the long thread that grew out of Aaron Gordon's proposal for a paper on King's "I Have a Dream". Aaron distrusted King: "The only reason that we repeatedly study about this man is because that the government and schoolboard or whoever thinks that his message is soft and won't really spark any desire into the minds of young blacks to start another movement to strive for equal rights and treatment in America" (10/21/93). Aaron knew both that his classmates would not welcome such sentiments and that he did not have the basis in this class for making such an argument. So he presented his community with a problem (that King's "joyous tone" was inappropriate), one they immediately recognized as important because it carried the kind of consequences most important to an academic community: they might have to change their mind about something deeply embedded in their conceptual and value structures. Aaron's classmates resisted this threat to their ideas in the same way that academic communities always do: they challenged the accuracy of his evidence ("He is speaking in a demanding tone to me" [Dorian Green]); they asked for additional evidence ("What are some evidences that show that he was talking in a joyous tone?" [Sangmin Lee]); they questioned the relevance of his evidence ("Aaron I have listened to the speech and even though they are hollering as if they were in church, there is...more tone of dissatisfaction, anger and positive energy, not e[x]actly joy" [Herman Spencer]); and they offered alternative conclusions ("Besides, if you think about it, ...when Baptist go to church they sing, laugh and cry and that never implies that they are not 'serious' because they are." [Amy Hendricks]). Aaron's thread turned out to be an important milestone in helping the class to recognize their ownership of the proto-disciplinary community they had created on InterChange.

3.3.4. CMC as a tool for building academic communities

In the work of building an academic community, CMC provided students three kinds of support. First, CMC defined a protected conversational space very different from the traditional classroom. That space bore a relation to the larger community of English studies, chiefly through the example, intervention, and approval of the teacher. But it was also safely peripheral. The space was theirs, maintained by their continuing efforts at community building within the class, and they thought of it as their primary locus for academic talk. When one of Simutis' classes once generated a particularly productive discussion in the traditional classroom, the students proposed that they adjourn to the computer classroom, since that was where such serious discussions belonged. Colomb encountered a similar phenomenon in a class using an e-mail discussion group: though there was significant interaction between the e-mail discussion and the classroom, some issues the students preferred to reserve for their electronic writing space.

Students' ownership of the electronic space was not personal, however. They might try anything in their space, but in order to survive above the noise, their words had to gain and hold the floor, just as in any scholarly community. Not only did their process of interaction resemble that by which scholarly groups maintain themselves, giving students some experience of academic inquiry, but it also generated a fund of questions, issues, and observations that could stand as the common knowledge defining a community of interest, a proto-disciplinary community, legitimate yet peripheral, in which students can have fully shared authority.

Second, CMC gave students a visible record of their conversations. During the sessions, the evolving transcript allowed students to move easily between participating and observing. As some ideas held the floor to become threads in the conversation, students could linger over them to see what might be valued by the larger community. But they could also jump in at any point to join a developing thread, thereby experiencing as well as seeing examples of successful participation. When students composed messages, the evolving transcript minimized the demands on memory and attention. Students could review the transcript for what had gone before and could safely ignore new messages without concern that they would miss something important.

After the sessions, the printed transcript allowed students to revisit and reflect on their conversations. In the traditional classroom, students used the transcripts to reconsider or expand on what they had said or, more importantly, to reflect on how the conversations had developed. By studying this trace of their disciplinary thinking, students developed a measure of conscious control and explicit understanding, making them both more effective and more comfortable with the process. Outside of class, the transcripts provided resources for writing papers and, more generally, for reflecting on the class. Students reported that they returned to the transcripts not only to glean material for their papers but also to relive the conversations, keeping alive their sense of community. Of course this is all possible with oral conversation, if one is practiced enough and knowledgeable enough that the demand on memory is not too high. But for students, the visible record improves not only the conversation itself but also their access to its lessons.

Finally, CMC provides a level of interaction, intermediate between speaking and writing, which for these particular students proved more enabling than either. The students reported, and their performance confirmed, the value of having the time to compose their messages as slowly as needed. And since responses came in minutes rather than seconds, students had time to consider each response as it arrived. They felt that they could be more thoughtful, which made them more comfortable about participating. In the heat of conversation students occasionally composed as quickly as they could type, but the pace was always far slower than oral conversation, and students felt little external pressure to perform on cue, especially since they were not required to interact face to face.

At the same time, the InterChange sessions had a level of immediacy that was in our judgment key to the success of the discussions. The pace was quick enough that students had no trouble sustaining conversational threads. Because of the pace, most turns were relatively short. Responses came just about as quickly as students could absorb them, and developing ideas had more chance to reflect those responses. More students could participate in a thread, which then more fully reflected a common understanding. We also believe that it mattered that students were together in the same room, making it easier to react to their colleagues as persons rather than as distant presences.

This mix of distance and immediacy was, we think, the one element that justified the expense in equipment and class time associated with synchronous interaction in a networked classroom. More fully-socialized students could have achieved the same benefits in the more distant medium of e-mail. While Simutis was teaching the target class, Colomb tested a similar pedagogy in an upper-level writing class for English majors. There we used an e-mail discussion list, with similar results and with less cost in equipment and no cost in class time. But the demands on students were greater. The slower pace and distributed locations put greater demands on students' understanding, memory, and commitment to the conversation. As a result, their messages were longer and in many cases more carefully composed, thereby further increasing the writing and reading challenge.

For the students in the target class, with their lack of familiarity and comfort with the material and with so many reasons to feel excluded, the immediacy of InterChange was probably necessary. In one comparison class, Lyle tried to duplicate the experience with class discussions, short response papers and other written notes, but abandoned the effort almost immediately. Without the power of an immediate response (or lack of response), the work of community building through writing proved too hard for those students.

3.4. Written conversation

Although many benefits of the InterChange sessions arose from their role in supporting the students' efforts to build an academic community, those sessions also provided students important opportunities for three kinds of writing practice: first, to practice the language of rhetorical and literary analysis without being hampered by concerns about correctness; second, to practice elements of text structure without concern for the character of their sentences; and third, to practice in an actual dialogue those dialogic elements that they would have to build into their formally monologic papers.

3.4.1. Practicing academic language

In order to write as a participant in an academic discourse community, even as a peripheral one, students need some fluency with its language. It is always a good idea to give students new to a discipline opportunities to use its language in a "low cost" writing environment, one in which they do not face strong demands for coherence or heavy scrutiny from a teacher. Generally, the most effective strategy is to assign paper genres that do not require students to formulate arguments or make and support points: journals, response papers, rough summaries, and other forms of "writing to learn". Not for basic writers, however. First of all, paper genres do not lower the cost enough. It has long been known that these students tend to have a history that leads them to labor over sentences, focusing excessively on the demands of correctness (Shaughnessy 1977). So much of the response to their papers focuses on problem sentences and so much of their instruction focuses on sentence grammar that writing in any paper genre becomes a matter of getting the right sentences on the page—an environment that encourages self-consciousness over fluency. Second, these students need practice in formulating arguments and making and supporting points, matters in which they typically have had least instruction and experience. As much as our students needed to become comfortable with the language of textual analysis, they also needed the kind of work that journals and response papers cannot provide.

In electronic written conversation, the students found a forum in which they could use the language of textual analysis without anxiety about their sentences. They didn't consciously think of themselves as writing sentences: they were posing problems, making points, offering evidence, asking questions about others' points, and so on. The more successful the discussion, the more quickly and effortlessly the students wrote. The one exception was the young woman who composed and then erased messages when the discussion had passed her by, but even she had the benefit of writing all those sentences she erased. All the others participated regularly. In the third session, the most prolific student posted 89 words, and half of the students posted at least 44. By the final session, the most prolific student posted 195 words, and half posted at least 68. Individual postings became longer and more complex through the semester. In the second session, the average posting was 34 words, and the longest was 79. By the end, the average posting was 73 words, and the longest was 201, by one of the quietest women in the class (who continued to be the most prolific writer in her new section the next semester).

During InterChange sessions, the teacher avoided any reference to surface features of sentences, and composed her own messages quickly, with no effort to revise. The students also ignored errors, except for a single episode of teasing:

> Dorian: Herman you need to learn how to spell. Since when do you spell the word "repetition" reputition.
> Herman: Dorian why are you trying to be funny early in the morning. Did I miss spell that.
> Dorian: I am being funny because I only got one hour of sleep, how would you act with one hour of sleep? (10/14/93)

The students were too engaged in the discussions to let their sentences slow them down. Nevertheless, as they gained experience and became more comfortable in academic discussion, they developed greater command over their sentences. Excluding obvious typing errors, the frequency of grammatical and mechanical errors declined by more than half from the first to the last transcript: in the first transcript 11% of the sentences had errors; by the last, only 5% had errors.

The value of a forum that deflects attention away from surface features of sentences was evident in the one departure from that practice. It occurred when the tutor joined an InterChange discussion of proposed problem statements and points for papers analyzing King's "I Have a Dream". Charles Gibson was explaining one of the more sophisticated arguments made all semester: that the repeated elements in King's speech served the same function as the refrains in classical Greek drama. In response to one of Charles' postings, the tutor slipped into old habits and asked, "Charles, could you combine your last 2 sentences so that you're making one point?" These instructions only confused Charles: "Kathy, Then how would I explain how King lead his audience?, because it would be hard to explain, with a 'and'." (10/21/93). Although the tutor explains that "and" is not the only way to combine sentences, Charles was silenced by this request. He had come to understand that his goal in these sessions was explaining, not worrying about the complexity of his sentences. It took another twelve turns before Charles would rejoin the discussion, and when he did, he responded only to those who had asked questions about his evidence. He never answered the tutor's question about sentences.

3.4.2. Practicing text structures

When students wrote papers, the teacher adopted a similar strategy of diverting attention away from a bottom-up, sentence-based method of composition. Students were taught a simplified text grammar and in writing their papers were encouraged to concentrate on matters of text structure. For the most part, InterChange sessions played little role in helping students control the formal arrangement of their papers. But they did allow students to rehearse the most important text-level "semantic" elements: the problem or question that would motivate their text, and the points and support around which it would be organized. These matters dominated the InterChange sessions, as shown by Table 1.

Table 1. Primary content of messages

	Total	Problems/Points	Support/Evidence	Questions for Others
1	105	14 (13%)	73 (70%)	4 (4%)
2	43	22 (51%)	14 (33%)	4 (4%)
3	115	6 (5%)	95 (83%)	11 (10%)
4	17	16 (94%)	0	0
5	36	19 (53%)	16 (14%)	0
6	55	33 (60%)	9 (16%)	6 (11%)
7	96	37 (39%)	0	27 (28%)
8	42	0	38 (90%)	2 (5%)
9	44	0	44 (100%)	2 (5%)
10	69	21 (30%)	34 (49%)	7 (10%)
11	82	0	78 (95%)	6 (7%)
12	77	13 (17%)	46 (60%)	16 (21%)
avg.	65	15 (23%)	37 (57%)	7 (11%)

Column 1 indicates the session number, with the total number of messages posted in column 2. Columns 3-5 indicate the number of messages in which the primary concern was information or questions about elements of text structure (based on word count messages with dual concerns were counted twice).

3.4.3. Practicing academic dialogue

The InterChange sessions enabled one additional form of writing practice: the practice of academic dialogue. CMC has been praised for fostering the Bakhtinian opposition "between the monologic centripetal forces of unity, authority, and truth and the dialogic centrifugal forces of multiplicity, equality, and uncertainty" (Faigley 1990:308). Our students' experience confirmed the importance of dialogue, although more in the line of Bakhtin's technical discussion of the role of dialogue in all speech (Voloshinov 1973). For us, the relevant distinction is not between monologue and dialogue—Voloshinov's analysis shows that all utterances are dialogic—but whether students writers recognize, acknowledge, and learn to manage the dialogic elements in their texts, even when they have the external form of monologue.

Most academic genres are formally monologic: they speak in one explicit voice; they are pointed texts, built around a single claim or result; they meet high standards of relevance, including only matters that help to make the point; and so on. Yet each of these formally monologic texts participates in an ongoing written and oral conversation. Each text is itself one turn among many, responding to its predecessors and anticipating responses in return. Some traces of that dialogue are obvious, such as the explicit and implicit responses to previous texts or the common closing strategy of looking forward to further research or new questions. Other traces of dialogue are less explicit but no less important. For example, the publication practices of academic communities put texts in dialogue with editors, peer reviewers, conference participants, and others.

Two of those less obvious traces played important roles in our pedagogy. When writers formulate a conceptual problem to which their text will respond, they put the text in dialogue with those for whom the problem has unacceptable consequences. If there is no one for whom an area of ignorance or misunderstanding is a problem, then there is no reason to find or provide an answer. In some fields, those problems tend to be widely known in advance, so that one enters the dialogue merely by raising them. In other areas, writers expend significant energy on defining a problem, explaining its importance, and finding readers willing to admit it to the conversation (MacDonald 1987; Kaufer and Geisler 1989). Another example: academic arguments normally address potential objections and contrary evidence, both explicitly and implicitly. Often those objections are drawn from prior literature, but just as often they are drawn from the writer's knowledge of other participants in the conversation (Latour and Woolgar 1979). In fact, when experienced writers engage participants they don't already know, they seek them out in order to elicit their concerns, which they then build into their texts (Blakeslee 1993).

When students write academic discourse, the problem is not that their natural, centrifugal tendency toward dialogue is constrained by the centripetal forces of unity, authority, and truth in academic genres. The problem is that they are too often denied the resources needed to achieve the kind of dialogue that makes academic discourse what it is. They have neither the interest nor the time and opportunity for the extended give and take of professional scholars, and they are usually not provided access to another forum more appropriate to their degree of knowledge and engagement. Their conversation is only with their teachers, who too often hide from them the contingent, contested nature of what they are learning (Graff 1992). These become powerful incentives for monologue, especially for first-year students, who have the added burden of overcoming the well-documented tendency of novices to crave singular truths and to shun the ambiguity and complexities that academic communities value (Perry 1981; Belenky et al. 1986; Rodgers 1990).

In the InterChange sessions, our students found a forum that could support an element of dialogue in their papers. They used the sessions to develop questions worth asking and problems worth writing about—which is to say, problems whose resolution mattered to at least some of their colleagues. They also used the sessions to try out arguments, to test their evidence, to ask their colleagues to add to their store of evidence, in the meantime discovering the kinds of questions and concerns they would have to address because they had become part of the common store of the community. These sessions served their proto-disciplinary community in much the way that the written conversations in the professional literature serve us. They created a history of conversation that gave a human context to the texts that they produced for a grade. Now that the class is over and some students have moved on to new sections without InterChange, they have complained how much they miss the transcripts as a source of ideas for their papers. We believe that as much as the ideas themselves, what the students miss is the dialogic connection of those ideas to the real concerns of a colleague.

4. Conclusion

In this investigation, synchronous electronic discussion in a networked classroom proved to be a valuable tool that allowed students to experience kinds of learning that they otherwise would not. Because the synchronous discussion was a novel writing environment for these students, it helped to create an atmosphere in which they could make a fresh start at learning to write, putting aside the habits of basic writers and the limited textual forms learned in high school. Because their written conversation was less immediate than oral conversation, it was less demanding and less threatening. Students could always take time—to observe and learn from others' performances, to study messages before responding to them, to think, and to compose their own contributions—all of which improved their performance and lessened their anxiety. Because the conversation was far more immediate than most other forms of writing, including some forms of CMC, it enhanced students' ability and willingness to become engaged. Sitting together in a room, engaged in producing a single transcript, students could more easily see themselves as a community of inquiry. Responses came quickly enough that they could see threads develop and join in as soon as they were ready. Because their conversation was visible, students could interact with it in a greater number of ways: they could read it, add to it, return to it, talk about it, make it an object of reflection and study, and finally write their papers out of it. Through the transcripts, both the evolving ones on the screen and the printed ones they took home, students were able, most for the first time in their lives, to experience academic writing not as a vehicle of information transfer but as a focal point and product of human interaction.

Some of these benefits are related to general features of CMC and might be expected in most classroom environments. But the major benefits were tied to the particular needs and abilities of this group of students and to the particular role created for CMC in the pedagogy and conduct of the class. We believe that for these students, the benefits outweighed the cost in equipment and class time, but we can also imagine that our judgment would be different in different circumstances—if, for example, the students had not been novices, or if CMC had been less fully integrated into the pedagogy. Before we can identify which variables might define the range of worthwhile uses of CMC in writing and other classes, we will need more examples, more detailed research, and much closer attention to the interactions among the technology, its users, their tasks, and their situations.

NOTES

1. The approach to text structure was adapted from the teaching materials known as the Little Red Schoolhouse, distributed by the Programs in Professional Writing at the University of Illinois at Urbana-Champaign and the Writing Programs of the University of Chicago. For a description, see Williams and Colomb (1990a, 1993). For an account of the text grammar, see Colomb and Williams (1986, 1987), Williams and Colomb (1990b), and Booth, Colomb and Williams (1995).
2. Real names are used in this chapter, at the request of the students.
3. A few "exercise" prompts were used early (e.g., "Summarize the main points in Lincoln's Second Inaugural Address"), as an unthreatening way to accustom students to Inter-Change. They generated diligent, but relatively unengaged responses, as is fitting for a mere exercise. Even when students disagreed and were encouraged to work out their differences, they had not yet come to a position in which they had any real stake in them.

IV: CMC and Group Interaction

Group Dynamics in an E-Mail Forum

Joan Korenman
University of Maryland Baltimore County

Nancy Wyatt
Penn State University, Delaware County Campus

1. Introduction

This paper reports a descriptive study of communication in an electronic forum, WMST-L (Women's Studies List); we used a case study approach to describe and analyze relevant aspects of communication practices. Joan Korenman, Associate Professor of English and Director of Women's Studies at the University of Maryland Baltimore County, started WMST-L as an unmoderated e-mail forum for Women's Studies teachers, researchers, librarians, and program administrators in May 1991. The forum has prospered and as of May 1994, had over 2700 subscribers.

The impetus for this study was our notion that the interaction on this electronic forum "felt" like the interaction in a group. How, we asked ourselves, could messages exchanged electronically, sequentially, and asynchronously be perceived by participants as group process? Were our perceptions of "groupness" shared by other participants? Did the interaction on WMST-L resemble processes generally attributed to groups? To answer these questions, we have looked to two areas of communication scholarship—the study of computer-mediated communication and the study of group process in face-to-face groups. We are interested in discovering to what extent traditional theories of group interaction can productively be applied to the study of computer-mediated communication in fora such as WMST-L.

There are basically two measures of "groupness", each of which corresponds to the perspective of the person making the judgment. The experiential measure of "groupness" is the feeling of participants in the interaction that they are members of a group; a group is a group because it feels like a group. The second measure of "groupness" can be inferred from observations made by persons outside the group; groups exhibit consistent patterns of behavior that can be described and measured, i.e., roles, norms, etc.

In describing group behavior, we ordinarily distinguish between rules for behavior, which are patterns of behavior specified by authority, and norms, which are patterns of behavior developed by the members through interaction. Robert's Rules of Order (1981) is a commonly recognized set of rules for group interaction used mainly by standing committees. Often groups which adhere to formal sets of procedures fail to develop experiential feelings of "groupness", largely because the formality of the rules militates against personal interactions in which emotional bonds of "groupness" can form. In actual practice, many groups modify formal rules to greater or lesser degrees for their own purposes; such modifications constitute norms of interaction. Officially prescribed rules of interaction are usually readily available, but norms are more difficult to identify, describe and analyze.

In general when new groups are formed, members bring to those groups their understanding of group norms from previous groups in which they were members. But groups may also develop norms that may be unique to that group through interaction. Participants in WMST-L may bring their understanding of group norms from previous face-to-face groups or from other computer-mediated communication interactions.

In our study, we examine the extent to which members of WMST-L follow the formal rules specified in the "WMST-L User's Guide" and the extent to which they develop norms for interaction on their own.

We are interested also in the degree to which WMST-L embodies scholars' predictions that computer-mediated communication enables and encourages communication across traditional hierarchical, social, institutional, and geographic boundaries (Hiltz 1982). Data for the study came from two main sources: we administered a ten-item questionnaire to all subscribers via e-mail in February 1993, and we analyzed the content of WMST-L logs over two separate six-month periods.

2. Questionnaire study

On February 1, 1993, Joan Korenman sent a ten-item questionnaire via e-mail to current members of WMST-L; nine of the items were open-ended (see Appendix). Ten days later, she sent a reminder along with another copy of the questionnaire. By mid-March, 192 completed questionnaires had been returned, 165 of them via e-mail; the remaining questionnaires were returned by U.S. mail.

3. Observation study

The notion of "observing" interaction in an electronic forum is problematic. Interaction in a computer-mediated forum such as WMST-L is conducted electronically, sequentially, and asynchronously; the usual methods of observation investigators use for face-to-face communication are impossible to implement in this context. Instead of observing behavior, we observe its consequences or results, which are the logs of participation collected electronically by LISTSERV software in the order in which messages are received by the mainframe computer, in this case at UMDD.

Transcripts of face-to-face communication are redacted, that is, they are records of communication and not the communication itself. None of the traditional nonverbal cues that accompany face-to-face interaction, including cues that indicate norms for appropriate behavior, are captured in redacted transcripts of discourse. Computer-mediated communication, however, has none of the traditional nonverbal channels of communication with which to convey meaning; the only data available to participants from which to draw conclusions about other participants and about group norms are the messages that appear daily in participants' electronic mailboxes. The nonverbal data available to participants in this forum are those implicit in all written communication: spelling, capitalization, punctuation, format, emoticons, etc. We argue, then, that the logs of WMST-L are not redacted transcripts of communication but the actual communicative interaction of the group. Reading the transcripts is the same as observing interaction in the e-mail forum.

A critic might argue that the "flow" of messages into and through a member's e-mailbox is an experiential aspect of participation on WMST-L that cannot be captured by simply reading the logs. For example, sometimes a topic will become "hot", and several messages addressing that topic will appear in quick succession. It might be difficult to reconstruct the experience of this interaction simply from reading the logs in sequence. Participants' experience of this flow of messages will vary, however, as a function of any number of factors that are largely unaccountable. Persons who read their mail daily will have a different impression of the flow of messages than will persons who read their mail only at irregular or widely spaced intervals of several days or even weeks. Persons who receive the digest form of WMST-L will have a different experience of the flow of message from persons who do not.[1] Since the "flow" of messages varies for different participants, we do not feel that our reading of the logs was significantly different from the "normal" list experience.

In analyzing the interaction in the logs of WMST-L, we used traditional methods of content analysis: identifying the factors in which we were interested, counting, and describing the occurrence of those factors (Smith 1988).

4. Patterns of participation on WMST-L

In describing and characterizing patterns of participation on WMST-L we are dealing with three separate groups. The largest group consists of all subscribers to WMST-L who receive and read the messages posted to the list. A recent count of this group reveals 2741 participants as of April 19, 1994. A second group consists of those persons who actively participate on WMST-L by sending messages to the list; this group is considerably smaller than the membership of the larger group and varies from month to month. The membership of the participating group can be determined at any time by counting the userids on the WMST-L logs. A third group, by far the smallest, is composed of those persons who completed and returned the questionnaires for this study. One difficulty in interpreting the data for this study arises in estimating the extent to which those who completed and returned the questionnaires accurately represent either the active participants or the general membership of WMST-L.

Respondents returned 192 completed questionnaires. Of these, 167 came from women, 18 from men; in seven cases, the respondent's sex could not be determined. By comparing userid (user I.D.) data from the questionnaires and names from those returned via U.S. mail to the userid data from the logs, we determined that approximately 48% of the questionnaires returned by e-mail were from persons who had sent at least one message to WMST-L during the six months preceding the administration of the questionnaires.

It is more difficult to estimate what percentage of the total membership of WMST-L this number represents. While the readership of the forum is recorded automatically by LISTSERV software, some persons may not be receiving mail for various reasons. To complicate things further, WMST-L is fed into some campus bulletin boards, and we have no idea how many people read WMST-L in that way, nor how many of those who do are subscribers. We have, therefore, no way of knowing to what extent these respondents are representative of the membership at large.

On February 9, 1993, the LISTSERV maintainer reported there were 1639 subscribers, of whom 1031 were receiving messages. Using the figure of 1031 as our base, we can figure a return rate for questionnaires at 18.6%. Out of 2741 current subscribers (April, 1994), 2277 (roughly 83%) are from the United States, 270 (9.8%) are from Canada, and the rest (roughly 7%) are from 32 other countries. Our 192 questionnaires (February, 1993) included 168 (87.5%) from the U.S., 19 from Canada (almost 10%), and five from other countries (2.6%).

We looked at the patterns of interaction on WMST-L from August 1991 through January 1992 and again from August 1992 through January 1993. We chose to begin our analysis in August 1991 because that was the month in which Korenman introduced the "WMST-L User's Guide". Korenman had a clear idea of the form she wished WMST-L to take, but new participants had their own agendas. Consequently, the initial few months were ones of working out the rules for interaction, a process that was complicated by the fact that many of the participants on WMST-L were not experienced in computer-mediated communication. Partly to assist these novice participants, Korenman drafted a User's Guide, which she sent in August to the membership of WMST-L for comments and revisions. She then distributed a revised version in September, and copies of the Guide were sent from then on to all new subscribers. In interpreting the interaction on WMST-L, we consider the "User's Guide" to represent prescribed rules of interaction.

In this section of the paper, we describe the patterns of communication on WMST-L without reference to the content of that interaction. Patterns of interaction form the structure within which communication takes place. Table 1 summarizes the interaction for these six months.

Table 1. Patterns of participation on WMST-L 8/91 through 1/92

Months	*Persons*	*Posts*	*Mode*	*Mean*
August 1991	28	51	1	1.82
September 1991	47	74	1	1.57
October 1991	77	190	1	2.46
November 1991	125	245	1	1.96
December 1991	117	267	1	2.28
January 1992	147	311	1	2.11
TOTAL	[322]*	1,138		

* Because some participants posted messages in more than one month, the total number of participants for the period reported here does not equal the sum of the participants in this table.

During the six months from August 1991 through January 1992, 322 participants posted 1,138 messages. Both participants and messages increased steadily over this period. Fewer persons posted messages in December, probably because many faculty and students are on vacation during that period, but the number of messages increased nonetheless. In no case was the median or mode of posts more than one. These figures argue for a general participation among members; the discussion was not dominated by a small group of contributors.

Five persons contributed messages during all six months in this period. The 196 messages posted by these five persons account for only 18.3% of the total messages posted from August 1991 through January 1992; these findings again support a claim for general participation on WMST-L.

Participation on WMST-L continued to increase in the next year; during the six months between August 1992 and January 1993, 528 persons posted 1,747 messages. Table 2 illustrates the increasing participation on WMST-L over this period.

A total of eight persons posted messages to WMST-L each month during the period from August 1992 through January 1993. In all, these eight persons contributed 18.6% of the total messages posted to WMST-L during this six-month period. Although the message traffic from one year to the next increased by 50% and the number of persons who posted during all six months increased by 60%, the percentage of messages posted by these "regulars" remained nearly the same. The membership of this group was also remarkably stable; four persons from the first six-month period posted messages regularly

Table 2. Patterns of participation on WMST-L 8/92 through 1/93

Month	*Persons*	*Posts*	*Mode*	*Mean*
August 1992	102	148	1	1.45
September 1992	133	259	1	1.94
October 1992	168	321	1	1.91
November 1992	201	431	1	2.14
December 1992	135	223	1	1.65
January 1993	193	365	1	1.89
TOTAL	[528]*	1,747		

* Because some participants posted messages in more than one month, the total number of participants for the period reported here does not equal the sum of the participants in this table.

during the second six-month period. The fifth person from the first six-month period posted messages during five of the six months between August 1992 and January 1993, and two of the persons who appear for the first time in Table 2 sent messages to WMST-L during five months between August 1991 and January 1992. We find a remarkable consistency of regular participation by a small group of persons, who apparently serve as the "core" of the discussion. This small core of regular posters contributes four times as often as the rest of the membership, who average one to two messages per month. Regular contributors to other e-mail discussions often exceed this average; Herring (1993a) reports that the regular posters on LINGUIST post eight times as often as the remainder of the membership. Nonetheless, the pattern of a small core of regular participants corresponds closely to the behavior of participants in face-to-face interaction (see, e.g., Hare, Borgatta, and Bales 1965).

We note parenthetically that two of the five persons who contributed messages during all six months from August 1991 through January 1992 are male. One of those men also sent messages during all six months from August 1992 through January 1993, and the other man sent messages during five of those months. Examination of the subscriber list for August 1991 reveals that men made up approximately 20% of subscribers at that time; a year later, as publicity about the list appeared in more women's studies publications and conferences, men constituted approximately 12% of subscribers. Though the numbers are too small to be significant, we note that men are represented among the consistent contributors in 1992 (1 of 8, or 12%) in almost exact proportion to their presence as subscribers. In this respect, their participation seems to diverge from the common pattern of male domination of communication interactions reported in previous studies (e.g., Kramarae & Taylor 1993; Herring, Johnson, & DiBenedetto 1992; Herring, This volume). More research would be needed to determine the extent to which male participation on WMST-L differs from that on other lists, and the significance of any such differences.

5. Discussion

In this section we address two research questions related to patterns of participation on WMST-L. The first focuses on the claim that computer-mediated communication encourages communication across social, geographic, professional, hierarchical, and institutional boundaries (Hiltz 1982).

5.1. Crossing boundaries

One of the questionnaire items asked respondents to identify their professions using a category scheme we provided. Tenured faculty (58 of 191 respondents, or 30.4%) made up the largest group. Next were untenured faculty (42; 22.0%), followed by graduate students (33; 17.3%), librarians (26; 13.6%), administrators (9; 4.7%), undergraduate students (2; 1.0%), and others (21; 11.0%). Since WMST-L was expressly designed for an academic usership, we were not surprised to find that most respondents are university faculty, graduate students, and librarians. Indeed, over half of the respondents are faculty. We were especially interested, however, in the rather large category of "other" professions, which were difficult to categorize. These professions included software designer, retired research psychologist at a museum, PBS TV news director, counselor, university secretary, research scientist, senior policy advisor for educational equity, computer engineer, technical editor, technical services assistant at library, physician, science writer, software engineer, project assistant to a committee on women in science, unaffiliated feminist researcher, post-doc in art and religion, continuing education office manager, computer science center consultant, National Women's Studies Association office manager, and research assistant. If this diversity is characteristic not only of those who returned questionnaires, but also of the membership at large, this finding supports a claim that communication across traditional professional boundaries is taking place on WMST-L despite the fact that the forum is specifically designed for and targeted toward women's studies academics.

Communication takes place across social and hierarchical as well as institutional boundaries in that tenured and untenured faculty, graduate students, librarians, and administrators ask and answer questions and discuss issues related to Women's Studies teaching, research, and administration. Participants are themselves aware of this phenomenon; one respondent noted: "[E]lectronic forums tend to quash many of the hierarchies implicit in much of academia. I like to see students getting responses from faculty they might never approach otherwise and vice-versa." We must qualify this claim by noting that although nearly a third of the respondents to the questionnaire were graduate students, there were only two responses from undergraduate students. If the respondents reflect WMST-L's membership, most of the interaction between students and faculty is on the level of graduate study.

Examination of the subscriber list reveals that members represent 48 of the 50 states in the U.S. Questionnaires were returned from universities in 37 states and Washington, D.C. Six questionnaires were returned from non-university sources within the United States. Additionally, questionnaires were returned from Australia, Brazil, Canada, Denmark, Ireland, and Switzerland; 19 questionnaires came from Canada and one questionnaire came from each of the other countries. We interpret these data to indicate that there is a wide distribution of participation across geographical but not institutional boundaries.

We have discussed the collaborative interaction occurring on-line on WMST-L, but an electronic computer-mediated forum also allows for private communication among persons who have met only through e-mail. We asked respondents to describe their correspondence with persons they had "met" through WMST-L. Well over half of the persons who answered this question (116 of 188; 61.7%) said they had corresponded privately with other members of the list more than twice. In all, 80.3% (151 persons) had corresponded at least once with another member of WMST-L whom they had met through the forum. Most of the persons who responded to this question said they had answered a question or responded to a request for resources privately. There were only a few accounts of extended personal or professional relationships, and one or two mentions of possible collaborative research studies that were initiated through this medium. (Indeed, this study is the result of a private communication sparked by interaction on WMST-L :-).)

We analyzed the topics of communication mentioned by respondents. Of the 146 people who indicated the topics of their private correspondence with persons they had met over WMST-L, 140 (92.7%) communicated about Women's Studies topics. We note, too, that nearly three-quarters of all respondents reported having corresponded about Women's Studies issues with other members of WMST-L whom they met through e-mail. These figures indicate a high degree of communicative interaction both on the list and off.

The question remains, however, whether the medium of e-mail is in itself the stimulus for this communication, or whether other factors are involved. It is possible that computer-mediated communication simply allows for another form of the professional collaboration already common among this group. We might argue that this collaborative bent was what led the participants in WMST-L to the forum and not the reverse. While the medium may allow for communication across boundaries, we might also argue that communication across boundaries characterizes Women's Studies faculty, staff, and students, and that they bring this collaboration to the new medium of computer-mediated communication. Comparison to similar studies in other fora may shed light on this question, and further research is certainly called for.

5.2. "Groupness"

The simple fact of communication among members of WMST-L, whether public or private, does not substantiate any claim for a feeling of "groupness" within this forum. We found two ways of investigating the extent to which persons within the forum felt themselves to be members of a group. Analysis of the content of the questionnaires revealed that persons often mentioned one of the "satisfying and useful" aspects of WMST-L to be a "sense of community". Additionally, many more members said that they enjoyed the discussion of Women's Studies issues and shared personal experiences reported on WMST-L. We took those statements to be evidence of the personal response to group participation that is said to characterize a feeling of group cohesion described by Brilhart and Galanes (1992:174) as "the common bonds and sentiments that hold a group together". Brilhart and Galanes report that cohesiveness is fostered partly by the extent to which members know and like each other as individuals. We argue that discussion of personal experience is an important element in the development of cohesion on WMST-L. Table 3 documents the responses from the content analysis of responses to the open-ended questionnaire item which asked respondents to list "useful and satisfying" aspects of WMST-L:

Table 3. Useful/satisfying aspects of WMST-L reported by respondents

Satisfactions	*Number*	*Percent of Respondents*
Information	129	67.2%
Discussion of Personal Experience	78	40.6%
Discussion of Pedagogy	69	35.9%
Sense of Community	43	22.4%
Announcements	31	16.1%
Restricted Focus	30	15.6%
Film Reviews	14	7.3%
Discussion of WS Programs	13	6.8%
Digest Form of WMST-L	13	6.8%
Increased Knowledge	13	6.8%
Consideration/Politeness	10	5.2%
Personal Contacts	7	3.6%
Other	22	11.5%

The response categories are not mutually exclusive. Some categories are clearly subsets of larger categories: announcements and film reviews are subsets of the more general category "Information". "Sense of Community" was specifically mentioned by 43 persons (22.4% of the respondents) as a satisfying aspect of WMST-L. We also interpret "Discussion of Personal Experience", which 78 respondents (40.6%) mentioned, as evidence that participants feel an emotional connection with the group; discussion of personal issues is generally considered an aspect of group cohesion (Brilhart & Galanes 1992). Interestingly, ten people (5.2% of respondents) mentioned consideration for other persons to be an aspect of the forum that they appreciated. We interpreted this to refer to the fact that WMST-L is relatively free from flames or emotional outbursts. A quick reading of the logs will reveal that differences of opinion abound on the forum, so there is no lack of topics that could give rise to flames were participants inclined to take offense.

5.3. Norms

We have discussed some evidence that points toward a feeling of "groupness" among the members of WMST-L. Another way of exploring the extent to which the interaction on this forum might be said to resemble group process is to look at how interaction on the forum is regulated. From an observer's perspective, can we identify consistent patterns of interaction that could be interpreted as norms?

Identifying the rules for interaction is relatively simple; the listowner sends out the "WMST-L User's Guide" to all new members and posts excerpts from the Guide regularly on WMST-L. These guidelines are drawn partly from rules common to many e-mail fora, and partly from suggestions offered by WMST-L participants themselves. The rules are intended as a common sense guide to make participation on WMST-L both simple and efficient; there are no official sanctions for disregarding these rules. Members are encouraged to end all messages with their name and e-mail address so that readers can respond privately if they so wish. This procedure is important because some nodes strip the headers when the messages are forwarded or posted to bulletin boards. When responding to a previous message, members are encouraged to include a short summary—a synopsis or direct quote—so that readers will be able to interpret the response. If the message header alone provides a sufficient context for the response, no summary is necessary. Members are reminded that messages to subscribe or unsubscribe should be sent to LISTSERV and that any questions concerning subscriptions or the forum should be sent to Korenman. The guidelines indicate that discussions relevant to Women's Studies teaching, research, and program administration are welcome, but that other lists exist for discussions of women's issues or feminist issues unrelated to teaching, research, or administration of Women's Studies programs. There are occasional on-line discussions of the proper application of these guidelines.

Using these guidelines as criteria, we coded the messages for the month of August 1991, when the "WMST-L User's Guide" was first posted, and the messages for the following August. If a message violated any one of these criteria, we coded it "incomplete".

Table 4. Complete/incomplete messages — 8/91 and 8/92

	August 1991	*August 1992*
Complete	27 (52.9%)	62 (40.8%)
Incomplete	24 (47.1%)	90 (59.2%)
TOTAL	51 (100.0%)	152 (100.0%)

This gross analysis gives the impression that participants on WMST-L are generally disregarding the "WMST-L User's Guide". But a look at specific comparisons of patterns of interaction to the individual rules for interaction, which appear in Table 5, reveals an interesting pattern:

*Table 5. Incomplete messages — specific criteria**

	August 1991	*August 1992*	*% Change*
Incomplete Signature	12 (23.5%)	44 (28.9%)	+ 5.4%
Inadequate Summary of Previous Message	16 (31.4%)	65 (42.8%)	+ 11.4%
Messages Meant for LISTSERV	3 (5.9%)	5 (3.3%)	- 2.6%
Messages Meant for Korenman	1 (2.0%)	2 (1.3%)	- 0.7%
Messages Meant for Individuals	3 (5.9%)	61 (40.1%)	+ 34.2%
Messages Meant for Another List	9 (17.6%)	12 (7.9%)	- 9.7%
Inappropriate/Inaccurate Headers	6 (11.8%)	17 (11.2%)	- 0.6%
Missing Headers	4 (7.8%)	1 (0.7%)	- 7.1%

* Because some messages violated more than one guideline, the totals in Table 5 exceed the total number of messages reported in Table 4.

This analysis reveals that in August 1992, there were fewer messages appropriate to other fora, and fewer messages had missing, inappropriate or inaccurate headers. At the same time, there were far more messages that should have been sent to individuals rather than to WMST-L, and more messages lacked recommended signatures or summaries of messages responded to. We might argue that the continued apparent disregard of the guidelines results from increased membership and turnover of membership. But members cannot plead ignorance of guidelines that are posted monthly, and that factor alone cannot account for the significant variance in patterns of failure to follow the guidelines.

We offer a different interpretation of these data. The data may indicate that participants have either learned or agreed to follow the rules related to appropriate content for WMST-L; by and large, they are sending LISTSERV messages to LISTSERV and messages unrelated to teaching, research or administration of Women's Studies programs to other discussion lists. But many of them continue to ignore three guidelines: signatures, summaries of previous messages to which they are responding, and posting messages addressed to individuals to the entire list. While some of this failure to follow the guidelines may result from difficulties with e-mail systems, the sheer number of entries in these categories argues against this interpretation. We suggest that the discrepancy between the behavior suggested by the guidelines and actual behavior illustrate a difference in how the communication on WMST-L is conceptualized.

5.3.1. Forms of discourse

The "WMST-L User's Guide" posits the messages in this forum as written discourse. In written discourse it is necessary to identify the source of a message and customary to identify the subject, usually at the beginning of a message. These message elements are both customary and necessary for clear understanding when the communication takes place asynchronously between persons separated geographically, hierarchically, and/or socially. We almost never send or receive a letter that begins, "You know you're absolutely right..." or "And another thing..." or that contains an answer to a question without reference to that question.

In oral, face-to-face discourse, however, formal practices are perceived as cumbersome and unnecessary; persons respond to questions or comments without prefatory remarks and almost never identify themselves as the source of a particular message. In most small group meetings or conversations among a group of friends remarks are exchanged freely, sometimes directed to the group and sometimes to individuals in the group. There are, in fact, usually two or more threads of conversation occurring simultaneously among members of a group on both official and unofficial topics. We observe that the discourse on WMST-L resembles more nearly this description of a small group meeting or conversation among friends than a written discourse conducted between correspondents or among scholars.

Some examples of oral discourse style posted to WMST-L will illustrate our point. Messages posted by Korenman follow the guidelines exactly and serve as a model for other participants:

> Earlier today, [Name deleted] asked for some information about
> witchcraft films that had appeared on WMST-L sometime last spring.
> Coincidentally, I've received several requests recently asking about
> messages that had appeared earlier. I'd like to remind people that it is

possible to do very specific database searches of the WMST-L archives. For example, to find a prior message about witchcraft films, you can do a search for messages about "witchcraft", or for messages that include BOTH "witchcraft" and "film", etc. You can search the entire archives or limit the search to a particular period of time. You can ask that the search include the entire message, or just the subject header.

Charles Bailey wrote a very clear, brief set of instructions for performing such searches on a list called PACS-L, but the instructions apply equally well to WMST-L. To get a copy of Bailey's instructions, send the following message to LISTSERV@UMDD or LISTSERV@UMDD.UMD.EDU:

GET SEARCH LOGFILES WMST-L

You will be sent a file (or a mail message, if you're on the Internet) called SEARCH LOGFILES. It contains Bailey's very useful instructions.

Joan Korenman Internet: korenman@umbc2.umbc.edu
Bitnet: korenman@umbc

By contrast, we argue that the following four examples of messages posted to WMST-L illustrate adherence to an oral, face-to-face style of interaction characterized by spontaneity and an assumption that people who are reading the words will be able to put them into the appropriate context:

1. I have probably said a variety of things about MacKinnon in different contexts, and for the life of me I can't figure out which one you're referring to -- so call me a space cadet!
2. My copy of the book has a 1971 copyright date with a 1973 reprinting.
3. no
4. and yet she doesn't show the women as convincing in the "sociopolitical" stye of governent as she might, pitting the two Pro-Matriarchs against ecah other then converting the bad one to good with no credible reason; but of course MXB always asserts (in Friends of Darkover books, repeatedly) that she's no feminist and someitmes sounds positivey vindictively anti-femi (aargh-communication interrupt!) and sometimes sounds positively anti-feminist. I find her an inetresting case of an author in growth/change: comparing Darkover Landfall with, for eg, The Shatttered Chain. [errors in original]

Oral discourse, more so than written discourse, is also characterized by the frequent reference to other participants by their given names, the use of names as terms of address, or the frequent use of "you" to refer to individuals engaged in the discourse. We analyzed 430 messages from August and September 1992; 49 messages were announcements by Korenman or messages intended for LISTSERV, which left us with 381 regular messages from participants. Overwhelmingly, messages that met the criteria specified above occurred as responses to previous messages, so we figured these categories both as a percentage of responses (270 messages) and as a percentage of the 381 regular messages. We found 40 messages that referred to another participant by name (14.8% of replies; 10.5% of total messages); 34 messages addressed another participant by name (12.6% of replies; 8.9% of total); and 47 messages addressed another participant as "you" (17.4% of replies; 12.3% of total). Participants on the list might get the impression of a conversation as they "listen" to the messages on their computer screens. Lacking data from other lists, we are hesitant to make claims about the meaning of most of these statistical measures. We believe, however, that the statistical evidence supported by examples indicates that to a large extent the members of WMST-L conceptualize the computer-mediated communication on this forum as a kind of pseudo-oral communication. The following discussion of our analysis of metacommunication bears on the issue of the interpretation of the nature of the discourse on WMST-L.

5.3.2. Metacommunication

Metacommunication is talk about talk. By looking at the ways in which participants discuss what is or is not appropriate on WMST-L, we can get an idea of what they think the norms are or should be. One way of identifying norms are to look at the metacommunication we generally label "apologies" and "complaints". When people realize they are violating norms, they often apologize for their misbehavior. When someone violates a norm, someone else may complain about the violation. By noting and analyzing such instances, we can identify common definitions of appropriate modes of behavior on WMST-L.

Examination of the logs from August 1992 through January 1993 reveals 90 apologies. Of these, 58 (64.5%) are related to the distinction between messages that should be sent to individuals and messages that should be sent to WMST-L. Participants seem to recognize the importance of sending some messages privately; the lack of inclusion of e-mail addresses so that people can reply privately where appropriate was the subject of 16 apologies (17.8%). When participants sent messages to the list that they meant to send privately or made it impossible for others to send messages to them privately, they apologized.

The topic of which messages should be sent privately and which should be sent to WMST-L also figured prominently among the 21 complaints sent to the list during this same six-month period. Nine of the 21 complaints (42.8%) objected to postings that should have been sent privately. The definition of which messages belong on WMST-L for the membership at large and which should be sent to individual members bears directly on the definition of the extent to which the interaction on the forum is defined as written or oral in nature. In oral communication, such messages are mostly appropriate, although they may be made *sotto voce* or possibly with appropriate nonverbal signals. In written communication, these messages constitute noise in the channel that interrupts discourse and irritates some readers. A continuing tension over the definition of the nature of discourse on WMST-L characterizes the interaction. (A different ongoing controversy, one concerning the list's scope, provided the subject for nine of the remaining twelve complaints.)

6. Conclusion

We return in our conclusion to the impression that was the impetus for this study; interaction on WMST-L feels like interaction within a group. We have identified the high rate of personal e-mail messages both on and off the list as one important characteristic of the communicative interaction that may contribute to this impression. These personal exchanges account in large part for the high number of messages sent to WMST-L emulating oral discourse, leaving readers with the impression that they are listening to a conversation instead of reading a series of memos. Examination of the logs has also revealed a core of participants who each contribute a few messages every month; their messages make up approximately 18 percent of the interaction in any given period. From their regular patterns of participation, these persons have undoubtedly developed public personae within the context of this forum. Their userids and discourse will have become familiar to WMST-L members and will provide continuity that contributes to a perception of conversation among a group of colleagues or friends. It is largely these oral discourse practices, we argue, that create the "sense of community" mentioned by respondents to the questionnaire.

It is also in large part these oral discourse patterns and personal messages that form the basis for complaints. Changes toward a more formal style of interaction are perceptible in the complaints about personal messages and in apologies of individuals who have sent personal messages through WMST-L.

One of the truisms of small group communication is the observation that as the size of the group meeting face-to-face increases, personal interactions among members tend to become more complex and to decrease, and the nature of the discourse becomes more formalized and rule bound (Brilhart & Galanes 1992). More discourse is directed toward the work of the group and less discourse is personal in nature, until finally the camaraderie and sense of community are lost entirely and the group becomes a collection of individuals who coordinate their behavior but who do not feel themselves to be connected to the group by emotional or psychological ties with other members. So far this process does not seem to have occurred on WMST-L; the question of whether such a process will overtake the participants on WMST-L remains to be seen. If not, this exception to the general rule may prove fertile ground for further study and theorizing.

We have addressed only in passing one aspect of WMST-L that may be an important factor in its growth and in the satisfaction of participants with the forum. Members of WMST-L are bound by common goals, assumptions, and vocabulary, but these are by no means conditions that are unique to WMST-L. WMST-L participants are, however, additionally bound to one another by the fact that as feminists, participants are very likely a minority in most other groups and organizations in which they must interact. WMST-L provides a safe place for the participants to discuss common interests and for them to receive encouragement and support from one another.

NOTES

1. WMST-L digest subscribers receive the day's messages arranged in bundles and distributed once each day.

Appendix

This is the questionnaire that was sent:

Nancy Wyatt (NJW@PSUVM), a professor of Speech Communications at Penn State, and I are collaborating on a research project concerning the uses people make of an e-mail list like WMST-L. We're interested both in the ways people have used the list and in what changes, if any, the list has helped bring about. We've devised a moderately short questionnaire that WE'D LIKE TO ENCOURAGE YOU TO FILL OUT AND RETURN EVEN IF YOU HAVEN'T PARTICIPATED ACTIVELY ON THE LIST (the questionnaire will follow these introductory remarks). All quotations from the responses will be kept anonymous, and the raw data will be kept confidential. We will be happy to share our findings with those who participate in the study; indeed, we may be turning to some of you to help us interpret our findings.

The questionnaire follows. I've set a "reply-to" header so that if you hit "reply", your response will be sent privately to me, not to WMST-L). If you'd prefer to send the questionnaire via snail mail, please send it to Joan Korenman, Women's Studies Program, UMBC, Baltimore, Maryland 21228-5398 USA. For us to be able to use your response, it must reach us by the end of February.

Many thanks.

Joan Korenman Internet: korenman@umbc2.umbc.edu
Bitnet: korenman@umbc

****

1. How long have you subscribed to WMST-L?

2. How did you learn about WMST-L?

3. What is your profession/job?

[If your position involves more than one of the following categories, please indicate the area of your PRIMARY RESPONSIBILITY with a "P" and the area(s) of SECONDARY RESPONSIBILITY with an "S".

_____ Tenured faculty

_____ Untenured faculty

_____ Librarian

_____ Administrator

_____ Graduate Student

_____ Undergraduate Student

_____ Other (please describe)

3a. What is your discipline or area of study?

4. Please describe your connection with women's studies.

5. Have you corresponded privately with any other members of WMST-L whom you 'met' through the list? Please describe briefly the nature of your correspondence with other members of the list.

6. Have you modified your views on any important topics or issues as a result of discussions on WMST-L? Please describe briefly the topics on which you modified your views and explain how and why you changed your views on these topics.

7. Have you modified your teaching philosophy or practice as a result of your participation on WMST-L? Please describe briefly how you modified your teaching philosophy or practice and how and why you changed them.

8. Which aspects of WMST-L do you find most useful and satisfying? Please explain why these aspects are important to you.

9. Which aspects of WMST-L have you found to be problematic or frustrating? Please explain why these aspects are important to you.

10. What else would you like to tell the researchers about WMST-L or your participation on that list?

Writing to Work:
How Using E-Mail Can Reflect Technological and Organizational Change

Oren Ziv
University of California, Berkeley

1. Introduction*

In this chapter, I present a case study of how three workers use e-mail to negotiate technological and organizational conflict that resulted from an article being drafted for a university newsletter. This case is taken from a qualitative study focusing on the relationships between writing and technological and organizational changes within workplaces. All of the general questions I ask center around the "new kinds of cultural dialogues" (Dyson and Freedman 1991:4) one might enter through writing when electronic communications are involved. These questions are:

1. How do people work together differently when electronic forms of communication are made available?
2. How do such technologies interact with the social patterns of the workplace?
3. How does the availability of electronic mail and other forms of network communication influence the hierarchical structures within the workplace organization?

These questions are all concerned with how workers use computer-mediated text to perform their jobs, and the effects this use has on the organizational structures of workplaces.

Popular claims of egalitarian effects of computer networking are often based on management hyperbole rather than research taking into account the perspectives of workers at various positions throughout an organization (cf. Wilke 1993). In order to address this deficiency, the present study closely examines three workers' perspectives on using e-mail in an attempt to make explicit some implicit notions of how writing with computer technology reshapes and is reshaped by organizational behavior within workplaces.

2. Background

2.1. Computer-mediated writing and organizational behavior

Although writing and computer-based communications are inexorably intertwined within the workplace, it is difficult to locate empirical research on how computer-mediated writing, in particular, has effected organizational behavior. Here, I briefly review two exceptions: one that looked at the differences between electronic mail and other forms of communication, another that examined the effects of computer-mediated communication on an organizational hierarchy.

Reder and Schwab (1989) studied how the use of e-mail shaped task-oriented workgroup behavior among technical professionals within a high-tech firm. These researchers found that computer-mediated communication does not have a uniform set of interactive or functional characteristics, as some of the earlier, less empirical literature on e-mail has implied. Instead, they found that professionals often used computer-mediated communication along with other types of communication for related sequences of interaction, where interactants' choices of vehicle were made in relation to their personal set of communicative strategies and tactics. The authors suggest that users ascribe active social meanings and evaluations to the use of computer-mediated communications technologies.

Sherblom (1988) examined all of the electronic mail files (N=157) received over several months by a middle level manager in the computer-communications services department of a large organization. In so doing, Sherblom found evidence that e-mail reflected and interacted with the hierarchical structure of the organization, impacting the communications system of the organization as a whole. In particular, Sherblom noted differences in form and function between those messages sent upward through the organizational hierarchy and those sent horizontally or downward. Sherblom concluded that "communication patterns are negotiated within a meaningful context that facilitates some social realities and discourages others" (51).

One difficulty with the existing literature on computer-mediated writing in the workplace is that much of it examines the writing of engineers, since they were the principal early adopters of the technology. Engineers and scientists may have more of a predilection for using the latest technology than other workers. For example, James Gleick reported in *The New York Times Magazine* (May 16, 1993) that when the phone rang during an interview with Arno Penzias, the Nobel laureate who directed research at Bell Laboratories, Penzias "grouse[d]:

why didn't the caller use electronic mail instead? Voice can be so retrograde, so intrusive." It is equally important, however, to examine attitudes toward the use of computer-mediated writing among a variety of different workers—such as managers, clerks, engineers, and laborers—in a variety of different work settings.

2.2 . *Writing as social dialogue*

In the following case study, I will examine how the computer-mediated writing of workers of a particular organization reflects their membership in a changing, hierarchical workplace culture. Underlying my investigation is the philosopher Mikhail Bakhtin's (1986) notion of the text as situated within social relationships. As Morson (1986) explains:

> Any patterned way of using language—any kind of text or genre—temporarily crystallize(s) a network of relations (p. 89) between themselves and other people; those relations include the author's sense of (a) her or his power and status vis-a-vis the other, (b) the purposes that have brought them together, (c) the topic of their discourse, and (d) the history of other conversations they have had. A particular kind of text, then, is an articulation of a particular kind of social relationship, of one's place in the ongoing social dialogue. (cited in Dyson 1992:5)

I assume, moreover, that examining the particular context of writing from the perspective of the participants involved is the best way to understand the nature of how writing and organizational change are linked.

3. Method

3.1. *Site and participants*

Michael, Brad, and Thomas[1] are members of the Technology Planning Services (TPS) team within the Telecommunications department of a major research university. The department, which includes approximately 45 employees, has recently undergone major organizational restructuring, which included becoming part of the university's Academic Information Systems (AIS) organization. Prior to this reorganization, Telecommunications was under the supervision of the vice chancellor of Business and Administrative Services (BAS). Now, as a department within AIS, it falls under the jurisdiction of the academic vice chancellor and the provost for Research, and specifically, the vice provost for Academic Information Systems (See Figure 1). All three focal subjects had been members of the department since before the reorganization.

There are noticeable differences between Telecommunications and the rest of AIS. Physically, Telecommunications is located on two floors of a modest office building a city block away from the university campus, while the majority of the AIS organization has offices on the same floor of the computer science building on campus. Telecommunications' carpeted and cubicle laden offices have a decidedly business-like feel to them; however, the rest of AIS is hard to discern from the academic departments that surround it.

TPS is one of four groups within Telecommunications. It is responsible for assessing and evaluating current and future voice communications technologies for the campus, managing local computer and information systems within the Telecommunications department, and marketing telecommunications services to the campus community. At the time of my observations, there were five members of the TPS team.

Michael, the associate director, manages TPS and reports directly to Cynthia, the director of Telecommunications. Michael is a European-American man who appeared to be in his early thirties at the time of my observation. He had already worked at the university for a number of years in administrative positions. Prior to reorganization, he was acting associate director of Communications in charge of Business and Finance. He clearly demonstrated an interest in the emerging technology that his team was in charge of investigating. At the same time, he also reported that he desires to build a cooperative team which allows for increased participation and provides the maximum opportunity for personal development to each of its members.

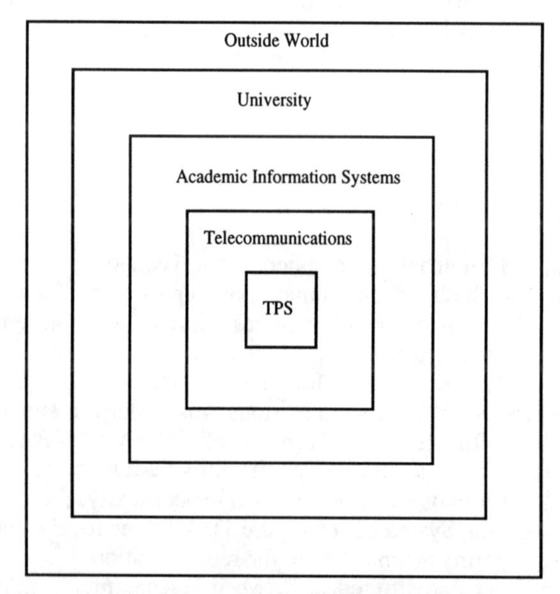

Figure 1. Social hierarchical frame

Brad is a European-American man who appeared to be in his late twenties at the time. He serves as an analyst. As such, he is directly responsible for investigating new telecommunications technologies and preparing written reports on both their short-term and long-range applicability for the campus. He also handles various automation and technology-related projects. Although Brad is adept at understanding technical topics, he majored in English, and not science or engineering, as an undergraduate. He said he "accidentally stepped into this", and was planning to leave the Telecommunication department in August in order to attend law school at the university. Brad voluntarily participates in team meetings more often than other members, and seemed particularly concerned with receiving and imparting information that could be valuable to the team.

Thomas, another European-American man, appeared to be in his mid-twenties. He dresses in a more traditionally business-like manner than other team members. As the marketing coordinator for Telecommunications, his role was formerly to conduct market research, develop and implement marketing plans, and perform other analytic tasks related to marketing activities. However, since the reorganization, practically all of Thomas's time is taken up revising the department's "recharge rates", the amount it charges campus customers to recover the costs for various telecommunications services. Thomas is very focused on a career in higher-education administration. He is an active participant in the campus staff assembly and in various management training programs.

3.2. Data collection

Data collection took place from March 15 through April 30, 1993. During this period, I observed three one-hour weekly team meetings, three one-on-one direct report meetings, conducted six open-ended interviews, and collected all of the e-mail messages sent by three of the participants. I also requested and collected—with mixed success—copies of printed documents produced by team members.

I made handwritten observation notes of meetings and interviews, and requested and received photocopies of memos, letters, and reports. I was able to collect e-mail messages from my focal subjects by copying onto a floppy disk all their e-mail messages, which had been automatically saved onto their computers' hard disks by their e-mail software. I ultimately collected 295 e-mail messages sent or received by my three focal subjects.

My goal in making internal sampling decisions was to find focal subjects who were representative of all the workers within the department as a whole. Ultimately, however, focal subjects were self-selected by their willingness to provide e-mail messages and printed documents, as well as by their and my success at scheduling interviews. As a result, the focal subjects—three white males—do not represent the gender and cultural diversity of the group.

My stance toward the group was that of a participant observer, maintaining the minimum amount of interaction necessary to enable me to observe in a naturalistic, unobtrusive way. At the same time, in order to foster participation, I presented myself to both the associate director and the group not just as a researcher studying issues of writing and technological change, but also as someone with over ten years of experience implementing computer technology within dynamic workplace environments. On a few occasions, when asked, I gave my opinion on certain computer technologies. I also used e-mail messages to coordinate many of my own interactions with the group in order to support my stance as a technologically-knowledgeable observer.

At the first team meeting I observed, I was introduced by the associate director, who assured the group that my role was not evaluative, and that he felt that my observations and analysis might help the group toward their own objectives. I explained to the group that their degree of participation in my study was entirely at their own discretion.

My basic data-gathering units were communicative events, which I sorted according to the communicative channel used by members of the group. These channels included face-to-face meetings, printed documents, and e-mail messages (See Table 1). By contrasting the use of e-mail with the use of these other communicative channels, I sought to understand both when and how e-mail communication takes place, and the social context that surrounds it.

Table 1. Communicative channels observed

Face-to-Face Meetings	*Printed Documents*	*E-mail*
Weekly team meetings	Handwritten notes	Direct messages
Direct report meetings	Formal memos	List postings
Informal conversations	Letters	Documents
	Reports	Downloaded information
	Project plans	
	Agendas	
	Meeting reports	

3.3. Data analysis

After reading through the collected documents, e-mail messages, and field notes, I decided to focus only on productive communicative activities where the focal subjects were active participants. This meant that I would closely examine the e-mail messages they sent, and not those they received or downloaded (electronically copied) from the campus network. I also examined the participation of each subject within the observed direct-report and team meetings.

Second, I analyzed each of the e-mail messages sent by the participants for characteristics related to my research questions and previous research on the use of e-mail (e.g. Reder and Schwab 1989, Sherblom 1988, Sproull and Kiesler 1991). These included (a) the date written, (b) the length of each message in lines, (c) the subject of the message as written in its header, (d) the communicative purpose of the message, (d) whether it was structured in paragraph or outline form, (e) the formality of the style of writing, (f) the identity of the addressee, (g) the addressee's organizational position, (h) at what hierarchical level the addressee's position was situated in relation to the sender, (i) the organizational affiliation of the addressee, (j) the type of message closing used, (k) the signature used, and (l) whether the message was written in response to a previous message.

Third, through inductive analysis, I developed a set of categories that characterized the communicative purposes found within the e-mail messages and printed documents, noting whether e-mail messages were written often, occasionally, or seldom for these particular purposes (See Table 2). These purposes will be illustrated through discussion of the case itself.

Fourth, I examined all of the field notes from interviews, direct-report meetings, and team meetings for evidence of communications for the above and other purposes. I added new purposes identified to the above list, and noted whether they were used often, occasionally, or seldom during these activities.

Fifth and last, I examined all the field notes, e-mail messages, and printed documents for evidence reflecting participants' perceptions of the organizational and technological changes taking place within the Telecommunications department. As a result of this examination, I identified the various communications regarding an article being written for the department's newsletter as particularly reflective of the relationships between the technological and organizational changes taking place.

In the following section, I first present background information leading up to my case study. Then I present the case of the article for the university newsletter, paying particular attention to the function of e-mail messages.

4. Findings

4.1. Fitting into a technology-centered culture

More than physical distance separated Telecommunications from the rest of AIS. According to Michael, the associate director, it is the least "technologically sophisticated" group in AIS. Telecommunications has traditionally functioned principally as a service organization, handling service orders and billing for campus telecommunications services, while contracting with the local telephone company to manage almost all of the technical aspects of the campus telephone system. As in the past, Telecommunications was responsible for all voice communications technology on campus, while Data Communications, an existing department within AIS, was responsible for computer networking. However, voice and data communications technology are quickly merging, and the reorganization of Telecommunications into AIS was a response to this technological change.

Table 2. Taxonomy of communicative purposes

Communicative Purposes	*E-Mail*	*Printed Documents*	*Team Meetings*	*Direct Meetings*
Acquiring Technological Expertise			=	
Assigning New Responsibilities				+
Collaborating and Cooperating			+	
Considering Cross-training			=	+
Considering Information Storage/Access			=	
Considering Site Location			=	
Delivering Documents	-	=	=	
Discussing Goals and Objectives		=	+	=
Discussing Hiring Process			+	
Discussing Information Sharing			+	
Discussing Using E-Mail	-		=	=
Establishing Links with AIS			=	+
Forwarding Information	+			
Handling Administrative Requests	=	=		
Improving Health and Safety			=	
Offering Feedback	=		-	+
Personal Correspondence	=			
Preparing Budget		=	+	+
Prioritizing Responsibilities			-	+
Providing Opinions	-		-	+
Reporting Information	+	=	+	+
Reporting Project Status	=		+	+
Requesting Action	-	=	-	+
Requesting Information	+		=	+
Reviewing Documents	-		-	+
Setting Schedules	-		-	+
Solving Computer Problems	+		=	+
Suggesting Meeting or Phone Call	+		-	

Key
Often + Seldom -
Occasionally = Not Observed

According to an article authored by the vice provost of AIS in the January-February 1993 edition of the *Campus Computing* newsletter, "The transfer of Telecommunications to AIS will enable both that organization and Data Communications to work more closely together to facilitate completion of the campus network....To complete this network requires the strong collaboration of different groups, taking the best from all available communication technologies and designing the best overall system for our extended campus community."

As the vice provost recognized, the merging of the university's voice and data communications resources was more than a purely technological challenge. It would require two campus organizations with very different cultures to learn to collaborate. By examining the use of e-mail as a communicative channel by TPS, one group within Telecommunications, I was able to observe some of the social forces at work as this group attempted to maintain control over its area of responsibility, while at the same time learning to adapt to the organizational culture of a more technologically-centered organization.

Far from adverse to new technologies or their organizational move into AIS, members of TPS were generally positive about the changes. Thomas felt that the department was now more protected from budget cuts. In fact, the group was using its new position within AIS to gain quick budget approval for upgrading Telecommunications' own computer equipment. At the same time, they pointed to a printed memo from the vice chancellor of Business and Administrative Services advising, "To protect our future, we must invest now in ideas that save money and avoid costs for the long-term. For example, we need to use computers instead of paper to provide and exchange information whenever possible." The purchase of new computers exemplified the group leveraging its transition between the worlds of AIS and BAS to improve the department's effectiveness and protect its long-term viability. During team meetings, Michael also suggested other ways that Telecommunications could make use of AIS resources, such as computer support personnel, to help in their own technology implementation efforts.

During the observation period, Michael joined a cross-departmental AIS committee chaired by Clyde, the associate director of Data Communications (Datacom). Michael's role on this committee would later play an important part in establishing Telecommunications' credibility for participation in joint activities concerning technology that crossed departmental jurisdictions.

4.2. The role of e-mail within AIS and Telecommunications

At our first meeting, Michael explained to me that e-mail was one of the most widely used forms of communication within the rest of AIS and very important for "fitting in with the culture" of AIS. He reported that other parts of AIS used e-mail extensively for communications both within workgroups and throughout the organization. In fact, the vice provost often distributed organization-wide notices by e-mail. The director and other associate directors of Telecommunications were already using e-mail. However, at the time of my observations only ten of the 45 total members of Telecommunications were using e-mail, six of whom were within TPS. Michael was using e-mail to a greater extent than any of the other members of the team. And while Michael encouraged the team to check their e-mail at least once a day, information was still generally "sent around" physically in the form of printed documents.

Although he wrote extensively using a computer, prior to the reorganization Brad felt it was better to speak in person with someone or talk over the phone than use e-mail. After the reorganization, Brad felt that using e-mail had been "informally mandated" within TPS: "It would be too backwards not to use it," he said in an interview. He felt using e-mail was important for departmental image. He reported that working with other AIS analysts on projects was pushing him to use e-mail more. His only quandary was whether he should include a greeting and closing within messages, since the e-mail system automatically included such information in the message header. His messages displayed how this uncertainty played out: first, including no signature; next, signing only his first name; then, both first and last names; back to first name only; finally, using a formal signature with his complete name, team, department, and telephone numbers. Other team members generally closed their messages with either their first names or initials. Brad's beliefs that e-mail was most useful for communications with people physically distant, as well as his uncertainty over the proper e-mail writing style, were shared by other members of the team as well as reflected by the communicative purposes for which team members used e-mail (See Table 2).

While Thomas did check his e-mail once a day, he principally used e-mail to download and store messages sent by others. He reported that he didn't have much interaction with anyone in AIS and pointed out that many of the people in BAS, with whom he still interacted, did not have e-mail accounts. He said at the time of my observation that he used e-mail more as a "social tool" in order to write to his father in Wyoming, because it was cheaper than telephoning.

4.3. The case of the ISDN article

Focusing on the social dialogue surrounding the publication of a particular article in the *Campus Computing* newsletter, I will now highlight how the use of e-mail reflected the organizational and cultural changes taking place within the Telecommunications department. The article focused on the plans by the campus to implement Integrated Services Digital Network (ISDN) technology, a particularly touchy subject, since this technology allows for data and voice communications to be transmitted over the same wiring, and thus blurs the lines of authority between Telecommunications and Data Communications.

During my first meeting with Michael on March 15, 1993, we discussed ISDN. He reported to me, "There is and will be tension on whose job this is." That same afternoon, several members of his team were attending classes sponsored by the telephone company in order to learn more about ISDN.

On March 16, 1993, Michael *forwarded*[2] an e-mail message to Cynthia, the department director, related to ISDN; the message was from an e-mail forum on the campus network for people concerned with personal computing issues. The author of the message was Wharton, the director of Datacom; in it he responds to press accounts of the university's involvement in the national "information highway" projects promoted by the Clinton Administration. He described AIS plans and progress for integrating ISDN technology for data communications, and referred people to the Telecommunications department if they were interested in voice communication applications. Wharton clearly wanted to project that the university was making substantial progress in this high-profile technology area.

During the first group meeting of TPS on March 18, 1993, ISDN was a central point on the agenda. Much of the meeting was dedicated to *reviewing and discussing written goals and objectives* for the Telecommunications department and the TPS group; these documents were part of the planning process being conducted throughout AIS. While other associate directors had drafted goals for their teams, Michael had drafted both the goals for his team and the department as a whole. Michael read through each of the Telecommunications department goals, stopping after reading, "Provide integrated voice, data, and video communication infrastructure and services by working with other departments in AIS and across the campus." He then commented, "This is the most controversial, whether it fits in with our mission."

The controversy over control of ISDN came to a head as a result of the circulation of a draft of the May-June issue of *Campus Computing* (see Appendix), the official university-wide communication organ of AIS, which contained an article explaining the campus plans for ISDN. Attached to the draft copy was a printed memo explaining who could revise the newsletter's text and *requesting action*: This memo is shown in Figure 2.

Reaction to the draft of this article lead to a heated e-mail exchange. It began when Michael recommended to the director on April 1, 1993 that she exercise her review authority *(providing opinions)* and ask that the article drafted by Datacom be held from publication and that another article be drafted by Telecommunications on the subject and be published in several months (See Figure 3). It is important to note that Michael's office was directly adjacent to the director's, yet he eventually chose e-mail as the communicative channel for making his recommendation.

Figure 2. Printed memo delivering documents and requesting actions

AIS Publications
291 Turing Hall
Re: Campus Computing, May-June issue

Attached is a draft of the May-June issue of Campus Computing for your review. Mark your comments directly on your copy and return it to 291 Turing Hall by the afternoon of Wednesday, April 7.

Directors and managers, review those sections or articles that touch upon your area of responsibility. Feel free to pass material along to your staff for further review.

If you are an author, review your article and let us know if you would like us to make any changes. If other reviewers suggest significant changes, we will let you know. Check your byline as well as any telephone numbers or electronic mail addresses that may appear in your article.

If you have any questions, please contact Emily at 64X-XXXX or Cindy at 64X-XXXX. Electronic correspondence about the newsletter should be sent to alan@turing.university.edu. This issue will appear in campus mailboxes around May 1.

The article deadline for the July-August issue is Friday, May 21.

Thank you for your help.

Michael's reaction to the draft of the article (shown in Figure 3) demonstrated a sensitivity to the service aspects of the ISDN technology. He was concerned that an article to the campus community on this subject should clearly focus on the benefits and details of subscribing to these services. He was also interested that the university's ISDN activities be represented to the campus community as jointly researched by Datacom and Telecommunications.

Figure 3. E-mail message providing opinions

Date: Thu, 1 Apr 93 10:18:03 PST
From: "Michael A. Graumann" <mag@ulink.university.edu>
To: parnasus@ulink
Cc:
BCc:
Subject: ISDN Article

Cynthia,

As I said, we should hold off on this article until we work out some major issues.
1. The article ought to be driven by the applications. That is, we ought to make clear to users what ISDN can do for them, what the costs will be, and when these services will be available.
2. We should not have two individuals in the article as contact persons for questions. This will only confuse people. We should identify one person in this department and then share the relevant inquiries with Datacom (see point 4 below).

3. There is nothing in the article about the fact that one can order these services from us now. We will need, again, to describe what is available and who to contact. (As for who to contact, as I have said, I am concerned about whether consulting services has the capability now to clearly process orders.)
4. In all of this we should be trying to think of how to make this as clear and easy for the customer as possible. We should, with this new service and opportunity, not fall into the same situation as exists when trying to establish a connection to the campus network. Let's design ISDN services so that we can have "one stop shopping". The article ought to reflect this. And we will need to do some planning before we can get this straight.
5. I think we should work out some joint research strategy with Datacom regarding applications which tie into the campus network. This can take a variety of different forms. We should at least find out what they have done and our thinking of in terms of these data applications.
6. I would recommend that Telecom draft a new article from scratch about ISDN to be published in the next 2-3 months.

Michael

Apparently, Michael's recommendations were acted upon by Cynthia, setting off a debate between Datacom and Telecommunications over whether to hold, revise, or run the article as it was. On April 13, 1993, an administrator in charge of *Campus Computing requested action* through an e-mail message to all parties concerned that they come to a decision on the article within a day. On the morning of April 14, 1993, Cynthia *forwarded* a message over the e-mail system to Michael, writing, "Let's discuss this and the next e-mail message I'm forwarding to you." The forwarded e-mail (Figure 4) was a very pointed response by Wharton to Cynthia and Michael's original concerns over the ISDN article, *requesting action, providing opinions,* and *suggesting a meeting.* (< Indicates that this text was copied from the addressee's previous e-mail message.)

Figure 4. E-mail message requesting action, providing opinions, and suggesting meeting

---

Received: from (128.32.211.2] by ulink.university.edu (5.64/1.33(web))
id AA05544; Wed, 14 Apr 93 07:43:03 -0700
X-Nupop-Charset: English
date: Wed, 14 Apr 93 06:43:39 PST ---om: "Cynthia Parnasus"
<parnasus@ulink.university.edu>
Sender: parnasus@ulink.university.edu
Message-Id: <24231.parnasus@ulink.university.edu> To: mag
Subject: Fw: RE: ISDN articles "pulled"

This needs to be read, we need to discuss in conjunction with the other e-mail I just sent you.
Cynthia
I'd suggest first thing this am after 9:30

From: mlw@flower.university.edu (Michael Wharton)
Tue, 13 Apr 93 17:51:03 -0700
To: parnasus@ulink.university.edu
Subject: RE: ISDN articles "pulled"

Cynthia, The article is not a general discussion of ISDN. It is a simple description of the fact we are using it to extend the campus network. It does say that additional services will be defined and made available later. The point in publishing it now was 1) to let people know we are using this technology, and 2) to let them know that it is not available to individuals at this time for general network access.

> 1. We should not have two individuals in the article as contact persons for questions. This will only confuse people. We should identify one person in the dept and then share relevant inquires and information.

I would have pointed them at Clyde since the article is about Datacom use of ISDN. However, you had added Graumann's name so I left it in.

>2. The article ought to be driven by applications. That is, we ought to
>make clear to users what ISDN can do for them, what the costs will be and
>when these services will be available. There is nothing in the article
>which indicates these services can be ordered now.

It was not intended to be a general article, as stated above. There is nothing else anyone can do with ISDN today. Why wait to tell them what we ARE doing?

>3. In all of this we should be trying to think of how to make this as clear
>and easy for the customer as possible. We should, with this new service and
>opportunity. Let's design ISDN services so that we can have "one stop
>shopping". The article ought to reflect this. and we will need to do some
>planning before we can get this straight.

I suppose we can wait until next February but it seem a waste. Again, the purpose of the article was to describe what Datacom is doing now.

> 4. We should work out some joint research strategy with Datacom regarding
> applications which tie into the campus network. This can take a variety of
> different forms. We should what you have done and are thinking of in terms of
these data applications.

I am not at all clear on what you mean by the above.

> I would like us to meet and resolve some of these issues and I believe this
> can be quickly. If you are of the same mind I'll have Judy schedule some
> time and the 4 of us can get together and get this resolved quickly?
> Cynthia

"Quickly" perhaps but not in time for the next newsletter. This article was "pulled" at your request last time. We had weeks to discuss it. The fact you are pulling it again is quite annoying.

By all means, ask Judy to contact Doreen and schedule something.

Wharton

Wharton's message, both in tone and substance, reflected the tension between Telecommunications and Datacom over the ISDN issue. Wharton wanted to inform the campus community about the progress his organization had made in what was a high-profile technology. His priority was to show his organization's technological leadership, and he seemed insensitive to Telecommunications' concerns over not being prepared to meet demands for these services. He also appeared reticent to share authority with Telecommunications over this technology.

After presumably discussing this e-mail message face-to-face with Cynthia, Michael sent her an e-mail message that included a draft message *(delivering documents)* for her to respond to Wharton. In it, she is to request only two substantial changes: (1) that Michael be made the only contact for further information on this technology and (2) that her name be added as an author to show the campus community that Telecommunications and Datacom are working together on ISDN.

Figure 5. E-mail message delivering drafted response to previous request

Date: Wed, 14 Apr 93 08:57:33 PST
From: "Michael A. Graumann" <mag@ulink.university.edu>
To: parnasus@ulink
Subject: ISDN Article

Cynthia,
Here is a message from you to Wharton.
MAG

Michael,
Here is what I propose.
Let's run the article now but make the following 2 changes.
1. Let's have only one contact for inquiries, which will be Telecommunications, but let's share all information about ISDN inquiries and begin a working group together on ISDN led by Snow and Graumann. Thus leave the Graumann information in and drop the Snow information. I will have Michael Graumann share ALL of the ISDN phone inquiries with Clyde and we will give Clyde access to the account isdn@ulink so that both he and Michael can see inquiries. Clyde and Michael can then work out who should handle what sort of questions as part of an overall joint effort to investigate and deploy ISDN applications. I strongly believe it is best for the campus to have only one contact person and to pool our efforts.
2. Add my name as one of the authors to the bottom of the article. This will show the campus that we are working on this together.
We should meet soon to discuss how we can pool our ISDN efforts. I will set up a meeting.

Cynthia

That Michael and Cynthia are carefully composing an e-mail message negotiating wording in a newsletter article highlights the importance of written communications for establishing the authority of Telecommunications within AIS.

Later that day, during a one-on-one direct report meeting, Michael reviewed the e-mail message from Wharton with Brad. Michael commented (*reporting information, reviewing documents,* and *providing opinions*), "He gets pretty sarcastic. His tone is nasty. We should be able to work this out together. Cynthia thinks Clyde [associate director of Datacom] will get upset over this." Brad responded (*offering feedback*) that he thought Datacom thought that "we want to jump in now that most the work is done." Michael agreed with Brad: "We should be careful about the way we present what we know and do. Hopefully, they can work with us."

That same day, Cynthia *forwarded* an e-mail message to Michael from Clyde, assuring Cynthia that he welcomed working with Michael on ISDN and other issues and that Michael "has fit right into" a committee Michael was already serving on (*establishing links with AIS*). The fact that Michael was able to "fit in" with the other members of AIS on this committee was important to Clyde and made him enthusiastic about working jointly with Telecommunications on other issues.

The following day, April 15, 1993, Michael *reported* during the TPS team meeting that the article on ISDN in *Campus Computing* would include bylines of both Cynthia and Wharton, although Wharton wrote the draft. He stated that the article offered some overall direction of who should provide what services. He also noted (*providing opinions*), "I'm not terribly pleased with the article as it's written now. It may raise a lot of questions. We'll have to get our act together on what services we're going to offer and what it's going to cost. It is an important set of technologies. It may have real impact on revenue and billing."

When the ISDN article was published in the May-June 1993 issue of *Campus Computing*, it did reflect the request that Michael be listed as the only source for further information; however, only Wharton's byline appeared on the article. This clearly established the limits of Wharton's interest in accommodating the concerns of Telecommunications.

On Monday, April 19, 1993, Brad sent an e-mail message to Michael who was home sick, but able to access his e-mail messages. In the message, Brad described a meeting with Thomas and Malcolm, another associate director within Telecommunications, regarding an internal document Brad was preparing for Telecommunications describing ISDN technology (*reporting information*): "At the 1:00 with Malcolm and Thomas, Malcolm explained what Cynthia wanted to see in the document. In general terms, she did not want to spend any time on applications which involve Datacom at all. She wanted to spend the seed money on projects which involved Telecom only. I reordered the list to Malcolm's specifications and deleted some references to Datacom." Whether in reaction to Wharton's obstinacy or for some other reason, Cynthia appeared to be no longer interested in researching ISDN cooperatively with Datacom.

To sum up, the directors and associate directors of Telecommunications and Datacom used e-mail for a variety of communicative purposes regarding the

ISDN article, including: *delivering documents, forwarding information, providing opinions, reporting information, requesting action, suggesting meetings*—and most importantly—*establishing links with AIS.* However, Michael's communications about the ISDN article with members of his TPS team, including Brad, were conveyed only through face-to-face meetings. Clearly, the choice of communicative channel was not influenced by physical proximity, since Cynthia and Michael have adjacent offices, while Brad and some other members of the TPS team have offices on a different floor. In fact, the only time physical location was the principal motivation for using e-mail was when Brad used it to communicate with Michael, who was at home sick. Instead, using e-mail appears to be motivated by the writer's desire to assimilate into the AIS culture. Because of their greater contact with others in AIS, Michael and Cynthia were more likely than Brad or Thomas to recognize the importance of using e-mail to fitting in with others in AIS. As director and associate director of their department, it is also much more critical to their professional success that Cynthia and Michael demonstrate that they are capable of making the transistion into an organization that is more technically oriented than the organization from which they came.

5. Discussion and implications

While the particulars of the ISDN case or the Telecommunications study cannot be generalized to all e-mail users in organizations, the examination of this case provides insights into the relationship between writing and technological and organizational change. In concluding, I address the three questions posed out the outset of the chapter. In so doing, I hope to highlight that neither writing nor workplace change can be adequately considered outside of the social contexts in which they are situated.

5.1. How do people work together differently when electronic forms of communications are made available?

During my study, TPS members used e-mail most for providing or requesting short answers and establishing the need for a meeting or phone call with AIS members outside of Telecommunications. In this way, the team was attempting to bridge the cultural gap between their previous organizational culture—that of the administrative organization of the university where interpersonal service was most highly valued—and the technologically-centered AIS. However, members of the TPS team were still more comfortable using printed documents, group meetings and face-to-face discussions for substantive communications within their own group.

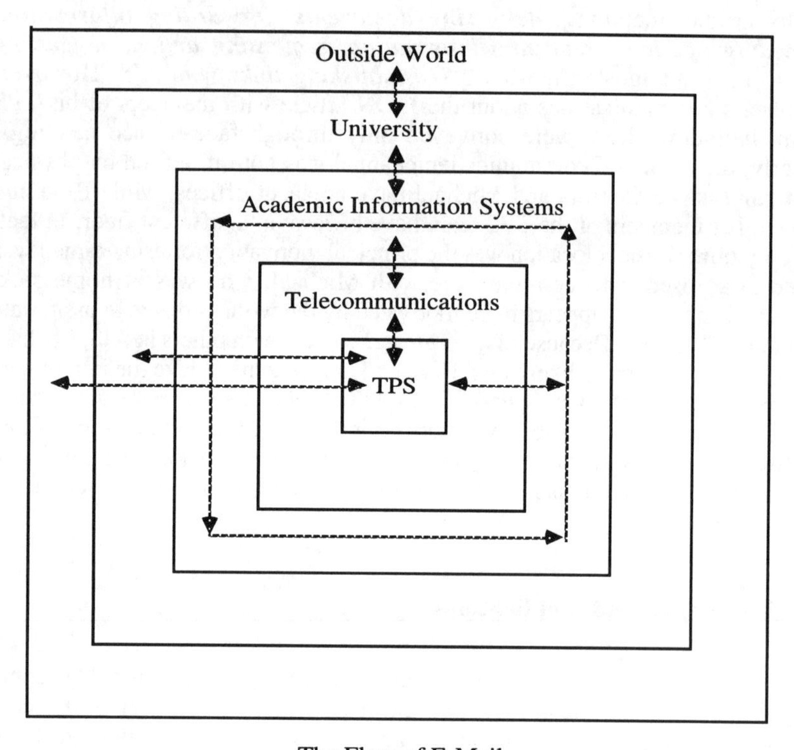

The Flow of E-Mail

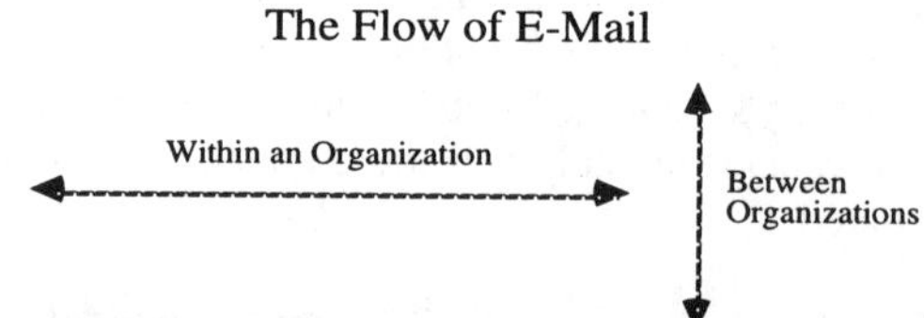

Figure 6. The flow of e-mail throughout the social hierarchical frame

Figure 6 shows how e-mail flowed in and out of TPS and Telecommunication, between TPS and Telecommunications, but flowed throughout AIS. The flow of e-mail within the university and in the outside world independent of AIS, TPS and Telecommunications is not indicated in this figure.

For TPS, using e-mail involved learning both physical and social technologies. The group was rapidly acquiring the knowledge and resources to adopt the use of e-mail to their own communicative practices. At the same time that the group was struggling to overcome problems with accessing the campus network and using e-mail software, it was also attempting to negotiate the structure, style and appropriate purposes of writing e-mail messages. As members of TPS later became more involved with others in AIS, their usage of e-mail would both increase and broaden in its purposes.

5.2. How do such technologies interact with the social patterns of the workplace?

For Michael, Brad, and Thomas, using e-mail was a social action. They ascribed active social meanings and evaluations to the use of computer-mediated communications technologies. E-mail was representative of the AIS culture. In fact, using e-mail was a way of affirming the value of the technology AIS managed. Members of Telecommunications perceived e-mail to be used broadly within AIS, and recognized that adapting their own communicative strategies and tactics to include e-mail was important to becoming part of the AIS culture.

5.3. How does the availability of electronic mail influence the hierarchical structures within the workplace organization?

E-mail did not flatten organizational hierarchies, but reflected and interacted with existing hierarchical structures. In Bakhtinian terms, examining the written interactions over the ISDN "temporarily crystallized" (Morson 1986, cited in Dyson 1992) the power relations being hammered out between and within Telecommunications and Datacom. The text of these e-mail messages is an articulation of the participants' relationships in an ongoing social dialogue. The messages reflect that organizational and technological change are not easily managed processes, but involve complex webs of very human relationships through which people are negotiating their new places in a particular social world.

ACKNOWLEDGMENTS

* Thanks to Anne Haas Dyson, Sara Warshauer Freedman, David Greenbaum, Glynda Hull, Patricia Philbin, and Harley Shaiken for their contributions and editorial suggestions.

NOTES

1. All names are pseudonyms.
2. Italics identify communicative purposes from Table 2.

Appendix

May-June 1993 Volume 3, Number 4
Campus Computing
Academic Information Systems, University of XXX
Networking

ISDN Promises New Communications Services

Telecommunication Services, through its new service contract with Pacific Bell, will soon be making available to the campus a new type of communications service based on the Integrated Services Digital Network (ISDN) standards. A good overview of this service is provided in the following article, which describes how this technology is being used at the University of Michigan. Telecommunication Services is now examining several new communication applications based on ISDN, while Data Communication and Network Services (Datacom) has been developing ways to use ISDN to increase connectivity to the campus network. We hope at least some of these services will be available by the end of this year.

ISDN provides two "channels", each of which can carry voice or data. For example, you could use one channel for your normal telephone service and have the other available simultaneously for data communication at speeds up to 64 kilobits per second (Kbps). We think this will be very attractive for University students, faculty, and staff who work from home or offices not connected to the campus network.

There are two factors which currently limit ISDN service availability. The first is that ISDN service is not yet widely available outside of the campus proper. Pacific Bell has stated that ISDN service should be available in most of the XXX Area by the end of 1994. However, even in locations where ISDN is available now, you cannot always place an end-to-end ISDN call to a distant ISDN subscriber because interoffice telecommunications systems may not yet be capable of supporting ISDN. Most of the campus should have this capability sometime in 1994.

The other consideration is the cost of the equipment needed to make use of ISDN service. Unfortunately, your existing telephones alone are not enough, and existing modems are not compatible with ISDN technology. You will need a Network Termination device (referred to as an NT1) and a Terminal Adapter unit (referred to as a TA). The NT1 is installed between the telephone service line and the wiring in your home. The TA connects to your home wiring and provides the attachment jacks for a terminal or computer and (optionally) an ordinary telephone. The current price of the two units together is around $1,000. We expect this price to drop as more service and equipment are sold.

Telecommunications and Datacom, working with Pacific Bell and Northern Telecom, are now investigating ISDN applications for the campus. These may include video-conferencing, telecommuting, connections to the campus network, and enhanced voice call management systems. For information about these services, contact either Michael Graumann, Telecommunication Services, XXX-XXXX, lsdn@ulink.university.edu or Clyde Snow, Datacom, XXX-XXXX, netinfo@ulink.university.edu.

Datacom is now using ISDN service on the campus to link local networks into the campus network. For example, the Millet Street offices of the Associate Vice Chancellor, Business and Administrative Services, and the Sciatic Avenue offices of Telecommunication Services are both connected to Turing Hall this way. We use both channels for data, thus achieving about 128 Kbps between campus and these locations. For comparison, this is approximately half the speed of Apple's LocalTalk network. The cost of this type of network-to-network connection with all the associated electronics is around $8,000.

Datacom is looking at ways to use ISDN to extend the campus network to individuals homes as well. This would be achieved by supporting the campus network protocols over one of the ISDN channels at the full 64 Kbps. The home computer then would become a node on the campus network with access to all the network resources just as if it were on campus, but with lower data connection speed.

Further articles will elaborate on Telecommunication Services and Datacom's plans for offering ISDN services. Michael Wharton

The Rhetorical Dynamics of a Community Protest in Cyberspace:
What Happened With Lotus MarketPlace

Laura J. Gurak
University of Minnesota

1. Introduction: Electronic rhetorical forums

In ancient Greece, as reflected in classical rhetorical theory, citizens engaged in public debate and distributed messages through the common gathering place of the *polis*. This idea has remained with us until only recently in the form of town meetings, often held in central public halls. In contemporary society, however, with its diverse communities dispersed over vast distances, the central town meeting place is no longer a viable option. Yet communication technologies provide a means to span the physical boundaries between local communities. Telephone, radio, television and most recently, computer-mediated communication (CMC) are some of the technologies giving a new shape to the forums where public debate takes place. These technologies are often examined for their technical components (speed, efficiency), but are less likely to be examined for the ways they impact human rhetorical interactions. For example, an on-line Congressional hearing with public comments may easily be labeled an "electronic town hall", but unlike traditional town hall meetings, participants never see each other face to face. How does electronic interaction change the rhetoric of debate in a democratic society?

This chapter offers a rhetorical analysis of one way CMC was used as a forum for protest, and of how a rhetorical community came together in this forum. In 1990, Lotus Development Corporation announced the impending release of a new product called MarketPlace Households. The product was a database containing direct marketing information on 120 million American consumers. Many people became concerned with the privacy implications of this product and used the global Internet network to orchestrate a protest against Lotus. In what was perhaps the first case of a "protest in cyberspace", the Lotus case provides an example of the rhetoric of an electronic forum, highlighting issues such as the speed of delivery and the ethos and discourse style of a rhetorical community linked only via a computer network. These features have important implications for how CMC can or cannot be used to increase public participation and decision making.

My overall argument is that rhetorical communities on computer networks can be socially and politically powerful, especially as networks continue to integrate and become available to a wider user group. Along with the potential to revive public discourse, however, computer-mediated debate can also present problems in terms of accuracy of information.

I begin my analysis by providing background on the Lotus case. Next, I examine the structure of the discourse from a rhetorical perspective, illustrating how the use of CMC helped an exigency come into focus quickly. I then examine the ethos and style of the protest postings and suggest that on computer networks, leadership style may take a different form. Next, I analyze the style of Lotus's postings and compare this style to the protest postings. Finally, I summarize my results and suggest implications for network development.

2. Background: The case of Lotus MarketPlace

On April 10, 1990, Lotus Development Corporation announced a "desktop information product" called Lotus MarketPlace. The product, a CD-ROM direct mail marketing database, was designed to run on Macintosh personal computers, thus giving small businesses easy and affordable access to direct marketing mailing lists. The product came in two editions: Lotus MarketPlace: Business and Lotus MarketPlace: Households. The business edition contained information on 7 million American businesses; the Households edition on 120 million individual American consumers from 80 million different households. Lotus MarketPlace: Households was a joint effort of Lotus and Equifax Credit Corporation, which provided the demographic data for the product (Lotus Development Corporation 1990).

In the months that followed, Lotus MarketPlace: Households was the subject of intense debate concerning its implications for personal privacy. Over 30,000 people contacted Lotus and asked that their names be removed from the database. The product, which had been scheduled to be released during the third quarter of 1990, was never released. On January 23, 1991, Lotus issued a press release announcing that it would cancel MarketPlace: Households due to "public concerns and misunderstandings of the product, and the substantial, unexpected costs required to fully address consumer privacy issues" (Lotus Development Corporation 1991). Later, Equifax issued a press release, announcing its "decision to discontinue sales of direct marketing lists derived from the consumer credit file" (Equifax Inc. 1991).

From Lotus' first announcement until months after it canceled the product, newspapers, news and computer magazines, the Internet, and various electronic bulletin boards and e-mail systems were full of discussions about MarketPlace: Households. In fact, computer-mediated communication was a critical forum in this case. Networks were a-buzz with discussions and debates about the privacy implications of MarketPlace. People posted the address and phone number of Lotus and Equifax and gave information about how to get names removed from the database. Some people posted "form letters" that could be sent to Lotus. Notices were forwarded around the net, re-posted to other newsgroups, and sent off as e-mail messages. In the end, the corporations and the network activists acknowledged the role that the networks played in stopping the release of MarketPlace. Some subsequently called it "[a] victory for computer populism" (Winner 1991).

3. Speed of delivery: CMC focuses the message

The past decade and a half has seen a build-up of general public concern about computer privacy. Books such as Burnham's *The Rise of the Computer State* (1980) and Laudon's *Dossier Society* (1986) criticized the large databases being amassed by government and private industry. The popular press, too, began to print stories about computers and individual privacy. By the late 1980s, magazine articles such as "'Big Brother Inc.' May be Closer Than You Thought", which described "[t]he latest threat: personal 'profiles' compiled from the widening web of databases" (Field et al. 1987:84), brought the issue into the public eye.

But the general public concern for computer privacy did not often translate into social action, since the problem seemed pervasive and without any identifiable agent. It was into this climate that Lotus MarketPlace was introduced, and, as one Lotus official put it, acted as a lightning rod for public concern about privacy.[1] One activist made a similar observation when he noted that the network participants were "like kindling waiting for a spark".[2]

It was not only the product but also the rapid and simultaneous nature of delivery via CMC that brought the controversy into focus. On November 14, 1990, the *Wall Street Journal* ran a story about MarketPlace, in which Lotus representatives explained the benefits of the product while computer privacy advocates expressed concern about the product. Immediately, network participants began posting notes containing excerpts of the *Journal* story. These notes quickly spread across the net. My research uncovered three such notes, all date stamped November 14. One posting was found on the RISKS Digest list and another on the Whole Earth 'Lectronic Link (WELL), where an entire discussion list, or forum, was established to talk about Lotus MarketPlace. A third posting also appeared in the RISKS Digest, but was actually an excerpt from an "unofficial electronic newspaper edited and published within Digital for Digital employees".[3] These notes, containing portions of the *Journal* article and comments by the author of the posting, quickly defined the protest and brought it into focus. By the next day, November 15, the conferences I analyzed were in full swing debating the merits of the Lotus product and suggesting ways of contacting Lotus.[4]

4. Community ethos and values in cyberspace

CMC was effective in defining this protest not only due to its speed and the simultaneous nature of its transmission, but also because the medium encouraged a sense of community by focusing the values of conference participants. These values are evident for example in one of the November 14 postings to RISKS Digest. The author of the posting is not in favor of MarketPlace and implies that the product has serious implications for personal privacy. I have highlighted passages in the text for emphasis.

> Date: Wed, 14 Nov 90 09:19:28 EDT
> From: Jerry Leichter <leichter@lrw.com>
> Subject: Police technology; mailing list hyperstacks
>
> The Wall Street Journal this week had two articles on privacy and technology that I thought RISKS readers might find of interest.
>
> On Monday (13-Nov; page A-1) it reports on some new technologies that are becoming available to the police.
>
> [Section describing first article edited out — LJG.]
>
> On Tuesday (14-Nov; page B1) the Journal reports on the controversy surrounding a product soon to be introduced by Lotus. Lotus Marketplace consists of a CD containing information on some 80,000,000 households, including names, addresses, shopping habits, likely income levels, and even a catagorization (by Equifax) into one of 50 catagories like "accumulated wealth", "mobile home families", "cautious young couples", and "inner-city singles". Also included is a program - apparently at least partly a Hypercard stack - that provides an interface to the system. The whole thing costs $695 for the program and an initial 5000 names; each additional 5000 names cost $400. How Lotus keeps you from using the other information on the CD is unclear - presumably, you sign a license and they come after you if you breach the terms.

In the next paragraph, the writer suggests that MarketPlace could be dangerous:

> The program Lotus provides does not allow you to look up a particular individual by name, *but of course if you know anything about him you can come up with a query that will find him and few others - and of course the unethical will hardly be stopped from developing their own search programs by the terms of a license agreement* (emphasis added).

This excerpt from the next paragraph exhibits the same ethos: a mistrust of potential abuse from a technical perspective:

> It astonishes me that anyone can imagine they can control how a small piece of plastic, indistinguishable from hundreds of like copies, will be used once it gets out into the world.[5]

Though some people did not agree that Lotus MarketPlace posed a privacy problem, most discussion adhered to a common distrust and dislike of the Lotus product. The protest attracted like-minded people to a public forum, a forum that spanned distance and time and allowed people of common values to come together. This sense of shared values and community has been noted by many network observers (Stone 1992; Rheingold 1993),[6] and in the Lotus case, continued throughout the entire net debate.

5. Leadership in a net-based protest

Soon after the net discussions about Lotus MarketPlace began, participants began suggesting ways of contacting Lotus. By as early as November 15, postings on all of the conferences I studied began to include Lotus's address and phone number. Eventually, Lotus's address, phone numbers, and even the e-mail address of Lotus's CEO were in wide circulation over the Internet, private e-mail, and internal company bulletin boards.

The protest against Lotus appeared in many ways similar to a traditional protest. People with common values and a similar agenda came together to send a message and push for change. Yet one striking aspect of the Lotus protest was its lack of any leadership in the traditional sense.

Most protests have some kind of organizational structure, with one or more persons assuming a leadership role. In the protest against Lotus MarketPlace, however, no one was officially the leader and there was no organized plan. Postings suggesting action against Lotus were mixed in and given equal weight among postings about many other issues related to computer privacy. For example, one issue of Telecom Privacy Digest contains an article about caller ID[7] along with articles about Lotus. Risks Digest's table of contents (1990: vol. 10, no. 61) also includes many topics, only the first two of which concern Lotus:

Police technology; mailing list hyperstacks (Lotus)
Privacy concerns about Lotus "Marketplace"
Kuwaiti citizen database
Gas pump inaccuracies?
"It's the computer's fault"
Re: Voting electronically from home
Re: Computer Mishap Forces shift in Election Coverage
Election coverage software
Re: Juicy 911 RISKS
Ada Remarks

On the WELL, where a special group was created for the exclusive purpose of discussing Lotus MarketPlace, conversations still spanned many topics. As with the above table of contents, the MarketPlace case was mixed in with other threads,[8] including one rather lengthy digression about the pros and cons of "junk mail", which then turned into a debate about the quality and purpose of the various mail-order catalogs received by many of the participants.

Yet even though MarketPlace was often only one of many threads on a given discussion forum, the protest was not without a structure. Rather than being led by an active leader with an explicit plan, the Lotus protest grew in phases, in response to the motivations of those who read and posted notes. Early postings provided Lotus's address and talked about possible action; later, "form letters" and other motivating notes were circulated widely both on the conferences and throughout cyberspace. In fact, one of these form letters itself took on a leadership role in the protest, suggesting that in cyberspace, certain texts can become dominant if they have community appeal.

In December and January, postings began taking on the quality of electronic chain letters. A few long, detailed notes were sent to multiple computer conferences and were forwarded and re-forwarded throughout cyberspace. These postings often included sample letters that others had sent to Lotus and that readers could presumably cut, edit, and paste for their own use. People sometimes added to or edited the material in the note before sending it out again to another person, mailing list, or conference. One such posting was the one that originated with Larry Seiler.

According to Seiler, a computer professional with a large Boston-based computer firm, his original note was based on one by another computer professional with a different company. Seiler downloaded this person's posting, added his own commentary, and e-mailed the resulting note to people both inside the company and on the Internet at other organizations.[9] From there, unknown persons posted and re-posted Seiler's letter to sites across the Internet. On the WELL, Seiler's letter showed up on December 20 containing a header and commentary indicating that the note had traveled to British Columbia, then to someone in Seattle, and finally on to the WELL. On December 30, another version of the Seiler note was posted to the Telecom Digest, this time having traveled from New Jersey. And on December 31, another edited version of

Seiler's note appeared in Telecom Privacy Digest.

The following excerpts from Seiler's letter show how the community's values about personal privacy were expressed. Seiler's posting, which I found on three conferences, contains two parts. After some prefatory remarks by the person re-posting the note, the first section contains Seiler's comments about MarketPlace and his response when he tried to contact Lotus. The second section contains a letter that he sent to Lotus.

In the first section, Seiler comments on the product. After describing his conversation with someone at Lotus, he summarizes his feelings about MarketPlace:

> GREAT! So not only do they have the audacity to print an estimate of your income (which could be quite damaging if they get it wrong, and is an intrusion into your privacy if they get it right), they also have space on the disk for arbitrary comments about you -- and they'll be selling this data in volume to mass marketing companies across the country!

The idea that "they'll be selling this data...across the country" directly reflects the concerns of others in the protest community about the lack of control they have over their personal data. Because the MarketPlace data was sold on a CD-ROM disk, making change or updates impossible, and because Lotus required people to request name removal rather than initially asking their permission to use their names, people felt angry and hostile. Although Lotus held a very different position, arguing that these data were already widely available through credit bureaus and marketing services, the Seiler note appealed to the values of a community concerned about the possibility of any additional infringements on their personal privacy.

Along with its appeal to shared values, this posting illustrates the sense of community felt among network participants. Commenting on the accuracy of his information about MarketPlace, Seiler (1990), in a preface to the form letter, states:

> In interviews, Lotus has said that individuals will NOT be able to correct their own entries, or even see what they are. I didn't try to confirm this in my call to Lotus, but I did confirm that the person who reported it -- Rich Salz of BBN -- has an excellent reputation on the internet. Also, everything he said that I checked with Lotus is absolutely accurate. Further, the Wall Street Journal has reported on it -- saying that the database has ages, marital status, and other such personal data as well.

Notice Seiler's confidence in information he obtained from someone with "an excellent reputation on the internet". Such faith in the Internet community was in fact a strong part of what kept the protest cohesive.

After this section of comments, Seiler appends the letter he sent to Lotus. The tone and voice of this letter, characteristic of "flaming" behavior,[10] also served to keep the protest moving by appealing to the participants' anger.

The letter begins with the salutation "Dear Marketeers" and goes on to state that he does not want his name listed in the MarketPlace database. After suggesting that "[a]s you have it set up, I think your "Household Marketplace" CDROM database is an incredible intrusion and ought to be illegal," the letter goes on in a similar tone to list four reasons why the product should not be released. Seiler then concludes with this paragraph:

> In conclusion, if you market this product, it is my sincere hope that you are sued by every person for whom your data is false, with the eventual result that your company goes bankrupt. That would be a pity, since you make many fine products. However, that is preferable to permitting you to spread rumors and encourage abusive business practices. It would be better if your chief officers went to jail, but that will apparently require new laws to be passed. If you persist in your plans to market this product, a lot of people will be pushing to make that happen. I suggest that you abandon this project while there is time to do so.
>
> Yours most sincerely,
> Larry Seiler[11]

While some participants thought the letter was "a bit intemperate and overstated",[12] it is likely that most people agreed with participant Bob Jacobson,[13] who called the letter "right on point", since the Seiler letter was widely distributed across the Internet. As Seiler's and other similar letters, with their angry tone and implied sense of community, circulated on the Internet, participants took up the cause. People wrote to Lotus, made phone calls, and re-distributed these letters across the net.

6. Credibility and network information

The rapid nature of delivery on the networks, combined with a sense of community and novel types of leadership, illustrate the potential for CMC as a forum for public participation and social action. Yet this "bottom-up" rhetorical form, where information is distributed at a grassroots level rather than from the top down, has a problematic side. How can participants be sure the information they receive is accurate? How can networks encourage true debate and discussion when the credibility of information is not possible to ascertain? How can communities with widely differing communication styles use the networks effectively?

In the Lotus protest, a large amount of the information distributed on the Internet about MarketPlace was inaccurate. Another form letter, similar to Seiler's, contained the following list of fields that it claimed were part of the Lotus database:

In one one [sic] database, the combined knowledge may include such things that we normally expect to consider private:

o family members' names, gender, and ages (!!)
o address and home phone number
o annual salary
o debt-to-earnings ratio
o net worth (house, cars, misc. household items)
o investment portfolio (stocks, CD's, etc.)
o self and spouse employer info
o health and life insurance plan info
o schools attended by my children
o kind of car(s) I own }
o kind of computer I own }
o kind of stereo equipment I own } from "warranty" registrations
o kind of video equipment I own }
o kind of household appliances I own }
o who knows what else?

In fact, most of the items included in this list were not included in the Lotus MarketPlace database. Although a composite of a person's spending habits and lifestyle was an included field in the product, the database did not contain individual fields for listings about a person's kind of car or stereo equipment. Yet this note, according to its introductory paragraph, also made the rounds on the Internet:

Dear Friends,

This message is being passed around the country via E-mail. The headers on this message included Maine, UC Santa Barbara, and IBM in Westchester. I've deleted them for your convenience but the prose (coming as it does from 10 different authors) is fractured.[14]

Not only does this note's "collaborative authorship" style make for fractured prose, it also allows each author to append or change information without reference to its source. Furthermore, because of the implicit sense of community and thus of a credibility in information gained from the networks, readers were inclined to believe this note's contents without checking.

Thus, along with the power of CMC for community building, there also exists the danger of inaccurate information being spread quickly.

7. A clash of communities in the cyber-forum

Another difficulty in using networks as forums for public deliberation is the way in which communities with vastly different rhetorical styles can potentially clash. For government or private industry, used to a formal mode of communication, interacting over the Internet can be a frustrating experience, since, as noted in the previous section, network postings often contain statements not subject to verification. Also, the emotive voice characteristic of the Lotus protest is in direct conflict with the more logical, business-like voice of corporate communications.

When Lotus Corporation realized that a protest was taking place over the Internet, they attempted to reply to some of the participants' concerns by posting a note of their own. This strategy was problematic. First, there was no way the company could track down each and every network posting in order to counter with a note of its own. As one Lotus official indicated, "[w]e just didn't have a coordinated strategy to fight the Internet."[15] The word *coordinated* is key here, since coordination and organization are crucial in business but are exactly what the Internet lacks. Organizations are familiar with a "top down" style of communication, where information is distributed from clearly identifiable sources (a public relations office or marketing department) out to a broader public. Yet the Internet, as noted earlier, operates in a "bottom up" fashion.

Second, even when Lotus did attempt to enter the forum, the corporation's note was written in a logical, business-like voice, which clashed with the more emotional tone of the protest:

> In response to recent messages that have appeared here about Lotus MarketPlace, we want to provide some hard facts that we hope will clear up some of the misinformation surrounding our product.
>
> [List of items included in the database]
>
> We hope that this clarifies any questions or concerns.[16]

In rhetorical terms, the Lotus note is logos-based: "hard facts" that will "clear up some of the misinformation..." After a listing of these facts, the letter ends with a standard business phrase: "[w]e hope that this clarifies any questions or concerns." The premise that a list of "hard facts" will somehow "clarify" the problem contrasts with the personal and emotive style of the protest. Protest participants were upset and angry, and were not interested in "hard facts". The emotional and cynical response to Lotus's posting indicates this clash in style:

> Perhaps the data is encrypted. Big deal. As another poster has pointed out, it's only a matter of time before your protection scheme is broken and made available to the unscrupulous public.[17]

Or this posting, referring to the idea that one could send in a phony name to test Lotus's claim that the data was protected from illegitimate use:

> If somebody will send me the $599, I'll be glad to try the experiment of sending in an order in the name of "A. Slimy Jerk". Just make your check out to me personally . . . after all, why shouldn't you trust me as much as you do Lotus.[18]

Thus, interlocutors using two very different styles tried unsuccessfully to communicate. Lotus did not engage the protest participants on their emotional rhetorical terms, and protesters were not interested in responding to a listing of "hard facts".

8. Implications for CMC and community action: Toward a rhetoric of public debate on networks

In January 1991, just nine months after the product's announcement and only two months after the network protest began full force, Lotus Development Corporation canceled the release of MarketPlace: Households. Clearly, this result demonstrates the effectiveness of CMC as a forum for public debate and social action. Since the time of the Lotus protest, this power has been recognized by government and corporations alike. Current discussions about widening the Internet to create a National Information Infrastructure (NII), interest in this project by most major corporations, and test projects such as an on-line Congressional forum speak to the potential of CMC for rhetorical interactions in the next century.

The Lotus case points toward some positive aspects of CMC but also indicates some areas that will need attention should CMC be used to encourage true debate and deliberation. On the positive side, the Lotus case clearly illustrates the power of a medium in which information can, with a single keystroke, be forwarded to thousands of readers. This delivery feature can quickly bring an issue into focus and can encourage the development of an instant community. Furthermore, CMC encourages the sharing of community values through a projection of an ethos that is readily identifiable by others on the network.

Yet these same features of speed and community which mark the unique rhetoric of computer-mediated communication may also encourage the promotion and spread of inaccurate information. In the Lotus case, for example, many of the messages that sped through the network contained exaggerated statements about the MarketPlace product. Therefore, while the sense of community based on common values about computer privacy was heightened by the postings, the computer conferences did not provide the most open forum for a debate about MarketPlace and computer privacy in general.

The Lotus case also raises more general questions about computer networks, questions that are critical as the United States begins to restructure the Internet and design a new information infrastructure for communication in the next century. This re-structuring is bringing with it a variety of suggestions for using networks for political discourse. For example, Vice President Gore has participated in an on-line discussion on the computer network Compuserve. However while many in government and industry welcome the coming of the "information superhighway" for its technical power and speed, we know very little about the nature of computer networks as places for deliberative discourse. Do CMC technologies encourage open debate? Do they encourage or discourage traditionally under-represented groups or dissenting voices?

In 1988, Zuboff asked similar questions about the early stages of factory automation and computer use in organizations. Arguing along the same lines as Winner (1986) and others who challenge the deterministic model of technological development, Zuboff suggested that the then-new computer technologies could be used in one of two ways. They could be designed and implemented to reinforce traditional hierarchical structures within organizations, or, on the other hand, they could be used to invent a new corporate structure that emphasizes participation and worker knowledge.

Computer-mediated communication and network technologies are currently situated in a historical place similar to that of the office computer systems Zuboff studied. The newly emerging network forums can be designed in a variety of ways, some of which will limit and control public dialogue, and others of which will encourage open debate and discussion. Careful and close analysis of debates such as the Lotus case provide evidence for how CMC functions as a rhetorical forum, and what it can and might become in the future.

NOTES

1. Janice Brown, personal telephone communication, March 23, 1993.
2. Marc Rotenberg, personal communication, December 4, 1992.
3. Jeff E. Nelson, electronic message to RISKS Digest, vol.10, no.61, Nov. 16, 1990.
4. For this study, I examined texts from four Usenet newsgroups (UNIX-based bulletin boards) and one forum from the Whole Earth 'Lectronic Link, or WELL. The WELL is a network based in Sausalito, California. For further discussion of my method and of the methodological issues I encountered when using cybertexts as research data, see Chapter Two in Gurak (1994).
5. Jerry Leichter, electronic message to RISKS Digest, vol. 10, no. 61, November 16, 1990.
6. Stone, for example, speaks of "virtual communities, passage points for collections of common beliefs and practices that unite people who [are] physically separated" (1992: 85).
7. The technology which displays the phone number of an incoming call.
8. The term "thread" is used on computer conferences to describe a theme of discussion that takes place within the larger conference topic. On a conference about privacy, for example, one might find threads about a number of privacy related topics. Threads are usually "tied" together not only by similar subject matter but also by similar, if not identical, subject lines.

9. Larry Seiler, personal e-mail communication, February 12, 1993.

10. Flaming, which Lea et al. (1992, 1989) define as "the hostile expression of strong emotions and feelings", has received much attention in the CMC literature. Herring's (1993a) study of gender in CMC suggests that flaming-style language may be a gender-based trait, a line of study which deserves more investigation. In the Lotus case, the flaming-style language helped keep the protest community focused and angry at Lotus.

11. Larry Seiler, electronic letter distributed to many sites on the Internet. Excerpted here from Whole Earth 'Lectronic Link computer network, Electronic Frontier Foundation conference, topic 71 (Lotus MarketPlace), 20 Dec. 1990. Message no. 154.

12. Tom Mandel, electronic message to Whole Earth 'Lectronic Link computer conference, Electronic Frontier Foundation network, topic 71 (Lotus MarketPlace), December 20, 1990. Message no. 155.

13. Electronic message to Whole Earth 'Lectronic Link computer network, Electronic Frontier Foundation conference, topic 71 (Lotus MarketPlace), December 20, 1990. Message no. 153.

14. Electronic message posted to Telecom Privacy Digest, vol. 2, no. 11, January 23 1991. Authorship of this message is unclear, composed as it was by many different participants.

15. Douglas Borchard, personal telephone communication, March 1, 1993.

16. Douglas Borchard, electronic message posted to comp.society Usenet newsgroup, January 3, 1991.

17. Tim Klein, electronic message posted to comp.society Usenet newsgroup, January 4, 1991.

18. George Mulford, electronic message posted to comp.society Usenet newsgroup, January 4, 1991.

References

Aguilar, G.
1992 *Catálogo de Resumenes 1990 - 1992 (Programa de Apoyo a Proyectos de Investigación y de Innovación Docente).* Mexico: DGAPA-UNAM.

Aiken, Milam W.
1992 "Using a group decision support system as a teaching tool." *Journal of Computer Based Instruction* 9.82-85.

Applegate, Lynda M.
1993 Quoted in "Computer links erode hierarchical nature of workplace culture," by John R. Wilke. *Wall Street Journal*, December 9.

Arms, V. (ed.)
1986 Special Issue on Computer Conferencing. *IEEE Transactions of Professional Communication* PC-29 (1).

Armstrong, David
1994 "Computer sex: Log on; talk dirty; get off: On-line services provide a virtual intimacy." *San Francisco Examiner,* April 10.A1-14.

Auferheide, Pat
1994 "The media monopolies muscle in." *The Nation,* January 3-10.1, 18-21.

Axelrod, Robert
1984 *The Evolution of Cooperation.* New York: Basic Books.

Bacchi, Carol Lee
1990 "The sexuality debates." *Same Difference: Feminism and Sexual Difference.* Boston: Allen & Unwin, 202-27.

Bakhtin, Mikhail
1968 *Rabelais and His World.* Cambridge: MIT Press.

Balka, Ellen
1993 "Women's access to on-line discussions about feminism." *The Electronic Journal of Communication* 3(1). Available from comserve@rpitsvm1.bitnet.

Balsamo, Anne
1993 "Feminism for the incurably informed." *South Atlantic Quarterly* 92.681-712. Reprinted in Dery (ed.) 1994b, 125-156.

Baron, Naomi S.
1984 "Computer mediated communication as a force in language change." *Visible Language* XVIII 2.118-141.

Barrett, Thomas and Carol Wallace
1994 "Virtual encounters." *Internet World*, November/December:45-48.

Bartle, Richard
1990 "Interactive multi-user computer games. Internal study for British Telecom." Electronic document. FTP: english-server.hss.cmu.edu

Batson, Trent
1988a "Ex cathedra: The 'pulpit model' of teaching and computer networks." Paper presented at the Twelfth National Institute on Issues in Teaching and Learning. Chicago, IL.

1988b "The ENFI project: A networked classroom approach to writing instruction." *Academic Computing* 2.32-33, 55-56.

Belenky, Mary F., Blythe M. Clinchy, Nancy R. Goldberger and Jill M. Taruk
1986 *Women's Ways of Knowing: The Development of Self, Voice, and Mind.* New York: Basic Books.

Benedikt, Michael (ed.)
1991 *Cyberspace: First Steps.* Cambridge: MIT Press.

Bennahum, David
1994 "Fly me to the MOO: Adventures in textual reality." *Lingua Franca*, May/June.

Berger, C. R. and R. J. Calabrese
1975 "Some explorations in initial interaction and beyond: Toward a developmental theory of interpersonal communication." *Human Communication Research* 1.99-112.

Besnier, Niko
1990 "Language and affect." *Annual Review of Anthropology* 19.419-51.

Biber, Douglas
1988 *Variation across Speech and Writing*. Cambridge: Cambridge University Press.

1991 "On the exploitation of computerized corpora in variation studies." In K. Aijmer and B. Altenberg (eds.), *English Corpus Linguistics: Studies in Honour of Jan Svartvik.* London & New York: Longman, 204-220.

1992 "On the complexity of discourse complexity: A multidimensional analysis." *Discourse Processes* 15.133-163.

Bitter, G. and R. Yohe
1989 "Preparing teachers for the Information Age." *Educational Technology* 29.22-25.

Blakeslee, Ann
1993 "Readers and authors: Fictionalized constructs or dynamic collaborations?" *Technical Communication Quarterly* 2.23-35.

Bochner, A. P.
1984 "The functions of human communicating in interpersonal bonding." In C. C. Arnold & J. W. Bowers (eds.), *Handbook of Rhetorical and Communication Theory*. Boston: Allyn and Bacon, 554-621.

Bolter, Jay David
1991 *Writing Space: The Computer, Hypertext, and the History of Writing*. Hillsdale, NJ: Lawrence Erlbaum Associates.

Booth, A.
1988 *Qualitative Evaluation of Information Technology in Communication Systems*. London: Taylor Graham.

Booth, Wayne C., Gregory G. Colomb, and Joseph M. Williams
1995 *The Craft of Research*. Chicago: University of Chicago Press.

Bornstein, Kate
1994 *Gender Outlaw: On Men, Women, and the Rest of Us*. New York: Routledge.

Brail, Stephanie
1994 "Take back the net! Don't let on-line's dirty little secret prevent you from exploring cyberspace." *On the Issues* 40.

Branwyn, Gareth
1993 "Compu-sex: Erotica for cybernauts." *South Atlantic Quarterly* 92.779-792. Reprinted in Dery (ed.) 1994b, 223-235.

Braun, Ludwig
1990 *VISION: TEST (Technology Enriched Schools of Tomorrow) Final Report*. Eugene, OR: International Society for Technology in Education.

Bright, Suzy
1992 *Suzy Bright's Sexual Reality: A Virtual Sex World Reader*. Pittsburg: Cleis Press.

Brilhart, John K. and G.J. Galanes
1992 *Effective Group Discussion*. (7th ed.) Madison: Wm. C. Brown Publishers.

Broadhurst, Judith
1993 "Lurkers and flamers." *Online Access* 8(3).

Brown, John Seeley, Alan Collins and P. Duguid
1989 "Situated cognition and the culture of learning." In *Educational Researcher* 18.32-42.

Brown, Penelope and Stephen Levinson
1987 *Politeness: Some Universals in Language Usage*. Cambridge: Cambridge University Press.

Bruckman, Amy S.
1992 "Identity workshops: Emergent social and psychological phenomena in text-based virtual reality." Master's Thesis, MIT Media Laboratory.

1993 "Gender swapping on the Internet." *Proceedings of INET '93*, The Internet Society, Reston, VA. FTP: media.mit.edu in pub/MediaMOO/papers.gender-swapping

1994 "Serious uses of MUDs?" Panel at DIAC 94. Cambridge, MA, April 23-24, 1994. FTP: media.mit.edu:/pub/asb/serious-diac94.txt

Bump, Jerome
1993 "Sexual difference and participatory pedagogy." Paper presented at the 44th Conference on College Composition and Communication. San Diego, California.

Burnham, David
1980 *The Rise of the Computer State*. New York: Random House.

Burns, Kate
ms. "Where men are men and women get nasty e-mail: Narratives of violence and frontier justice on the Internet." May 24, 1994. Department of Literature, University of California, San Diego.

Butler, Judith
1990 "The force of fantasy: Feminism, Mapplethorpe, and discursive excess." *Differences: A Journal of Feminist Cultural Studies* 2(2).105-25.

1993 *Bodies that Matter: On the Discursive Limits of "Sex."* New York: Routledge.

Campbell, K.K.
1994 "Attack of the cyber-weenies." *Wasatch Area Voices Express (W.A.V.E.), Women's Edition* 1.5. Available from wave@cc.weber.edu.

Cantarero, M.
1993 "Critical thinking and ESOL." *GELI Newsletter* 3(1), February. Havana: GELI.

Carlstrom, Eva-Lise
1992 "Better living through language. The communicative implications of a text-only virtual environment, or welcome to Lambda." FTP: parcftp.xerox.com in pub/MOO/papers

Carter, R.
1987 *Vocabulary: Applied Linguistic Perspectives*. London: Unwin Hyman.

Castaños, F., P. González, and M. Meagher
1991 *Proyecto de Investigación: Aprendizaje Cooperativo de L2 vía Telecomunicationes en el Bachillerato*. Mexico: UNAM.

Cathcart, R. and G. Gumpert
1983 "Mediated interpersonal communication: Toward a new typology." *Quarterly Journal of Speech* 69.267-277.

Cavazos, Edward A.
1994 "Intellectual property in cyberspace: Copyright law in a new world." In E. Cavazos and Gavino Morin (eds.), *Cyberspace and the Law: Your Rights and Duties in the On-line World.* Cambridge: MIT Press.

Chafe, Wallace and Jane Danielewicz
1987 "Properties of spoken and written language." In R. Horowitz and S.J. Samuels (eds.), *Comprehending Oral and Written Language.* New York: Academic Press.

Cherny, Lynn
1995 *The MUD Register: Conversational Modes of Action in a Text-Based Virtual Reality.* Unpublished Ph.D. dissertation, Stanford University.

Cherny, Lynn and Elizabeth Reba Weise (eds.)
Forthcoming *Wired Women: Gender and New Realities in Cyberspace.* Emeryville, CA: Seal Press.

Chesebro, James W.
1985 "Computer-mediated interpersonal communication." In B.D. Ruben (ed.), *Information and Behavior.* New Brunswick, NJ: Transaction Books, 202-222.

Chung, C.-S.
1992 "Electronic mail (E-mail) usage in low-context and high-context cultures." Paper presented at the annual meeting of the Speech Communication Association, Chicago, IL.

Cicero, Marcus Tulins
1986 *De Oratore.* Landmarks in Rhetoric and Public Address. Southern Illinois University Press.

Clark, Rex and Mary Hocks
Forthcoming "Writing about literature with hypertext." In M. Rosenberg (ed.), *Teaching with Hypertext.* Houghton, MI: Computers and Composition Press.

Coates, Jennifer
1983 *The Semantics of the Modal Auxiliaries.* London: Croom Helm.

1993 *Women, Men and Language.* 2nd ed. London: Longman.

Cody, R. and J. Smith
1991 *Applied Statistics and the SAS Programming Language.* Englewood, NJ: Prentice Hall.

Collins, Allan, John Seely Brown and Susan E. Newman
1989 "Cognitive apprenticeship: Teaching the crafts of reading, writing, and mathematics." In L. Resnick (ed.), *Knowing, Learning, and Instruction: Essays in Honor of Robert Glaser.* Hillsdale, NJ: Lawrence Erlbaum Associates, 453-94.

Collot, Milena
1991a "Electronic language: A pilot study of a new variety of English." *Computer Corpora des Englischen* 5 (1-2).13-31.

1991b The situational features and textual dimensions of electronic language. Unpublished master's thesis, TESL Centre: Concordia University, Canada.

Collot, Milena and Nancy Belmore
1993 "Electronic language: A new variety of English." In J. Aarts, P. de Haan and N. Oostdijk (eds.), *English Language Corpora: Design, Analysis and Exploitation.* Amsterdam & Atlanta, Ga.: Rodolpi, 41-56.

Colomb, Gregory G. and Joseph M. Williams
1986 "Perceiving structure in professional prose." In L. Odell and D. Goswami (eds.), *Writing in Non-academic Settings.* New York: Guilford Publications, 87–128.

1987 *Discourse Structures.* Technical Report #3. Writing Programs: University of Chicago.

Condon, Sherri
1986 "The discourse functions of OK." *Semiotica* 60.73–101.

Condon, S., C. Cooper and H. Grotevant
1984 "Manual for the analysis of family discourse." *Psychological Documents* 14.1, Document no. 2616.

Cook, Kevin and Dan Lehrer
1993 "The Internet: The whole world is talking." *The Nation*, July 12.60-66.

Cooper, C., H. Grotevant and S. Condon
1982 "Methodological challenges of selectivity in family interaction: Addressing temporal patterns of individuation." *Journal of Marriage and the Family* 44.749–754.

Cooper, Marilyn M. and Cynthia L. Selfe
1990 "Computer conferences and learning: Authority, resistance, and internally persuasive discourse." *College English* 52.847-869.

Coulthard, Malcolm
1985 *An Introduction to Discourse Analysis.* 2nd edition. London: Longman.

Crystal, D. and D. Davy.
1969 *Investigating English Style.* London & Harlow: Longmans, Green & Co. Ltd.

Cukier, W.
1993 "Panning for gold in the data stream has its rewards." *The Globe and Mail* (Canada), 28 September.

Curtis, Pavel
1992 "Mudding: Social phenomena in text-based virtual realities." *Proceedings of DIAC92.* FTP: parcftp.xerox.com in pub/MOO/papers/DIAC92

Curtis, Pavel and David A. Nichols
1993 "MUDs grow up: Social virtual reality in the real world." FTP: parcftp.xerox.com in pub/MOO/papers

Daft, R. L. and R. H. Lengel
1984 "Information richness: A new approach to managerial behavior and organization design." In B. M. Staw and L. L. Cummings (eds.), *Research in Organizational Behavior*, volume 6. Greenwich, CT: JAI Press, 191-233.

1986 "Organizational information requirements, media richness, and structural determinants." *Management Science* 32.554-571.

Daisley, Margaret
1994 "The game of literacy: The meaning of play in computer-mediated communication." *Computers and Composition* 11.107-119.

Danet, Brenda
1992 "Books, letters, documents: Implications of computer-mediated communication for three genres of text." Unpublished manuscript, Noah Mozes Dept. of Communication and Journalism: Hebrew University of Jerusalem.

Davis, Erik
1994 "It's a MUD, MUD, MUD, MUD world." *Village Voice*, Feb 22.42-44.

Dawes, Robyn
1980 "Social dilemmas." *Annual Review of Psychology* 31.169-193.

Delgado, E., M. Meagher, P. Ryan and M. Valenzuela
1993 *Informe Final de Investigación Cualitativa, Aprendizaje Cooperativo de L2 vía Telecomunicaciones en el Bachillerato: Tres Estudios de Caso.* Mexico: UNAM.

DeLoughry, Thomas J.
1993 "Guaranteeing access to the data highway." *Chronicle of Higher Education,* Nov 3. A23.

Dern, D. P.
1992 "Applying the Internet." *Byte* 17(2).111-118.

Dery, Mark
1994a "Flame wars." In M. Dery (ed.), *Flame Wars: The Discourse of Cyberculture. South Atlantic Quarterly* 92(4).559-67.

1994b *Flame Wars. The Discourse of Cyberculture.* Durham: Duke University Press.

Díaz Guerrero, R. and M. Salas
1975 *El Diferencial Semántico del Idioma Español.* Mexico: Trillas.

Dibbell, Julian
1993a "Code warriors: Battling for the keys to privacy in the Info Age." *Village Voice*, Aug 3.33-37.

1993b "A rape in cyberspace." *Village Voice,* Dec. 21.36-42. Reprinted in Dery (ed.) 1994b, 237-261. FTP: parcftp.xerox.com:/pub/ MOO/papers/VillageVoice.txt..

1994 "The prisoner: Phiber Optik goes directly to jail." *Village Voice,* January 11.44.

Dijk, Teun van
1980 *Macrostructures: An Interdisciplinary Study of Global Structures in Discourse, Interaction and Cognition.* Hillsdale, New Jersey: Lawrence Erlbaum Associates.

DiMatteo, Anthony
1990 "Under erasure: A theory for interactive writing in real time." *Computers and Composition* 7.71-84.

1991 "Communication, writing, learning: An anti-instrumentalist view of network writing." *Computers and Composition* 8.5-19.

Douglas, J. Yellowlees
1994 "'Nature' versus 'nurture': The three paradoxes of hypertext." In P. T. (ed.), *The Social and Interactional Dimensions of Human-Computer Interfaces*. New York: Cambridge University Press.

Durlak, J. T.
1987 "A typology for interactive media." In M. L. McLaughlin (ed.), *Communication Yearbook 10*. Newbury Park, CA: Sage, 743-757.

Dworkin, Andrea
1981 *Pornography: Men Possessing Women.* New York: Perigree, and London: Women's Only Press.

1988 *Letters from a War Zone.* London: Secker and Warburg.

Dyson, A. H.
1992 "Whistle for Willie, lost puppies, and cartoon dogs: The sociocultural dimensions of young children's composing or Toward unmelting pedagogical pots." (Technical Report No. 63.) Center for the Study of Writing, University of California, Berkeley.

Dyson, A. H. and S.W. Freedman
1991 "Critical challenges for research on writing and literacy: 1990-1995." (Technical Report No. 1-B.) Center for the Study of Writing, University of California, Berkeley.

Echols, Alice
1983 "Cultural feminism: Feminist capitalism and the anti-pornography movement." *Social Text* 7.34-53.

Edelsky, Carol
1981 "Who's got the floor?" *Language in Society* 10.383-421.

Elmer-Dewitt, Philip
1994 "Battle for the soul of the Internet." *Time*, July 25.50-56.

1995 "On a screen near you: Cyberporn." *Time*, July 3.38-45.

Erhard, Jean
1994 "Digital rights." *Internet World*, November/December.79-81.

Equifax Inc.
1991 "Equifax discontinues sale of direct marketing lists derived from consumer credit file." Press Release. Atlanta: Equifax Inc.

Faigley, Lester
1990 "Subverting the electronic workbook: Teaching writing using networked computers." In D. Daiker and M. Morenberg (eds.), *The Writing Teacher as Researcher.* Portsmouth, New Hampshire: Boynton/Cook Publishers, 290-311.

1992 Fragments of Rationality: Postmodernity and the Subject of Composition. Pittsburgh: University of Pittsburgh Press.

Ferrara, Kathleen, Hans Brunner, and Greg Whittemore
1991 "Interactive written discourse as an emergent register." *Written Communication* 8(1).8-34.

Field, Anne R. et al.
1987 " 'Big Brother Inc.' may be closer than you thought." *Business Week,* February 9.84-86.

Fishman, Pamela M.
1983 "Interaction: The work women do." In Barrie Thorne, Cheris Kramarae, and Nancy Henley (eds.), *Language, Gender, and Society.* Rowley, Massachusetts: Newbury House.

Fowler, Roger and Gunther Kress
1979 "Critical linguistics." In R.G. Fowler, G. Kress, A.A. Trew and R.I.V. Hodge (eds.), *Language and Control.* London: Routledge and Kegan Paul.

Fox, Dennis R.
1985 "Psychology, ideology, utopia, and the commons." *American Psychologist* 40(1).48-58.

Frecerro, Carla
1990 "Notes of a post-sex wars theorizer." In M. Hirsch & E. Keller (eds.), *Conflicts in Feminism.* New York: Routledge, 305-25.

Furher, Urs
1993 "Behavior setting analysis of situated learning: The case of newcomers." In S. Chaiklin and J. Lave (eds.), *Understanding Practice: Perspectives on Activity and Context.* Cambridge: Cambridge University Press, 179-211.

Furlong, M. S.
1989 "An electronic community for older adults: The SeniorNet network." *Journal of Communication* 39(3).145-153.

Garnsey, R. and A. Garton
1992 "Pactok: Asia Pacific electro-media gets earthed." Paper presented via the Adult Open Learning Information Network Conference, Australia.

Garside, R.
1987 "The CLAWS Word-tagging system." In R. Garside, G. Leech and G. Sampson (eds.), *The Computational Analysis of English: A Corpus-Based Approach.* London: Longman, 30-41.

Gaudio, Rudolf P.
1994 "Sounding gay: Pitch properties in the speech of gay and straight men." *American Speech* 69(1).30-57.

Gibson, William
1984 *Neuromancer.* New York: Ace Books.

Godwin, Mike
1994a "The law of the net. Sex and the single sysadmin: the risks of carrying... graphic sexual materials." *Internet World*, March/April.56-62.

1994b "The Feds, and the Net: Closing the culture gap." *Internet World*, May.66-69.

1995a "alt.sex.academic.freedom." *Wired*, February.72.

1995b "Cops on the I-way." *Time*, Spring.62-64.

1995c "The long arm of the law." *Internet World*, March.78-80.

1995d "Running Scared." *Internet World*, April.96-98.

1995e "Net backlash = fear of freedom." *Wired*, Auguest.70.

1995f "Artist or criminal? *Internet World*, September.96-100.

1995g "Philip's folly." *Internet World*, October.102-104.

Goffman, Erving
1974 *Frame Analysis.* New York: Harper and Row.

1981 *Forms of Talk.* Philadelphia: University of Pennsylvania Press.

Graddol, David and Joan Swann
1989 *Gender Voices.* London: Basil Blackwell.

Graff, Gerald
1992 *Beyond the Culture Wars: How Teaching the Conflicts Can Revitalize American Education.* New York: Norton.

Grindstaff, Laura and Robert NIdeffer
1995 "Cuming soon on CD-ROM." *Speed* 1.2. Available on the World Wide Web at http://www.arts.ucsb.edu/~speed

Gross, M.
1972 *Mathematical Models in Linguistics.* London: Prentice Hall.

Gruber, Sibylle
1995 "Ways we contribute: Students, instructors, and pedagogies in the computer-mediated writing classroom." *Computers and Composition* 12.61-78.

Gudykunst, W. B.
1988 "Uncertainly and anxiety." In Y. Y. Kim & W. B. Gudykunst (eds.), *Theory in Intercultural Communication.* Newbury Park, CA: Sage, 123-156.

Gudykunst, W. B. and S. Ting-Toomey
1988 *Culture and Interpersonal Communication.* Newbury Park, CA: Sage.

Gudykunst, W. B. and T. Nishida
1984 "Individual and cultural influence on uncertainty reduction." *Communication Monographs* 51.23-36.

Gudykunst, W. B. and Y. Y. Kim
1984 *Communicating with Strangers: An Approach to Intercultural Communication.* New York: Random House.

Gumpert, G.
1990 "Remote sex in the information age." In G. Gumpert and S. L. Fish (eds.), *Talking to Strangers: Mediated Therapeutic Communication.* Norwood, NJ: Ablex, 143-153.

Gumpert, G. and S. J. Drucker
1992 "From the Agora to the electronic shopping mall." *Critical Studies in Mass Communication* 9.186-200.

Gurak, Laura J.
1994 *The Rhetorical Dynamics of a Community Protest in Cyberspace: The Case of Lotus MarketPlace.* Unpublished Ph.D. dissertation, Rensselaer Polytechnic Institute.

In press "The multi-faceted and novel nature of using cyber-texts as research data." In Teresa M. Harrison and Timothy D. Stephen (eds.), *Computer Networking and Scholarship in the 21st Century University.* Albany: SUNY Press.

Hall, E. T.
1976 *Beyond Culture.* New York: Doubleday.

Hall, Kira
1994 "Bodyless pragmatics." In M. Bucholtz, A.C. Liang, L. Sutton, and C. Hines (eds.), *Cultural Performances: The Proceedings of the Third Berkeley Women and Language Conference.* Berkeley Women and Language Group, 260-277.

1995 "Lip service on the fantasy lines." In K. Hall and M. Bucholtz (eds.), *Gender Articulated: Language and The Socially Constructed Self.* NY: Routledge.

Halliday, M.A.K.
1978 *Language as Social Semiotic: The Social Interpretation of Language and Meaning.* London: Edward Arnold Ltd.

1985 *Spoken and Written Language*. Sydney: Deakin University.

1991 "Corpus studies and probabilistic grammar." In K. Aijmer and B. Altenberg (eds.), *English Corpus Linguistics*. London: Longman.

Haraway, Donna
[1985]1990 "A manifesto for cyborgs: Science, technology, and socialist feminism in the 1980s." In K.V. Hansen and I.J. Philipson (eds.), *Women, Class, and the Feminist Imagination*. Philadephia: Temple University Press, 580-617. (Reprinted from *Socialist Review* 80.65-107.)

Hardin, Garrett
1968 "The tragedy of the commons." *Science* 162.1243-48. Reprinted in G. Hardin and J. Baden (eds.), *Managing the Commons*. San Francisco: Freeman, 16-30. (1977)

1974 "Living on a lifeboat." *BioScience* 24. Reprinted in G. Hardin and J. Baden (eds.), *Managing the Commons*. San Francisco: Freeman, 261-279. (1977)

Hardy, Henry H.
1993 "The future of text based virtual reality." Electronic document. FTP: english-server.hss.cmu.edu

Hare, A. Paul, Edgar F. Borgatta and Robert F. Bales (eds.)
1965 *Small Groups: Studies in Social Interaction*. New York: Knopf.

Haskel, Lisa
Forthcoming "Cyberdyke." *Lesbian Others*. London: Cassell Press.

Hawisher, Gail and Cynthia Selfe
1990 "Letter from the editors." *Computers and Composition* 7.5-14.

Heritage, John
1984 *Garfinkel and Ethnomethodology*. Cambridge: Polity Press.

Herring, Susan C.
1992 "Gender and participation in computer-mediated linguistic discourse." Washington, D.C.: ERIC Clearinghouse on Languages and Linguistics. ED345552.

1993a "Gender and democracy in computer-mediated communication." *Electronic Journal of Communication* 3(2). Special issue on Computer-Mediated Communication, ed. by T. Benson. Available from comserve@rpitsvm.bitnet. Reprinted in R. Kling (ed.), *Computerization and Controversy*, 2nd ed. New York: Academic (1996).

1993b "Macrosegmentation in postings to two electronic 'lists'". Paper presented at the Georgetown University Round Table on Languages and Linguistics, Presession on Discourse Analysis: Written Texts, March 1993.

1993c "Men's language: A study of the discourse of the LINGUIST list". In A. Crochetière, J-C. Boulanger, and C. Ouellon (eds.), *Les Langues Menacées: Actes du XVe Congrès International des Linguistes*, Vol. 3. Québec: Les Presses de l'Université Laval, 347-350.

1994 "Politeness in computer culture: Why women thank and men flame." In M. Bucholtz, A.C. Liang, L. Sutton, and C. Hines (eds.), *Cultural Performances: Proceedings of the Third Berkeley Women and Language Conference.* Berkeley: Berkeley Women and Language Group, 278-294.

1996 "Posting in a different voice: Gender and ethics in computer-mediated communication." In C. Ess (ed.), *Philosophical Perspectives on Computer-Mediated Communication.* Albany: SUNY Press, 115-145.

Forthcoming "Critical language research on the Internet: Some ethical and scholarly considerations." In J. Thomas (ed.), Special Issue on Ethics in Cyberspace Research. *The Information Society*, March 1996.

Herring, Susan, Deborah Johnson, and Tamra DiBenedetto
1992 "Participation in electronic discourse in a 'feminist' field." In K. Hall, M. Bucholtz and B. Moonwomon (eds.), *Locating Power: Proceedings of the Second Berkeley Women and Language Conference.* Berkeley Women and Lg. Group, 250-262.

1995 "'This discussion is going too far!' Male resistance to female participation on the Internet." In M. Bucholtz and K. Hall (eds.), *Gender Articulated: Language and the Socially Constructed Self.* New York: Routledge.

Hiltz, Starr Roxanne
1982 "Experiments and experiences with computerized conferencing." In R.M. Landau, J.H. Bail, and J.H. Siegman (eds.), *Emerging Office Systems.* Norwood, NJ: Ablex, 182-204.

1986 "The 'virtual classroom': Using computer-mediated communication for university teaching." *Journal of Communication* 36.95-104.

Hiltz, Starr Roxanne and Murray Turoff
1978/1993 *The Network Nation: Human Communication via Computer.* First edition Addison-Wesley; second edition MIT Press.

Hodge, R. and G. Kress
1988 *Social Semiotics.* Cambridge: Polity Press.

Holderness, Mike
1993 "Assault on the interface." *Times Higher Education Supplement,* December 24.

Horton, Mark et al.
1993 "Rules for posting to Usenet." Electronic document. FTP: rtfm.mit.edu

Ito, Gloria
1991 "El papel de la cultura dentro del aprendizaje de una lengua extranjera." *Estudios de Lingüística Aplicada*, no. 14. Mexico: CELE-UNAM.

Jeffreys, Sheila
1990 *Anticlimax: A feminist perspective of the sexual revolution.* New York: New York University Press.

Jerome, Marty
1994 "Avoiding bodily harm on the national infobahn." *Boston Globe*, June 5.B32.

Johansson, S.
1991 "Times change, and so do corpora." In K. Aijmer and B. Altenberg (eds.), *English Corpus Linguistics.* London: Longman.

Johansson, S., E. Atwell, R. Garside and G. Leech
1986 *The Tagged LOB Corpus Users' Manual.* Bergen: Norwegian Computing Centre for the Humanities.

Johansson, S., G. Leech and H. Goodluck
1978 *Manual of Information to Accompany the Lancaster-Oslo/Bergen Corpus of British English, for Use with Digital Computers.* Dept. of English: University of Oslo.

Jones, Steven (ed.)
1995 *Cybersociety: Computer-Mediated Communication and Community.* Thousand Oaks, CA: Sage.

Jourard, S. M.
1971 *The Transparent Self.* 2nd edition. New York: D. Van Nostrand.

Just, M.A. and P.A. Carpenter
1980 "A theory of reading: From eye fixations to comprehension." *Psychological Review* 87.329-354.

Kantrowitz, Barbara
1994 "Men, women and computers." *Newsweek*, May 16.48-55.

Kaplan, Nancy and Eva Farrell
1994 "Weavers of webs: A portrait of young women on the Net." *The Arachnet Electronic Journal on Virtual Culture* 2(3). FTP: byrd.mu.wvnet.edu/pub/ejvc/KAPLANV2N3

Katz, Alyssa
1994 "Modem Butterfly: The politics of online gender bending." *Village Voice,* March 15.39-40.

Kaufer, David and Cheryl Geisler
1989 "Novelty in academic writing." *Written Communication* 6.286-311.

Kenner, H.
1989 "Out my computer window." *Harper's Magazine,* November.76-80.

Kerr, Justin
1993 "Digital love." Available from The BLINK Web, j-germuska@nwu.edu.

Kiesler, S., D. Zubrow, A.M. Moses and V. Geller.
1985 "Affect in computer-mediated communication: An experiment in synchronous terminal-to-terminal discussion." *Human Computer Interaction* 1.77-104.

Kiesler, Sara, Jane Siegel and Timothy W. McGuire
1984 "Social psychological aspects of computer-mediated communication." *American Psychologist* 39.1123-1134.

Kim, Min-Sun and Narayan S. Raja
1991 "Verbal aggression and self-disclosure on computer bulletin boards." Paper presented at the International Communication Association, Chicago, IL. Washington, D.C.: ERIC Clearinghouse on Languages and Linguistics. ED334620.

King, Storm
Forthcoming "Proposed ethical guidelines for using Internet research data in the social sciences." In J. Thomas (ed.), Special Issue on Ethics in Cyberspace Research. *The Information Society*, March 1996.

Kirkup, G. and C. von Prümmer
1990 "Support and connectedness: The needs of women distance education students." *Journal of Distance Education* 1(2).9-31.

Kittredge, Richard and John Lehrberger (eds.).
1982 *Sublanguage: Studies of Language in Restricted Semantic Domains.* Berlin & New York: de Gruyter.

Kollock, Peter and Marc Smith
Forthcoming *The Sociology of Cyberspace: Social Interaction and Order in Computer Communities.* Thousand Oaks, CA: Pine Forge Press.

Kramarae, Cheris (ed.)
1988 *Technology and Women's Voices: Keeping in Touch.* New York and London: Routledge and Kegan Paul.

Kramarae, Cheris and H. Jeanie Taylor
1993 "Women and men on electronic networks: A conversation or a monologue?" In H.J. Taylor, C. Kramarae and M. Ebben (eds.), *Women, Information Technology, and Scholarship.* Urbana, IL: Center for Advanced Study, 52-61.

Kremers, Marshall
1990 "Sharing authority on a synchronous network: The case for riding the beast." *Computers and Composition* 7.33-44.

1993 "Student authority and teacher freedom: ENFI at New York Institute of Technology." In B. Bertram, J. Kreeft Peyton and T. Batson (eds.), *Network-Based Classrooms: Promises and Realities.* Cambridge: Cambridge University Press, 113-123.

Kroker, Arthur
1993 *Spasm: Virtual Reality, Android Music, Electric Flesh.* New York: St. Martin's Press.

Kroker, Arthur and Marilouise Kroker
1993 *The Last Sex: Feminism and Outlaw Bodies.* New York: St. Martin's Press.

Krol, Ed
1992 *The Whole Internet User's Guide & Catalog*. Sebastapol, CA: O'Reilly & Associates.

Lakoff, Robin Tolmach
1975 *Language and Women's Place*. New York: Harper Colophon Books.

Landow, George
1989 "Hypertext in literary education, criticism, and scholarship." *Computers and the Humanities* 23.173-198.

Forthcoming (ed.) *Hypertext and Literary Theory*. Baltimore: Johns Hopkins University Press.

Lanham, Richard A.
1993 *The Electronic Word: Democracy, Technology, and the Arts*. Chicago: University of Chicago Press.

Latour, Bruno and Steve Woolgar
1979 *Laboratory Life: The Construction of Scientific Facts*. Princeton: Princeton University Press.

Laudon, Kenneth C.
1986 *Dossier Society: Value Choices in the Design of National Information Systems*. New York: Columbia University Press.

Laurel, Brenda
1990 (ed.) *The Art of Human-Computer Interface Design*. Reading, MA: Addison-Wesley.

1991a "Virtual reality design. A personal view." In S.K. Helsil and J. Roth (eds.), *Virtual Reality. Theory, Practice and Promise*. Westport, CT: Meckler.

1991b *Computers as Theatre*. Reading, MA: Addison-Wesley. Revised ed. 1993.

Lave, Jean
1993 "The practice of learning." In S. Chaiklin and J. Lave (eds.), *Understanding Practice: Perspectives on Activity and Context*. Cambridge: Cambridge University Press, 3-32.

Lave, Jean and Etienne Wenger
1991 *Situated Learning: Legitimate Peripheral Participation*. Cambridge: Cambridge University Press.

Lea, Martin and Russell Spears
1991 "Computer-mediated communication, de-individuation, and group decision-making." *International Journal of Man-Machine Studies* 34, 283-301.

Lea, Martin, Tim O'Shea, Pat Fung and Russell Spears
1992 "'Flaming' in computer-mediated communication: Observations, explanations, implications." In M. Lea (ed.), *Contexts of Computer-Mediated Communication*. New York: Harvester Wheatsheaf, 89-112.

Leap, William
Forthcoming "Performative effect in three gay English texts." In A. Livia and K. Hall (eds.), *Queerly Phrased: Language, Gender, and Sexuality*. New York: Oxford University Press.

Leary, Timothy
1990 "The interpersonal, interactive, interdimensional interface." In Brenda Laurel (ed.), *The Art of Human-Computer Interface Design*. Reading, MA: Addison-Wesley, 229-233.

Levi, Margaret
1988 *Of Rule and Revenue*. Berkeley: University of California Press.

Lewis, Peter H.
1994 "Persistent e-mail: Electronic stalking or innocent courtship?" *New York Times*, September 16.B18.

Li, J., J. Seu, M. Evens, J. Michael, and A. Rovick
1992 "Computer dialogue system (CDS): A system for capturing computer–mediated dialogue." *Behavior Research Methods, Instruments, & Computers* 24.535–540.

Licklider, J.C.R., Robert W. Taylor, and Evan Herbert
1968 "The computer as a communication device." *Science and Technology: For the Technical Men in Management*, April.21-31.

Longacre, Robert E.
1992 "The discourse strategy of an appeals letter." In W. Mann and S. A. Thompson (eds.), *Discourse Description: Diverse Linguistic Analyses of a Fund-Raising Text*. Amsterdam: John Benjamins, 109-130.

Lotus Development Corporation
1990 *Lotus Marketplace*. Press Release. Cambridge: Lotus Development Corporation.

1991 *Lotus, Equifax Cancel Shipment of Lotus MarketPlace: Households*. Press Release. Cambridge: Lotus Development Corporation.

Ma, Ringo
1992 "The role of unofficial intermediaries in interpersonal conflicts in the Chinese culture." *Communication Quarterly* 40.269-278.

1993 *Saying "yes" for "no" and "no" for "yes": A Chinese rule*. Paper presented at the annual meeting of the Speech Communication Association, Miami, FL.

MacDonald, Susan Peck
1987 "Problem definition in academic writing." *College English* 49.315-31.

MacKinnon, Catherine
1987 *Feminism Unmodified: Discourses on Life and Law*. Cambridge: Harvard University Press.

1993 *Only Words*. Cambridge: Harvard University Press.

Magid, Lawrence J.
1994 "On-line neighborhoods you might want to avoid." *Los Angeles Times*, May 11.

Mann, William, Christian Matthiessen and Sandra A. Thompson
1992 "Rhetorical structure theory and text analysis." In W. Mann and S. Thompson (eds.), *Discourse Description.* Amsterdam: John Benjamins.

Marvin, Lee-Ellen
1995 "Spoof, spam, lurk, and lag: The aesthetics of text-based virtual realities." *Journal of Computer-Mediated Communication* 1.2. Available on the World Wide Web at http:/shum.huji.ac.il/jcmc/vol1/issue2/vol1no2.html

Maslen, Geoffrey
1993 "An Australian university examines the issue of electronic-mail abuse." *The Chronicle of Higher Education,* Sept 1.A53.

1994 "Archaeologist wins defamation suit over material put out on Internet." *The Chronicle of Higher Education*, April 27.A30.

Mason, R.D.
1989 *A Case Study of the Use of Computer Conferencing at the Open University.* Unpublished Ph.D. dissertation, IET, Open University, UK.

Matheson, Kimberly
1992 "Women and computer technology: Communicating for herself." In M. Lea (ed.), *Contexts of Computer-Mediated Communication.* New York: Harvester Wheatsheaf, 66-88.

Matray, K.
1991 *Educational Telecomputing as an Instrumental Alternative in K-12 Education: A Meta-Analysis.* San Jose: San Jose University.

May, W.
1967 "Test of generality of affective meaning systems." *XI Congreso Interamericano de Psicología.* Mexico: UNAM.

McCormick, N.B. and J.W. McCormick
1992 "Computer friends and foes: Content of undergraduates' electronic mail." *Computers in Human Behavior* 8.379-405.

McGuire, W.J., S. Kiesler, and J. Siegel
1987 "Group and computer-mediated discussion effects in risk decision-making." *Journal of Personality and Social Psychology* 52.917-930.

McLaughlin, Margaret L.
1984 "Turn-taking, gaps, and overlaps in conversational interaction." Chapter 3, *Conversation: How Talk is Organized.* Beverley Hills: Sage Publications.

Meagher, Mary Elaine
1993 *Informe Final de Investigación Cuantitativa, Aprendizaje Cooperativo de L2 vía Telecomunicaciones en el Bachillerato.* Mexico: UNAM.

Messick, David M. and Marilynn B. Brewer
1983 "Solving social dilemmas." In L. Wheeler and P. Shaver (eds.), *Review of Personality and Social Psychology*, Vol. 4. Beverly Hills, CA: Sage, 111-144.

Metz, J. M.
1992 "Computer-mediated communication: Perception of a new context." Paper presented at the Speech Communication Association, Chicago, IL.

Moonwomon, Birch
1995 "The writing on the wall: A border case of race and gender." In K. Hall and M. Bucholtz (eds.), *Gender Articulated: Language and the Socially-Constructed Self.* New York: Routledge.

Moran, Charles
1991a "We write but do we read." *Computers and Compostion* 8.51-61.

1991b "Using what we have." *Computers and Composition* 9.39-46.

Morson, G.S.
1986 "Introduction to extracts from 'The problem of speech genres'." In G.S. Morson (ed.), *Bakhtin: Essays and Dialogues on his Work.* Chicago: University of Chicago Press, 89-90.

Murray, Denise E.
1988 "Computer-mediated communication: Implications for ESP." *English for Special Purposes* 7.3-18.

1991 "The composing process for computer conversation." *Written Communication* 8(1).35-55.

Nakamura, Lisa
1995 "Race in/for cyberspace: Identity tourism and racial passing on the Internet." *Works and Days*.25-26.

Nwoye, Onuigbo
1993 "Social issues on walls: Graffiti in university lavatories." *Discourse and Society* 4(4).419-442.

Offutt, A. Jeff et al.
1992 "Hints on writing style for Usenet." Electronic document. FTP: rtfm.mit.edu

Okabe, R.
1983 "Cultural assumptions of East and West: Japan and the United States." In W. B. Gudykunst (ed.), *Intercultural Communication Theory.* Beverly Hills, CA: Sage, 21-44.

Olaniran, B.
1992 "Computer-mediated communication (CMC): A look at intercultural implications." Paper presented at the Speech Communication Association, Chicago, IL.

Olson, D.
1977 "From utterance to text: The bias of language in speech and writing." *Harvard Educational Review* 47.257–281.

Olson, Mancur
1965 *The Logic of Collective Action: Public Goods and the Theory of Groups.* Cambridge, MA: Harvard University Press.

Ong, Walter
1982 *Orality and Literacy: the Technologizing of the Word.* New York: Methuen.

Osgood, C.E.
1952 "The nature and measurement of meaning." *Psychological Bulletin* 49(3).197-237.

Osgood, C.E., G.J. Suci, and R.H. Tannenbaum
1957 *The Measurement of Meaning.* Urbana: University of Illinois Press.

Ostrom, Elinor
1990 *Governing the Commons: The Evolution of Institutions for Collective Action.* New York: Cambridge University Press.

Paolillo, John C.
1995 "Code-switching on the Internet: Panjabi and English on soc.culture.panjab." Paper presented at the Georgetown University Round Table on Languages and Linguistics, Presession on Computer-Mediated Discourse Analysis, March 1995.

Perry, William, Jr.
1981 "Cognitive and ethical growth: The making of meaning." In A. Chickering (ed.), *The Modern American College.* San Francisco: Josey-Bass.

Perse, E. M., P. I. Burton, E. S. Kovner, M. E. Lears, and R. J. Sen
1992 "Predicting computer-mediated communication in a college class." *Communication Research Reports* 9.161-170.

Petersen, Julie
1994 "Sex and the cybergirl: When Mother Jones stepped out onto the electronic superhighway, so did a few cyberpigs." *Mother Jones*, May/June.

Peyton, Joy Kreeft
1989 "Computer networks for real–time interaction in the writing classroom: An annotated bibliography." *Computers and Composition* 6(3).105–122.

1990 "Technological innovation meets institution: Birth of creativity or murder of a great idea." *Computers and Composition* 7.15-32.

Pioch, Nicholas (pioch@grasp1.univ-lyon.fr)
1993 "A Short IRC Primer." Available in the /irc directory of many ftp sites.

Plant, Sadie
1993a "Beyond the screens: Film, cyberpunk, and cyberfeminism." *Variant* 14.12-17.

1993b "The future looms: Weaving women and cybernetics." *Broad Sheet: Free Contemporary Art Magazine* 22.3.

Forthcoming *Beyond the Spectacle: The Matrix of Drugs and Computers.* New York: Routledge.

Pollatsek, A. and K. Rayner
1989 "Reading." In M.I. Posner (ed.), *Foundations of Cognitive Science.* Cambridge, MA: MIT.

Popkin, Cathy
1992 "A plea to the wielders of academic dis(of)course." *College English* 54(2).173-181.

Poster, Mark
1990 *The Mode of Information.* London: Basil Blackwell.

Quarterman, John
1990 *The Matrix: Computer Networks and Conferencing Systems Worldwide.* Bedford, MA: Digital Press.

Quirk, R.
1960 "Towards a description of English usage." *Transactions of the Philological Society* 40-61.

Quirk, R., S. Greenbaum, G. Leech and J. Svartvik
1985 *A comprehensive grammar of the English language.* London & New York: Longman.

Quittner, Josh
1994 "Johnny Manhattan meets the Furry Muckers." *Wired,* March.92-97, 138.

Raymond, Eric (ed.)
1993 *The New Hacker's Dictionary* 2nd ed. Cambridge, MA: MIT Press. Also available as "The on-line hacker jargon file" (ver. 3.0.0). Electronic document. FTP: rtfm.mit.edu

Rayner, K.
1977 "Visual attention in reading: Eye movements reflect cognitive processes." *Memory and Cognition* 9.225-236.

1978 "Eye movements in reading and information processing." *Psychological Bulletin* 4.443-448.

Rayner, K. and S.A. Duffy
1986 "Lexical complexity and fixation times in reading: effects of word frequency, verb complexity, and lexical ambiguity." *Memory and Cognition* 14(3).191-201.

Reder, S. and R.G. Schwab
1989 "The communicative economy of the workgroup: Multi-channel genres of communication." *Technology and People* 4(3).177-195.

Reid, Elizabeth M.

1991 *Electropolis: Communication and Community on Internet Relay Chat.* Senior Honours thesis, University of Melbourne, Australia. FTP: english-server.hss.cmu.edu

1995 "Virtual worlds: Culture and imagination." In S. Jones (ed.), 164-183.

Rem, Kathryn

1994 "Log on to proper cybersocial graces." *San Diego Union-Tribune*, November 10.

Rheingold, Howard

1991 *Virtual Reality.* New York: Simon & Schuster.

1993a "A slice of life in my virtual community." In Linda M. Harasim (ed.), *Global Networks: Computers and International Communication.* Cambridge: MIT Press, 57-80.

1993b *The Virtual Community: Homesteading on the Electronic Frontier.* Reading, MA: Addison-Wesley.

Rice, Ronald E. (ed.)

1984 *The New Media: Communication, Research, and Technology.* Beverly Hills, London, New Delhi: Sage Publications.

Rice, R. E. and D. Case

1983 "Electronic message systems in the university: A description of use and utility." *Journal of Communication* 33(1).131-152.

Rice, R. E. and G. Love

1987 "Electronic love: Socioemotional content in a computer-mediated communication network." *Communication Research* 14.85-108.

Riel, M.

1989 "Telecommunications: A tool for reconnecting kids with society." In B. Feinstein and B. Kurshan (eds.), *Proceedings of the International Symposium on Telecommunications in Education: Learners and the Global Village.* Eugene, OR: International Society for Technology in Education.

Robert, Henry M.

1981 *Robert's Rules of Order, Newly Revised.* Glenview, IL: Scott, Foresman and Company.

Rodgers, Robert F.

1990 "Recent theories and research underlying student development." In D. G. Cramer (ed.), *College Student Development: Theory and Practice for the 1990's.* Alexandria, VA: American College Personnel Association.

Romano, Susan

1993 "The egalitarianism narrative: Whose story? Whose yardstick?" *Computers and Composition* 10.5-28.

Rosch, W.L.
1987 "The modern modem: Bridge to the on-line world." *PC Magazine* 6.

Rose, Helen Trillian
n.d. "Frequently Asked Questions." Electronic document. Available on the Usenet newsgroup alt.irc.

Rosenshine, Barah and Joseph Guenther
1992 "Using scaffolds for teaching higher level cognitive strategies." In W. J. Keefe and H. J. Walberg (eds.), *Teaching for Thinking.* Reston, VA: National Association of Secondary School Principals.

Rubin, Gayle
1984 "Thinking sex." In C. Vance (ed.), *Pleasure and Danger: Exploring Female Sexuality.* Boston: Routledge & Kegan Paul.

Rumelhart, David E.
1980 "Schemata: The building blocks of cognition." In R.J. Spiro, B.C. Bruce & W.F. Brewer (eds.), *Theoretical Issues in Reading Comprehension.* Lawrence Erlbaum, 33-58.

Rusiecki, J.
1985 *Adjectives and Comparisons in English: A Semantic Study.* London: Longman.

Sabourin, Conrad F., with Rolande M. Lamarche
1994 *Computer Mediated Communication Bibliography*, Vols.1 and 2. Montreal/ Hudson: Infolingua.

Sacks, H., E. Schegloff, and G. Jefferson
1974 "A simplest systematics for the organization of turn–taking for conversation." *Language* 50.696–735.

Sagan, Dorion
1995 "Sex, lies, and cyberspace." *Wired*, January.78-84.

Salzenberg, Chip et al.
1992 "What is Usenet?" Electronic document. FTP: rtfm.mit.edu

Saukkonen, Pauli
1989 "Interpreting textual dimensions through factor analysis." *Glottometrika* 11.157-171.

1993 "Grammatical structures as indicators of textual dimensions." In A. Crochetière, J.-C. Boulanger, and C. Ouellon (eds.), *Les Langues Menacées: Actes du XVe Congrès International des Linguistes.* Québec: Les Presses de l'Université Laval.

Savetz, Kevin M.
1993 "MUDs, MUDs, and glorious MUDs." *Internet World*, November/December.46-51.

Schank, Roger C. and R. Abelson
1977 *Scripts, Plans, Goals and Understanding.* Hillsdale, New Jersey: Lawrence Erlbaum Associates.

Schegloff, E. and H. Sacks
1973 "Opening up closings." *Semiotica* 8.289–327.

Schegloff, E.A., G. Jefferson and H. Sacks
1977 "The preference for self–correction in the organization of repair in conversation." *Language* 53.361–382.

Schelling, Thomas
1960 *The Strategy of Conflict.* Cambridge, MA: Harvard University Press.

Schiffrin, Deborah
1987 *Discourse Markers.* London: Basil Blackwell.

Schneider, M. J.
1985 "Verbal and nonverbal indices of the communicative performance and acculturation of Chinese immigrants." *Internat'l. Journal of Intercultural Relations* 9.271-283.

Schwartz, John
1994 "A terminal obsession." *The Washington Post,* March 27.F1-F4.

Schwarz, Jerry et al.
1993 "Answers to Frequently Asked Questions about Usenet." Electronic document. FTP: rtfm.mit.edu

Searle, John
1975 "Indirect speech acts." In P. Cole and J.L. Morgan (eds.), *Syntax and Semantics.* Vol. 3: *Speech Acts.* New York: Academic Press.

Sedgwick, Eve Kosofsky
1993 *Tendencies.* Durham: Duke University Press.

Seiler, Larry
1990 Electronic message and form letter to Lotus Development Corporation. Re-posted to Whole Earth 'Lectronic Link computer conference, Electronic Frontier Foundation conference, topic 71 (Lotus MarketPlace). 20 Dec. Msg. no. 154. 19:27 PST.

Selfe, Cynthia L. and Paul R. Meyer
1991 "Testing claims for on-line conferences." *Written Communication* 8(2).163-192.

Seu, J., R. Change, J. Li, M. Evens, J. Michael and A. Rovick
1991 "Language differences in face–to–face and keyboard–to–keyboard tutoring sessions." *Proceedings of the Cognitive Science Conference.* Hillsdale, NJ: Lawrence Erlbaum Associates, 576–580.

Shaughnessy, Mina
1977 *Errors and Expectations: A Guide for the Teacher of Basic Writing.* New York: Oxford University Press.

Shea, Virginia
1994 *Netiquette*. San Francisco: Albion Books.

Sherblom, J.
1988 "Direction, function, and signature in electronic mail." *Journal of Business Communication* 25(4).39-54.

Short J., E. Williams and B. Christie
1976 *The Social Psychology of Telecommunication*. London: Wiley.

Sirc, Geoffrey and Tom Reynolds
1990 "The face of collaboration in the networked writing classroom." *Computers and Composition* 7.53-70.

1993 "Seeing students as writers." In B. Bertram, J. Kreeft Peyton and T. Batson (eds.), *Networked-Based Classrooms: Promises and Realities*. Cambridge: Cambridge University Press, 138-160.

Smith, Judy and Ellen Balka
1988 "Chatting on a feminist network." In C. Kramarae (ed.), *Technology and Women's Voices*. New York: Routledge and Kegan Paul, 82-97.

Smith, Mary John
1988 *Contemporary Communication Research Methods*. Belmont, CA: Wadsworth.

Smolowe, Jill
1995 "Intimate strangers." *Time*, Spring.20-24.

Spafford, Gene et al.
1993a "List of active newsgroups, Parts I & II." Electronic document. FTP: rtfm.mit.edu

1993b "List of moderators for Usenet." Electronic document. FTP: rtfm.mit.edu

Spears, R., M. Lea and S. Lee
1990 "De-individuation and group polarization in computer-mediated communication." *British Journal of Social Psychology* 29.121-134.

Spender, Dale
1992 "Information management: Women's language strengths." In K. Hall, M. Bucholtz, and B. Moonwomon (eds.), *Locating Power: Proceedings of the Second Berkeley Women and Language Conference*. Berkeley Women and Language Group, 549-559.

1995 *Nattering on the Nets*. Australia: Spinifex Press.

Spitzer, M.
1986 "Writing style in computer conferences." *IEEE Transactions of Professional Communication* PC-29(1).19-22.

Springer, Claudia
1994 "Sex, memories, and angry women." In M. Dery (ed.), *Flame Wars: The Discourse of Cyberculture. The South Atlantic Quarterly* 92(4).713-733. Reprinted in Dery (ed.) 1994b, 157-177.

Sproull, Lee and Sara Kiesler
1986 "Reducing social context cues: Electronic mail in organizational communication." *Management Science* 32.1492-1512.

1991a "Computers, networks and work." *Scientific American* 265(3).116+.

1991b *Connections: New Ways of Working in the Networked Organization.* Cambridge: MIT Press.

Steele, Joshua
1969 *Prosodia Rationalis; or, an Essay towards establishing the Melody and Measure of Speech, to be expressed and perpetuated by peculiar Symbols.* English Scholar Press.

Steinfield, C. W.
1986 "Computer-mediated communication in an organizational setting: Explaining task-related and socioemotional uses." In M. L. McLaughlin (ed.), *Communication Yearbook 9.* Newbury Park, CA: Sage, 777-804.

Stenger, Nicole
1991 "Minds as a leaking rainbow." In M. Benedikt (ed.), *Cyberspace: First Steps.* Cambridge: MIT Press, 49-58.

Sterling, Bruce
1986 "Preface." In B. Sterling (ed.), *Mirrorshades: The Cyberpunk Anthology.*

Stone, Allucquere Rosanne
1991 "Will the real body please stand up?: Boundary stories about virtual cultures." In Michael Benedikt (ed.),*Cyberspace: First Steps.* Cambridge: MIT Press, 81-118.

1992 "Virtual systems." In John Crary and Sanford Kwinter (eds.), *Incorporations, Zone 6.* New York: Urzone, 609-621.

Sutton, Laurel
1994 Using Usenet: Gender, power, and silence in electronic discourse. *The Proceedings of the 20th Annual Meeting of the Berkeley Linguistics Society.* Berkeley: Berkeley Linguistics Society, Inc.

Svartvik, Jan (ed.).
1990 *The London-Lund Corpus of Spoken English.* Lund: Lund University Press.

Swales, John
1990 *Genre Analysis.* Cambridge: Cambridge University Press.

Tannen, Deborah
1979 "What's in a frame? Surface evidence for underlying expectations." In R. Freedle (ed.), *New Directions in Discourse Processing*. Norwood, New Jersey: Ablex.

1982 (ed.) *Spoken and Written Language: Exploring Orality and Literacy*. Norwood, NJ: Ablex.

1990 *You Just Don't Understand*. New York: Dell Books.

1994 "Gender gap in cyberspace." *Newsweek*, May 16.52-53.

Taylor, H. Jeannie and Cheris Kramarae
Forthcoming "Creating cybertrust from the margins." In Susan Leigh Star (ed.), *The Cultures of Computing*. Oxford: Basil Blackwell.

Taylor, H. Jeannie, Cheris Kramarae and Maureen Ebben (eds.)
1993 *Women, Information Technology, and Scholarship*. Urbana: Center for Advanced Study.

Taylor, Michael
1987 *The Possibility of Cooperation*. Cambridge: Cambridge University Press.

Templeton, Brad
1991 "Emily Postnews answers your questions on netiquette." Electronic document. FTP: rtfm.mit.edu

The American Internet User Survey
1996 Available on the World Wide Web at http://etrg.findsvp.com/features/

Thomas, Jim (ed.)
Forthcoming Special Issue on Ethics in Cyberspace Research. *The Information Society*, March 1996.

Thompson, Diane
1988 "Interactive networking: Creating bridges between speech, writing, and composition." *Computers & Composition* 5.17-27.

Tierney, John
1994 "Porn, the low-slung engine of progress." *The New York Times* (January 9) 2(1).18.

Ting-Toomey, S.
1985 "Toward a theory of conflict and culture." In W. B. Gudykunst, L. P. Stewart, and S. Ting-Toomey (eds.), *Communication, Culture, and Organizational Processes*. Beverly Hills, CA: Sage, 71-86.

1987 "A comparative analysis of the communicative dimensions of love, self-disclosure maintenance, ambivalence, and conflict in three cultures: France, Japan, and the United States." Paper presented at the Internat'l Communication Assoc., Montréal.

1988 "Intercultural conflict style: A face-negotiation theory." In Y. Y. Kim and W. B. Gudykunst (eds.), *Theories in Intercultural Communication.* Newbury Park, CA: Sage, 213-235.

Turkle, Sherry
1988 "Computational reticence: Why women fear the intimate machine." In C. Kramarae (ed.), *Technology and Women's Voices.* New York: Routledge and Kegan Paul, 41-61.

Turkle, Sherry and Seymour Papert
1990 "Epistemological pluralism: Styles and voices within the computer culture." *Signs: Journal of Women in Culture and Society* 16(1).128-157.

Turoff, Murray and Starr Roxanne Hiltz
1977 "Meeting through your computer." *IEEE Spectrum,* May Issue.

Unattributed
1992 "Computer porn prompts outcry." *The Globe and Mail* (Canada), 20 July.A5.

Ure, J.
1971 "Lexical density and register differentiation." *Applications of Linguistics: Selected Papers of the Second International Congress of Applied Linguistics, Cambridge, 1969.* Cambridge University Press.

Valverde, Marianne
1989 "Beyond gender dangers and private pleasures: Theory and ethics in the sex debates." *Feminist Studies* 15(2).237-54.

Van Der Leun, Gerard
1995 "Twilight Zone of the Id." *Time*, Spring.36-37.

Van Gelder, Lindsey
1990 "The strange case of the electronic lover." In G. Gumpert and S. L. Fish (eds.), *Talking to Strangers: Mediated Therapeutic Communication.* Norwood, NJ: Ablex, 128-142.

Vantses, Martine
1991 "Rousse flamboyante. Fantasmes et réalités du Minitel Rose." *Les Temps Modernes* 535.91-114.

Viljanen, Lea and Hari Husa
n.d. "How to behave on IRC." Electronic text available on the Usenet newsgroup alt.irc.

Volosinov, V. N.
1973 *Marxism and the Philodophy of Language.* Trans. by Ladislav Matejka and I. R. Titunik. New York: Seminar Press.

Von Rospach, Chuq et al.
1993 "A primer on how to work with the Usenet community." Electronic document. FTP: rtfm.mit.edu.

Wajcman, Judy
1991 "Technology as masculine culture." *Feminism Confronts Technology.* University Park: Pennsylvania State University Press, 137-61.

Walther, J. B.
1992 "Interpersonal effects in computer-mediated interaction: A relational perspective." *Communication Research* 19.52-90.

Walther, J. B. and J. K. Burgoon
1992 "Relational communication in computer-mediated interaction." *Human Communication Research* 19.50-88.

We, Gladys
1994 "Cross-gender communication in cyberspace." *Electronic Journal of Virtual Culture* 2(3). FTP: byrd.mu.wvnet.edu/pub/ejvc/WEV2N3

Weidlich, Thom
1994 "Is stubborn e-mail Romeo a stalker? Case may put anti-stalking laws on trail." *National Law Journal,* June 20.A7.

Wilke, J. R.
1993 "Computer links erode hierarchical nature of workplace culture." *The Wall Street Journal,* December 9.A1, A10.

Wilkins, H.
1991 "Computer talk." *Written Communication* 8(1).56-78.

Williams, Jospeh M. and Gregory G. Colomb
1990a "Articulating top-down." In T. Fulwiler & A. Young (eds.), *Programs that Work: Writing across the Curriculum.* Portsmouth, N.H.: Heineman/Boynton/Cook, 83-113.

1990b *Style: Toward Clarity and Grace.* Chicago: University of Chicago Press.

1993 "The case for explicit teaching: Why what you don't know won't help you." *Research in the Teaching of English* 27.252-264.

Wilson, David L.
1993a "Electronic riches are free on the Internet, but some worry about the consequences." *Chronicle of Higher Education,* July 28.A18-20.

1993b "Gate crashers." *Chronicle of Higher Education,* October 20.A22-23.

1993c "Suit over network access." *Chronicle of Higher Education,* November 24.A16.

Winner, Langdon
1986 *The Whale and the Reactor.* Chicago: University of Chicago Press.

1991 "A victory for computer populism." *Technology Review* May/June.66.

Woodland, J. Randal

1995 "Queer spaces, modem boys, and pagan statues: Gay/lesbain identity and the construction of cyberspace." *Works and Days*.25-26.

Yates, Simeon J.

1993a "Speech, writing and computer conferencing: An analysis." In R.D. Mason (ed.), *Computer Conferencing: The Last Word?* Victoria: Beach Holme.

1993b *The Textuality of Computer-Mediated Communication: Speech, Writing and Genre in CMC Discourse*. Unpublished Ph.D. dissertation, Open University, UK.

1993c "Gender, computers and communication: the use of computer-mediated communication on an adult distance education course." *International Journal of Computers in Adult Education and Training* 3(2).21-40.

Yum, J. O.

1988 "The impact of Confucianism on interpersonal relationships and communication patterns in East Asia." *Communication Monographs* 55.374-388.

Zimmerman, Don and Candace West

1975 "Sex roles, interruptions and silences in conversation." In B. Thorne and N. Henley (eds.), *Language and Sex: Difference and Dominance*. Rowley, MA: Newbury House, 105-129.

Zipf, G.K.

1935 *The Psycho-Biology of Language: An Introduction to Dynamic Philology*. Cambridge, MA: MIT Press.

Zita, Jacqueline

1992 "Male lesbians and the postmodern body." *Hypatia* 7(4).106-24.

Zuboff, Shoshana

1988 *In the Age of the Smart Machine: The Future of Work and Power*. New York: Basic Books.

Index of Names

Index of Subjects

In the PRAGMATICS AND BEYOND NEW SERIES the following titles have been published thus far:

1. WALTER, Bettyruth: *The Jury Summation as Speech Genre: An Ethnographic Study of What it Means to Those who Use it.* Amsterdam/Philadelphia, 1988.
2. BARTON, Ellen: *Nonsentential Constituents: A Theory of Grammatical Structure and Pragmatic Interpretation.* Amsterdam/Philadelphia, 1990.
3. OLEKSY, Wieslaw (ed.): *Contrastive Pragmatics.* Amsterdam/Philadelphia, 1989.
4. RAFFLER-ENGEL, Walburga von (ed.): *Doctor-Patient Interaction.* Amsterdam/ Philadelphia, 1989.
5. THELIN, Nils B. (ed.): *Verbal Aspect in Discourse.* Amsterdam/Philadelphia, 1990.
6. VERSCHUEREN, Jef (ed.): *Selected Papers from the 1987 International Pragmatics Conference. Vol. I: Pragmatics at Issue. Vol. II: Levels of Linguistic Adaptation. Vol. III: The Pragmatics of Intercultural and International Communication* (ed. with Jan Blommaert). Amsterdam/Philadelphia, 1991.
7. LINDENFELD, Jacqueline: *Speech and Sociability at French Urban Market Places.* Amsterdam/Philadelphia, 1990.
8. YOUNG, Lynne: *Language as Behaviour, Language as Code: A Study of Academic English.* Amsterdam/Philadelphia, 1990.
9. LUKE, Kang-Kwong: *Utterance Particles in Cantonese Conversation.* Amsterdam/ Philadelphia, 1990.
10. MURRAY, Denise E.: *Conversation for Action. The computer terminal as medium of communication.* Amsterdam/Philadelphia, 1991.
11. LUONG, Hy V.: *Discursive Practices and Linguistic Meanings. The Vietnamese system of person reference.* Amsterdam/Philadelphia, 1990.
12. ABRAHAM, Werner (ed.): *Discourse Particles. Descriptive and theoretical investigations on the logical, syntactic and pragmatic properties of discourse particles in German.* Amsterdam/Philadelphia, 1991.
13. NUYTS, Jan, A. Machtelt BOLKESTEIN and Co VET (eds): *Layers and Levels of Representation in Language Theory: a functional view.* Amsterdam/Philadelphia, 1990.
14. SCHWARTZ, Ursula: *Young Children's Dyadic Pretend Play.* Amsterdam/Philadelphia, 1991.
15. KOMTER, Martha: *Conflict and Cooperation in Job Interviews.* Amsterdam/Philadelphia, 1991.
16. MANN, William C. and Sandra A. THOMPSON (eds): *Discourse Description: Diverse Linguistic Analyses of a Fund-Raising Text.* Amsterdam/Philadelphia, 1992.
17. PIÉRAUT-LE BONNIEC, Gilberte and Marlene DOLITSKY (eds): *Language Bases ... Discourse Bases.* Amsterdam/Philadelphia, 1991.
18. JOHNSTONE, Barbara: *Repetition in Arabic Discourse. Paradigms, syntagms and the ecology of language.* Amsterdam/Philadelphia, 1991.
19. BAKER, Carolyn D. and Allan LUKE (eds): *Towards a Critical Sociology of Reading Pedagogy. Papers of the XII World Congress on Reading.* Amsterdam/Philadelphia, 1991.
20. NUYTS, Jan: *Aspects of a Cognitive-Pragmatic Theory of Language. On cognition, functionalism, and grammar.* Amsterdam/Philadelphia, 1992.

21. SEARLE, John R. et al.: *(On) Searle on Conversation.* Compiled and introduced by Herman Parret and Jef Verschueren. Amsterdam/Philadelphia, 1992.
22. AUER, Peter and Aldo Di LUZIO (eds): *The Contextualization of Language.* Amsterdam/Philadelphia, 1992.
23. FORTESCUE, Michael, Peter HARDER and Lars KRISTOFFERSEN (eds): *Layered Structure and Reference in a Functional Perspective. Papers from the Functional Grammar Conference, Copenhagen, 1990.* Amsterdam/Philadelphia, 1992.
24. MAYNARD, Senko K.: *Discourse Modality: Subjectivity, Emotion and Voice in the Japanese Language.* Amsterdam/Philadelphia, 1993.
25. COUPER-KUHLEN, Elizabeth: *English Speech Rhythm. Form and function in everyday verbal interaction.* Amsterdam/Philadelphia, 1993.
26. STYGALL, Gail: Trial Language. *A study in differential discourse processing.* Amsterdam/Philadelphia, 1994.
27. SUTER, Hans Jürg: *The Wedding Report: A Prototypical Approach to the Study of Traditional Text Types.* Amsterdam/Philadelphia, 1993.
28. VAN DE WALLE, Lieve: *Pragmatics and Classical Sanskrit.* Amsterdam/Philadelphia, 1993.
29. BARSKY, Robert F.: *Constructing a Productive Other: Discourse theory and the convention refugee hearing.* Amsterdam/Philadelphia, 1994.
30. WORTHAM, Stanton E.F.: *Acting Out Participant Examples in the Classroom.* Amsterdam/Philadelphia, 1994.
31. WILDGEN, Wolfgang: *Process, Image and Meaning. A realistic model of the meanings of sentences and narrative texts.* Amsterdam/Philadelphia, 1994.
32. SHIBATANI, Masayoshi and Sandra A. THOMPSON (eds): *Essays in Semantics and Pragmatics.* Amsterdam/Philadelphia, 1995.
33. GOOSSENS, Louis, Paul PAUWELS, Brygida RUDZKA-OSTYN, Anne-Marie SIMON-VANDENBERGEN and Johan VANPARYS: *By Word of Mouth. Metaphor, metonymy and linguistic action in a cognitive perspective.* Amsterdam/Philadelphia, 1995.
34. BARBE, Katharina: Irony in Context. Amsterdam/Philadelphia, 1995.
35. JUCKER, Andreas H. (ed.): *Historical Pragmatics. Pragmatic developments in the history of English.* Amsterdam/Philadelphia, 1995.
36. CHILTON, Paul, Mikhail V. ILYIN and Jacob MEY: *Political Discourse in Transition in Eastern and Western Europe (1989-1991).* Amsterdam/Philadelphia, n.y.p.
37. CARSTON, Robyn, Nam SUN SONG and Seiji UCHIDA (eds): *Relevance Theory. Applications and implications.* Amsterdam/Philadelphia, n.y.p.
38. FRETHEIM, Thorstein and Jeanette K. GUNDEL (eds): *Reference and Referent Accessibility.* Amsterdam/Philadelphia, 1996.
39. HERRING, Susan (ed.): *Computer-Mediated Communication. Linguistic, social, and cross-cultural perspectives.* Amsterdam/Philadelphia, 1996.
40. DIAMOND, Julie: *Status and Power in Verbal Interaction. A study of discourse in a close-knit social network.* Amsterdam/Philadelphia, 1996.
41. VENTOLA, Eija and Anna MAURANEN, (eds): *Academic Writing. Intercultural and textual issues.* Amsterdam/Philadelphia, 1996.
42. WODAK, Ruth and Helga KOTTHOFF (eds): *Communicating Gender in Context.* Amsterdam/Philadelphia, 1996.